CW00621546

CULTURE AND MANAGEMENT IN THE AMERICAS

CULTURE AND MANAGEMENT IN THE AMERICAS

Alfredo Behrens

STANFORD BUSINESS BOOKS
An imprint of Stanford University Press
Stanford, California

Stanford University Press
Stanford, California
© 2009 by the Board of Trustees of the
Leland Stanford Junior University.
All rights reserved for English language.

Printed in the United States of America on acid-free, archival-quality paper

Library of Congress Cataloging-in-Publication Data

Behrens, Alfredo, 1951–
  Culture and management in the Americas / Alfredo Behrens.
      p. cm.
  Includes bibliographical references and index.
  ISBN 978-0-8047-6014-0 (cloth : alk. paper)
  1. Management—Social aspects—Latin America. 2. Latin America—Civilization.
I. Title.
  HD70.L29B44 2009
  302.3'5—dc22

                                                        2008036647

Designed by Bruce Lundquist
Typeset by Classic Typography in 10.5/15 Adobe Garamond Pro

Special discounts for bulk quantities of Stanford Business Books are available to
corporations, professional associations, and other organizations. For details and
discount information, contact the special sales department of Stanford University
Press. Tel: (650) 736-1783, Fax: (650) 736-1784

Jonathen!

Let this be

the beginning

of a long friendship!

JH

2004

CONTENTS

FOREWORD

H OW DOES CULTURE MATTER when it comes to management? This substantive and complex issue has rarely been addressed from a Latin American perspective. Indeed, the general, working assumption appears to be that culture does not really matter very much. The world is populated by people motivated by very similar aims and methods. Yet this book by Alfredo Behrens is an erudite, engaging, and provocative challenge to the modern orthodoxy. Behrens has a number of powerful arguments to make: notably, that the universalistic view of humanity—at least in its economic dimensions—is both naïve and misleading. One manifestation of the orthodoxy is the raw transplantation of models of behavior and management from North American to South American locations. This practice, Behrens argues, is doomed mostly to failure and confusion. He points to substantial economic costs to the reliance on this model, such as a tendency for firms and workers to be less productive than elsewhere, and other associated signs of inefficiency. In its place, Behrens suggests, systems of management and organization that take into account long-lasting social or cultural attributes are warranted. In making these arguments, Behrens draws on historical precedent and patterns. He gains inspiration from a variety of intellectual traditions and methods—including history, economics, management, and psychology—and marshals his claims carefully and intelligently. The result is a challenging yet readable and enjoyable treatise. I have no doubt that it will find much resonance and will stimulate a lively and important debate in the Americas and elsewhere.

SIMON COMMANDER
director, Centre for New and Emerging
Markets, London Business School
   and
senior adviser, European Bank
for Reconstruction and Development

ACKNOWLEDGMENTS

THROUGHOUT MY LIFE, many people have contributed to this book even before I settled to the idea of writing it up. I am in their debt. But quite a few people must be acknowledged by name because they shared with me their experience and insights as I was writing the book. Exchanges with Leda Machado and contributions from Carlos Francisco Hargreaves were most meaningful, as I learned a great deal through their vast experiences as executives at Brazilian and North American corporations. To the late Emmanuel (Manolo) Prado Lopes, I owe much of my understanding of the pleasure of being Brazilian. In this last sense, conversations with Roberto Teixeira da Costa were also most valuable.

I shaped my initial ideas about this field while preparing for a short course by invitation of Anne Nemer, director of the Global EMBA at the Katz Graduate School of Business. For a couple of years, I also benefited greatly from colleagues during my affiliation with the London Business School's Centre for New and Emerging Markets. Simon Commander continued to read advance versions of this book and contributed significantly to creating a crisper and more well-rounded argument. Jonathan Eaton, Sue Watt, and Tracy Ellis, librarians at the London Business School, helped me bridge the distance while working in São Paulo, where I had the assistance of Vania Choi, librarian to the Fundação Escola de Comércio Álvares Penteado.

Theodore Zeldin, of Oxford's St. Antony's College and the Project MUSE, kindly offered encouragement and comments on early versions of my work, as did Shalom Schwartz of the Hebrew University of Jerusalem. My colleagues from the Universidad de San Andrés in Buenos Aires, Ernesto Gore and Sebastian Steizel, and their colleagues at a seminar in Buenos Aires, helped me hone my perceptions on Argentina and its business culture. Francisco Leguizamón of INCAE Business School kindly furnished me with INCAE's work on the rich history of Grupo San Nicolás in El Salvador. To Ramiro Podetti, of the Universidad de Montevideo, I owe much of my understanding of the mythical dimensions of Peronism in Argentina. To Barbara Barrett, former president at Thunderbird School of Global Management, I owe my gratitude for her fine comments and generous encouragement regarding her perceptions on the usefulness of this book for North American business leaders engaged in Latin America.

IBMEC São Paulo, where I lectured on cross-cultural management from 2005 to 2008, offered a most stimulating environment. To my students there, and currently to those at Fundação Instituto de Administração's (FIA) International Executive MBA, I owe my gratitude for showing the dedication in class that they did, in spite of outside jobs and family obligations. I am also very grateful to FIA's International Executive MBA program leader, Professor James Wright, for so generously accepting me to voice ideas that he may not espouse himself, and for his time in allowing me to hone them in discussions with him. I particularly wish to thank my students Mauro Persona, Luciana Amiki, Clarisse Barreto, Djalma Cerino, Adriana Bonora, and Samantha Cafero, and the teams they led, for the excellent quality of their work. Flavio Cabaleiro and Hernan Armbruster, while students with IBMEC São Paulo, devoted a considerable amount of their scarce time to contributing their international executive experience, and their comments have found their way into this book.

The initial version of this work in Portuguese would not have been possible without the unyielding support of IBMEC São Paulo's leader, Claudio Haddad, and the EMBA coordinator Alexandre Duarte, who initially encouraged me to write it. Also, FIA director and professor James Wright, supported the rest of the work to bring this book to publication by Stanford University Press.

I am also indebted to my editor, Geoffrey Burn with Stanford University Press, for his elegant and unwavering encouragement to produce a relatively shorter and more cogent argument. In fact, this book is half as long as the Brazilian edition, despite containing new information. Geoffrey's collaborators there, Jessica Walsh, Judith Hibbard, and Dave Horne, were always a pleasure to work with, as was Mary Barbosa, the copyeditor appointed by the press. Mary added an inordinate amount of dedication and cultural understanding to her qualities as a wordsmith and to bringing this book—thought out in Portuguese and Spanish—to a readability in English that I could not have accomplished alone.

Yet, as I close, I realize that mentioning all of the people above is only a poor tribute to what I owe them, and no tribute at all to those whom I do not mention. My deepest gratitude goes out to all.

WHO SHOULD READ WHAT
IN THIS BOOK

THIS BOOK SEEKS TO AWAKEN the need to develop managerial techniques that are attuned to the cultures of the people being managed. The lack of such adaptation may be responsible for a significant part of the lower productivity found in many developing countries.

If your management work involves an interaction between Latin America and either North America or Europe, you are likely to find some food for thought in at least parts of this book, if not all of it.

Asian and African executives and students, on the other hand, may find little of relevance in the following pages. This is because the focus of the book is on the interaction of people in three cultural clusters: North America, represented by the United States; Europe, represented largely by England and the southern European countries; and the so-called Latin American countries, here represented largely by Argentina and Brazil.

I would encourage management students and executives in any part of the Americas to read the whole book. Those with a firm schooling in the social sciences may want to just skim over Parts One and Two. Part Three should be read by all. While it may contain insufficient traditional history to satisfy many readers in the New World, the selection of facts in this section was nonetheless driven by a unique cultural perspective, central to this book on management. Those initiated in cross-cultural management may dispense with Part Four, which can also be skimmed over by executives of any region, although executives may want to refer to this section occasionally for some crucial definitions.

Students of development studies in any region may find some unusual perspectives throughout the book, even in the general background of Part One; but they will derive most use from Chapters 9 and 10, and all of Part Five.

Finally, some students of Latin American literature or cultural anthropology may find interesting avenues for their own research in this book, which blends work in those fields with managerial needs.

Whatever part of the book you decide to read, I hope you will have fun doing so and that it may awaken something in you.

Please share with me your thoughts. Many thanks for reading this work.

ALFREDO BEHRENS
www.alfredobehrens.com

	Culture and Management in the Americas				
	Part One	Part Two	Part Three	Part Four	Part Five
Graduate Students in:					
Management	Read	Read	Read	Read	Read
Development	Read	Browse	Browse	Read	Read
Social sciences	Read	Browse	Read	Browse	Read
Executives from:					
Europe	Browse	Read	Read	Browse	Read
Americas	Read	Read	Read	Browse	Read

Legend: ▓ Read   ▒ Browse

QUICK READING GUIDE

CULTURE AND MANAGEMENT IN THE AMERICAS

COUNTRIES OF THE FUTURE, FOREVER?

The real voyage of discovery consists not in seeking new landscapes but in having new eyes.

Marcel Proust

THIS IS A BOOK ABOUT how culture shapes management and the economic development of countries. Specialization has led us to inadequate interpretations of social processes such as economic development or even management. Neoclassical economics has left out most of what matters, and management has lazily followed its methods; a too-high level of abstraction has led managers to believe that people are the same whether they were brought up in Boston or in Patagonia. They are not. Moreover, I contend that at least part of the observed lower productivity of the region is due to the fact that Latin Americans are managed as if they were North Americans, and this cultural disconnect may shed some light on the question posed by 2004 Nobel Prize–winner Edward C. Prescott, regarding why Latin American economic development has lagged 75 percent behind the leader for over a century.[1]

Yet this book is not all about efficiency. It is also a call to search for new ways of working together that will offer people the chance to enjoy work more because the workplace will be less punishing and because hierarchy will be more responsive, even encouraging people to engage more in modern collective pursuits such as technological research. This new work environment should reduce the reward for socially deleterious behavior such as roguery, helping to increase the level of trust that is necessary for networks to prosper beyond family-based circles.

Within this generation, Latin Americans have been through "dirty wars," medical doctors have seconded as torturers, and teachers and journalists have been jailed. Elections were suppressed or their results cooked, people were tossed into the sea from planes, newspapers were shut down, poets were persecuted, and guitar players had their fingers broken. Not everywhere, not all of the time, but malfeasance has been too pervasive and too extended for us to comfortably brush it under the carpet.

Latin America is a region of the world renowned for its close family ties; Iberians, Italians, Greeks—Mediterranean people at large—already knew, since the nineteenth century, the sorrow of families broken apart because their countries could not support their offspring. During that generation, large numbers of southern Europeans began emigrating to Latin America, the inhabitants of which now leave. Knowing that emigration is a temporary phenomenon does not make it any easier on the soul or on the pocket.

The Latin American culture is not a culture of the survival of the fittest, it is not finely attuned to pecuniary incentives, and it is not inclined to praise individual initiative as easily as elsewhere. Despite these differences, large enough to be obvious to all, Latin Americans are being managed as if they had all of those traits. They are being managed as foreigners in their own land.

This is what this book is about. It is focused on how Latin Americans can reengineer their talents to be able to be more effective in a globalized world. It is not a question of turning Latin Americans into North Americans or Japanese, but of bridging the gap of understanding between "us" and "them" and of turning into strengths what currently look like weaknesses.

I hope that after reading through you may grow to believe that the differences between Latin Americans and others are mostly related to perceptions of the enactment of values. Differences in values exist to the point that, when measurable, they may even be statistically significant, but it seems to me that some effort in respectful understanding of the reasons behind the different values and their enactments will go a long way toward improving the efficacy of management of Latin Americans and toward helping the latter develop their own managerial techniques.

I do not claim to be an expert on much of what I write about. Rather, if you find no better guide, just accept me as you would a knowledge integrator. This book brings together several conjectures; a few of these may lead to worthy avenues that some readers will wish to pursue. If this book should stimulate further reflection, that will be enough of a reward for me.

WHY THE MISMATCH?

Much of my argument holds that Latin America's productivity lag is the partial result of poor management. I do not contend that managers are short of talent, far from it. What I contend is that there has been too little research to adapt managerial practice to local cultures. Much of what is known today as high managerial theory is no more than a collection of techniques derived from observation of non–Latin Americans. Those techniques have rendered textbooks that are used in Latin American business schools as if their recommendations needed no adaptation.

Take Brazil as an example; today's top cadre of executives was trained between twenty and thirty years ago. When these executives were working toward their MBAs, there were basically fourteen business schools offering graduate studies in Brazil. These employed two hundred PhDs, 55 percent of whom were trained abroad. Of those, 70 percent were trained in the United States.

Four business schools offered doctorate degrees, but only two of these received top rankings from the local accreditation agency. Together, these two best-ranked schools accounted for almost two-thirds of all advanced-degree business scholarship in Brazil; one school was based in Rio de Janeiro, the other in São Paulo. The share of foreign textbooks used in these two schools hovered at around 80 percent and showed a tendency to grow year on year.

Only half of the authors of business textbooks published by the largest two Brazilian publishing houses were Brazilian. The share of local authors would be vastly smaller if foreign publishers were taken into account. Yet even the books authored by Brazilian writers did not, at the time, seem to reflect much Brazilian experience, consisting mostly of collections of foreign essays or reviews of the literature produced by foreign authors.[2]

In all, Brazil's current managerial elite was either trained abroad or trained at home by teachers mostly trained abroad, and who led their students to read mostly foreign literature. Today the picture in Brazil is different; regional input is more significant and reflects more local effort. But, given the training of the teachers, the bias stills favors foreign outlooks on local problems. Worse, Latin American business schools are blindly following North American staffing and teaching practices on what may be a wrong track: favoring the hiring of scholars over practitioners, distracting students from their real-world business objectives by mimicking the tools and teaching methods of a mature practice in the USA, and disregarding the focus and styles of early-twentieth-century North American business school teaching. That instruction was more fitting to what was then a new field in the United States.

Business teaching is still a new field in Latin America, but when the field was emerging in North America, U.S. workers were the focus of observation. Hardly anyone observes Latin American workers today. Furthermore, Latin American business schools may be adopting training techniques that fit poorly the transitional nature of our societies. Case study–based teaching is in itself a case in point. Latin American students expect questions they can deliver answers to. Teaching based on case studies presupposes a degree of autonomy that the average Latin American student may not have developed nor is likely to find in the work environment. Perhaps using the case-study method suits elite training schools catering to the manpower needs of globalized industries in Latin America, such as financial services, yet the technique is being emulated by other schools that have neither the teachers nor the students to fit it.[3]

Foreign management techniques may work for those who have learned to act as if they were foreigners themselves; these people are our local versions of the Davos Man.[4] But they are too few. It is true that the education of this lot may help them benefit from FILO employment (first in, last out), conferring to their styles an aura of success and desirability. But this is a very small share of our population, perhaps not even 1 percent.[5] It is too low a number to guarantee the consistent leadership necessary to modernize relations at work.[6] The other 99 percent will still be encumbered by such obstacles as the standard English-language PC keyboard. Of course, once one learns to hit the Esc key when one is in trouble, all will be fine, but it also helps to figure that out faster if one knows what "Esc" stands for. It is this worldliness that is lacking in the vast majority of the Latin American population. Increasingly, our people are washed away to jobs that require little knowledge of the modern world, where pay is poor and helplessness is insidious.

This book is only cursorily interested in how the cultural environments of Latin American populations are responsible for the psychological differences of the diverse groups. Rather, I assume here that cultural environments shape attitudes sufficiently to warrant the need for developing specific management techniques for different groups. I argue that these distinct environments were partly inherited from the diverse populations that populated these countries, partly contributed by those that landed in the New World—willingly or unwillingly—and partly a result of the interaction of all of these, both within these societies and between them and the larger world.

The resulting environments conditioned an adaptive fit between the personality characteristics of the populations and their environments. This is why today we associate cultural traits with national territories, which encourage, or even enforce, those adaptive fits.[7] Such pigeonholing may overlook the significance of national boundaries, which were drawn often in disregard of cultural boundaries. Instances of this are found in Africa, as well as in Europe and in the Andean region. Yet by and large, given the information at hand, it will suffice to fully associate cultures with nations, allowing for the cultural heterogeneity to be found in any one country.

Some of this book is also concerned with explaining how Latin Americans are different, both among themselves and from other peoples, as well as how they are similar, including to North Americans, especially to Southern North Americans. After all, Latin American cultures today, in addition to their indigenous stock, have cultural tributaries quite similar to those of the United States and Canada: Italians, French, Spaniards, Portuguese, and Africans populated Latin America in different proportions than those witnessed in North America, but the peoples of both regions are nonetheless much alike in their origins. Even descendants of Scandinavians and Germans are to be found in South America, albeit less frequently than in Minnesota, but again, they share the same heritage and cultural stock. Also, large regions of both South and North America veered toward plantation economies early on. This historical detail, with its tangential enslavement of Africans, even today gives rise to pervasive cultural similarities that I will deal with in greater detail further on. This common heritage may be one reason why the Brazilian bossa nova rhythm, for example, was so quickly accepted among North American jazz lovers, triggering a mutual enrichment of rhythms that quieted the despair of the purists.

Latin America was already populated when the first Portuguese and Spaniards arrived, and despite the striking depopulation through death and abuse that the encounter triggered, indigenous populations are still very numerous and contribute substantially to the region's cultural diversity, as is manifest in the wide range of Spanish-language accents found all around Latin America. To that population segment, we must also add those who were forcefully brought to the New World, mostly from Africa. I will bypass both of these groups, the indigenous and African populations, only because I do not know enough about their original cultures. The fact that I do not know more about these ethnicities even at this stage of my life is also a reflection on the Latin American culture and the ways that we are educated and informed. I could attempt to overcome the handicaps of my upbringing, but these are many, and having arrived at the point of crafting this book has already been an ordeal.

STRUCTURE OF THE BOOK

This introductory chapter focuses on culture and its relevance to development and organizations, including business organizations. Culture, I argue, provides the backdrop that, like motivation, steers the choices to be made. Once basic choices are determined, development will follow its natural path. In making the fundamental societal choice of allocating large landholdings to an elite few, for example, the natural outcome is that power will be concentrated, relationships will be nonegalitarian, paternalism will be key, and selflessness and sacrifice will be held as virtues.

Parts One and Two are meant to provide readers with a referral point for understanding the developmental paths and business management options that I will present in later chapters. Overall, these first sections do not attempt to show original work except in the selection of the ideas presented.

Part One, "Culture and the Americas," introduces the topics of culture and other basic categories of this book. It delves into issues such as stereotypes and religion, particularly in the latter's relationship to development paths, and includes the role of modern symbols, such as the luster of Davos and its meaning for the allocation of talent. Readers who are well versed in the histories of the countries considered may only gloss over Part Two, "Cultural Tributaries of the New World," while readers in the Americas may want to read this section as a refresher and because it addresses specific issues that economists may have overlooked, such as the political and economic significance of the Black Plague, or the attitudinal proclivities of Spain and Portugal at the time of the Reconquista, or the prevalence of Spanish tradition in today's southern Europe.

Part Three, "Cultures of the New World," focuses on the United States, Argentina, and Brazil. Again, no citizen of any of these countries will learn much that is new about their nation's history, except as occurs from the selection of the material. There are no war stories. This part mostly informs about a selection of people espousing ideas or actions that shaped their countries. Argentina's intellectual history, for example, is portrayed through the personalities of Mariano Moreno, Rosas, Alberdi, Sarmiento, and the Peróns; certainly, this is not all that one needs to know about Argentina, but much of the country's history that is not expressly mentioned in this book is the result of the ideas of these personalities, or the containment thereof.

Part Four, "Cross-Cultural Management: The Toolbox," delves into the main contributors to the field of cross-cultural management. Geert Hofstede is, of course, prominent in this section, as are Fons Trompenaars and Shalom Schwartz. The addition of Mary Douglas to this list may surprise some, but I believe that the elegant conciseness of her contributions provides a structuring afterthought to the field.

Part Five, "Measuring the Impact of Culture on Management," deals with the managerial implications of all of the previous efforts. It begins by focusing on leadership issues as seen from the northern perspective; it moves on to criticize the lack of resolution shown on leadership styles, as shaped by Latin American culture; and it proposes a literature-based alternative for portraying the most acceptable leadership and managerial styles congruent with those cultures. Subsequent chapters focus on the adequacy of North American management techniques for dimensions in Latin America such as managerial control, teamwork appraisal and compensation, communication patterns, or even strategic choices such as outsourcing to single-purpose companies and debt-structure options. Finally, I suggest research avenues that may lead to more effective management in populations that are so diverse from their North American counterparts.

CULTURE AND
THE AMERICAS

T HIS SECTION INTRODUCES THE focal issue of this book, suggesting that effective management depends on attuning its instruments to the culture of the people it purports to manage. However, the focus of this part is to level the ground, introducing concepts such as culture and stereotypes, the meaning and extent of the concept "Latin America," and the role of Iberian Catholicism in the formation of the Latin American mind.

CHAPTER I

THE DAVOS MAN
OR THE GAUCHO?

I invent nothing, I rediscover.

Auguste Rodin, 1840–1917

MUCH TO THE DISMAY of the Davos Man, modernization does not necessarily mean adopting the Davos
culture. More often than not, modernization means a return to indigenous
values, as in Bolivia's Evo Morales, or the popular appeal of Peru's Ollanta
Humala. Such is also the case with Islam and Asian values. The Davos Man,
powerfully connected as he is, is not the spearhead of evolution. He is merely
a slim developmental option, and not necessarily the one with the greatest
chance of success in Latin America.

In Latin America one has seen, at the outset of this millennium, the backlash against globalization. The populations of Argentina, Bolivia, Brazil, Ecuador, Panama, Uruguay, and Venezuela, for example, elected governments
more attuned with local values than with international ones.

WHAT IS CULTURE?

By *culture*, some people may refer to the more or less tangible manifestations
of a place—such as its art, literature, architecture, music—and its folk culture. To political scientists, culture means the values, attitudes, orientations,
philosophy, and weltanschauung of a people. To anthropologists, culture has

•

a much broader sense and comprehends all of the above plus the symbols and way of life of a society, its family and social structures, its functional stratification, and the institutions it operates through.

Furthermore, culture is not static, it is the expression of interference, dialogue, and negotiation. Culture is used and produced; it flows. National identity is not static; it is grounded in everyday life. Yet there are limits: its evolution is slow.

Clifford Geertz, the renowned cultural anthropologist, refers to culture as a web, for it tenuously surrounds people, conveying the limits of the acceptable. But a web recalls a spider, thus the web is threatening because it is spun by a purposeful living creature with the aim of trapping us. Consider this Geertz-like web definition of culture: "Culture [means] an organized body of rules concerning the ways in which individuals in a population should communicate with one another, think about themselves and their environments, and behave toward one another and toward objects in their environments."[1] The definitions are many, partly because culture is difficult to apprehend. One feels culture rather than sees it; and, notably, one feels it only through the contrast of different cultures. Someone who is born and raised in a single culture without exposure to any other is unlikely to develop the concept of culture.

Culture also is expressed in the attitudes of a people. People can be more easily assertive in cultures where individuals are expected to clearly say what they want—such as American Donald Trump refusing to accept a small tree as a token of appreciation from the city of New York for his contributions to charities. The tree, Trump said, would not adequately reflect his demeanor; he wanted a sequoia instead, the tree that grows to be the highest in the world.

Culture also rules in the background, such as through moral stances that render some peoples more prone to guilt and others to shame. Individualist cultures tend to be more guilt ridden, while in collectivist cultures, shame has a higher guiding prominence.[2] Among the former, individuals are expected to be responsible for their actions, and they tend to feel guilty only for wrongdoing that they have direct control over. They suffer no more liability than that. On the other hand, in collectivist countries, where "face" is more important, an individual feels shame even for liabilities not under his or her control, such as congenital physical impairments.[3]

Literature carries messages that shape us, as do our parents and schooling systems, and as do our friends, through interaction. We gradually learn how to work, what to work for, and what to respect, including other people's property. When we do not respect it, we meet with the sticky side of the Geertz web; we are entrapped. The judicial system, with its laws and enforcement, as well as its eventual inefficacy, is a manifestation of our culture, like our art and our buildings. Those are the visible expressions of our culture.

STEREOTYPES, THE CULTURAL SHORTCUT

Once we become aware of different cultures, we try to apprehend their constellations of expressions through stereotypes. Despite their negative connotations, cultural stereotypes have a place in social interaction. They help us fit scant and fragmented information into a jigsaw puzzle that we can draw sense from. Structuring information within a stereotype is no different from the generic process of cognition.

Stereotypes are useful as long as we are flexible and willing to accept that the facts can be at odds with the stereotype, and we must also be willing to adapt the stereotype to the new information. Stereotyping may be a lazy way of proceeding, but it is painfully real. Moreover, stereotypes may guide behavior, even in the wrong direction. To this effect, it is useful to illustrate with the case of New York's Mad Bomber.

The Mad Bomber scare resulted from a series of bombs that exploded in public places in New York during 1956 and 1957.[4] The type of bomb and associated details led analysts to identify a "signature" in the bombings, and it was assumed that one individual was responsible. A lengthy opinion survey was conducted, revealing that most people believed the Mad Bomber to be a white male. Many readily offered explanations like "only men are intelligent, bold, and nervy enough." Upper-class and female respondents, in contrast, would more readily finger women as the Mad Bomber, offering explanations like "women can be stupid and dangerous." Most believed that the Mad Bomber was an atheist because of the consensus that a religious person would not be able to do what the bomber was doing. Some respondents asserted that the Mad Bomber was a Protestant because his plot was directed against the majority of the New York population: Catholics and Jews.

Other responses suggested that, in the case of a prolonged threat without apparent cause, the population could resort to prejudice and project motives of the transgression onto specific subgroups. This was apparent with regards to religion as well as to nationality. Germans and Italians tended to see the Mad Bomber as Russian; some Russians and Italians tended to see him as German, while most Russians tended to see him as Italian. Explanations to justify assigning one nationality over others suggested that the Mad Bomber would be Russian because "Russians and communists are nonbelievers in God and they throw bombs." The alleged ferocity of Poles was enough to attribute that nationality to the Mad Bomber, and Italians were also targeted because "Italians are hotheaded." A few believed that the Mad Bomber might be Egyptian and attributed their choice to the "Egyptian sneakiness."[5]

CULTURE AND NATIONAL IDENTITY: WHICH LATIN AMERICA?

The Latin America tag—and its implicit us-them dichotomy—may be a nineteenth-century European misnomer, and it hides an even greater misconception: the so-called Latin countries are not all alike. Argentina, Chile, and Uruguay show scant precolonial underpinnings. Paraguay is sometimes thrown into this Southern Cone for reasons of being part of an agricultural economy extending along the Paraná River. Paraguay differs from the other three countries mainly due to its strong indigenous population. Perhaps southern Brazil could be added to this cultural group as well. That region of Brazil belongs to the same river basin, with similar weather and agricultural orientation and similar traditions—not least among them the habit of sipping yerba maté—and a stronger European immigration background than is found in the rest of Brazil.

We also have the mainly Andean countries where the pre-Columbian cultures still have a significant impact: Bolivia, Peru, and Ecuador. Mexico is also a country with a strong indigenous heritage, besides a two-thousand-mile shared border with the USA, which certainly subjects it to an interesting but different cultural symbiosis. Puerto Rico is another stand-alone country, part of the old Spanish empire, yes, but under American tutelage for a century now. Neighboring Cuba is part of Latin America, of course, but after narrowly escaping Puerto Rico's fate, it succumbed to another relatively alien regime. Then we have Colombia and Venezuela, which were one nation until 1830; they are different, yes, but similar in values, particularly among their coastal populations. Then, of course, we have Brazil, separated from the rest by jungles, language, and a particular blend of nationalities, among which the presence of the African Negro is substantial. This historical and economic clustering is strong enough to register statistically, as argued by Lenartowicz and Johnson.[6] The former Guianas and Belize are largely overlooked by all, encrusted in the region as evidence of former colonial rivalries, which also color the Caribbean.

It no longer suffices to argue that Latin America is a "tenable hypothesis," justifying the lumping of all countries into one cluster. When it comes to culture and management, the various nations may be different enough to deserve specific research, which needs to be developed. The purpose of this book is not to recommend management techniques for all of the regions but to reveal that the cultural differences may be large enough to merit research specific to each culture. In that sense, it suffices to focus more deeply on two Latin American countries in order to illustrate the point. The United States, Argentina, and Brazil are the focus of this book, and when Latin or South America is mentioned, it is not with the intent of arguing that the same comments apply to all countries but rather to remind the reader of the breadth of the argument: management must be congruent with people's vital beliefs in order to be effective.

CULTURAL TIDES: HOW DID THESE PLACES COME INTO BEING?

The Americas are lands with many cultures. In the North, national unity was brought about under the hegemony of the predominant culture, that of the original British settlers. Waves of subsequent immigrants were woven into this culture, which evolved in response to the immigrants. This is why we now can distinguish a "Brit" from a "Yankee," especially when we hear them speak English.

Still, the predominance of the English language, from whatever source, as a main element of the North American culture today implies a European heritage that brought with it the Christian religion and mostly Protestant values. These values were crystallized in documents such as the Declaration of Independence and the U.S. Constitution, which express the underlying values of equality, liberty, individualism, rule of law, entrepreneurship, and democracy.

In the case of much of Latin America, the Iberian settlers and local indigenous peoples initially formed the predominant culture. Indigenous peoples were found more densely in today's Mexico and Central America, Ecuador, Peru, Bolivia, and Paraguay. To these cultures were added those of Africa (during the seventeenth to nineteenth centuries) and southern Europe (during the late nineteenth and early twentieth centuries), very much as happened in the United States. Some Asian peoples settled along the Pacific coast, mainly Chinese in Peru. On the Atlantic shore, Brazil absorbed a large influx of Japanese immigrants in the early twentieth century that settled mostly in the Southeast, creating the largest Japanese community outside of Japan.

Africans were enslaved and drawn to the Americas from the western coast of Sub-Saharan Africa to the southern United States and eastern South America, particularly Brazil, where they were settled from the Northeast down to the Southeast of Brazil in such high numbers that, according to one prominent historian, Luis Felipe de Alencastro, Brazil could not have existed without Africa, particularly Angola. The emphasis placed on Brazil's Atlantic coast—given both the slave trade and the export of sugar to Europe—means that Brazil was less integrated with the rest of Latin America than it was with Africa.[7]

Beyond headcount and geographical origins, the values transferred by a people to their new home are crucial in defining the resulting culture. Shared values and attitudes act as tangible manifestations of culture, and this common understanding allows us to know what to expect of another person—as regards, for instance, respect for the order of arrival in the forming of lines.

An acceptable level of trust is also a cultural manifestation that varies from culture to culture. In some cultures, people trust more readily than in others. There may be good reasons for this, as seen in the expression "once bitten, twice shy." Societies with poor law enforcement enable wrongdoers to get away with malfeasance more frequently. The lower risk associated with the penalty may prompt individuals to take advantage of others; accordingly, the proverb "opportunity makes the thief" *(occasio facit furem)* dates back to Roman times, as does "believe in no human" *(ne humanus crede)*. A lower threshold of trust makes business transactions more guarded, adding unnecessary attrition to business and to company growth. One may seriously wonder whether such lack of trust eventually led to the demise of the Roman empire and subsequently flowed into Latin America through its immigrants, mostly southern European Catholics.

Culture also impacts organizations, including the business world. The values of a culture thus influence the way business is conducted, from small business transactions to industrial corporations. Interpersonal trust is an important element of values and attitudes and, as an expression of culture, varies much among countries. Francis Fukuyama has argued that where the scope of trust is broad, such as in the United States, Germany, and Japan, countries are more able to develop large-scale organizations; whereas in countries with a narrower scope of trust, the size of corporations is likewise limited, and these remain largely family owned, as in Italy, France, and Spain as well as in the locations where those populations have migrated to, such as Brazil and Argentina.

Cultures frequently crystallize their messages in sayings or proverbs like those in the previous examples. Benjamin Franklin's aphorism, "time is money," is a cultural expression that speaks directly to the Protestant work ethic, wherein idle time is better spent productively and—by implication—to fulfill the Lord's mandate. This particular sentiment is unlikely to fit as well in Catholic environments, where work is not as readily identified with devotion to the Lord. Such aphorisms are cultural shortcuts that, like memes, gain a life of their own, at once teaching generations and helping to bind societies together, while also differentiating them from other societies.

The pull of a common culture can make or break large geographical areas. Consider the almost tectonic shifting after the fall of the Soviet bloc. Previously, Europe was divided by an Iron Curtain. Countries such as Austria, Finland, and Sweden that were located behind it through no choice of their own had little option but to be neutral. Others chose to suppress their disputes for fear of a greater menace, such as that of the Soviet Union. For this reason, Greece and Turkey suppressed their cultural animosity and sided with the North Atlantic Treaty Organization (NATO)—to them, the lesser of two evils.

As the Iron Curtain was drawn apart and Russia's influence pulled back several hundred miles to the east, Austria, Sweden, and Finland, plus the Baltic Republics, Poland, the Czechs, the Slovenians, and the Croatians, all approximated the European Union. Simultaneously, the Christian Orthodox are experiencing stronger ties among themselves. This movement is clustering Bulgaria, Serbia, and Greece into an "orthodox entente," with the Greek president going as far as claiming in 1997: "Today we do not face any threat from the North. . . . Now, those countries have the same religious beliefs as we do. Today we face a cunning threat from the West . . . from the Papists and the Protestants."[8]

Samuel Huntington may be right when he argues that the centripetal attraction of similar cultures may explain the success of the European Union and Mercosur, as much as it explains the lower yields of less culturally homogeneous collective efforts, such as the North American Free Trade Area (NAFTA) or the Asia-Pacific Economic Cooperation (APEC).

THE IBERIAN ORDER HAS NO BOTTOM LINE

Over two hundred years of a slow technological developmental path, plus five decades of World Bank and IMF prodding, should have made most discerning Latin Americans aware that there are alternative ways of getting where Latin America presumably wishes to be.[9] The Iberian roots of the region's heretofore plodding approach to corporate growth may even be traceable to a Mediterranean ethos, and certainly the Latin American organizational path is identifiable as different from the Anglo-Saxon one, as well as from that of the Renaissance.[10]

The shores of the Iberian Peninsula were not washed by the waves of reform that shaped the modern world. The Protestant Reformation bypassed the Iberian World, as did the industrial and scientific revolutions. During the three hundred years from the expansion to the Americas until the loss of the colonies, the Iberian Peninsula remained authoritarian, stratified, elitist, and hierarchical, and it reinforced traditional patrimonial values intimately associated with Catholicism, including its notion of "flock."[11] Here, then, lies the difference between the Anglo-American experience and the Iberian American one.

It was the Protestant Reformation, with the ensuing deification of avarice as an acceptable moral pursuit for achieving the common good, that alienated the Iberian Peninsula from the Anglo-American experience. This alienation persists today in the New World and is reinforced by an Anglo-Saxon insensitivity fringing on contempt for the psychological foundations of corporatist

Catholic societies. These societies vie for an all-encompassing moral order that guarantees continuity, consolidated in a cohesive organization in which individuals guide their behavior by a shared code of honor ruling this life and the afterlife. The integration of the social and ethical worlds adheres to the foundations of a modern Catholic society in which hierarchy is functional, as espoused by Thomistic-Aristotelian thinkers during the Spanish Golden (sixteenth) Century.[12] There is nothing intrinsically wrong with this concept—it managed to be successful for hundreds of years and was prevalent in Europe from the sixteenth through the eighteenth centuries—but it has fallen out of fashion. The same applies to chivalry, honor, and loyalty, all of which are pre-capitalist virtues that—unable to reach a price—have been devalued, leading the most pecuniarily oriented to believe that such virtues are better suited to history books.

However, despite the common roots, positivism in Latin America led *to* the scientific method, while in Europe and the United States, positivism stemmed *from* the scientific method. As the theory in vogue in Latin American education in the late nineteenth century, the scientific method raised pragmatism to levels previously unknown to Latin Americans. Hence the backlash expressed in Rodó's *Ariel* in 1900,[13] the Iberian American response to the Anglo-American experience—as guided by rampant utilitarianism that is empiricist and inductive as well. In the Iberian order, in contrast, facts such as the interest rate, for example, are weighed according to their fit within a chain of logic stemming from an abstract concept of justice.[14]

This explains why Iberian America is more adroit with logic and discourse than with empiricism and pragmatics; why the word—and dexterity with it—is more highly valued than the thing it represents; why verbal acrobatics, as in political discourse, are more highly appreciated than the mechanics of the projects proposed by that discourse.[15] Unfortunately, the preceding predilections also explain the Iberian order's pervasive contempt for applied work, which appears to be culturally deprived of nobility.[16]

The liberal viewpoint would state that the Iberian order's aversion to work, particularly manual labor, hindered—and still hinders—development. The Latin American perspective, however, holds that the Iberian order ensures a cohesive society in which everyone knows his or her place—leading children to respect their parents and teachers—and in which the elderly are taken care of by their families. Within the Iberian order, the individual has no role but to serve the group and abide by the general will. This view of society is an inherently conservative one, in which divine justice delegates power to the ruling class and thus ensures the harmony of an organic whole. This may be why Latin Americans have not taken as wholeheartedly as Northerners to Montesquieu and the separation of powers, to the American insistence on "checks and balances," or to the overriding corporate concern for efficiency and the bottom line.

This inherent Iberian stance is frequently taken to be an expression of cultural inferiority rather than an expression of a resilient and functional moral tradition, one that renders the Iberian society more collectivist and cohesive and less prone to individual antisocial behavior. It also explains why Latin Americans are frequently staggered and flabbergasted when confronted with details of extremism in Anglo-Saxon behavior, ranging from the bizarre predilections of serial killers to random shooting sprees on school campuses, and with the havoc wreaked by the legacy of Puritan attitudes toward sex and alcohol. Granted, Iberian Americans often live in extremely violent environments, yet the typical act of violence can be argued to derive more from economic hardship than from alienated individuals.[17]

When the Iberian political organization is accepted under this light, rulers such as Primo de Rivera and Franco ("*Generalísimo* by the grace of God") in Spain, Mussolini in Italy, or Oliveira Salazar and Marcello Caetano in Portugal are not exceptions, but expressions of the rule.[18] The exception was the Spanish Republic, and its defeat in 1939 restored the victors' concept of the divine order. It is not by chance that Spain accepted the third restoration of the Bourbon monarchy in 1975, given that an enlightened monarchy is considered the ideal government within the Iberian order. Nor is it by chance that the nineteenth-century Argentine dictator Juan Manuel de Rosas was called the "Restorer of the Law," because the Iberian New World did not seek to denounce Iberia but rather to reformulate its rule according to the new evidence, as seen in the installation of Napoleon's brother as ruler of Spain (1808–13). Even Juan Bautista Alberdi, a foe of Rosas, would dismiss northern European philosophy, preferring that of southern Europe, "the land of our origin and our heritage, in whose intellectual initiative we have a right to share."[19] It is also in accordance with the Iberian order that Justo Sierra would advocate for Mexico a dictatorship à la Porfirio Díaz, because, despite believing in freedom, Justo

Sierra also believed in inculcating order to the Mexican organism—through the power of a strong government—because order would ensure that Mexico would not fall into anarchy. Mexican positivism reinforced the authoritarian background, and lent credence to the hard-line *pan o palo* (bread or the club) approach favored by Porfirio Díaz. Incidentally, Díaz's coarse incentive and punishment system turned him into an early behaviorist who governed with the support of his Comtian acolytes, *Los Científicos* (scientists), who believed that government ought to be left to those who understood the complexity of the matter. Díaz's grip on Mexico was folding just as scientific management had taken hold in the United States. It is unlikely that the Mexicans, having just freed themselves from the rule of one set of *Científicos*, would so quickly fall for another brand.

Iberian Americans did not really want to break with the old regime, which is why there was so little political change in the region during the nineteenth century. From Mexico to the Patagonia, local heroes toyed with the idea of propping up monarchies. Conservative Mexicans actually went as far as installing one under Maximilano de Hapsburgo in 1864–67. The Argentines, lacking an adequate European suitor, considered establishing an Incan monarch as supreme ruler.

Republican forms were adopted, but they were of the authoritarian variety. Societies remained permeable to the winds of change, but change was not earth shattering or fundamental in the North American or European sense. By the twentieth century, the established authorities sought to accommodate the pressures for meritocratic advance with the overruling need to guarantee harmony and organicity, for these were the values that allowed a healing sense of belonging to surface, rather than bowing to conflict and alienation. Peoples' representatives in Argentina, Brazil, and Mexico were realigned, fitting the collectivist heritage, according to function—business, unions, intellectuals, religion—rather than conceding to the perceived divisive tactics of rootless individuals pursuing blind self-interest in markets guided by an "invisible hand." It should also not be surprising that many associations, such as unions, became dependent on the state—to which they owed the reason for their existence: to resolve conflict rather than to create it.

This was also the time of large, state-led projects, for, within the Iberian order, entrepreneurial activity is not necessarily undertaken by isolated individuals.

After all, the New World, Anglo or otherwise, has been indebted to state-led entrepreneurial activity ever since Isabella sponsored Christopher Columbus's maiden voyage. This is what legitimizes—except in the eyes of the World Bank or the Davos Man—Latin America's state-run oil companies or the Brazilian government's decision to build an aeronautical industry from scratch by capacitating labor at its national Aeronautical Technology Institute—which led to the success of Embraer, now a world leader in midsized passenger jet planes. State-owned corporations were sufficiently bad-mouthed during the Cold War, but they seem to have also been an engine of growth in many Latin American countries.

By the first half of the twentieth century, positivism was being rejected, for, as expressed by Argentine Alejandro Korn, Iberian America believed sufficiently in the nature of humankind to value life more than economics. World War II and the ensuing preeminence of the USA blighted the luster of Iberian propositions. Yet the basic organic Iberian concept never disappeared from Latin American culture. If anything, the Iberian order was renamed and lives on, as in politics through Christian Democratic parties, or in religion through theology of liberation. It also has bared its teeth—as during the military rule in Argentina (1975–83) and Brazil (1964–85)—with fire and torture, thus invoking the times of the Holy Inquisition.

The appeal to organic integration still permeates kinship relationships in Latin America, as seen in the patron-client dyad of business relationships or the frequent government use of family imagery, in which nepotism is viewed in the context of the benevolent ruler overseeing the safety of all the national family. This, we will see, was the appeal of Juan Domingo Perón in Argentina, or of Getúlio Vargas in Brazil, as well as of Arnulfo Arias in Panama. The business leader is seen under the same light, and allusions to father-son style relationships are frequent in Brazilian enterprises.[20]

SUMMING UP: BELONGING OVERRIDES PERFORMANCE

The friendly reader may have noted in the preceding section a considerable tour de force to present under a kinder light some traits of the Iberian culture that are generally frowned upon by the Davos Men. The kinder light is merely suggesting that these allegedly negative traits are but part of a discarded framework that has shed its glamour. However, the framework has not lost its relevance for managing Iberian Americans, as indeed has been shown over and over again when they are left to manage themselves.

To non-Iberian analysts, focused more narrowly on the bottom line, the Iberian order "shackles" the business development of Iberian America. This seems to be the conclusion of Eugene McCann in 1964 when he noted the dearth of Iberian American business management literature.[21] He interpreted this gap to reveal Iberian Americans' belief that management is an art form, unteachable and unlearnable. Like most non-Iberians, McCann failed to realize that, in the mind of an Iberian American, an enterprise is only part of the larger organism of society, and that companies must fit into a higher order for which the purpose is the satisfaction of a societal goal. A corporation, therefore, must quench the individual's thirst for belonging and security.

Efficiency is not paramount to an Iberian American, particularly if it is to be achieved at the expense of solidarity and loyalty—the lack of which leads to the alienation of the worker. Because North America's scientific orientation has tended to narrow its interests, that region's analytical backdrop fostered a climate that is inimical to the sociological and psychological foundations of Catholic societies, and ultimately numbing of any effort to understand them.[22]

PART TWO

CULTURAL TRIBUTARIES OF THE NEW WORLD

Much of what happened after the conquest can be understood
and even predicted from a thorough grasp of how the societies
involved were constituted immediately prior to contact.

James Lockhart and Stuart B. Schwartz, Early Latin America[1]

THIS SECTION TRACES the cultural roots of the New World. To this effect, the most relevant cultures of Europe are briefly characterized. This section of the book cannot replace history books; it only purports to make readily accessible information that I believe is crucial to understand how managerial techniques came into being in the United States and not in Latin America. Once in place, those techniques would reflect cultural attitudes that are more aligned with the United States than with Latin America.

In this book, managerial techniques are taken to be North American, particularly from the United States. While this may seem as a shortcoming to Europeans, the loss is likely exaggerated. In Latin America, business management is mostly a North American practice. Other hard choices were made. The European cultural roots of the New World, as represented in this section, are limited largely to England in the United Kingdom, and to Spain, Portugal, and Italy because of these countries' more significant population contributions to the New World. These are the countries whose cultural history I will briefly review in the next few chapters.

I describe how culture was shaped in three of the largest countries in the New World. My overarching purpose is to explain attitudes toward work and organizational preferences. This is why I will be emphasizing issues that historians may consider of lesser historical significance, while some economists may frown upon the scarcity of quantitative evidence. What you will read in this section is not original work except in the selection and organization of the material. I will focus mostly on ideas and how they shaped societies.

I do not start in all countries at the same time. I may refer to England before Abelardo's time, but only barely. With regards to Italy, I highlight history that is less commonly known among people in the New World, such as the fact that much of Southern Italy was under Spanish rule for a considerable amount of time, and was highly fragmented during other periods. Nor do I end each country's story everywhere in the same year, though I finish shortly after World War II, largely because it was then that the formation of much of Latin America's current leadership was completed.

This section will highlight ideas and concepts, but only inasmuch as they helped to shape culture—that web of attitudes and rituals that characterizes societies. That is why I can span a millennium of English history in a couple of pages, by focusing on events that portray a culture of individualism and freedom that would discourage despotic power, harbor religious tolerance, and spin off the North America that we know today. I will also focus on the role of technology as a barometer of attitudes of mastery or submission.

In this sense, my particular brand of intellectual history is very practical; I will guide you through the ideas and events that shaped political theory, economic development, and the organization of production. Even then, I will not venture in Europe farther beyond the four countries that I consider to be the main contributors, in terms of population, to New World culture: England, Italy, Spain, and Portugal. Following my interpretation of these nations, I will contrast their cultural attitudes toward work at the close of the section.

Historical regurgitation notwithstanding, this is largely pioneering work. If it succeeds in opening new research avenues, I will be content in knowing that my efforts will be expanded on, rounded off, and carried forth by future interpreters.

CHAPTER 2

ENGLAND

Law in origin was merely a codification of the power
of dominant groups, and did not aim at anything that
to a modern man would appear to be justice.

Bertrand Russell

E NGLAND IS PART OF AN ISLAND, and as such one would
expect it to be culturally insular, but it is not. It is true
that England did not have to contend with the influx of cultures as dissimilar
as those that battled over Spain, but England was influenced by many cultural
tribes. Once the Roman empire broke down, the eastern parts of the British
Isles were overrun by predominantly German tribes stemming from as far
north as Jutland, hence the Anglo-Saxon core. Under Christian monks, as late
as the seventh century, England began indirectly unifying the territory of the
British Isles. By the ninth century, Scandinavian raiders were brought under
control. In many ways, the British Isles reflect all of these influences, evident
even in the English names for the days of the week.[1]

Christianity reached England some four hundred years before a French
king helped consolidate Catholic rule. Nonetheless, Christianity was always
mostly a French concern, irradiated as it was through St. Augustine in the
South—sent by Pope Gregory the Great in 597 A.D.—and in the North via
followers of the French-trained Irish monk, St. Patrick. The French brought
Catholicism to the island and, in 1066, their feudal regime as well—the same
structure they had planted in Italy with such different institutional and social

results. The bitter English inter– and intra–royal family disputes—clouded by religious ones—were not more vicious than anywhere else, but England did find specific solutions that have made it culturally distinct—in particular, the limitations to monarchic rule, with the ensuing impact on the rule of law and human rights, and the peculiar relationship it crafted to accommodate religion with state. Both particularities spilled over to the New World, to its colonies in North America as well as to the countries with which it traded farther south. It is on these institutional specificities, so different from those in Portugal, Spain, and Italy, that we will concentrate our attention, for in those differences may lie the explanation to the different patterns of social and business cultures between Anglo-Saxon America and the rest of the New World.

FRENCH ENGLAND

The crowning of William as king of England in 1066 hailed the beginning of a new dynasty. The Normans were now in control, and they introduced French feudalism—as well as a new nobility, a new religion, and a new ecclesiastical hierarchy. The Saxon earldoms disappeared and their great estates were redistributed to Norman and Breton landowners. Rents in the way of barley and ale would no longer suffice. The feudal regime required that any vassal cooperate with the demands of the mounted knights. Under French rule, the military function was outsourced. This arrangement, which was peculiarly Norman, provided King William with an inexpensive army, but it also created a new ruling class.

Administrative control would also be more exacting. The *Domesday Book*, began in 1080, was the most complete record of resources ever attempted. Its purpose was to assess the region's existing goods and the amount that could be collected by the crown. To produce the *Domesday Book*, King William sent his men to every shire to record all land and holdings "to the last pig."[2]

Overall, the Norman regime lasted four hundred years. Its outsourcing of military services dispersed power and brought about its share of warring knights and bitter power disputes that weakened central power, allowing for the burghers (commoners) to increasingly establish limitations to monarchic rule. For instance, bishops at a Great Council in 1197 at Oxford refused levies on barons to finance war abroad.[3] Limitations on monarchic rule took the institutional form of Parliament at the time of Henry III (1216–72).

Initially called the Great Council and attended by nobles and bishops (House of the Lords) and representatives of the burghers (House of the Commons), these two entities would meet to confer, or "parley" (note the similarity with the French *parler*, precursor of *parliament*). At Parliament sat commoners for the first time. In one sense, the Great Council of 1197 was a political development of even greater significance than the ensuing Magna Carta (1215).

The Magna Carta primarily protected the interests of barons against the king. While it did not satisfactorily address military service, the charter did open a flank for the gentry and smaller landholders to take part in the political debate, particularly with regards to taxes, from 1299 on. Later, the clergy and merchants negotiated a larger say. It was clear by the time of Edward III (1312–77) that English kings were forced to come to terms with the new political society that was brewing in England. Rule by consensus had been established de facto.

THE BLACK PLAGUE INTERMEZZO:
"BROTHER ABANDONED BROTHER"[4]

The Black Death pandemic wiped out at least a third of the European population between 1347 and 1348. Notably, the two centuries that preceded it facilitated rapid spread of the pandemic. The years between 1000 and 1250 were years of plenty. The average temperature had increased by about one degree Celsius, helping to yield abundant harvests. Europe's population doubled, universities were founded, and no major wars erupted. Cities grew in size and power, and information and trade flowed increasingly easily. So did the plague when it struck, arriving probably from Caffa, piggybacking on rats aboard trading vessels. According to Josiah Cox Russell, "the decline produced by the plague reduced the population probably about 50 percent by 1400."[5]

Europe was no longer on sure footing when the plague arrived. Poor harvests during 1315 and 1316 had triggered famine and wars. Cities could not take care of themselves as readily, and the greater population density would facilitate contagion. When the Black Death struck, affecting mostly the adult population, the social fabric broke down. Scapegoating was rampant and fell most harshly on Jews.[6]

Previous experiences with plagues had taught people that death came from beyond. Thus it was only natural to refrain from contact with others.

Fire arrows were thrown at ships attempting to dock; travelers were kept out of cities. Europe closed up on itself. High death rates bloated cemeteries. Too small to receive all of the dead, these were supplemented by ad hoc solutions: the Rhone was consecrated and bodies were dumped in it; in Florence, mass graves accommodated corpses: "the dead were laid out, layer upon layer just like one puts layers of cheese on lasagna."[7] All to no avail; by the time the plague had infected all of Europe and moved east toward Russia, what was left was altogether different.

Because the plague required proximity to ensure contagion, the greater the population density, the harder it was hit. Its sweep deprived the social system of the former repositories of administrative skills and cadres of intellectuals that concentrated in these centers. For these reasons, the social order after the plague was conceivably less conservative, if not better or more efficient. Moreover, the higher death rate among the elite left an open door to social innovation.

The ensuing labor shortage shifted power from the nobility to the peasants. Parliaments everywhere would seek to cap the windfall gains of peasants, leading to peasant revolts like that of England in 1381. Yet some scholars argue that the plague's impact was far worse. By destroying the balance of power that held society together, the plague ushered in the reign of greed. Custom was no longer a reference; chivalry lost its glamour.

BACK TO THE HISTORY OF ENGLAND

On the cultural side, a parliamentary act of 1362 determined that English would be the official language in pleadings in law courts. French-speaking lawyers resisted the new law, but English was increasingly used in matters of protocol, helping to standardize the written English language. Chaucer's *Canterbury Tales* in the late fourteenth century is a reflection both of the impact of Norman influence in English and of the wider reading market for the English language.[8]

The Catholic Church was meeting increasing resistance in England. John Wycliffe (1324–84) argued that the Bible, not the church, was the true guide to faith, and he was the first to translate the Bible into English.[9] A significant popular revolt, led by Jack Cade in 1450, drove the point home to the English royalty: the people possessed a force to be contended with.[10] While England, still insular, focused on local issues, Constantinople was captured by Moslems in 1453—a world event that, by blocking land routes with Asia, would trigger the discovery of the New World. English royalty, meanwhile, believed it had more immediate problems at hand. The War of the Roses, an English war of succession, broke out in the mid-fifteenth century and lasted for three decades, virtually exterminating the English aristocracy, as the fortunes of the noble class vacillated repeatedly from victory to defeat. This did not wholly stop England; despite the turmoil, John Cabot sailed from Bristol in 1497 and landed in North America while searching for a northern passage to Asia.

All this was happening at a time when the Catholic kings installed throughout Spain's empire were consolidating their powers and expanding toward both the New World and Southern Italy, amid stifling competition from the Turks, who were uncontrovertibly defeated by a Spanish fleet at Lepanto in 1571.

It was also a time of religious upheaval. As the teachings of Martin Luther were spreading to all of Europe, the floodgates of the Reformation were fully opened. Henry VIII was at odds with the (Spanish) pope over his wish to marry Anne Boleyn, and he challenged the pope with the authority of the Reformation Parliament, convened for the first time in 1529 and effectively putting an end to the medieval English church in 1533.

If only by the density of talent produced, the late Tudor period proved to be, if not a Renaissance, certainly the beginning of England's modern era. Within a century of the birth of Edmund Spenser (1552), we also saw Milton, in poetry; Christopher Marlowe, Ben Johnson, and William Shakespeare, in poetry and drama; and William Byrd, in music. Thomas More and Francis Bacon authored philosophical enquiries that pushed the limits of humanism and cognition, giving seed to the disenchantment of society by ushering out alchemy and astrology and clearing the path for the scientific method, such as later would be espoused by Isaac Newton, born in 1643.

The reign of Elizabeth I (1533–1603) saw the consolidation of British international power. This would rest on the capacity to finance international expansion and on the ability to manage a shipping fleet. The opening of the Royal Exchange in London offered a suitable trading place for Antwerp bankers fleeing the Spanish Duke of Alba's repression (1567–73) of Dutch resistance to the harsh dominion of Spain's Philip II. As many as twenty thousand Protestants of the Low Countries may have died under the Duke of Alba. These stirrings laid the foundation for a staunch financial pole to develop in London, which was not toppled even by the Great Fire of London that burned four-fifths of the city to the ground in 1666.

ENGLAND ADOPTS THE MORALS OF THE LATECOMER

By the time England was ready to break its isolation, the world had been partitioned by the pope without England's input. The island country could not expand by adhering to the rules designed by others to favor themselves; it was in England's interest to develop a navy and construe its own engagement rules.[11]

A competitive navy was promoted through on-the-job training. Hence, compulsory fishing days were increased from two to three times a week, ensuring the development of seafaring skills. Although these sailors would initially be no more than pirates, their dexterity at sea contributed immensely to lay the foundations of Britain's later vast overseas empire. Once ready to sail, England would not observe—and not only for religious reasons—the papal grant of 1493 splitting the New World between Portugal and Spain. Nor would England take notice of the Treaty of Tordesillas signed between Spain and Portugal a year later, effectively partitioning the New World and the Asian one for the benefit of Spain and Portugal. This is how Britain's Sir Francis Drake came to circumnavigate the globe (1577–80), sixty years after Magellan's El Cano feat. The Genoese John Cabot had reached Newfoundland under the British flag just five years after Columbus. It takes time to learn by doing, but Britain was catching up and would no longer need Genoese nationals to lead its navy.

SEVENTEENTH-CENTURY ENGLAND

England would not, however, make much of John Cabot's discovery for almost one hundred years. Nor was Sir Francis Drake's New Albion colonized, or San Francisco Bay, claimed for England during Drake's voyage around the world. After a couple of failed colonization attempts, religious separatists settled Plymouth in 1620. They drew up the Mayflower Compact establishing that it would be the will of the colonists—rather than the crown—that would determine the government.

Seventy years earlier, Spain had already founded Mexico's National University. Even Buenos Aires and Recife, on the Atlantic, and Lima, on the Pacific, were founded some eighty years before the Pilgrims settled Plymouth.

In 1628, the reign of Charles I (1625–49) was further restrained by the Petition of Right, the clauses of which would find their way into the United States' Bill of Rights and amendments to its constitution. The Petition of Right emphasized ancient rights of the English people, insisting on freedom from arbitrary arrest and imprisonment, nonparliamentary taxation, the enforced billeting of troops, and martial law.[12] It effectively freed British subjects from relying on "trust of the Royalty" as the sole source of justice.

The long English tradition of freedom of religious choice was also being shaped into popular movements. In 1644 the seven General Baptist churches issued the London Confession, claiming that men are free to obey their own conscience and understanding. In 1647 the Quaker leader George Fox began preaching under the conviction of the "inner light." The civil war, and the republican commonwealth that followed it, provided the political background for this period of intense religious disquiet and social disorder.

THE REVOLUTION OF 1648–1657

The middle classes neutralized the absolute power of royalty during a series of civil wars between parliamentarians and royalists. But more important, this revolution asserted the rights of individuals to profess their religion of choice,[13] to analyze and interpret the Bible according to their own cosmogony, and to freely chose pastors of their own faith as well as guaranteeing the autonomy of their parishes and towns. No doubt Cromwell destroyed some castles in Ireland and victimized the Catholics, but the revolution aimed neither at destroying the old regime nor, certainly, the lords' rights to their lands. Moreover, it supported dispossession by the nobility of communal lands by means of the Enclosure Acts, which displaced so many peasants and set them at the mercy of the town-based manufacturers. What the English Civil War did conquer were some very basic rights to the individual's intellectual autonomy, and this was to prove no small matter. For instance, the unrest undermined the doctrine of the divine right,[14] which would still haunt Spain well into the Franco regime, until 1975, and perhaps beyond.[15]

HABEAS CORPUS

The Habeas Corpus Act of 1679 severely limited police discretion in detaining people, as jailers would now be obliged to produce a reason for detention. Furthermore, it limited the time that a prisoner could be detained without trial and, once set free, prevented him or her from being tried twice for the same offense. Centuries of prisoner abuse and intimidation over the powerless were delegislated in a single stroke. The Habeas Corpus Act found its way into the legal framework of many countries, including the United States.[16]

By 1690 John Locke had given shape to the theory of limited monarchy in *Two Treatises of Civil Government*. Trust in Parliament did not mean universal suffrage of men and women, which would come only in the twentieth century. Enfranchisement was very limited to a very powerful class whose fortune was based mostly on trade, and interest in the latter shaped foreign policy. Seventeenth-century England was a nation poised for international expansion. For instance, Parliament founded the Bank of England in 1694 to fund the cost of the Nine Years' War with France. Also, as from 1698, the granting of trade monopolies would no longer be a royal dispensation but an act of Parliament. This paved the way for the East India Company and the expansion of British influence, underwritten, as from 1688, by the Lloyd's Coffee House, which would provide marine insurance for overseas trading.

In 1697 Britain began to keep records of the gap between its imports and its exports, improving significantly over the *Domesday Book*. Keeping tabs on the "balance of trade" would allow better understanding of the flow of goods, which was crucial to a land increasingly dependent on international trade. Exploration was also supported. Mapmaker and explorer James Cook (1728–79) made three trips to the Pacific Ocean, mapping its main coastlines.

BRITISH POWER

The increased wealth brought about by international trade would allow the flourishing of an intellectual class of remarkable accomplishment. Isaac Newton's *Mathematical Principles of Natural Philosophy* (1687) and his *System of the World* (1686) saw their English translation from Latin three decades later. David Hume (1711–76) shaped British empiricism. Adam Smith (1723–90), with *An Inquiry into the Nature and Causes of the Wealth of Nations*, created the discipline of economics by stressing the individual's egoistic drive as the source of progress—including the progress of free trade and capitalism—in opposition to Rousseau's preference for an altruistic individual interested in the common good.

Engineering feats responded to the needs of transportation and manufacture. The harnessing of steam power by James Watt in the 1760s would not only provide the necessary energy, it would also change the landscape, displacing factories from fast-flowing highland rivers to the lowlands, closer to coal mines and markets. England would also now need to cope with the nurture and management of its own innovation: mechanical engineering became a profession, iron took the place of wood in industrial machinery, and invention was making incursions into the new machine tool industry as Henry Maudslay developed the all-metal lathe (1784, 1797) and James Nasmyth developed the steam hammer (1838).[17]

The industrialization of iron was in itself telling of the pace of innovation. Darby's coke-smelting process was a significant technological innovation, and coke-fueled furnaces were put in place in the 1760s. Watt-designed steam engines were pumping air into the smelting process and freeing smelters from the vagaries of rainfall that affected the flow of the streams previously relied on for power. Advances were piecemeal and rarely depended on only one innovation, which in any case were only rarely deployed in the form they were initially offered. For all its zigzagging, innovation had allowed the doubling of iron output in half a century. In the hundred years preceding 1847, the output of English pig iron had multiplied a hundredfold. Near the end of the nineteenth century, pig iron output was equivalent to that of continental Europe and America; England had become ironmaster to the world.

England and the United States would be the first to navigate with steam-driven engines in the 1780s. Rail-based steam carriages would appear in the early nineteenth century. This was the apex for transportation engineers of the stature of Isambard Kingdom Brunel (1806–59), with his construction of a network of bridges, viaducts, and tunnels and his celebrated suspension bridges. Brunel was also the designer of famous ships. The *SS Great Western*, launched in 1837, was the first steamship in transatlantic service, while the *SS Great Britain,* launched in 1843, was the world's first screw propeller–driven, iron-hulled, steam-powered passenger liner.

By then, England was well into the industrial revolution and suffering opposition to it.[18] Luddites were damaging machines in a symbolic attempt to redress the exploitation of workers. While the Luddites were not revolutionaries, they were remarkably successful.[19]

But even by the mid-nineteenth century, England still was not an industrial urbanized society. Steam power, for which the first patent was taken in 1769, became industry's primary energy source only in 1820. Nonetheless, by 1851, agricultural output amounted to just 20 percent of the nation's total production, although half the population still lived in the countryside. Of those that lived in urban zones, 15 percent resided in towns with fewer than twenty thousand inhabitants. Let there be no doubt as to England's industrial might by the mid-nineteenth century, yet its provincial character and narrow range of occupations remained significant.[20]

England's late nineteenth century ceases to be our focus, as the emigrants to the New World had mostly departed by then. England continued to increasingly influence the New World, though to a lesser degree through significant migrations that would shape New World societal or business organizations.

Despite England's awe-inspiring technological development, nineteenth-century America was already leapfrogging its parent. The United States was mechanizing production in the face of an inelastic labor supply. An American could but amass wealth as a ready source of prestige. England, in contrast, could offer many prestige-inducing roles, but entrepreneurship was not among them: "There is a general argument . . . that the English social structure and English public opinion were less favorable than the American to entrepreneurship, less favorable both to the recruitment of ability and to full exertion of ability once recruited."[21]

SUMMING UP: THE CURBING OF ABSOLUTISM IN ENGLAND

This history of England may incur the sin of selecting self-serving examples to argue my point. But I will leave that judgment to others. In boiling down one thousand years into a few pages, I have attempted to highlight an indomitable tension among the English people: that of preserving their autonomy of thought while still taking part in something larger than themselves. There is no doubt that England witnessed absolutism and its barbarism just as many other countries did, but the English people showed an unrepentant disposition to preserve their right to individual choice.

The initial four hundred years of French absolutism since the Battle of Hastings (1066) did little more than expose Catholicism to the English people; the French could not impose it. To a considerable extent, the English chose what to absorb of Catholicism and of the foreign power they could not repel. In defending their autonomy, the English sought to curb the power of absolutism. The Great Council of 1197 and the Magna Carta of 1215 are the first among many important milestones, while the movement that inspired them continued to seek limits on absolutism and succeeded in establishing the parliamentary system (1265), ultimately leading to the Petition of Right (1628), the Habeas Corpus Act (1679), and the Whig triumph (1688).

By Chaucer's time (1343–1400), the English were capable of asserting themselves in their own language, not more than half a century after Dante wrote his *Divine Comedy* in Italian. Unlike the Italians, the English succeeded in preserving their individual autonomy from an absolutist ruler of their own.

Thus dissent became second nature to the English people, allowing numerous interpretations of Christianity to flourish and eventually be expressed with even greater autonomy in the New World, where the inherited right to choose would eventually lead to the American Revolution.

The circumstances of thought that generated a movement expressing itself in a document as far reaching as the Bill of Rights are rare in human history. In the sense that any historical document can be viewed as an act in a play, the USA's Bill of Rights (1791) would be deemed act 3; act 2 would be the Whig triumph (1688), "government altogether on the consent of the people," while act 1 would be the defeat of the English people by the French at Hastings (1066), effectively making the English foreigners on their own land and thus driving their beliefs and values underground and making passive resistance a way of being. The people's hard learning of the ways of resistance is at the historical root of English antiauthoritarianism.

This defiant nature would manifest itself in Wycliffe's "poor preachers" as well as in the Quaker Bristol episode of 1656—the protagonist of which, James Nayler, preached an egalitarian liberation theology of the time—and in Jack Cade's lightning attack on London in 1450. Resistance galvanized the lower classes into social movements with religious overtones that sought not to overturn regimes but rather to secure local and individual autonomy. The young Voltaire would return from his exile in England marveled by the pluralist capacity of the English in hosting so many creeds living in peace with each other.

Coexistence was not always easy, and America, the vast expanse across the ocean, was the valve that defused animosity. Penn's sagacity allowed him to see the practical reward of religious tolerance: prosperity. Philadelphia was, at the time of the American Revolution, the second-largest city of the British empire. Jefferson and Madison would later advocate similar tolerance to their fellow Virginians. The crown would also promote tolerance in the colonies by partitioning the land among groups with notoriously low tolerance of each other.

Religious ferment is what allowed the Quakers to produce a Tom Paine, who would agitate in England for higher wages and later accept Benjamin Franklin's invitation to Philadelphia, where he became the American Revolution's most-read pamphleteer. His *Rights of Man* was a colossal best seller. It would not have been so in the absence of an avid audience. Tom Paine was at the pinnacle of a movement that would lead to the structuring of the United States and its business practices. In Chapters 13 and 14, I will draw on the symbiotic relationship between author and public to support my depiction of the cultural traits of Argentines and Brazilians.

One can maintain that a business organization should accommodate the libertarian ethos among its collaborators, but one must realize that business draws its collaborators from society and, as such, reflects the values of that society. English society and its North American offspring are societies that value dissent, individual autonomy, and self-consciousness; they engage in social contracts ruled by a higher authority that citizens are called on to interpret. A business organization made up by these people is necessarily different from another that does not value this mix of attributes with the same emphasis.

CHAPTER 3

SPAIN

It would be tiresome to ask me not to want what Heaven wishes,
destiny mandates, reason begs, and above all, my will desires.

Don Quixote

S PAIN AND PORTUGAL were no exception to the ruthlessness
of life in feudal Europe. Yet they were exceptional in many
ways, not least in that they were occupied by Moslems over a period of several
centuries. Both Spain and Portugal were lands with long coastlines, rendering a
population familiar with sailing. Both were lands protruding into the Atlantic
with little chance of expanding eastward, where competition was strong—by
land, from the French and Germans and, by sea, from the Turks.

Both Spain and Portugal were naturally inclined to look westward for
expansion. The timing of the expansion corresponded to the end of centuries
of warring over consolidation among the Catholic kingdoms as well as to
driving out the "infidels." At the time of the annexation of the New World, the
Catholic kings of both countries expelled the Jews (1492, from Spain; 1496,
from Portugal). The full expulsion of the Moslems would come a century later,
in the first decade of the seventeenth century.

In Moslem Spain, control of the land by Christians was confined to the
North, where the Cantabrian mountain range made the region less interesting to the Moors. Dominion of this area ceded Christian control of the pilgrimage route to Santiago de Compostela, religiously on a par with Jerusalem
and Rome.

South of the Cantabrian Mountains and west of the Pyrenees, Christians coexisted with Moslems, as they had for the centuries since the Moslem invasions of Iberia early in the eighth century. Cohabitation was not always peaceful. Incidentally, the term "cold war" was first used in the thirteenth century by Spanish Catholics to describe an uncomfortable coexistence with peninsular Moslems. Yet the Moslem occupation was not altogether regrettable. Moslems had brought knowledge to a land with few harbors and "whose soil is thin—and not even that uniformly well watered," in the words of the classical geographer Strabo.

The cultural activity of Moslems had peaked in the tenth century, when the Caliphate of Córdoba could boast of a library holding some four hundred thousand volumes, including works by some of the more significant philosophers in Europe. Moslem-induced irrigation allowed the growth of oranges and rice, which entered the diet of the Christians along with the Arabic language, which came to dominate literature and philosophy.[1] Nonetheless, the Caliphate began to dissolve under pressure from northern Catholic kingdoms and its own internecine succession difficulties.

In the thirteenth century, Christian kingdoms pressed south, leaving only the kingdom of Granada under Moslem control. Religious intolerance undermined coexistence, and Jewish people began to be regarded as aliens. In 1341 there were massacres of Jews in Seville, Valencia, Toledo, and other important cities.

In their drive southeast, the forces of the kingdom of Aragon secured the coast of Iberia along the Mediterranean. Naval power was built on the wealth from trade surpluses with Italy and southern France. Barcelona and Valencia were the seafaring hubs that supported the retention of the Balearic Islands and the conquest of Sicily (1282) and Sardinia (1323–24) as well as mainland Naples (1435). In only four centuries, the kingdom of Aragon had almost single-handedly unified much of Spain and built a Mediterranean trading empire.

The onslaught of the Black Death (1348), which wiped out as much as two-thirds of the population in some areas of Europe, led to a severe scarcity of manpower in Spain. Because Spain was less densely populated and its cities were smaller, the spread of the Black Death must have been slower and its mortality rates less acute. However, historical records indeed point to a labor shortage that would determine an important production choice: cattle rearing on extensive landholdings was favored over labor-intensive agricultural activities.[2] This choice also spurred the consolidation of large landholdings. Smaller tracts within the large ones were also consolidated and dedicated to cattle, which would ultimately discourage specialization, concentrate power, and constrain the growth of the domestic market. Spain would not produce many of the goods its people sought, leading to a rise in imports, which in turn required exportable surpluses in order to meet their costs.

The centuries of warfare for the Reconquista—literally, Spain's reconquest of its land from the Moslems—could not have helped to encourage tolerance. The Jews were expelled from Spain in 1492, as the Moors would also be in 1609–10, with an additional loss of between 350,000 and 600,000 people, perhaps 10 percent of Spain's population at that time. These religious persecutions, perpetrated in Spain and abroad (in mid-sixteenth-century Flanders, for example) helped disseminate the perception of a level of intolerance inimical to the development of science and technology.

It was also in 1492 that Castile would finance the trip of Columbus to what became the New World. Trade with the New World, coupled with the fall of Constantinople (1453) would lead to a decline in the relative importance of the Mediterranean trade, where the kingdom of Aragon had its commercial base. The merge by the Catholic kings of Castile and Aragon (1474–1516) would benefit both. Aragon would bring into the bargain the Roman peninsula, with its proximity to the seat of the Catholic church and its bases in the Mediterranean, a bulwark against Ottoman expansion. Castile would bring its commercial expertise with northeastern Europe and its rights to the New World. It turned out to be a most successful merger.

Queen Isabel, through Columbus, found much more than she had hoped for. The annexation of the lands in the New World meant that Europe would focus on a developmental pattern that would gravitate less on the Mediterranean and more on the Atlantic Ocean. Given the transportation technologies of the time, the occupation of the New World would be more intensive on its coastline. Furthermore, the northern shores of the New World would be preferred for their greater proximity and accessibility over the more distant South.

The riches brought from the New World would lead to an enhanced role for Spanish monarchs. The succession of the Habsburgs brought Charles V, grandson of Fernando and Isabella, to the core of European politics in 1516, precisely at the sensitive time of the Protestant Reformation, triggered by Martin Luther in 1517. The reign of Charles V placed Iberia in control of some of the wealthiest regions of Europe: Flanders, Franche-Comté, and ultimately Milan (1535–40). Even the Austrian and German empires were to be placed under Spanish rule, that of Ferdinand II, Charles's brother.

Spain's most glorious phase is commonly placed between the signings of the treaties of Cateau-Cambrésis and Westphalia, or 1559 and 1648, respectively.[3] Besides Basque iron ore, Spain's cloth manufacture—based in Córdoba, Segovia, and Cuenca—rivaled those of northern Europe in the early sixteenth century. Yet from Segovia's peak of six hundred looms in 1580, only half of them were in operation a century later. Output had dropped further, to only one-third of the region's previous eighteen thousand measures of cloth per year. The decline in production was also evident in the shipping industry. Foreign vessels carried only 5 percent of the trade with the New World during the early sixteenth century, yet by 1588 these accounted for up to 20 percent.

The de-skilling of Spain was noticeable among the Renaissance intellectuals, particularly those notable for strategic analysis and competitiveness, like the Italian Giovanni Botero (1544–1617): "No country is more lacking in crafts and industry."[4] Seventeenth-century wars and religious persecutions had shaped foreigners' perceptions that Spain's proclivities were more attuned to warfare than to the industries that thrived under peace, such as science and fortifying infrastructure. Incidentally, the quote from Don Quixote at the opening of this chapter alludes to his own stubborn preference for the martial arts over more cultured pursuits.

The riches reaped from the Atlantic trade never quite benefited the hinterland. Spain was naturally short of navigable rivers, and the authorities had made little effort to alter natural matters. Lack of proper roads, for instance, would lead to long delays in internal communications. A trip from Valencia to Madrid (about two hundred miles) would take five to seven days in the early seventeenth century. Still, a century later the trip from Barcelona to Madrid (nearly twice the distance) would take a fortnight.

The economic decline had many culprits, not least among them the *carestia*, or inflation, expressed in the increase in the price of bullion. The Spanish empire was overextended, fighting too many wars in northern Europe and installing sons on Italian thrones. Philip II had retrenched his European expenditures, concentrating on raising revenue from his Atlantic operations. On that front, Spain was inclined to lay its hands on as much precious metal as possible. The abundance of the latter led to inflated prices. Payment delays favored the debtors, rewarding old sins such as idleness, sumptuous consumption, and simple greed.

Still, the reasons for the decline cannot have been purely inflationary or political. Spain was suffering from what came to be known in the twentieth century as the "Dutch Disease": large positive trade balances would increase domestic prices of nontradable goods, vis-à-vis foreign ones, discouraging local manufacture. Solid physical reasons also played a role. For instance, forever short of manpower, Spain was now short of masts as well. Indeed, the tall masts required by larger vessels now had to be imported from the Baltic, and rigging equipment was also in short supply. The Marquis of Ensenada, "father" of the Spanish navy that was launched in the mid-eighteenth century, was commended for producing the most comprehensive survey of population and property yet undertaken in Spain.[5] Far-reaching as it was, it came seven centuries after the *Domesday Book* carried out by the French conquerors in Britain, and no use was made of the Spanish accomplishment.

HONOR AND KNOWLEDGE

By the late eighteenth century, Spain was having second thoughts, not only on economic management but also on the appropriateness of its values and institutions. In 1775, Minister Campomanes criticized the exaggerated emphasis on hereditary honor and privilege in detriment of application to goals. Warfare and defense were among his major concerns in terms of their drain on resources that could otherwise be applied to education and technology—in order, as Campomanes would put it, to differentiate the Spanish people from the hordes of untrained and unproductive Moroccans. A few generations before Spain's collapse, Campomanes had pinpointed Spain's most significant handicap: the lack of education of its population. Even as late as 1940 only two-thirds of the Spanish population was literate, representing an illiteracy rate that was twelve times higher than that of the United States, for example.

By 1787, Spain had a population of slightly over ten million, rendering a density of 20.6 inhabitants per square kilometer, or 40 percent of that of France at the time. According to British historian James Casey, an average of four thousand young men left every year to the New World, totaling close to two hundred thousand by 1591 and constituting a considerable drain on manpower.[6] Furthermore, the pull of the Atlantic ensured that whatever population was left in Spain was gathered along the coastline, accentuating the sense of solitude and abandonment of the Spanish hinterland.[7]

SCIENCE AND ARTS

Spain's contribution to technology centered on navigation. Whether in the design of sails and hulls, in their maintenance, or on cartography, the daring navigators learned by doing and amassed a competitive edge that they would hold for a couple of centuries. However, these were not advances that could percolate to the inland regions, which derived little benefit from the technological advances in navigation.

Circumscribed as the plagues may have been, they ravaged the populations in the cities where they hit. Very much as in the Black Death epidemic of the fourteenth century, social order was undermined in affected Spanish centers as well. A sense of disillusionment consequently permeated the arts, be it literature or painting, as seen in El Greco's saints, presented in attitudes of contrition or spiritual meditation, such as in the *Repentant Magdalene, Saint Peter in Tears, the Penitent Saint Jerome, Saint Dominic in Prayer,* or *Saint Francis in Meditation.*[8]

Spanish art found expression mostly in religious forms. Cathedrals were "religion in stone." Pious paintings depicted Catholic selflessness. It was the art that warring landlords would be willing to pay for at a time that physical strength took precedence over reflection.

ADMINISTRATION OF JUSTICE

Latin America is deemed hierarchical in its social organizations and plagued by patron-client relationship styles. Does this stem from an Iberian tradition at the time of colonization? It could well be, but if so, what was the nature of the relationship of Spain's common citizen with authorities? If the latter enjoyed unrestrained power, one would find in Spain's administration of justice the seeds of the hierarchical social arrangements in modern Latin America. However, the answer seems to be more complex.

At least since the time of Isabel de Castilla, Spanish royalty had sought to ensure a fair administration of justice. This trend was particularly consolidated during the reign of Philip II, to the point that to visitors in the late sixteenth century, Spanish administration of justice seemed fairer than most in Europe, as expressed by the moral philosopher Pineda in 1589 or by Barthelemy Joli, who pointed out that the law in Castile "does not spare the great ones as it does in France."[9]

What sort of administration of justice was this that leveled the mighty with the weak? It appears that the administration of justice was but the secular arm of Catholicism, seeking to hold together the flock by inhibiting animosity, as might be bred by unfairness or unfettered aggression. Cerdán de Tallada noted that law was instituted in order to help men become good, so they may "enjoy in peace and quiet their property, and that no one make bold to harm another, rather that they should treat one another with the love and harmony of Christian people."[10]

Castillo de Bobadilla's treatise illustrates a wide range of economic management functions of the *corregidor*: feeding the poor, public works maintenance, fixing prices in the market, and enforcing the quality of goods sold.[11] Even the Nueva Recopilación, the law code of Castile of 1567 and reiterated in 1640, is a blend of religion, morals, and law that to the modern layman would seem rather theocratic, which perhaps it was.[12]

The good of the commonwealth of Catholics may have been at the root of Spain's justice system and the leveling of Spanish society to one of fairness. Yet knowledge, as individually accessible through reading, did not fall within the standard of fairness deemed necessary. Spanish education remained in a pitiful state well into the Regency period (1833–43), meaning that by the late nineteenth century less than 15 percent of the population knew how to read.

As late as 1877, two-thirds of males and over four-fifths of women remained illiterate. The press effectively became an alternative to party politics during the Regency period, and its impact on public debate and the outcomes of elections was significant.[13] So much so that by 1900 a newly created Ministry of Public Instruction determined that all students should attend school through age nine. Yet illiteracy rates for men and women only dropped to 30 and 38 percent, respectively, by 1940.[14]

By the last quarter of the nineteenth century, Spain had become a fractious country living complacently off an imperial self-image that could no longer be sustained. The country was brought to a most rude awakening in 1898 when it lost most of its navy in a humiliating defeat at the hands of a relative newcomer to world affairs: the United States. That year came to be known to Spaniards as the Year of Disaster.[15]

Spain tottered thereafter until the Republic lost to Franco and the nation closed up for almost four decades, stopping in time. By 1950, illiteracy rates in Western Europe averaged 4 percent, but Spain's own illiteracy rate was over four times that, and higher still than the rates of Argentina and Uruguay. At the same time, life expectancy in Spain was sixty years, ten years less than the Western European average and lower than in Argentina and Uruguay.[16]

Spain's defeat in the Spanish-American War and its subsequent folding up under Franco led Latin America to figure out its own way forward. Spain's influence in Latin America had already taken root, and it was largely more beneficial than is usually acknowledged.

In particular, the administration of justice in colonial Spain should be viewed under a kinder lens. Spain's own administration of justice does not appear to have favored the oligarchy. In contrast, it showed signs of being a fair and impartial system. The fact that the administration of justice was less effective in the colonies than it was in Spain seems to be an unintentional result of the general disorganization of civil rule that "the crossing" conditioned. Organizations in the New World were poor replicas of their counterparts in Spain. Nonetheless, it is worth looking at a couple of the institutions that transferred the Spanish social order to the New World.

SOLIDARITY IN SECULAR ASSOCIATION

We have seen how Catholic Spain sought to create a commonwealth through the administration of justice. This sense of the common good would find expression in secular organizations such as the *hermandades* (brotherhoods) and *cofradías* (guilds). These societal institutions represent the unique Spanish focus on the community that promises group identity and collaboration and for which emotion is the only agglutinate.[17]

I am less interested in the ethnographic account or the diversity of the *cofradías* and *hermandades* than in their pervasiveness in Spanish culture as expressions of a binding, collective social device that illustrates Spanish Catholic proclivity to associability and teamwork. Their transfer to the New World also incorporated the *gremios* (labor guilds). In all, what we have at hand is a constellation of institutions that characterize Spanish colonial administration because they fit into a larger pattern of orientation toward a perceived commonwealth. Thus, such annual events as the Yucatan's *gremio*-sponsored festival parades provide "the functions of social integration, identity, and prestige of the festival tradition."[18]

The significance of the *cofradías* lies not only in their relevance as the conqueror's tools of social administration but also in their acceptance by the indigenous population. This is what made them so effective in the Hispanic New World and reveals a relatively comfortable juxtaposition of cultural traits. In both the indigenous and the Spanish Catholic cultures, personal sacrifice for the greater commonwealth was desirable to the point that it led to the individual acquiring honor by surrendering the private good to the communal good.[19]

This system of social colonial control and integration was frequent not only in Mexico but also throughout Hispanic America, including in the Andean region, where it found support in traditional kinship systems: "The ayullus [traditional kin groups] managed to revitalize themselves by functioning as *cofradías*."[20]

In Latin America, this revitalized role of the church had an important influence on the organization of thousands of forced resettlements of Indians in what were known as *reducciones*. The *cofradía* was a central part of life in these "new Indian towns," just as it had been in the towns of traditional Spain extending as far back as the old kingdom of León in the fourteenth and fifteenth centuries.[21]

It is worth insisting on drawing readers' attention to the integrative roles of spontaneous social institutions such as the ones mentioned above, because they reflect both a demand and a function. They are still vital today, and they offer an example of popular management that historically has been culturally acceptable to the population.

SUMMING UP: SPAIN

As Islam took over Spain and Portugal around the eighth century, Christians were displaced to the mountainous North that held the pilgrimage routes to

Santiago de Compostela, a destination on a par with Jerusalem. Moslem peninsular culture was considerably advanced and relatively tolerant, and Christians and Moslems maintained an uneasy coexistence for centuries. Tellingly, the term "cold war" is said to have been coined in these early times.

As the hold of the peninsular Moslems weakened and Christians pushed south, Christians inherited an increasing share of the land. The manpower shortage brought about by the Black Plague exacerbated the problem of an already sparse labor pool, causing Christians to abandon Moslem-implanted agriculture and resort to cattle rearing as they advanced toward the Southeast. The kingdom of Aragon secured the Mediterranean Iberian coast and expanded toward Southern Italy and Sicily. The kingdom of Castile secured the North and the West until the Reconquista was complete in 1492. Jews were expelled from Spain as the New World was being discovered, and the last Moors were expelled in 1609. Spain lost close to 10 percent of its population with these expulsions. Along with the people went their crafts and techniques.

However, Spain would become the Catholic bastion against the Protestant Reformation. Intolerance, such as that which galvanized Spain's population in the centuries-old battle of the Reconquista, found a new enemy in the Protestants. Hierarchy was consolidated, power was concentrated, freethinkers were persecuted, and the medieval church strengthened its hold over the populace, who were given only limited education. This is how Spain arrived in the New World, bound up in a Scholastic, medieval Catholic Church.

Yes, the conquistadors were in search of gold, not God. They brought God with them. The gold and silver extracted from the New World would allow Spain to purchase goods, garner support, and expand its power into Europe. But the de-skilling of Spain was also significant. Local nontradables appreciated in value, thus adding pressure to local prices and further draining Spain's capacity to supply itself, in addition to the manpower losses to the New World and to the plague. By the sixteenth century, Spain was at the core of Europe. Its soft diplomacy ensured the backing of the Catholic Church, and Spain took it upon itself to combat the Protestant Reformation, in the best intolerant Spanish tradition. This was Salvationist Spain, a nation with a religious mandate, proselytist and unrepentant at that, in both the Old and the New Worlds.

By the late eighteenth century, Spain was overstretched. With labor always in short supply, the nation now lacked the necessary materials for outfitting its fleets as well. Its leading thinkers were suggesting the unthinkable: privilege should be subject to achievement, instituting a paradigm shift that diverted resources to education and technology development and spawned a more equitable distribution of economic activity across the country—rather than concentrating it along the coastline, where the risk of losing even more citizens to the allure of the New World was greatest.

Nonetheless, little was done in terms of education in Spain, which arrived in a pitiful state to the late nineteenth century and, as a final blow, suffered defeat by the United States in the war over Spain's last colonial possessions.

Colonial power was dwindling, but Spain—nor, we will see, Portugal—could not easily abandon the trappings of an era; instead, it simply ground to a halt. When Spain fell, her achievements were all but buried under the burden of her many ills.

Yet Isabel de Castilla had ensured a fair administration of justice and had set a precedent that was consolidated under Philip II. *Corregidores* in the New World would control prices, stamp out extortion, fix water supplies, and check the quality of goods traded. In all, they were seen as a royal extension of the king and queen, who could be counted upon to protect the vulnerable, in the best Catholic tradition.

This sense of the common good was also sustained by societal organizations such as the *hermandades* and *cofradías*, which offered group identity and a structure for collaboration. These spilled over to the New World, where they found acceptance among the collectivist-oriented natives, for whom individual honor stemmed from surrendering private gain to the communal one.

To the nascent Spanish-speaking Latin American countries, independence from Spain was a political developmental stage, an opportunity to refocus, to put an end to the colonial yoke and keep a larger share of the pie. In the process, they would have to reorganize themselves, and the Spanish culture they had already inherited indelibly shaped the solutions to the new problems.

CHAPTER 4

PORTUGAL

Man cannot discover new oceans unless he has the courage
to lose sight of the shore.

André Gide

T HE PORTUGUESE WOULD always feel under threat of
the Moors and of their Spanish neighbors. This menace
shaped much of Portugal's history, from the defensive alliances it would make
with England to the international ventures it would engage in. To some extent,
Portugal never overcame that encirclement anxiety: water everywhere and an
expansionist Spain where the frontier was dry. As late as 2004, Portugal's prime
minister was quoted as stating that the nation must overcome its inferiority
complex regarding Spain.[1]

THE BECOMING OF PORTUGAL

Similarly to Spain, the weakening of the Córdoba Caliphate allowed a gradual
southern expansion by Christians, who took Lisbon from the Moslems in 1147.
Following succession turmoil, an Anglo-Portuguese alliance was confirmed
by the Treaty of Windsor in 1386, which provided Portugal with a bulwark
against Spain and freed Portuguese explorers to embark on maritime exploration. Portugal's solution to its eastern frontier problem would mean that from
that point forward Spain would have to look over its western back in any con-
frontation with England. To Portugal, however, securing its own eastern back

meant it was now safe to expand overseas and to seek an oceanic route to the Indies. The success of the Atlantic passage provided Portugal's King John I a valve to defuse popular discontent and progressively restrict the power of the Cortes (Portuguese parliament). By the end of his reign, sessions of the Cortes were called ever more sparingly.

PORTUGUESE EXPLORATION AND EXPANSION

Portugal's capture of Ceuta (1415) led the Portuguese to believe it would be possible to control North Africa by occupying it. It was one thing to beat the Moors on Portuguese land, however, and quite another to beat them on Moorish land. The ensuing adventure over Tangier and Arzila in 1437 was a military fiasco as well as a political one. Portugal would conquer Tangier and Arzila only in 1471.

Yet possession of Ceuta must have boosted Portuguese morale and given them the courage needed to explore the African coastline. Prince Henry founded the first school of navigation at Sagres in 1419 and sponsored the voyage around Cape Bojador in 1434. The discoveries of the Islands of Madeira and the archipelago of Azores came in 1442, Senegal three years later, and the Cape Verde Islands in 1446. Four years later, Bartolomeu Dias sailed around the Cape of Good Hope. Vasco da Gama finally reached India in 1497, beating Spain in the quest.

Indeed, to European contemporaries, the discovery of the route to India was more significant than that of the New World by Christopher Columbus. Vasco da Gama's voyage was the climax of almost a century of expansion around the African coast and represented an unprecedented show of daringness, endurance, and heroism. That excursion opened for Portugal the trade with the East that Europe had lost with the fall of Constantinople in 1453.

Vasco da Gama's voyage was an immediate success, and it changed the course of European history. The *São Gabriel* brought with it what Vasco da Gama had set out to find: a route to pepper, nutmeg, cinnamon, cloves, and precious stones.[2] The Portuguese were triumphant during the sixteenth century. Daringness had paid off. Europe would now turn itself toward the Atlantic, and Lisbon became Europe's commercial hub. Venice declined amid the Mediterranean's lost luster, until almost four centuries later when the Suez Canal would shortcut the route around the Cape of Good Hope in 1869.

In 1496, under pressure from Spain, the Portuguese king Manuel I ordered the expulsion of all Jews. In an about-face, apparently under the pragmatic advice of counselors concerned with the projected economic losses, within a short time the king decided to suspend the expulsion, provided that all Jews converted to Catholicism. Jews were given the assurance that for a period of twenty years they would not be persecuted. This is how synagogues came to be transformed into churches. Jewish ghettoes were abolished, and converted Jews were addressed as new-Christians. Assimilation was slow and was punctuated by several rough episodes, such as the Lisbon mutiny of 1506, during which new-Christians were persecuted and two thousand died.

The decision to expel the Jews from Portugal, depriving the Portuguese of crucial financial and commercial know-how, came precisely at a time when Portugal was establishing itself to make commercial use of the expansion into Asia. Many Portuguese Jews settled in the Netherlands, where their knowledge of Portuguese affairs would provide the Dutch with a competitive advantage.

The false unity sought under forced conversion led to the formation of two Portugals—the old-Christian Portugal: dogmatic, repressive, and averse to innovation; and the New-Christian Portugal: concealed, distrustful, and messianic, which could never quite trust that it was on equal footing with old-Christian society. Portugal would have to learn to live with this division, which would extend on into modern times.

In the meantime, the Portuguese continued to advance in their trade routes, establishing ties with Goa, in India (1510), Malacca, on the Malay Peninsula (1511), today's Indonesia (1512–14), China (1517), and Japan (1542). In 1557 the mandarin of Canton would grant Portugal the use of the peninsula of Macao for trading purposes. To Portugal, Brazil was no more than a savage coastline made Portuguese by the presence of a crucifix. Portugal's attention would not return to the Brazilian coastline until its hold on the Asian trade was contested by the Dutch.

Portugal's Atlantic expansion spanned six hundred years and is marked by three phases: the Asian phase lasted until the late sixteenth century when Portugal turned its concentration from Asia to Brazil, where the competition was less fierce. The Brazilian phase lasted until the early nineteenth century when, upon Brazil's independence, the African phase began, lasting until the late twentieth century. By the early nineteenth century, however, Portugal was no longer a significant European player.

Nonetheless, a century and half of Asian trade is a long time, long enough for Portugal to benefit from and spread trade benefits over a large share of the population. It is not by chance that the end of Portuguese civil unrest coincides with the beginning of the Asian expansion. However, riches gained through trade shifted the locus of economic activity from the farm to the port, making it difficult for Portugal to continue to produce sufficient goods for its own sustenance. Wheat would now be imported and less wine exported. The nobility would gain preeminence, particularly because without the Jews the merchants prospered, although they remained noncosmopolitan at a time of growing international trade, when international connections were increasingly important.[3]

Portugal's decline in Asia came about for many reasons. Some authors are tempted to attribute it in part to Portugal's zealous Catholicism, a spillover from Spain through John III's wife, sister to Charles V, king of Spain and Holy Roman Emperor. The Inquisition was introduced into Portugal in 1536, lasting through 1821, while education was entirely in the hands of the Jesuits as from 1540.

Other important reasons besides religion could be brought to bear. In hindsight, it is even surprising that Portugal was the nation to reach Asia by sea. Although the feat was undoubtedly the work of intrepid and entrepreneurial sailors, merchants, and kings, Portugal's size was small relative to the ordeal. Voyages to Asia took over six months and were subject to many perils.[4] While initially the Moors in control of Indian trade would flee under threat of Portugal's cannons, later they would respond in kind, or more. Moreover, maintaining multiple commercial outposts on the route to Asia was a drain on manpower to a small country, which piled on new colonies without making the strategic decision to move out of others.

But if the Portuguese purpose was not a mere commercial venture but rather the mission of a nation advancing Catholicism, could Portugal have abandoned any colony, including the North African ones? In fact, the tiny nation was in full Salvationist stance and could barely have devoted any thought to dropping North Africa. During the Cortes session of 1562, the councilors resolved to maintain the North African fortresses, even if it meant gutting the budget of the University of Coimbra, "which ought to be extinguished as it is detrimental to the kingdom."[5] Sadly, this illustration points to the importance Portugal attached to its overseas possessions at the expense of higher learning.

The Inquisition contributed to the lack of enlightenment. Portugal had too small a share of Protestantism to justify an Inquisition. The Inquisition was originally motivated by opposition to the Jewish population, although it had pecuniary motives as well, perhaps even more than religious ones. About ten people per year were burnt at the stake during the first 140 years of the Inquisition; the vast majority was accused of Judaism. Besides cruelty, the Inquisition had three anti-intellectual legacies: the elimination or "neutralization" of a large share of inquisitive people; intellectual censorship as manifested in the banning of books; and the culture of denouncement, with its implicit aversion to free thinking and, consequently, innovation. The Inquisition had yet another poor dividend: it deprived Portugal of one-third of its merchant class.[6]

PORTUGUESE MESSIANIC ATTITUDES: SEBASTIANISM

There was a cobbler in Troncoso who was so coarse that the Inquisition in 1534 deemed him only fit to be a shepherd. Yet the cobbler wished to write verses, preferring to choose words for their sound rather than for their meaning, which in any case would mostly escape him. His themes were pastoral and evocative, telling of prophetic plights against the powerful, corruption, and general societal sins. He based much of his writing on his Bible readings and regional legends, from which he got his messianic twist. His rhapsodies were so wild that the verses could be read to hold various meanings, though quite often to hold none at all. However, the allusions to the return of a messiah caught the attention of the Inquisition at the time of the persecutions against the Jews. The cobbler was indicted but found to be so alien to conspiracy that he was set free, although forbidden to write again, assuming that this would put an end to his influence.

Meanwhile, the religious zealot, King Sebastian, died in battle at Alcácer Quibir, Morocco, in 1578. As no gentleman could vouch to have seen his lord succumb without assistance, the legend grew that the king had disappeared in battle and that he would return to right all wrongs. The prophecies of the cobbler were then read with a new meaning, which would grab and hold the public's imagination until today. Many impersonators of King Sebastian were spotted and executed, yet it all added to the popular belief that he was around the corner. The cobbler was revered as a saint, and an altar with his image was built in his birth city. King John IV was obliged to state that he would turn over the crown to King Sebastian, should he appear. Modern versions of Sebastianism express the belief that desired events will take place by earnestly wishing for them.

Messianic Judaism had caught the imagery of the Portuguese as well as of the Jews: at times of collective plight, the Messiah will return to redeem the sufferers without their individual effort. According to Hermano Saraiva, Portugal can be divided into two groups: those, like the Jews, who await the Messiah; and those who continue to wait for King Sebastian. At the time of the Napoleonic invasions, in 1808, half the city of Lisbon had come under the grip of King Sebastian, according to João das Neves. The myth of King Sebastian was carried to the New World by immigrants. It was adopted there and fueled the messianic movement led by Antonio Conselheiro in the Brazilian Northeast, until it was suffocated by the Brazilian army in 1897, at the cost of many thousands dead.

PORTUGAL LOSES GROUND

Upon occupying Recife (1630), the Dutch had quickly learned that the sugar industry needed a reliable supply of slaves and that the occupation of Brazil would be worth little without them; thus they invaded Luanda (1641), in Angola. By the time the Portuguese got Recife and Luanda back (1654), the Dutch had learned enough about sugar production to move it to the island of Curaçao. Holland now also had the former Portuguese African colony of Guinea as a stable supply of slaves and could compete with the Portuguese in sugar production, which is what they had set out to do when they invaded Recife.

The Dutch had only a skeleton fleet when Spain took over Antwerp in 1585. But fifteen years later they were trading on the west coast of Africa. By 1650, Holland was a major international trading power, though they never devoted more than 15 percent of their seafaring capacity to non-European destinations. The Dutch also competed with the Portuguese in Asia, where they evicted Portugal from the East Indies, today Indonesia. They traded in salt with northern Venezuela, as they could no longer dry their herring with Portuguese salt, and in sugar, through the Sephardic network that had been expelled from Spain and Portugal.[7] Dutch privateering also took its toll on the Portuguese Asian fleet, adding to its decimation by the weather and the Moors. Even if the direct Dutch-inflicted losses were not great, Dutch pressure was forcing the Portuguese to sail under inappropriate weather conditions. Almost a quarter of the Portuguese fleet was lost on the way to Asia or back; risk averse the Portuguese were not.

During the first years of the seventeenth century, twenty-two ships per year were leaving Lisbon for Asia, compared to thirteen ships per year from Amsterdam. The Dutch fleet peaked in 1650, when its relevance declined vis-à-vis the increasing participation of both England and France.

This is how the Portuguese were gnawed at the fringes across the centuries. The string of defeats must have persuaded them that the Asian venture was either too risky, too competitive, or both. In 1572 that epic history was told by Camões in *Os Lusíadas*. The Brazilian phase of Portuguese expansion begins next, and lasts until the first half of the nineteenth century, after Portugal had invested more than two hundred thousand souls in Brazil; but this story is told in Chapter 8.

In November 1807, Napoleon invades Portugal and the royal family leaves for Brazil, arriving in 1808. Once Napoleon was ousted in 1814, Portugal resumes its course, but Brazil declares independence in 1822. Portugal then focuses on Africa, until its longest-living ally, England—in breach of the long-standing 1386 Treaty of Windsor—issues an ultimatum in 1890 regarding Portuguese dominion of Masson and Niassa in Africa, which posed an obstacle to Britain's intent to build a railroad from Cairo to Cape Town. Portugal thus refrains from its claim of territories known today as Zambia, Zimbabwe, and Malawi and from its aim to unite by land its colonies of Mozambique and Angola, in southeastern and western Africa, respectively.

The ultimatum came as an embarrassing shock to a nation that had ignored its repeated incapacity to establish the rule of law in its African possessions. Over much of the nineteenth century, Portuguese apathy permeated writers' assessments of Africa and of Portugal itself. Images of Portugal's decadence surfaced in the works of several authors, in particular those of the "Generation of 1870," known as Life's Vanquished. Eça de Queiroz was a forceful presence in this intellectual circle, which also counted Antero de Quental and the historian Oliveira Martins among its members. According to Eça de Queiroz's *Revista de Portugal*, the nation's African dominions were to be merely contemplated, for Portugal lacked the means or the initiative to effectively rule them.[8] To Antero de Quental, Portugal was to blame for the loss of Brazil.

Long before England's ultimatum, Portuguese perceptions of the nation's African dominions were tinged by pessimism and weakness. According to Trajano Filho, with this vision of themselves, when meekness was turned into virtue, these are the Portuguese emigrants that arrived at the Brazilian coastline.[9] The British ultimatum to Portugal accelerated the demise of the monarchy, and Portugal adopted the republican form of government in 1911.

SUMMING UP: PORTUGAL

Portugal has a relatively quiet history, with few feats in the arts to boast of, few in the sciences; but it does have to show for itself a remarkable audacity in over a century of exploration of the African coastline, as well as the feather in its cap of beating Columbus to India in 1497. One century would sire almost four generations of explorers, advancing, registering, and innovating sails, masts, hulls, and location devices. It was not merely a matter of perseverance, it was also one of courage.

Like Spain, Portugal was also a Salvationist nation. It carried forth a religious mission, which is why it held on to Moslem outposts that offered little in return in terms of trade or logistic support, draining resources such as those earmarked for the University of Coimbra.

The same Salvationist stance would lead to the expulsion of the Jews, despite the loss in trading skills that their departure entailed, particularly at a time when the maritime route to Asia had recently been opened. Yet the Portuguese sailed on and were the first to establish trade between China and Japan. There were daunting losses but also enough riches to attract Dutch competitors, backed by the Jews that had been expelled from Portugal.

Dutch competition on the Asian route diverted Portugal's attention to Brazil, until then much neglected. In fact, Brazil was occupied principally to keep it free from the threat of the French, Dutch, and Spanish. Since the time of its inception, Brazil would see the outside world as a threat rather than an opportunity.

Brazil's mineral riches came at a good time, and the territory provided a safe haven for Portugal's royalty when it came under threat by Napoleon. To Brazil, economically, hosting the royal family was a bonus. Becoming the seat of the empire led to the improvement of its infrastructure, the liberalization of trade, the advancement of education and research, and—frequently overlooked—the territorial integrity of the nation, as Brazil never fragmented politically like the Spanish colonial region did.

Brazil also inherited from Portugal the amiability that characterizes trading nations, along with the awe and mysticism that accompanies explorers and adventurers. This is how Sebastianism, an expression of fatalism, took hold in Brazil, adding to the sense of weakness inherited from the Portuguese, whose courageous efforts in discoveries were surreptitiously overridden by more powerful agents.

With Brazil's independence, Portugal diverted its interests to its African colonies. No longer able to leverage the riches of Brazil or those of trade to develop the colonies, Portugal folded into complacency until Britain issued its ultimatum in 1890, ending five hundred years of protection under the Treaty of Windsor. For centuries, Britain had enabled Portugal to embark on the maritime exploration of Africa, and with the ultimatum it reminded the Portuguese where the locus of power gravitated.

ITALY

I TALY WAS IN TURMOIL in the late nineteenth century. Low labor-absorption rates gave rise to a generation of restless youth. About half of all Italian gross emigration in the 1890s went toward other European countries, but the other half helped to populate the New World. Italy, Spain, and Portugal were among the European countries that supplied over fifty emigrants to the New World for every thousand inhabitants. Emigrants in the late nineteenth century were mostly young, unskilled men who emigrated alone, without families—young men who displayed a low dependency rate or a "near-zero drag" cost, in current Silicon Valley labor market terminology.[1] The predominant type of Italian emigrant testifies to the economic drive pushing Italy's people abroad; the exodus was in response to the low local absorption capacity of an economy that had experienced a surge in population in the fourth quarter of the nineteenth century. While only Spain's population increase faltered in the mid-nineteenth century, all three countries, and particularly Italy, failed economically in the late nineteenth century, driving large segments of their populations abroad.[2]

THE RISE OF CITY-STATES

The demise of the Roman empire in the late fifth century led to a period of power fragmentation that limited organizational capabilities. Some cities benefited from location advantages, such as ports with significant trade like Venice and Genoa. As cities became more powerful they vied for greater autonomy, which, during the eleventh century permitted the consolidation of an intricate web of communal governments. These subsequently fostered the leadership of a burgher class whose power rested on trade, banking, and at times the textile industry. Some of the northern cities best known today—Florence, Venice, Genoa, or Milan—concentrated sufficient power to become independent city-states, which weakened the aristocracy and the feudal regime on which it rested.

The diminished imperial and papal authority throughout the city-states allowed the flourishing of ideas and humanist attitudes that fostered the Renaissance. Power disputes in the cities continued, nonetheless. Victorious families would institute a dictatorial rule. This is the case of the Viscontis in thirteenth-century Milan, followed by the Sforzas in the mid-fifteenth century not long after the Medicis had secured their rule over Florence.

The consolidation of power within the cities would lead to the expansion of their areas of influence and to intercity disputes. Mercenary leaders were frequently called to intervene in favor of one prince or another, in wars that weakened the cities. Trade revenues in the region had suffered since the fall of Constantinople in 1453, strengthening the Turks, who waged wars against Venice for much of the sixteenth century. The debilitation of the cities continued until they fell prey to Charles VIII of France in 1494, two years after the beginning of the annexation of the New World.

SICILY

The South suffered a different fate. Unlike the North, with its vigorous trading poles, the South experienced a long period of feudal regimes brought about initially by the Normans, who began settling in the South in the eleventh century, at the same time they were invading England. This regime was extended in the thirteenth century under the German house of Hohenstaufen, which established one of Europe's most powerful states in Palermo.

The deepening of feudal rule led to secession in 1282 by Sicily, which fell under Spain's Peter III of Aragon. The kingdom of Aragon would reclaim the continental kingdom of Naples in the fifteenth century, when the kingdoms of Naples and Sicily were reunited under the kingdom of the Two Sicilies. This was the period when Spain was consolidating its control over the Iberian Peninsula, expelling the Moors and expanding to both the New World and southeastern Europe, including Rome.

SPANISH ROME

The influence of Spain in Rome during the sixteenth through the eighteenth centuries has been largely neglected, but it was significant to the point that about one-third of the Roman population was Spanish during much of that period.[3]

Continental Italy had been acquainted with Spanish rule since Alfonso the Magnanimous of Aragon conquered Naples (and Sicily) in 1442. Spanish presence, neighboring the papal states to the south, brought it considerable clout over the papacy. This is how the Borja family quickly ascended the ecclesiastical hierarchy and how Alfonso Borja became Pope Calixtus III in 1445 (through 1458). Alfonso had urged his nephew Rodrigo Borja to come to Rome, and this latter was made cardinal at the age of twenty-six. By then, the Borjas had been in Rome long enough to have their last name Italianized to Borgia. Rodrigo Borgia was elected Pope Alexander VI in 1492, as the Spanish empire's Catholic kings were expanding into the New World. With a Spanish pope in Rome and a flourishing Renaissance court in Naples, Spain wielded significant influence over papal affairs and Southern Italy, including over the latter's cultural traditions.

Nobody expressed more clearly this threat to cultural traditions than the pope's nephew, Cesare Borgia, who staged a bullfight in front of St. Peter's Basilica in 1424. After killing six bulls, the last with a sword with which he cut off the bull's head in one blow, Cesare only confirmed—in the eyes of the crowd—the notorious roughness of the thousands of Spanish soldiers under his command.

The initial largesse of Fernando and Isabella in becoming the benefactors in 1480 of St. Pietro's church and convent in Rome had now turned into a relationship of conquest as the Spanish expanded their empire. Charles V— king of the Holy Roman Empire and of Spain, and grandchild of Fernando and Isabella—added Milan to his possessions. So strong was Spain's influence that Charles V prevented the pope from conceding to the divorce of England's King Henry VIII from his Spanish wife, Catherine, ultimately leading to the birth of the Anglican Church.

By the time Charles V's son, Philip II, acceded the throne in 1557, Spain was well established as the dominant force in Italy. To the east, however, Suleiman the Magnificent, sultan of the Ottoman empire, ruled from Baghdad to Hungary and was stopped only at Vienna in 1529 by Christian forces led by Ferdinand I, archduke of Austria and brother of Charles V. Turkish ambitions over Europe were sobered considerably after the Turks were defeated at sea by Spain, in the 1571 battle of Lepanto. By the late sixteenth century, Spain would rule uncontested over the western Mediterranean as well. Its naval fleet there numbered close to one hundred ships, helping to keep the Ottoman threat at bay and thus offering the papal state the protection it could get nowhere else. This was the time of "soft Spanish imperialism" over the papal states.

The Borgias married into nobility, and tens of thousands of Spaniards came to Rome, including ambassadors, such as Garcilaso de la Vega, father of the renowned poet; clerics; courtiers; painters, such as Diego Velázquez; and writers, such as Miguel de Cervantes. The Spanish presence in Rome was so large that the city incorporated traditional Spanish versions of celebrations such as Easter and Corpus Domini. Spain's influence also was obvious in its eight Catholic cardinals, up from two just a few decades earlier and which constituted roughly 20 percent of all of the church's cardinals. The heightened number of canonized saints also illustrates Spanish influence. While no Spanish saint had achieved canonization in the sixty years preceding that of the Franciscan Diego de Alcalá of Spain in 1588, half of the twenty-seven saints canonized over the next hundred years were Spanish.

By 1550, Habsburg Charles V, king of Spain, had occupied nearly all of Italy. Mexico City was then twenty-five years old and Buenos Aires was just a year younger. Plymouth, landing spot of the Mayflower Pilgrims, would not be founded for another seventy years. Upon the abdication of Charles V, Philip II inherited Italy, which would remain under Spanish rule until Austria took over during the War of the Spanish Succession (1701–14). Yet the kingdom of the Two Sicilies—comprising the entire southern half of the peninsula and Sicily—would once more be under Spanish Bourbon control in 1735.

RISORGIMENTO

The Italian appetite for unification began to be expressed by nationalist revolts such as the Carbonari movement in the 1820s. Unification would come gradually, sparked off from Sardinia and eventually advancing to the south under the leadership of Giuseppe Garibaldi, who abolished the Spanish kingdom of the Two Sicilies in 1860–61. This was Garibaldi's third surge as a warrior for Italian unification. During his first attempt, he was caught and condemned to death. Garibaldi managed to flee to Brazil in 1834, where he engaged in civil wars in the Brazilian South and in Uruguay.

Garibaldi returned to Italy in 1854 and defeated the Austrian forces in the Alps in 1859. He subsequently regained Sicily in 1860 and Naples in 1861, effectively putting an end to the Spanish kingdom of the Two Sicilies. Italy was fully reunited under King Victor Emmanuel II in 1871, when Rome was chosen as its capital city.

United for the first time in centuries, Italy would have a long way to go. Unification of disparate dialects would effectively separate even its emigrants to the New World, let alone their larger cohorts back at home.

SUMMING UP: ITALY

There was no Italy, so to speak, for well over a millennium, from the fall of the Roman empire until its reunification. Fragmentation was the rule; independent cities and dialects were its expression. Spain had imposed a limited sense of unification in Southern Italy for much of the previous four centuries.

It should thus be no surprise that Iberian attitudes were familiar to the Southern Italians who migrated to Buenos Aires and São Paulo in droves. It is also natural to expect that Southern Italians would transport to the New World their institutional knowledge of societal organization.

Robert Putnam has suggested that the predominant trait of the Southern Italian institutional arrangement can be characterized as a low proclivity to establish horizontal alliances that would generate effective collaboration and foster the type of progress, equality, and respect that one recognizes in developed societies.[4] Southern Italians, argues Putnam, were victimized over centuries by foreign ruling elites that favored vertical ties of dependence, such as those between the feudal lord and the peasant, as these allowed the perpetuation of dependence and exploitation that might be threatened by horizontal ties of solidarity.[5] This vertical arrangement would later translate into what sociologists and anthropologists would call patron-client relationships, which are so pervasive in Latin America.

Both Sicily and England were invaded by the Normans at roughly the same time and endured their occupation nearly as long, considering both the French and Spanish occupations. Both societies suffered the yoke of similar foreign feudal arrangements, yet England ultimately developed a more significant array of institutional devices to curb absolutism than Sicily did.

It is possible that Southern Italians did develop the horizontal relationships that give rise to solidarity, but that these were too narrow in scope to foster institution building. The necessary degree of societal trust was hampered by the legacy of the foreign feudal regime. But Southern Italians developed a tradition of family-based horizontal relationships that allowed them to navigate in a hostile feudal environment.

Vertical relationships of the of patron-client sort were and still are more prevalent in Southern Italy than in the North. Southern immigrants to the New World arrived in their host countries with a tendency to develop or favor such ties under a varying degree of authoritarianism.

The inward solidarity developed in opposition to the Other gave rise in the United States to the Mafia, which is historically associated with the Southern Italian community. Perhaps the immigrants' feelings of alienation in the U.S. environment made them prey to organized crime. Yet it is interesting to note the lack of a parallel installment of the Mafia in Argentina, Brazil, or Uruguay—three countries that were also major recipients of Southern Italian immigrants. The fact that the Iberian societal arrangements of these countries were closely aligned with the immigrants' experiences provides one explanation why Southern Italians would fit in more readily in Latin America than they would in North America.

The difference in how Italians fit in, in North and South America, cannot be easily brushed aside. It is most relevant to the managerial message of this book. Southern Italians migrating to the United States fell into an alien organizational setting and responded by closing up among themselves. Accordingly, workers who are managed by foreign methods may behave like exiles in their own country and adopt strategies that will hinder organizational performance, as the Mafia did.

PART THREE

CULTURES OF THE NEW WORLD

W HILE PART TWO SOUGHT to trace the cultural roots of the New World to its nearest sources, the Mediterranean and Britain, this section seeks to characterize the culture of the New World, represented here by Argentina, Brazil, and the United States. The purpose of this section is not to provide a history class but rather to contextualize management in Latin America as being more representative of U.S. culture than of either Argentine or Brazilian culture. Management as practiced in the United States today is relatively alien to Latin Americans.

In the case of the USA I begin with the Pilgrims and the first successful colony at Plymouth, in today's Massachusetts. I will move on to the significance of the transcendentalist movement and the birth of the American nation, its drive westward, and its efforts toward unification. I trace the significance of these efforts in the building of the American character and the persistence of regional differences between the nation's North and South, particularly as expressed by the Little Rock crisis. I will explore the roots of those regional differences by examining their styles of land distribution and organization of production. It is by means of these different cultural manifestations that I will later approximate cultural attitudes of the Southern United States to those of Latin America, bridging a gap that is frequently understated.

I will devote less attention to the history of Argentina, except as can be told through the ideas of its prominent characters. I will begin with Mariano Moreno, in deference to both his prominence and his truculence, and move on to Rosas, Alberdi, and Sarmiento, opposites all, but significant in their impact on the formation of Argentina. I will devote more attention to Sarmiento than to the others because I believe his efforts on behalf of education were largely responsible for what Argentina is today. Inspired and aided by the North American transcendentalists, Sarmiento was Latin America's foremost educator, rendering a nation one century later with four Nobel laureates to its educational credit. A fifth Nobel Prize, to Adolfo Pérez Esquivel for Peace, in 1980, owes its differential solely to Pérez Esquivel's own personal courage in the war against the nastier side of Argentina's cultural heritage. A degree of intolerance has stalled Argentina in the last century, fragmenting it into bickering factions and hindering its capacity to transform knowledge into a technology that its industry may put to good use. This has led to stagnation and social strife, rendering a country that opened the current millennium with a revolving door, through which five presidents passed in a single fortnight.

I then turn to Brazil, as large as it is different. I argue that Brazil was not colonized but kept, drawing attention from the Portuguese only when their interests in Asia were challenged by competitors. Moreover, the royal family's move to Brazil thwarted Brazil's political development, just as the emotional development of an adolescent would be stalled if the entire family were to move into his or her freshman dorm. Brazil has since lingered behind, its individuals shy of entrepreneurial initiative when that means challenging foreigners in their own land. Brazil has hosted a sizable foreign manufacturing industry but has mostly failed at exporting manufactured goods. I argue that this is the result of the lack of a symbolic pact that would lead Brazilians to unite around a common goal, thereby integrating themselves into the concept of a nation and building an effective judiciary that might free them from patron-client relationships.

I then illustrate how these three nations' main characteristics were unwittingly nurtured by their forefathers: nations of small farmers in North America and of large landholdings and absentee landlords in South America. The former bred the dispersion of power that enabled democracy to flourish, along with competition and the accumulation of wealth. Meanwhile, the countries we are observing in South America concentrated power, refined authoritarianism, and consolidated the power of groups rather than of individuals. Which style is better is a matter of choice, but the results are facts to be contended with and not, as is the current method, ignored by attempting to manage the people of both cultures in the same way.

CHAPTER 6

UNITED STATES
OF AMERICA

The greatest discovery of my generation is that a human being
can alter his life by altering his attitudes.

William James, 1842–1910

ENGLISH INTEREST IN COLONIZING America was no
greater than its scant interest in its territorial discoveries.
The first Puritans arrived in North America aboard the *Mayflower* a hefty 130
years after the discovery of the New World.

English Protestants left England in search of religious liberty. Their views
on theology had political counterparts, and they imprinted upon the region
a distinctive political arrangement: the town meeting. Although only men of
property could vote, reflecting the Protestants' origins in English law, the town
meeting practice allowed the New England settlers strong familiarity with
political participation. The participative politics encouraged local solutions to
communal problems—such as an education provision, which to this day remains
locally or state based, except for higher education. This participative policy was
firmly grounded in an egalitarian work ethic: settlers working the wilderness in
conjunction made collaborative initiatives mandatory. The need for cooperation
required setting aside special privileges, rendering all people equal.

At the time of the American Revolution, 95 percent of the U.S. population was made up of farmers, and the equal footing implied in this statistic
meant that the egalitarian principle would permeate all of the nation's future

institutions. At the time, American egalitarianism was selective; it did not include Negroes, many of whom joined ranks with the British against American Revolutionaries. During the Gold Rush, incidentally, this egalitarian attitude would spawn great resentment among miners against Southern gentlemen "digging" for gold by means of their slaves.

Because land was relatively cheap, specialized labor would be scarce and crafts would be slow to develop and organize. The first printing press arrived in Massachusetts in 1638, and the second one only in 1674. The first presses utilized movable type, which would remain in short supply until 1768, when the first type foundry entered into business in Connecticut.[1]

Settlers in New England did not become known for their agricultural produce. By the mid-eighteenth century they had turned to trade, domestic and international enterprises, fishing, and shipbuilding. New Englanders earned a reputation for inquisitiveness, ingenuity, thrift, and solid work. This industriousness was crucial during the war for independence, when New Englanders turned to manufacturing and churned out such products as rifles, clothing, and clockworks. The drift from farm life to urban trades shifted perspectives and led to a religious backlash that became known as the Great Awakening and aimed at restoring the colonies' initial religious fervor.

THE BREAKUP WITH ENGLAND

The settlers faced all odds and paid few taxes, but as of 1651 the British began seeing the colonies as a source of riches that could cover more than the cost of the colonies' own defense. England sought to raise more cash by taxing its colonies and to contain defense costs by constraining their expansion westward. Conflict over these impositions by the crown rapidly cascaded from what was initially a tax issue into a war over independence.

The American Revolutionaries blended their settlers' experience with the political thought of John Locke and strove for a democratic republic. In 1776, Tom Paine, an English polemist whom Benjamin Franklin had invited to Pennsylvania, published the liberationist pamphlet called *Common Sense*. Paine rejected negotiations with the British and proposed complete independence. *Common Sense* became a best seller among a people who wanted to keep for itself a greater part of its work. America was showing its independence in many ways, not least of all through technological innovation.

Independence in the production of basic materials was being accomplished, as well as in the arts. Stephen Foster, born in 1826, is believed to be the first American composer to focus on New World rhythms: "Oh! Susanna," is one of his best-known compositions.

FORGING A NEW NATION

The independent spirit of North Americans would make them distrustful of government. Farmers were scattered and isolated, promoting individualism and self-reliance. The constitution they drafted for themselves assuaged those fears. Following Montesquieu's musings, they sought separation of government into three independent branches: executive, legislative, and judiciary, each with built-in checks and balances on the other. Ten amendments, known as the Bill of Rights—inspired by England's precedent of 1628, the Petition of Right— sought to protect individual liberties. The Bill of Rights protects citizens' rights to freedom of religion and speech, including freedom of the press; the right to gather in public places; and the right to protest government. It mandates that no authority can stop or search a citizen without good cause or search a home without authorization, and against cruel and unusual punishment.

The purchase of Louisiana from Napoleon in 1803 and subsequent re-moval of the French meant that America could reach the Rocky Mountains over land. Only the Spanish colonies in California would stand between the United States and the Pacific. Meriwether Lewis and William Clark caught the imagination of the American public in the newspapers when they tracked the route to the Pacific in their 1804–5 expedition. When the cowboy was king, Lewis and Clark followed the Missouri River and subsequently crossed the Rocky Mountains, arriving at the Pacific Ocean in Oregon. The nation's population was then close to seven million. It would reach almost ten million in 1820 and over seventeen million by 1840.

The economy would also grow rapidly. Britain was in the midst of its industrial revolution, and its textile mills required ever-increasing amounts of cotton. Eli Whitney invented the cotton gin in 1793, and by 1860 the United States supplied almost two-thirds of the world's cotton consumption, grown in the South through slave labor. Whitney's greatest contribution to American technology, however, was not the cotton gin—it was interchange-able parts.

Indeed, Whitney's cotton gin, pervasive as it became, would not have the capacity to permeate other industries that his Uniformity System came to have. The Whitney concept of standardizing production techniques and mechanisms in order to render the parts interchangeable was close to a technological revolution. As would be the case with so many important inventions in the future, Whitney's invention was conceived in response to a defense contract. Whitney initially agreed in 1798 to deliver muskets to defend the United States against a possible French invasion. Neither materialized, not the French attack nor the timely delivery of muskets. Yet his claim to the contract was granted because it promised to lead to a degree of standardization that would enable the division of large projects into subcomponents that could then be commissioned to numerous suppliers and assembled by others. Repairs would be facilitated, particularly under the duress of war. Arms procurement inducing a technological industrial revolution based on speed, uniformity, and precision would thus forever shape what became known as the American production system, which two hundred years later encircles the globe.

Newspaper publishing was already significant in the 1820s, when close to twenty-five daily newspapers and four hundred weeklies were being published. American dominance would liberate its artists from European styles; it also had the benefit of focusing literature on the American scene. Edgar Allan Poe launched American fiction in short stories with *The Masque of the Red Death* in 1835. His contemporary, Nathaniel Hawthorne, who orbited around the Peabody sisters[2] and Ralph Waldo Emerson, would become famous for *The Scarlet Letter*, a stark cry against the intolerance of Puritan morals. Hawthorne deeply influenced his friend Herman Melville, who explored themes in *Moby-Dick* such as evil and man's struggle against the elements as well as the soul-searching ignited by these musings.

In 1836, Ralph Waldo Emerson published *Nature*, in which transcendence into the natural world could provide an order without organized religion. Emerson's novel and lectures influenced many, among them Henry David Thoreau, author of *Walden*. Emerson's and Thoreau's writings reinforced American individualism and self-reliance. These members of the intellectual elite were among the thinkers that the Argentine Domingo F. Sarmiento would draw from during his trip to the United States to meet Horace Mann, "father of public education." That Bostonian intellectual elite would shape Sarmiento's outlook on the world, a world in which the USA had replaced Europe as a source of knowledge-based solutions.

In Chapter 7 we will see the importance that the Peabody sisters and intellectuals gravitating around the transcendentalist movement had for a receptive Argentine in the person of Sarmiento, avid for solutions for a new country. In Chapter 16 we will explore the managerial impact of American obsessions, such as those depicted in Melville's *Moby-Dick*.

As the northern United States industrialized around New England and the mid-Atlantic states, coal mining boomed as well. Transportation requirements grew, and the steady upgrading of its infrastructure sought to bring costs down: Lake Erie was linked to the Hudson River by canal in 1825, and the first railroad began construction in 1828. Improvements in transportation would cut travel time. In 1790 it took, on average, six weeks to reach the Great Lakes from New York City. By 1860, that amount of time would get one anywhere on the continent east of the Rockies.

In 1838, John Deere invented the steel plough. The self-governing windmill made its appearance in 1854, allowing wind power to be captured more efficiently. Barbed wire was patented in 1874, which helped promote cattle rearing and agriculture. By the early nineteenth century, innovation in the United States was surprising European visitors. The USA was still no rival to Europe in science, but labor was relatively scarce and wages could not elicit the interest of the adventurers who had crossed the Atlantic on the promise of cheap land. Wherever manpower could be replaced mechanically, it would be.[3]

The discovery of gold in California was announced in September of 1848, triggering the Gold Rush and boosting California's population to 250,000 by 1852, just two years after its elevation to statehood. California's great distance from New England was an effective barrier to the entry of goods manufactured in the East and effectively kick-started the development of local industry. The discovery of gold and the ensuing Gold Rush left vacancies on the East Coast, adding to North America's pull in Europe, particularly among those fleeing the Irish famine resulting from the potato blight of 1848–49. About 1.6 million Irish immigrants arrived between 1847 and 1854, settling mostly along the East Coast and in Philadelphia.

THE CIVIL WAR

"All men are created equal" read the Declaration of Independence. Nonetheless, to the 1.5 million slaves in the United States, those words must have sounded hollow. The U.S. Civil War is customarily attributed to the slavery issue, but the looming realities of regional imbalances and tariff disputes between the country's North and South were also prominent causes. Moreover, these same issues of discrepancy capture the image of most Latin American countries still today. In the United States the industrialized North would benefit from tariff protection for its nascent industries, while to Southerners, higher tariffs meant only more expensive imported goods and little to no benefit to their competitive agricultural output.

The Civil War was the reflection of a rapidly industrializing North's need for secure markets, and the humanitarian aside of abolition provided the rallying cry. Moreover, much like the Spanish empire after the Reconquista, the USA's North was ready for expansion. Manifest Destiny, the belief that democracy and freedom must be spread by shore-to-shore expansion, now turned to the southern United States. Years of fighting the Indian wars that plagued the western expansion, particularly since the 1790s, had seasoned a Northern army that could now be diverted to fight the South, which the North outnumbered four to one in military-aged men. The Civil War claimed 600,000 lives and devastated the South by the time it was over, in 1865.

Land was the American currency. Parcels were offered to immigrants in return for military service. By the end of the war, 20 percent of the Union Army were recent immigrants. Newcomers from Europe poured into the United States, seeking a better life and also lured by the Homestead Act of 1862. This act enabled the government to offer 160-acre parcels of land to anyone willing to till it for five years.

Prompt and fair access to land instigated a "perennial rebirth" under the auspices of the promise of plenty to those willing to work hard. Expediency and fairness were paramount, as expressed by Frederick Jackson Turner in the 1890s in his interpretation of the success of American society based on its capacity to attract and blend immigrants at the frontier.[4]

The American psyche was imbued with the pioneer spirit that remains vital today. The availability of vacant land at a time when land was the source of riches drove millions to the United States, where they fended for themselves, worked cooperatively whenever possible, and primarily sought viability in their endeavors. This sense of efficacy permeated such institutions as the jury and justice systems, which were prone to quick fixes like death by hanging. The pioneer spirit also engendered a practical orientation and distrust of intellectuals. Hofstadter has traced these roots to the absence of institutions hospitable to intellectual pursuits and to sectarian religious competitiveness.[5] These values were later crystallized in American business society. In the Hofstadter sense, religion and the business ethic have swayed the American consciousness toward a disdain for intellectual pursuits.

AMERICA AFTER THE CIVIL WAR

Winning the war would prove easier than eliminating discrimination against people of African descent. During 1866 and 1867, the newly formed Ku Klux Klan terrorized African Americans, frightening them into not voting, and antagonized Jews, Catholics, and immigrants as well.

Yet the Civil War was over, and the encouragement of immigration through offers of land would lead us to believe that America would forever be a land of farmers; which it was, until 1890, when for the first time industrial output exceeded agricultural output. One significant difference between the U.S. and Latin American versions of land occupation is that in the United States land was allocated to immigrants for cultivation on relatively small plots. This, at a time when tillable land was scarce in Europe, helped to make the United States a land of immigrants—a trait maintained until the late 1990s, when the nation's share of foreign residents hovered around the centennial yearly average of 7 percent. It may seem low, but it is not.

Entitling people to land grants meant there would be fewer paid farmhands and, most notably, that mortgage credit could be advanced to farmers—factors that gave homesteaders both an incentive to mechanize agriculture and the means to access credit.[6] This also boosted the industry of agricultural products, such as meatpacking in Chicago, which added to the overall demand for steel and transportation services.

By the late nineteenth century, American inventiveness had expanded beyond agriculture. The 1876 Centennial Fair in Philadelphia attracted over eight million people to view the country's progress. Two of America's most significant inventors were present: Alexander Graham Bell exhibited the first telephone, and Thomas Alva Edison showed the automatic telegraph.

The American character seems imbued with a significant dose of entrepreneurship. Whether this stems from Protestantism is debatable, but it is frequently argued that Calvinist ethics, strong among the *Mayflower* Pilgrims, may be at the root of American entrepreneurship, in the sense that Calvinism stresses hard work and accumulation as the way to honor God. How much is due to religion and how much to greed is hard to separate. After all, the fantastic wealth amassed by the "robber barons" in the late nineteenth and early twentieth centuries is hardly attributable to a religious mandate. No American growth at all would have been possible without the entrepreneurial spirit of the Spanish Catholic kings in sponsoring the voyages of exploration. Therefore, despite the admirable efforts of Max Weber in 1905, and of his followers since, accumulation as a result of Protestant fervor is not necessarily a satisfying answer to entrepreneurship. Indeed, the influence of literacy, as closely associated with Protestantism, may shed the most light in the effort to explain the roots of American entrepreneurship.[7]

Yet one good reason does exist to ascribe the triumph of America to Protestantism, as well as Judaism: both are religions that stress local government over the papal centralization that characterizes Catholicism. Local solutions favor a fair apportionment of surplus, a circumstance that encourages inventiveness and inquisitive thinking in addition to competitiveness. Competition spurs the fast adoption of innovation, including new methods of production. Such was the case with the adoption of the electric motor as a source of power. This invention not only further unshackled production from the forced proximity to waterfalls, as the steam engine had already begun to do, but it also invited new plant layouts: electric wires could now be drawn where power was needed, thereby freeing the production line from the pulley system that, by definition, enforced a straight line of production.

Mass production of consumer goods helped to revolutionize the American way of life. This, in essence, would be Henry Ford's contribution in 1913—adoption of the moving assembly line. This method brought parts on a conveyor belt to workers specialized in specific tasks. Ford's procedures proved that industry could proceed along alternative paths, inspiring industrial managers to rethink their processes in search of greater efficiency and lower costs.

Yet there were "good" and "bad" corporations. The latter had to be reeducated, and the time was ripe for business schools. Wharton was the first, in 1881. Dartmouth and the University of Wisconsin added business schools in 1891. Harvard's business school was founded in 1908, and by 1939 there were 120 business schools in the USA.

In 1900, America's output of steel was larger than Britain's. In the second half of the nineteenth century, the railway network expanded from 9,000 to 190,000 miles, which meant that America had more rail mileage than the whole of Europe.[8] The boost to the railroad network came through the allocation of public land for railroad construction in 1862. Rail construction increased the demand for coal, iron, and steel. By 1869 it was possible to board a train on the East Coast that would deliver passengers and goods on the West Coast. The world's first transcontinental railroad was completed, expanding markets and settlements. This prosperity would expand to the southern United States, where the textile industry blossomed alongside cotton.

The corporate structure encouraged the mobilization of capital needed to deploy inventions such as the electric light bulb or the telephone. Neither Edison nor Bell were entrepreneurs by trade, but neither wasted any time in securing the protection that their patents allowed them. The Edison Electric Light Company was chartered in 1878, eventually leading to today's General Electric Company. The Bell Telephone Company was founded in 1877. Twenty years later, American Telephone and Telegraph (AT&T) owned and operated the Bell system.

In the days before electricity, entertainment had to be live. Many American entertainers who later became famous through movies or records got their start in vaudeville theaters, such as W. C. Fields, Buster Keaton, Sophie Tucker, Al Jolson, and the Three Stooges. It was not until the dissemination of electricity in the late nineteenth century that music publishing prospered, with many firms based in New York City. Motion pictures also were enabled by the expansion of electricity service.

The growth of industrialization also meant better salaries and opportunities for entertainers. Until the early 1900s, movies had been a European domain, with Europe supplying close to 50 percent of cinema consumption in the USA. It is not surprising that New York would be the main market. By 1908 over five hundred movie theaters dotted New York City, and this was before talkies.

Many immigrants, particularly Jews, found employment in the U.S. film industry in the early 1900s. As is the case with many new, creative industries, cinema was less affected by discrimination. Jews, barred from other occupations by racial prejudice, made their mark in film. They first captured the niche of showing short films in storefront theaters; later, the likes of Samuel Goldwyn, Adolph Zukor, Louis B. Mayer, and the Warner brothers ran the movie studios. The studios relocated to California, where they would be met by a more hospitable climate—both physically, for shooting films outdoors, and businesswise, because of California's more tolerant attitude toward Jewish immigrants. Whether on the East Coast or the West, the United States claimed the industry by 1920, when European films had virtually disappeared from the USA. Market size determined the opportunity for the increased cost per film, driving European competitors away. Europe could not achieve similar scales because its home markets were fragmented into several languages and because of its small distribution networks.[9]

When booming, the film industry was churning out films like the automotive industry was cranking out cars. But, unlike the car industry, film managed to attract some of the most creative talents. For example, *To Have and Have Not* (1944), famous for pairing Humphrey Bogart and Lauren Bacall, was written by two future Nobel laureates: Ernest Hemingway, who authored the novel on which the film was based, and William Faulkner, who adapted it to film.

With growth came concentration and restrictive trade practices that the U.S. government, true to its egalitarian bias, attempted to curb. By 1887, interstate commerce would control railroad rates. The Sherman Antitrust Act of 1890 banned business agreements "in restraint of trade or commerce." Despite the competition-enhancing efforts, John D. Rockefeller of the Standard Oil Company became one of the richest men in America, and Andrew Carnegie built a vast empire of steel mills, despite having arrived as a poor Scottish immigrant.

EXPANSIONIST AMERICA

U.S. frontiers had been stable since the Mexican War (except for Alaska, added in 1867). But expansion creates its own rationale, and a spirit of expansion that would spill over the U.S. frontiers would sweep the nation by 1890.

In response to dreadful accounts of Spanish atrocities suppressing a revolt in Cuba, America went to war with Spain over Cuba in 1898. Much to the old Spanish empire's surprise, the war was short and to its disadvantage. When it was over, Spain had relinquished the remnants of its empire. This is how the United States came to rule over Cuba, Puerto Rico, the Philippines, and Guam. Shortly afterward, the USA left Cuba, except for the Guantanamo base it still holds today. Self-government was granted to the Philippines in 1907, though full independence did not come until 1946. Puerto Rico remains in a strange limbo even today; its citizens are liable to be drafted into wars they cannot vote on.

The Spanish-American War was no more than a skirmish to the victor. But it proved to the world that the United States was now a power to be reckoned with, capable of operating in several theaters simultaneously. The war also persuaded the USA of the need to move its naval fleet swiftly from ocean to ocean.

In a further display of power and determination, in 1903 President Theodore Roosevelt leveraged a local independent movement in Panama to fast-forward that country's secession from Colombia and secure for the American Corps of Engineers the power to build a canal across Panama, as well as to manage it for ninety-nine years. The Panama Canal was completed in 1914 and returned to Panama in 2000. During much of that century, the United States was committed to keeping the sea routes to the canal trouble free. Unfortunately, this meant a lot of trouble to the countries it sought to stabilize, such as Guatemala, Nicaragua, Panama, and Santo Domingo.

SHAPING THE ENVIRONMENT

Steel, urban concentration, and America's flair for the new led to an unmistakable American contribution to architecture: the skyscraper. Twenty years after the invention of the elevator emergency break (by Elisha Otis in 1852), over two thousand elevators had been installed in hotels, office buildings, and commercial centers. The skyscraper would take another decade. The thrusting lines of the skyscraper have since portrayed the power of America's imposing and audacious entrepreneurial drive, to the tragic point of becoming the target of anti-American terrorists in the early twenty-first century.

Radio broadcasts began in the 1920s and by the end of that decade had helped create larger markets for entertainment. This process of market unification would also have strong political impact. Radio networks were purposefully used to create a common U.S. culture. The Radio Act of 1927, still debated today, led to broadcasters enjoying fewer First Amendment rights than newspapers.

IRONING OUT THE CREASES

Despite the force of its expansionism, the United States was also looking inward and struggling with its domestic problems. Adam Smith's laissez-faire had argued for small government, but unbridled individualism was causing trouble as well as progress. About half of all industrial workers lived in poverty. In addition to museums, universities, and private libraries, there were also slums. In 1910 the U.S. population had reached ninety-two million. Brazil, of roughly the same size, would take another seventy years to reach a similar population size.

Innovation coupled with business. The Wright brothers first flew their plane in Kitty Hawk, North Carolina, in 1903, and by 1909 they had established the Wright Company with funding from J. P. Morgan and Cornelius Vanderbilt. Patent litigation consumed much of the Wrights' energy and jeopardized the U.S. technological lead in aviation.

Unlike its European counterparts, the U.S. government did not come to the aid of the nascent aviation industry. European armed forces were rapidly establishing airborne forces while the U.S. military was rejecting aviation. Despite its incursions into nearby lands, the United States was isolated by large masses of water and did not yet see itself as a power in need of airborne machinery hampered by faulty engines.

World War I would change this. In view of the emergency, the U.S. government stepped in to suspend the patent litigation that was stalling American aviation, backing a patent pool and reducing royalties to 1 percent. The Manufacturers' Aircraft Association was set up to coordinate aircraft manufacturing in the United States during the war.

The United States resorted to conscription to build an army of a standing similar to that of its navy, but it took a full year to deploy significant troops in Europe, and a full seventeen months before a U.S. contingent began an offensive against German troops, just two months before Germany surrendered. Isolationism alone would not preserve the United States. Preparedness, which was lacking in 1916, would do more to preserve U.S. neutrality. This lesson may have guided U.S. military policy during the rest of the twentieth century. Yet even in 1939, as World War II loomed, the U.S. Air Corps had only 26,000 troops; the British Royal Air Force had almost four times that number, and the German Luftwaffe almost twenty times. The United States had largely remained an isolated country that did not see a military purpose for air warfare.

THE CRASH OF WALL STREET

In early 1929 the illiteracy rate achieved a new low of 6 percent of the population, but the American economy began to falter. Demand for new cars fell, and housing construction faltered. The Wall Street crash of October 1929 led to bank failures, bankruptcies, and depressed business expectations. The crash depressed the world economy, and by 1932 industrial production in the United States had dropped by 50 percent, U.S. exports were at one-third of their 1929 level, and close to a quarter of the labor force was unemployed.

The pioneer spirit, which had fueled the economic boom for over a century, eventually played against the USA; President Hoover would not establish a countercyclical unemployment compensation that could have shortened the depression by supporting aggregate demand. He believed, along with much of the country, that making people dependent on public support would undermine the "rugged individualism" and resourcefulness that had made America what it was.

Franklin Delano Roosevelt took over in 1932. The debate over the size of the sphere of government is a recurrent theme in U.S. politics that we will return to. Roosevelt's policies, framed under the call for a New Deal did not provide immediate relief. Industrial output returned to 1929 levels only in 1939, and only the mobilization for World War II restored full employment.

THE SIGNIFICANCE OF WORLD WAR II

The United States was initially neutral in the conflagration that took over Europe in 1939. But the lesson of World War I on how long it could take to mobilize America to fight in Europe had not been forgotten. Roosevelt sought to turn the USA into "the arsenal of democracy," and in January 1941 he asked Congress for the Lend-Lease Act, empowering him to reinforce with supplies the defense of any country critical to the United States. This enabled the nation to mobilize without yet entering into war. The Japanese attack at Pearl Harbor in December of the same year triggered direct U.S. involvement in the war.

The war's boost to industry was significant. Aircraft production jumped from only 2,000 in 1939 to 96,000 in 1943. Similarly to the effect of World War I on granting power to women, the wartime shortage of labor helped the black American population to mobilize politically.

THE LITTLE ROCK CRISIS

Two centuries after the initial tobacco plantations were planted in Virginia, 13 percent of the U.S. population are descendants of former African slaves.[10] The nation is still contending with the legacy of the plantation system that allowed the Southern slavery-based colonies to survive into the eighteenth century.

The U.S. Supreme Court's 1954 ruling, *Brown v. Board of Education of Topeka*, initiated the desegregation of schools, which had been judged "inherently unequal." However, in support of the segregationists, Governor Faubus ordered the Arkansas National Guard to surround Little Rock Central High School to prevent nine black students from attending a "whites only" school. In response, President Eisenhower ordered the 101st Airborne Division into Little Rock to uphold the Supreme Court decision and ensure the safety of the "Little Rock Nine." Half a century later this is history, but it is still too recent to be taken lightly.

Positive law—as expressed from the high normative content of the constitution down to its enforcement in the streets by the police—must express the living beliefs of the people in order not to be resisted. When the law is divorced from living beliefs, as it was in Little Rock in 1957, positive law as expressed in Supreme Court rulings, for example, must be upheld by force. Fairness is less the issue than is congruence: congruence between the law and the living beliefs of the people.

The Little Rock crisis, as it came to be known, is a clear example of the core message of this book, for managerial techniques must be similarly congruent with a people's culture in order to be effective. Otherwise, exaggerated controls and constant reinforcement will be required to impose the will of management, to the detriment of overall performance.

The Little Rock crisis exhibited the case of a federal ruling in disagreement with the living beliefs of a substantial number of Southerners, although they represented the minority when compared to society at large. This local population was substantial enough to block the enforcement of the law, although the beliefs of the majority rightfully prevailed. Still, force must be used sparingly or society fragments, as it already had during the U.S. Civil War, less than a century earlier.

When an organization remains whole but one segment of its members resents the imposition of views in disagreement with its living beliefs, it may resort to underground sabotage, as happened in Southern U.S. society through the Ku Klux Klan.

In business, this lack of congruence between the culture of a people and the managerial ethos under which they are expected to work may lead to similar behavior, ranging from lack of engagement to outright sabotage. All forms of resistance lead to lower productivity. On the other hand, decisive action to seek congruence bolts people into action, as expressed in the telegram of appreciation sent to President Eisenhower by the parents of the nine black children at Little Rock.[11] Those parents were expressing the views of most African Americans, who would now have renewed faith in the white majority's willingness to redress injustice.

Bold antisegregation and affirmative action legislation during the second half of the twentieth century sparked a significant increase in the social mobility of African Americans. While less of a political milestone than a cultural barometer, it may be interesting to point out that in 1965 the first African American woman was featured on *Playboy*'s centerfold page. By then, even the media could tell that the worst of segregation was over. African American college enrollment had doubled by 1970,[12] and three decades later one-third of African Americans of college age were enrolled in higher education.[13] Black activist professor Angela Davis of the University of California, Berkeley, would come into prominence in the late 1960s and early 1970s; in 1987, Toni Morrison—later a Nobel laureate, in 1993—became the first African American professor at an Ivy League university (Princeton University). The ascent was also signaled by one African American member of the Supreme Court in the 1990s, two secretaries of state at the dawn of the twenty-first century, and, in 2009, the first African American president.

Desegregation of schools in 1957 was only the beginning; education had helped African American upward mobility. The Army's demobilization also played its part. The GI Bill of Rights enacted by Congress in 1944 vastly expanded access to higher education through financial aid for war veterans. By the end of 1955, the GI Bill had sponsored more than two million war veterans in college. The percentage of women in U.S. colleges had also grown, representing 54 percent of all degrees awarded in 1993, up from 24 percent in 1950.[14]

POSTWAR AMERICA

The end of World War II would disclose a new reality. Europe had been ravaged and impoverished, as had the Soviet Union, having also taken an expansionist path. Soon the Soviet Union would consolidate power over several countries along its vast frontier. This was the time of Churchill's reference to an Iron Curtain and to the rise of the fear of communism in the United States, leading to infamous displays of intolerance during the McCarthy era of "witch hunting" and communist bashing.

Postwar Europe had troubles of its own. Europeans sought to reestablish their prewar spheres of influence, but they could no longer manage on their own. England and France took over the Suez Canal in 1956 but were rebuked by the USA. A weakened Europe called for a larger U.S. role. The United States stepped in with Britain's help in Greece and Turkey, and on France's side in Vietnam. In the Far East, trouble was brewing as well. China fell into a civil war that would be won by the Communist side, and Korea would call for U.S. intervention.

The postwar period, with the Cold War in progress and the Korean War begun in 1950, saw a stepped-up public expenditure in research and development. Former liberal universities, such as California, Stanford, Johns Hopkins, and MIT, were drawn into war-related projects. The aeronautics Douglass Corporation funded the think tank RAND (its name derived from "research and development"), which employed close to eight hundred people during the 1960s and sold nearly $13 million in research projects to the air force each year.[15]

Eventually, this interventionist stance would lead the United States to its own war in Vietnam. By now, the USA was definitely the most universalist among the Western countries. However, under the Cold War the Soviet Union managed to occupy the role of freedom fighter ally. The United States lost its libertarian role, and in what became known as the third world, it would opt for containment rather than freedom, siding with all the wrong kids on just about any block, whether it was Somoza in Nicaragua, Castillo in Guatemala, Mobutu in Congo, Pinochet in Chile, or Savimbi in Angola.

Hispanic migration to the United States boosted the share of Catholicism in the "land of many faiths." Yet it will be a long time before this immigration wave challenges the three-faith model in vogue in the 1950s, that Americans come in three flavors: Protestant, Catholic, and Jewish, in that order. In the 1990 census, Protestants of all denominations numbered 140 million; Catholics, 62 million; and Jews, 5 million.

SUMMING UP: UNITED STATES OF AMERICA

The United States was blessed by an initial immigrant pool that cherished literacy and religious tolerance, traits that would spill over to the general independence of mind and inquisitiveness that came to characterize Americans. The high density of institutions of higher learning in New England today is the legacy of its early settlers. The United States generously opened its plains to immigrants, who came by the thousands. Farmers were favored, and the frontier honed their skills, determination, and a sense of self-reliance—for there was not much else to rely on. Because land ownership was not concentrated, power was not either, leveling the ground for the rise of competitive markets. Unrestrained competition by ambitious individuals made its mark on early America, helping to develop materialistic values.

Land ownership enabled rural credit to flourish, with land as collateral. Investment in agriculture ensured a steady demand for machinery and a thriving local industry, which was avid for labor-saving solutions.

Where slavery depressed wages, as in the American South, technology and education were in lower demand. A more complacent, patriarchal, agriculture-exporting society developed in this region, which took less interest in protective tariffs for industry than the North did. The ensuing Civil War ensured the predomination of the Yankees, or Northerners, but did not blur the cultural frontiers. Segregation remained rampant in the South for well over a century after the end of the Civil War.

Industry developed steel, steam enabled the locomotive, and rails connected the Atlantic to the Pacific. Economic activity spread across the continent, and clusters of progress appeared: cars around Detroit, the film industry in sunny

California. By then, the inquisitive, tinkering American mind was applying electricity to telecommunications.

An inward-looking continental United States would revert frequently to isolationism. Manifest Destiny was ascribed to the country's economic interests, and these remained regional into the early twentieth century, when U.S. resolve would lead it to meddle in the internal affairs of Caribbean countries. Only when U.S. economic interests broadened under the threat of war did the nation become politically active around the world.

By then, the United States had excelled in the sciences, its artistic expressions had achieved world recognition, and its production methods were referenced internationally, including those in management. Today its business schools are the longest standing and its academic literature the most prominent and pervasive across the world, particularly in developing countries that adopted the American business model with little adaptation. Although talk of business cultural convergence gained some ground, not even the USA is monolithic. Civil war was unable to suppress the country's internal differences, nor will non-American cultures voluntarily change; thus the idea of business cultures meeting halfway across a global negotiating table is wishful thinking, at best.

America's extraction and history formed self-reliant, inventive individuals whose freethinking religious origins led to an effective, trust-building judiciary and a preference for small government. Where individual efforts were not enough, ad hoc organizations were quick to form. U.S. managerial traits are based on these characteristics and demonstrate resolve, directness of speech, candidness and transparency in decision making, competitiveness, meritocratic staff selection and promotion, innovation, and pecuniary incentives. America's success has led to its managerial practices being emulated elsewhere, where business practitioners invariably do not find the same cultural backdrop that granted their success at home.

CHAPTER 7

ARGENTINA

AUDACITY HELPED THE SPANIARDS and Portuguese to embark to the New World, and their coarse background ensured their survival on little but pure grit. Their intolerance would help them ignore the pain imposed upon the indigenous populations and, later, the slaves. Their religion also legitimized taking bounty over the Other. When the Reconquista was over, land was no longer scarce in Spain or Portugal. But gold was. Gold was the tradable commodity par excellence and was sought at any expense. Where gold was not to be found, silver would suffice, as it did in Potosí, then in Alto Perú, now Bolivia. The rest of the land was to be used to support the gold or silver mining operations.

This was so much so that the oldest continuously inhabited cities in Argentina lie in the hinterland—where they supported Potosí—at that time more advanced than Buenos Aires. This is how the first Argentine university came to be set in Córdoba in 1613, at about the time the English Pilgrims founded Plymouth. Thus the economy of the River Plate area became tied to the incursions on the gold-rich Andean setting. The Spanish proclivity to large estates for extensive cattle rearing predominated in the New World, initially as a means of supplying food for the workers and mules for transportation in support of the gold and silver extraction operations.

Trade was monopolized to favor the Iberian rulers. Their descendants would benefit over those born on American soil (*criollos*), who would ultimately resent their exploitation and implicit rejection. It would take a long while for the criollos to realize that, despite not being Indians, they were not accepted as true Iberian stock. This awakening was accelerated by Napoleon's entry into the Iberian Peninsula in 1808, interrupting the historical line of authority of the Spanish royalty for the next five years while the royal family remained captive in France, which understandably played havoc with loyalties in the viceroyalty of the River Plate, as well as elsewhere. This was the time of Mariano Moreno as the educated criollo secretary of the junta who, in the absence of a Spanish king, reclaimed authority in Buenos Aires in 1810.

The ensuing Argentine Republic would end up with only half of the territory that its viceroyalty was entrusted with at the time of separation from Spain. This was no doubt a hefty loss, testifying to the fractiousness of Argentina's birth. Moreover, Argentina controlled less than a third of what would ultimately become its territory, as a great portion of it was in the hands of natives. Buenos Aires, capital of the viceroyalty for only a couple of decades, had approximately fifty thousand inhabitants and, after Córdoba, was Argentina's second-largest city. Córdoba was better integrated with the silver mines of Potosí, in today's Bolivia, than with Buenos Aires, and communications between the two cities passed through the city of Rosário across a narrow strip of territory that could be considered under Buenos Aires' control. The rest was "Indian land."

Even control of Buenos Aires was at stake, where the junta was unwittingly shaping Argentina's future and where resentment of Spain was growing to the extent of frowning upon Spanish customs such as dress and salutations. Bullfighting was banned in 1812, and unmarried Spanish nationals were asked to return to Spain, a decision later overturned on account of all the broken marriage promises this would entail. This is the setting in which Mariano Moreno was becoming a leading intellectual.

MARIANO MORENO (1778–1811)

Moreno came into political life in May 1810 as secretary of the first governing junta, whose members protected monopolist trade with Spain. But this was less than a year after he had authored *Representation of the Farmers and Laborers*, a text supporting free trade.

Moreno is now recognized as having also authored the secret "operational plan" espousing authoritarian reform of nascent Argentina while still with the junta, which was largely formed by monopolist traders from Buenos Aires. In effect, he may be considered the precursor of authoritarianism in Argentine politics. He allegedly proposed sanguinary measures against opponents as well as delation, torture, executions, and dissimulation against the English and Portuguese.[1]

The fiery Moreno, a lawyer who founded the first weapons factory in Argentina as well as the first public library, clashed with the more conservative Saavedra Lamas, leading member of the junta. Moreno, at age thirty-three, was dispatched to London as ambassador but died en route, perhaps poisoned.

Moreno's early endorsement of violence by the constituted authority is merely an early expression of the criollos' degree of comfort with the violence of their inherited culture, that of Spain, where intolerance of the Other had been manifest for centuries, or at least since the discordant coexistence with the Moslems was first called a "cold war" in the thirteenth century.

This underlying bellicosity, with occasional bouts of ferocity—addressed to the natives in particular—consumed Argentina during much of the nineteenth century. The instability had regional rather than internecine overtones. The provinces along the Paraná River, as well as the city of Buenos Aires, were better integrated with world trade than the hinterland was. International trade provoked prominent adversarial issues, particularly against the elites settled in Buenos Aires, who controlled the country's single international port. The hinterland was another story. Córdoba's significance, and particularly the cities of northern Argentina, Tucumán prominent among them, retreated with the downsizing of silver activity in Bolivia. Downsizing never comes easily: the second and third governors of Tucumán were beheaded by their successors.

Yet Argentina enjoyed a plentiful supply of inexpensive food and a relatively homogeneous urban population—the indigenous population excepted. No person was to be born a slave in Argentina as from 1813. These factors pre-empted organized internecine movements against the elites of the sort that Brazil witnessed in Recife, Salvador, and Rio de Janeiro during the nineteenth century. Nonetheless, the uneasy predominance of Buenos Aires over the provinces along the Paraná River, and the disparity with the hinterland, ensured only an uneasy truce that was forcefully wrought under Rosas.

JUAN MANUEL DE ROSAS (1793–1877)

Juan Manuel de Rosas governed or influenced Argentina for over two decades, until he was toppled in 1852 by Urquiza following a Unitarian[2] appeal—which in one sense must have reflected the country's trend toward even greater institutionalization after seventeen years under Rosas.

It is still hard to find a balanced view of Rosas.[3] It can safely be said that he was an intuitive, pragmatic man from the hinterland who distrusted educated city people. His intuition was the backbone of his political pragmatism, which sought to consolidate an Argentine nationality through the glorification of local culture. This gave new social salience to the peon, the gaucho, and the Negro, and also knocked the traditional white elite of Buenos Aires down a notch. Rosas is reported to have respected those who moved with ease among the upper classes, yet he felt they erred in their deprecation of the lower classes, the rural workers, and all those who could be counted as people of action.

When left to his own, Rosas would frequent the taverns in Negro neighborhoods in Buenos Aires, much to the white elite's horror. This may be why the taverns were rounded up by Urquiza's troops and the Negro population handed over to the Brazilian funders of Urquiza's successful uprising against Rosas. Carretero asserts that the descendants of former slaves rounded up by Urquiza's forces were themselves enslaved by Brazilians in the province of Entre Rios.[4]

Rosas began as a farmer and ended up in exile in the United Kingdom. In running his estates in Argentina, he acquired a firm grip of the psyche of the gaucho he sought to protect. Rosas was proud to say on occasion that he had become one of them. Always a pragmatist, he secured accommodation with the native Indian population through low-level bribes. Rosas saw little purpose in an accelerated institutionalization of Argentina, even to the point of neglecting education. To Rosas, neutralizing the insubordinates was sufficient.

Rosas himself was a man of action, and his hegemony was consolidated by a relentless control of the press, the dismissal of civil servants not entirely on his side, and the mandatory use of identifying elements, such as the color red, and compulsory mottoes, such as *Federación o Muerte* ("Federation or Death"), written on all official correspondence, and "Long live the Federation and death to the savage Unitarians!" At one time, Rosas broke off with the Jesuits, who refused to have his image placed on church altars. He also instituted a praetorian guard, Sociedad Popular Restauradora (popularly known as the *mazorca*), which intimidated civilians into compliance and was responsible for thousands of killings.[5]

JUAN BAUTISTA ALBERDI (1810–1884)

Alberdi's claim to fame is varied, though he is most remembered for having created the juridical bases for a "feasible" initial republic, with an eye to a later "ideal" republic. His apex came during the period of consolidation of the republic, during the second half of the nineteenth century. In the first half he got himself into all sorts of trouble.

It was Rosas's authenticity that initially appealed to Juan Bautista Alberdi, who saluted Rosas for what he saw in him: "the capitulation of the exotic to the national, of plagiarism to spontaneity, of the extemporaneous to the timely . . . the triumph of the majority over the minority."[6]

In his 1837 *Fragments*, Alberdi saw in the Pampas region the true source of the wealth reflected in the cities: "the smallest farmer, the yeoman, the humble gaucho, are wealth, to our population, to our European civilization, more important than all our writers, orators, however pretentious they may sound."[7] This is the Alberdi that could have provided Rosas, although a man of action, the informed worldliness that Rosas lacked.

Yet Alberdi's intellectual roots were French, at a time of resentment against colonial Spain. When the French Admiral Leblanc opened fire on Rosas's positions in 1838, Francophile Alberdi—with his allegiances split between the local caudillo Rosas and the French squadron—could not but side with France's worldly humanism. Alberdi initially sought exile in Montevideo, from where he would denounce Rosas as a barbarian. Alberdi's split from Rosas deprived Argentina of an alliance that could have saved it from decades of barbarism. But Rosas would pay no attention to refined intellectuals.

Perhaps Rosas could never have taken on Alberdi, who, in his most xenophobic 1853 writings, would claim that "to populate a land is not to civilize it but to brutalize it if it is peopled with Chinese and Asian Indians, with African Negroes."[8]

An Alberdi who despised his own people would hardly be fully loved in Argentina or elsewhere, which is a pity, for it was Alberdi who foresaw the importance of size and alliances for competing internationally. He realized early that the breakup of the Spanish colonies in the New World would result in weak countries subjected to the power of the stronger ones. If political alliances were not possible among the weaker countries, perhaps commercial alliances could impose a degree of economic strength that would benefit all of the member nations. Alberdi was the first to see that the weakening centripetal forces of the former Spanish empire could be overcome by something like a German Zollverein (customs union). Perhaps because he was familiar with Chile from his years in exile there, he saw a role for Chile in his Zollverein—but not for Brazil. Also a pragmatist, the later Alberdi favored a feasible Argentina, rather than an ideal one. His realism captured the essence of the solution to Argentina's weak institutionalization during the second half of the nineteenth century.

As in the case of Moreno, it is hard to depict an Alberdi one would want to dine with. In fact, before sitting down together, we would have to ask, which Alberdi?—just as one would also have had to ask, which Moreno? or even, which Sarmiento?—to whom we now turn.

DOMINGO FAUSTINO SARMIENTO (1811–1888)

To nineteenth-century Argentina, the frontier epitomized all that was wrong: the frontier was a brutal place where might prevailed over justice. Only the cities could provide the guidance and the strength necessary to overcome the hinterland barbarians. Europe, through urban Argentina, could provide the civilizing input. That was Alberdi's position.

Rather than Europe, Sarmiento chose New England for inspiration, but neither Alberdi nor Sarmiento, least of all the latter, saw in the Argentine frontier the opportunity for a new social foundation for the nation. In their eyes, Rosas, a product of the hinterland, had served as a case in point for shunning that uncouth region and turning instead to the cities for inspiration and opportunity.

As with Alberdi, Sarmiento's legacy is multifaceted; he was also an educator, an ambassador to the United States, and president of Argentina. Yet Sarmiento's platforms were more coherent and practical than Alberdi's. Neither one could tolerate the other, but both would help to shape Argentina's psyche of today.

Sarmiento was born in San Juan, in the foothills of the Andes, from a mother of African ancestry. He helped out at the family grocery store while also reading the history of Greece and Rome. Sarmiento clashed with the local governor over the founding of his newspaper and thus sought exile in Chile. There, he wrote his masterpiece: *Facundo: Or, Civilization and Barbarism* (1845).[9]

The book tells the true story of the life of a rural leader, Juan Facundo Quiroga, during the decades of unrest that followed Argentina's independence from Spain. Sarmiento's *Facundo* is centered on what he perceived was the fundamental division in Argentina: civilization or barbarism. To Sarmiento, civilization lay in the cities and barbarism in the hinterland, unlike the North American frontier myth that idealized the untamed wilderness.

To Sarmiento, the lawlessness of the hinterland was due to the irrepressible gaucho, who on horseback and in groups (*montoneras*) would attack cities and, on occasion, even the regular army. Facundo Quiroga was an actual leader of *montoneras* whose deleterious action Sarmiento experienced in San Juan as a child. In Sarmiento's romanticized *roman de la terre*, Quiroga became the protagonist. In fact, the book was an indictment against Rosas, also from the hinterland, though Rosas himself was an archenemy of the real-life Facundo Quiroga.

It is no wonder that Sarmiento opposed the populist Rosas and his proclivity to live by the standards of the gaucho. Once Rosas was ousted, Sarmiento advised the successor, President Bartolomé Mitre, "not to spare gaucho blood." President Mitre waged a police war seeking the extermination of the "indolent, rebellious, drunkard, and barbarian gaucho."[10] Besides facing direct combat by Mitre's army, gauchos were also drafted to frontier duty. José Hernandez would later decry this in what became the foundational Argentine poem, "Martin Fierro," about which we will see more in Chapter 15, particularly for its depiction of the prevailing Argentine style of male leadership.

The Chilean government commissioned the exiled Sarmiento to learn what worked and what did not work in European public education. In Europe, Sarmiento read *Report of an Educational Tour,* published in 1846 by the U.S. educator Horace Mann, and decided that the United States was where he should go to learn what South America needed in terms of public education.

Sarmiento traveled to the USA and met with Mann to learn his views on education, both agreeing on the benefits of equal education for all. Upon Sarmiento's later return to the United States as ambassador, he sought out Mary

Mann (née Peabody), who introduced Sarmiento to Ralph Waldo Emerson, Henry Wadsworth Longfellow, and other intellectuals of similar standing. Sarmiento and Peabody would exchange over two hundred letters over a period of twenty years. The letters have been annotated in a book titled *My Dear Sir*, as Peabody would almost invariably address Sarmiento.[11] By then, Sarmiento was a continental figure, consulted by the Mexicans on constitutional matters, symbolically presiding over the U.S. Senate, and inspiring educators such as Varela in Uruguay and Terreros in Venezuela. Sarmiento was a doer; his motto was "To do, even if wrong, but to do." He was also fond of Benjamin Franklin and displayed a bust of Franklin in his office, occasionally calling himself "Franklincito," or little Franklin. The University of Michigan granted Sarmiento an *honoris causa* doctorate. Later, his mistakes would be held against him, and his detractors in Argentina would disparagingly refer to Sarmiento as the "Michigan doctor."[12] It is no wonder that a U.S. president would one day refer to Sarmiento to remind Argentines of the close historical links between both nations, as President Clinton did when visiting Buenos Aires in 1997.

MARY PEABODY MANN (1806–1887)

Mary Peabody was the middle sister of three daughters in a family from Salem, Massachusetts. She married Horace Mann (1796–1859), America's foremost educator at the time.

All three sisters were members of a pioneering network of American intellectuals. The elder sister, Elizabeth, started the kindergarten movement in the United States. She later became a prominent member of Ralph Waldo Emerson's transcendentalist movement and edited the movement's magazine, *Dial*, from 1840 to 1844. Elizabeth also worked with William Channing and Amos Bronson, the latter being the father of Louisa May Alcott, author of *Little Women*.

Sophia Peabody, the youngest of the sisters, married Nathaniel Hawthorne, who later authored *The Scarlet Letter*. Hawthorne was a school friend of Henry Longfellow as well as of Franklin Pierce, who would later become the fourteenth U.S. president (1853–57).

Mary Peabody, whom Sarmiento would refer to as "my guardian angel," was instrumental in introducing Sarmiento to the best that the Boston-Salem-Concord area had to offer. This is how Sarmiento also met the astronomer

Dr. Benjamin Gould, who wished to study the Southern sky and ultimately secured an appointment to create the Astronomy Observatory in Córdoba. Dr. Gould arrived in Córdoba with his wife, Mary Quincy, of the lineage of early U.S. presidents. Dr. Walter Gould Davis, a scientist member of Gould's entourage, later founded over eighty meteorological stations in Argentina, many of which would become part of the National Meteorological Institute (INIMET).

It was through these acquaintances that Sarmiento was able to secure the help of sixty-five "brave young American teachers" to travel to Argentina in support of Sarmiento's efforts to establish a teacher's training school. Interestingly, Sarmiento insisted on an all-female entourage, for, as part of his vision of the United States as the ideal path to the future, he also wished for the teachers to impart their examples of what a modern woman should be like. Sarah Eccleston (1840–1916) led the North American teachers' efforts in Argentina.

UNIFICATION

The political hegemony of Buenos Aires, Argentina's only port of note, had been long contested, and it was only under Bartolomé Mitre that a consolidated leadership was achieved. This resulted in the 1860s in stifling the independent caudillos, whose power was dwindling as wool gained prominence in the market and sheep farming advanced ever deeper into the hinterland. Electoral fraud, an unwritten constitution, and seeking solutions to other practical problems in lieu of intellectual niceties all helped to keep Argentina united under a loose confederation of provinces, with Buenos Aires in the privileged position of international relations hub.

The railway system benefited from British investment, and a postal system was put in place. The introduction of wire fences innovated cattle-rearing techniques and prevented crops from being trampled by livestock. Windmills made possible the irrigation of formerly dry areas, contributing to greater productivity. Technological advances such as meat refrigeration and the steamship, coupled with massive population growth in Europe, would induce a revolution in Argentine business and agriculture. In 1870 the Sociedad Rural Argentina gathered Argentine ranchers and offered a hefty reward for the development of a means of transporting refrigerated meat to Europe. In 1876 the French engineer Charles Tellier built the first refrigerated ship, the *Frigorifique*, which sailed from Buenos Aires two years later with a load of frozen beef. In response to European tastes, Argentina would begin to favor cattle rearing over sheep rearing. As with management practices, not all imported technology would work as well in Argentina as it did in England. Buenos Aires wasted two years and many resources drilling for water under the advice of an English entrepreneur, who expected to find underground water in Buenos Aires just as he had done in England.[13]

WAR OF THE TRIPLE ALLIANCE AGAINST PARAGUAY (1864–1870)[14]

Although the fighting took place mostly in neighboring Paraguay, to Argentines the war against Paraguay was too close for comfort. Argentina, Brazil, and Uruguay joined forces to halt Paraguay's incursion into Brazil in response to the latter's intervention in Uruguay, with Argentina contributing the lion's share of the draftable population. In addition, Buenos Aires was the allied powers' port of entry, and the city inhabitants initially rallied with logistical and moral support for the troop movement. Later, Buenos Aires would suffer a cholera epidemic and, in 1871, yellow fever, which decimated the city's population. The stricken neighborhood of San Telmo was abandoned by the wealthy, who relocated to the Barrio Norte and conferred to it the architectural style that still characterizes Buenos Aires today.

By then, Argentina had seen many wars, but demobilization proved difficult, thus it would not be surprising that its military aggressiveness was redirected against a less dangerous enemy: its native population. The Desert Campaign of 1878–79, led by the future President Roca, opened up the Patagonia and boosted Argentina's agrarian economy, albeit at the expense of the indigenous population. The name given to the military action was actually a misnomer drawn from an attitude, or the consensus that the war theater was a metaphorical desert by reason of being occupied by natives.[15] The end of the Desert Campaign is what historian Félix Luna believes can be called Argentina's foundational year,[16] just as the end of the U.S. Civil War might signal a historical watershed for the United States.

EDUCATION IN ARGENTINA

Sarmiento's public school system is largely credited for Argentina's relatively high level of intellectual achievement. Yet there were postcolonial precursors as well, as education ranked high on the agenda of the 1810 junta, for instance.

Manuel Belgrano was responsible for the creation of the military's School of Mathematics when the junta was scarcely three months old. Rosas, on the other hand, predictably represented a step backward in educational matters.

During Sarmiento's presidency (1868–74), he established over one hundred public libraries, reformed educational methods, and also encouraged advances in the sciences: in 1872 he founded the Sociedad Científica Argentina (Argentine Scientific Society) and a year later the Academia de Ciencias (Academy of Sciences) in Córdoba, this latter initially directed by the renowned German scholar in zoology and paleontology, Carlos Burmeister, and renamed the National Academy in 1878.

Nicolás Avellaneda was Sarmiento's minister of education and, upon succeeding Sarmiento, continued his educational work during his own term. Prior to 1880, under President Julio A. Roca, primary education was ruled to be compulsory and free. By the turn of the century, Argentina had surpassed a 90 percent literacy rate, virtually turning on its head the 82 percent illiteracy rate recorded in the 1869 census.

This level of excellence, propped up by American intellectuals but driven by Argentines, set Argentina on an educational path that would eventually lead to three Nobel laureates in the sciences in the twentieth century: Bernardo Houssay in physiology of medicine (1947), Luis Federico Leloir in chemistry (1970), and César Milstein in medicine and physiology (1984). All three graduated from the University of Buenos Aires, although Milstein transferred there from National Southern University in Bahia Blanca. An earlier Nobel Peace Prize was awarded in 1936 to Carlos de Saavedra Lamas for his work to eliminate force as an instrument of international territorial disputes. While Saavedra Lamas's work was of a more political nature, his leadership on international matters can be attributed to his high level of scholarship. Saavedra Lamas was also a graduate of the University of Buenos Aires.[17]

Education in Argentina led to a pinnacle in the sciences as nowhere else in Latin America (or in Spain or Portugal, for that matter), which also indicated a broad population base of people who could read and write. With the highest literacy rate in Latin America, readership of newspapers and magazines in Argentina rose sharply.

In 1910 the bookshops that are today so characteristic of the Buenos Aires landscape were then few and selective. Nonetheless, the years between 1917 and 1925 saw the peak of weekly romances, which were printed in the thousands.[18]

Caras y Caretas was a magazine combining humor, art, literature, and current events that was founded in 1898 and lasted nearly four decades. By 1926 the Argentines would consume two-thirds of all of the newspapers circulating in Latin America. By then, wide readership also sustained magazines dedicated to radio broadcasting, local theater, and literature. Among the latter, *Sur*, headed by the wealthy intellectual Victoria Ocampo, would open its pages to international trends and to some of Argentina's most prominent writers, such as Jorge Luis Borges.[19]

IMPACT OF IMMIGRATION

As Buenos Aires boomed, European immigrants poured into the city, boosting the population from 90,000 in 1869 to 670,000 in 1895, when almost half the city was foreign born. A third of the population in the hinterland was also foreign born. Still, not only was this group relatively less numerous, but it also faced greater cultural resistance. Argentina had inherited extensive agricultural lands from Spain, but relatively few small plots were available for foreigners to buy. With its large landholdings, the hinterland had also inherited Spain's patriarchal family organization: conservative, tradition oriented, and religious.

On the other hand, Buenos Aires was the Babel, open to the world, prematurely rich, fast paced, and thirsty for modernity. Italy provided the most immigrants, initially from the northern region and later also from the South. Spain came in second, mostly with Basque nationals—to whose input Maria Seoane attributes the Argentine propensity to insubordination to whoever is not a member of the "tribe." Other immigrants were mostly Germans, French, and Central Europeans. Such an influx of immigrants would have a massive cultural impact, some of which may be appreciated in the Italianate architecture of public buildings and the colorful tenement houses of the Genovese in La Boca, along the River Plate.

The elite were bound to France, and French architecture styles of the late nineteenth or early twentieth century pervade the structures erected for the elite. Yet the Italian taste for elaborate colors and shapes, in addition to the Boca, could be appreciated in the sanctuary-like Barolo Palace.

By the early twentieth century, Buenos Aires boasted over seventy theaters. The Lumiére brothers' *Arrival of a Train* was the first public film exhibition in Buenos Aires, in 1896. The Teatro Colón, third largest in the world, was built in 1908. Opera would also separate immigrants from the local elite. While the former preferred Italian composers, the latter preferred Wagner. When Argentina celebrated the centennial of its independence, in 1910, only New York outranked Buenos Aires in size in the New World. By then, Buenos Aires had gas and electricity and modern sewers. By 1913, Argentina's gross domestic product was among the world's ten largest, ahead of France and Germany; the population of Buenos Aires had reached 1.3 million and moved about in a subway system.

The immigrants brought with them more than just tastes and styles. They also brought attitudes, many of them conflicting, and an anarchist movement also took hold in Argentina. Although immigrant workers would find jobs that helped them attain a social mobility that their forefathers had lacked in Europe, they were not granted Argentine nationality. Subsequently, immigrants became active in unions but not in politics. This paradox would only be resolved when universal and compulsory suffrage for adult males became law under President Roque Saenz Peña in 1912.

Voting rights granted the descendants of immigrants sufficient power to elect President Hipólito Yrigoyen, the son of an illiterate French Basque immigrant. The political ascent of the immigrants would usher in a larger and more interventionist government that tinkered with the management of the railway system, the ports, and health services and even founded the first state oil company in Latin America: Yacimientos Petrolíferos Fiscales (YPF).

Nonetheless, this would not quench unrest. Anarchists would provide little respite to Yrigoyen, and unions continued to agitate throughout the country. Yrigoyen's government sought to hold a delicate equilibrium between repression and arbitration of disputes, but it was far from successful. Yrigoyen's police attacked the Talleres Vassena metallurgical strikers, leading to the Tragic Week events of January 7–11, 1919. Strikers demanding an end to the eleven-hour workday plus rest on Sundays were attacked by police and the paramilitary Patriotic League, as were Jews and synagogues, yielding over seven hundred dead and three thousand wounded. The Liga Patriótica (Patriotic League) was supported by Leopoldo Lugones, whom I will return to shortly.

Two years later, in 1921, the Yrigoyen army suppressed a wool workers' union in the Patagonia, with the resulting loss of over one thousand strikers' lives. The size and ferociousness of the repression were remarkable. Workers were asked to dig their own collective graves before being shot into them. Other workers were locked in barns that were subsequently set on fire. Some years later, a German anarchist would take revenge by killing Lieutenant Colonel Varela for his leadership in the Patagonian massacre.

LEOPOLDO LUGONES (1874–1938)

The Wall Street crisis of 1929 only made matters worse for Yrigoyen's second presidency, which ended in a coup. This was to be the first of a long series of coups for Argentina. Now, migrants into Buenos Aires would arrive in droves from the hinterland, no longer from abroad. The capital's share of the country's total population would increase from 12 percent in 1936 to almost 30 percent in 1947. These less-educated and less-worldly newcomers, hungry for jobs, would by necessity be less open to the world and more focused on satisfying basic needs such as food and shelter. These were the migrants who would seek the protection of Perón in the 1940s.

Yet the most significant issue of this first military coup is that the conservative regime would give Argentina a new role for the intellectual Leopoldo Lugones, whose career spanned a large share of the political spectrum over four decades.

A descendant of a long-established family in Córdoba, with roots known to extend back to sixteenth-century Peru, Lugones grew up among the proud criollos of Córdoba. In Córdoba, during the time he wrote for *Pensamiento Libre*, an atheist and anarchist daily, he also founded a branch of the Socialist party, leaving soon thereafter for Buenos Aires. Once there, Lugones lost his faith in Marxist rationalist conceptualizations and became more concerned with replacing social class with the nation as the driving force. Already in 1896, Lugones challenged the notion of universal suffrage and equality as installing the rule of mediocrity, advocating instead a hierarchical society led by intelligence and knowledge.[20] In this, Lugones was the victim of positivism and not unlike Mexico's *Científicos,* who backed dictator Porfirio Díaz.

By 1903, Lugones had unequivocally drifted to the right and was known as an incendiary orator and polemist. *La Guerra Gaucha* (1905) was one of his nationalist instruments used to give voice to an Argentina still lacking an identity.[21] In 1907, Lugones had his only child and began publishing romances and poetry. He also wrote a very readable *História de Sarmiento* (1911) along the stylistic lines of *La Guerra Gaucha*, addressing Sarmiento as "a work of nature, the peak of a mountain signaling direction." After his second trip to Europe, in 1911, Lugones chose to focus on gaucho literature, inspiring his most famous disciple, Jorge Luis Borges, who would initially salute Lugones as Argentina's best writer. This is Lugones' most interesting phase; in *El Payador* (1916) he elevates José Hernández's "Martin Fierro" to its current standing as Argentina's foundational poem.[22]

In *El Payador*, Lugones declared his dissatisfaction with a democracy that espoused "everything for the people, but without the people," preferring rule by an illustrious oligarchy that he effectively sided with during the ousting of President Yrigoyen. Argentine critics have been very unforgiving, and Lugones has since been generally despised as a scribe of the authoritarian bureaucracy.

Yet Lugones' work is permeated with a strong love for Argentina. In canonizing Martin Fierro, Lugones praised the archetypical gaucho as the prototype Argentine. The fact that Fierro was a transgressor meant no ideological risk, for Lugones praised the gaucho at a time when there were no gauchos left, at a time when Argentina had ceased to be attractive to immigrants, and at a time when the nation's immigrants were old enough to have great-grandchildren, like Lugones himself.

Lugones nonetheless had succeeded in transforming the image of a drunkard, insubordinate, and irrepressible gaucho into a national hero. That Argentines were willing to accept Martin Fierro as the epitome of their national identity has two important implications: first, that they were so thirsty for an identity as to accept even a socially undesirable character as an icon, and second, that the divisive forces within Argentina were strong enough to require a symbol so long dead that it no longer presented a threat.

Moreover, the choice of a gaucho as a national symbol signaled just how much Argentina had closed up. The gaucho, after all, had been persecuted in the 1860s as representing all that was wrong in a society that sought to integrate itself into the modern world, which Sarmiento believed was no longer European but North American. This had been the stance taken by Sarmiento when he advised General Mitre to manure Argentine soil with gaucho blood. Domingo Faustino Sarmiento, since Lugones' era—although largely in spite of Lugones—began to be widely seen as detrimental to nationalism. Lugones' Argentina signaled the beginning of the closing of the Argentine mind.[23]

Internationalist cultural inertia would still be manifest in personalities such as the minister for foreign affairs under President Augustín Pedro Justo, Saavedra Lamas, who would secure the first Nobel Prize for Argentina in 1936.

Bear in mind that both men, the Martin Fierro propagandist Lugones and the internationalist Saavedra Lamas, were associated with the coup that deposed President Yrigoyen. Yrigoyen was a leader who represented a completely different sort of gaucho. His demeanor was reclusive, shy, lacking in charisma, and reserved in gestures.[24]

Speaking of Argentina's small elite, Saavedra Lamas, Justo's foreign minister, was a descendant of the Saavedra who ousted Mariano Moreno in 1810. President Justo was the father of Liborio Justo, founder of Argentina's Trotskyite party and godfather of Mario Roberto Santucho, who in turn became head of the People's Revolutionary Party (Ejercito Revolucionario del Pueblo, or ERP), Argentina's main urban guerrilla movement. Leopoldo Lugones—who wittingly or unwittingly played the role of Augustín Pedro Justo's scribe—had only one son, Polo Lugones, who became police chief of Buenos Aires and would achieve notoriety for inaugurating the use on detainees of the electric rod, which had formerly been reserved for cattle. Polo Lugones would have a daughter, nicknamed Piri, who became a *montonera* (member of the Peronist urban guerrilla movement), and before being "disappeared" in the "dirty war" of the 1970s she would introduce herself as the granddaughter of the poet and the daughter of the torturer. Piri Lugones married the renowned writer Rodolfo Walsh, who also was "disappeared."

There is more. President Yrigoyen, as we have seen, was removed from power by President Justo's elite. When Perón took over, he put them aside, but when he was similarly ousted, the next generation of the same elite that had ousted President Yrigoyen regained power: Adalberto Krieger Vassena was the minister of economics of the government that removed Perón from office as well as grandson of the owner of Talleres Vassena, whose workers' strike had led to the Tragic Week repression by Yrigoyen in 1919. During Justo's presidency, the governor of the province of Buenos Aires was Federico Martinez de Hoz. His son, Alfredo, became President Vidella's minister of finance around the time of Argentina's "dirty war." Half a century after President Justo had removed Yrigoyen from power, his minister of war, Basilio Pertiné, returned to the inner ruling circle via his granddaughter, the wife of President Fernando de la Rúa, the first civilian president after the "dirty war" came to an end.

This account only skims the surface of the tight family networks that ruled Argentina, but it sheds some light on the social breakthrough that came with Perón, to whom we now turn.

JUAN DOMINGO AND EVITA PERÓN

Economically, Argentina's Golden Age was over, but it was still too soon for Argentines to fully understand this fact. The economy tottered while the Communist party leaders zigzagged between Hitler and the Allies, stymieing the unions in the absence of a clear direction. In this political void, Juan Domingo Perón's leadership flourished, and he became president in 1946. His wife, Evita, was only twenty-six years old when she emerged onto the political scene and just thirty-three when she died in 1952.

The couple's message sought to elicit support by offering protection to those most in need of it. Industry and farms would no longer serve the profits of the rich. Jobs, food, health, and help would be made available to all. Juan took care of the macro policies and Evita, of the micro ones. Under Perón, transportation, banks, and utilities were nationalized; the number of hospital beds increased; and food staples were subsidized. Evita Perón's foundation looked after individual needs: from eyeglasses for singer Mercedes Sosa to sewing machines for homebound housewives.

Perón's detractors, and there are many, focus on the totalitarian nature of his style—closer to Egypt's Nasser than Italy's Mussolini—or on the unsustainability of his policies, which rested more on the collective satisfaction of needs than on individual motivation and capacity to serve them.

Nonetheless, to Perón's credit, he was the first in Argentina, since Alberdi one hundred years earlier, to see that small independent nations had little chance of competing in a world increasingly aligned with superpowers. This was the concern behind his call for Brazil's Vargas and Chile's Ibáñez del Campo to collaborate in increasing one another's limited powers. Indeed, Perón is likely to have financed at least part of the electoral campaigns of both Ibáñez del Campo and Vargas.[25] His call came four decades too early, but the gist of Perón's idea was implemented in Mercosur when his early vision—that size matters—became obvious to all.[26]

The phenomenal popular support of the Peróns' management of Argentine affairs may stem precisely from this collaborative stance, more befitting of the local culture than the individualist "survival of the fittest" doctrine offered by the more conservative spectrum of Argentine politics.

Sociologists and political scientists argue that Latin American populism is an organizational maneuver to improve the well-being of the masses without provoking a complete rupture with the past, such as communism might have implied. This may very well be so, although it would define populism while explaining neither its strength nor how it works. Let us only skim the surface, for we will return to the subject in Chapter 12 when discussing leadership in the Latin American context.

Populism seeks to forge father-image or mother-image relationships with the poor. Take the Perón couple, for example; they understood this well and did address the needs of the poor—as Vargas did in Brazil, with labor laws that straightjacket the Brazilian labor market still today.

Forget for a moment the class consciousness that fuels class struggle, particularly at a time when communist leaders, during World War II, did not quite know what they stood for. Like all populist leaders, Juan and Evita knew well, putting it bluntly, that the poor want to become rich, end of story.

Evita's mediating force had some real support, garnered through the foundation she ran largely by means of a tax on workers' salaries. The foundation's yearly intake was close to $200 million, much of that spent on such endeavors as supplying sewing machines to women and dentures to the toothless.

Ecuador had given women the vote in 1929; Brazil and Uruguay, in 1932. Evita also supported the enfranchisement of Argentine women, who voted for the first time in the election of 1951, massively in Perón's favor.[27] The poor found their chance, their ray of hope, in the Peróns through a simple process of identification.[28] Advertisers know this method well; only the college educated choose to ignore it. This is why Perón would remove his tie when addressing the poor—Evita taught him that trick.

That so many Argentines were willing to surrender their judgment to a manufactured image should be very telling of their ardent desire for protection and belonging. Despite the loyalty of significant intellectuals, Perón did not become an intellectual icon of the stature of Alberdi or Sarmiento. The

Peronist movement belonged to the masses, not to intellectuals; judgment was suspended, love of the brethren pursued, death to the infidels sought. Scientists were chased into exile while Jorge Luis Borges was demoted from his job at the municipal library and appointed inspector at poultry markets. Undoubtedly that decision must have been taken by a reader of Borges's "The Art of Verbal Abuse." Yet Borges was relatively protected by his international stature; his sister, however, was imprisoned and threatened throughout the Peronist period.

Without a doubt, Perón's style of governing was violent. Once deposed, he only regretted not using even more force. With Perón in exile in 1956, in a retribution befitting his style, a Peronist insurrection was suppressed by General Aramburu and resulted in the execution of thirty Peronistas. While Perón remained in exile, his image came to mean many things to different people. Moreover, Evita's image offered a second pole of identification, breaking the president's monopoly on the Peronist imagery as evoked in the statement by the *montoneras* direct-action group: "If Evita were alive, she would be a *montonera*."

The Perón brand had worn out substantially in two decades of absence, and his return could make it or break it. It broke it. Perón returned in 1972 to a great fiasco. Rival Peronist factions, at what was meant to be a two-million strong welcoming party at Ezeiza, killed three hundred people in a shooting spree. Fractious movements continued until Perón expelled the Peronist Youth organization from a workers' rally in 1974, driving the youth movement underground.

With Perón dead and his third wife, Isabelita, running for office, the Peronist government was overthrown in 1976 by a military uprising that would install one of the most violent persecutions in Argentine history, leading to the disappearance of possibly thirty thousand people. A bomb in the Israeli embassy killed twenty-nine people in 1992, and in 1994 an attack on the Jewish community center AMIA killed ninety-six. Unfortunately, these continuing frightful attacks against dissidents and minorities are merely an expression of the underlying ferociousness that runs through Argentine politics. Paramilitary tactics have been instrumental in Argentine politics for over a century. They were first proposed in Mariano Moreno's Operational Plan and later put into practice by Rosas's *mazorca,* by the Patriotic League, and by Perón, until the military took its gloves off and became directly involved in the "dirty war."

Moreno advocated the use of force against opponents. This intimacy with the use of violence would be espoused not only by the dictator Rosas but publicly endorsed by President Sarmiento, by President Yrigoyen's police and military, particularly in the Patagonia, and by Perón and his followers—not to mention by the military men of the mid and late 1970s. The nation's capacity to accept violence may explain why untold thousands of people were allowed to "disappear" at the hands of the state in the mid-1970s. The threat is still present, in an allusion to its renewed recourse by a bishop of the military as recently as 2005.[29] A darker side to this national characteristic is Argentina's attitude toward the Other. We have seen that the nation saw in the gaucho Martín Fierro an archetypical figure with many virtues, and this idolization implied a xenophobic shift in response to growing immigration. Persecutions of Jews in Argentina may be a further reflection of the same fear; just as in the 1919 Yrigoyen onslaught against strikers at Talleres Vassena, Jews were also overrepresented among the "disappeared" by the military at the end of the same century.[30]

Why has all of this happened in Argentina, otherwise so refined? It is a difficult question that begs an answer, however painful. Argentina does not seem to have succeeded in integrating its population as well as North America did and continues to do. Perhaps the early-twentieth-century civic pedagogy of José Ramos Mejías—focused on the exaltation of nationhood at the primary school level—has not rendered the type of unifying fruits he might have wished. Compulsory military service, particularly if it meant serving under an aggressive military, was counterproductive too. After all, Argentina has embarked not only on internecine struggles but also on international ones, having intermittently been embroiled in boundary disputes, or even war, with Chile, Britain, and Uruguay in just the last quarter of a century.

SUMMING UP: ARGENTINA

Argentina stands head and shoulders above the rest of Latin America, a credit to the higher educational standard of its citizenry. Five Nobel laureates—three in sciences, a field in which the rest of Latin America can boast of none—testify to the difference.

Yet Argentina is also prominent in the brutality exercised against its internal opponents—albeit perhaps not a brutality that exceeds that of so many of its neighbors. What makes Argentina's so exceptional is that it festers amid an otherwise exceptionally cultured society.

Rosas was comfortable at the frontier and espoused all that was wrong to someone like Sarmiento, who looked to the United States for revolutionary inspiration. Perhaps at no other time were North American ideals as close to vindication in Latin America as they were under Sarmiento. He recognized in the United States the vision, the resourcefulness, the ideals, and the wherewithal to institutionalize nation building with civility. Sarmiento thus embarked on a program of emulating American education, from public schooling to public libraries and with an injection of American teachers as well.

Sarmiento was not alone; he had supporters and many followers. Yet they might have achieved as much as they did, and more, without resorting to violence. Violence was always present, and it remains so a century and a half later. Perhaps because of the divisiveness that Sarmiento's use of force engendered, his ethos did not percolate as deeply as it needed to in order to transform knowledge into collaborative pursuits of the type that technology requires. Argentina's achievements in knowledge remain circumscribed to an elite: Nobel laureate Leloir was a cousin of the wealthy intellectual Victoria Ocampo, who lived a few blocks away from Nobel laureate Houssay, with whom Leloir began to study after a casual introduction. We have seen where Nobel laureate Saavedra Lamas came from. Only Nobel laureate Milstein was a newcomer, Jewish and far from rich. Except for Milstein and Pérez Esquivel, the Nobel lot hardly represented the social extraction that would build factories and employ and uplift thousands. When Perón took office, he roughed up the elite, like Rosas had. Houssay and Leloir headed abroad for some time, as did Milstein. Sarmiento had been defeated, and so had North American ideals. The Spanish collectivist-messianic tradition, with its inclusiveness and its suspicion of the Other, was reenacted. Leaders would be protective, subordinates would expect protection, and the collectivity would gain prominence over the individual. Violence would ensure conformity where it was found lacking. Martin Fierro and Perón would come to epitomize the most acceptable leadership style, at least in terms of sheer numbers of adherents.

CHAPTER 8

BRAZIL

THE PORTUGUESE WERE NOT in Brazil to work with their hands beyond what was necessary to pocket riches. If someone else could take on the drudgery of work, the Portuguese would gladly pay for it. Slavery remains an open wound in Brazil's history. We might as well start with its implications, as this is not the place to delve into historical milestones but rather to explore the framing of attitudes toward work and organizations.

Slavery was practiced extensively in Iberia before the Portuguese colonization of Brazil. When Portuguese rulers began to lose interest in the Asian trade, then disputed with the Dutch, they turned their attention to Brazil. It took them three decades to do something about the Brazilian landmass, and the shortage of manual labor led the rulers, rather lazily, to split it into thirteen captaincies and to hope for the best. Between 1532 and 1650, thirty-seven villas and towns were founded, only seven of them by the crown.

Sugarcane took root in Brazil, but it does not seem that the Portuguese promoted it for any other reason than to affirm a foothold in the region. For, if sugar was to require the heavy import of slaves from Africa, Portugal could have done better keeping the slaves in Africa and cultivating sugar there, as it had been doing for decades on the Atlantic islands west of Africa. It was not until 1600, when Brazil hosted 160 sugar mills, that the colony's production surpassed that of the Portuguese islands off Africa. Sugar was to foot the bill for keeping Brazil populated with people who would defend the land from other European suitors. Thus the ocean came to be seen, justifiably, as more of a threat than an opportunity, and this fearful or suspicious attitude would ultimately deprive Brazilians of the audacity necessary to seek markets abroad.

Befitting a nation known for maritime commerce, all of the Portuguese settlements were located along the coast, and Salvador, Bahia, with its welcoming bay, became the central port. This is where the first Jesuits landed in 1549.

EDUCATION

In all aspects, whether teaching the Indians, the slaves, or their masters, the Jesuits were Brazil's foremost educators for 210 years—from the time the first six members disembarked in Salvador and founded Brazil's first primary school within a fortnight, until the order's expulsion in 1759. Upon the death of the order's founder in 1560, the Company of Jesus had been in Brazil for twenty-one years and had founded five primary schools in the main cities along the coast south of Salvador, including São Paulo, and three colleges, in Recife, Salvador, and Rio de Janeiro, where they were able to confer the bachelor of arts degree. With never more than twelve members at a given mission, the Jesuits achieved what they did by leveraging a highly motivated cohort of sympathizers.

The Jesuits were most effective at winning over the souls and minds of the Indians. In the first place, nobody excelled more than the Jesuits at learning the native Tupi-Guarani language. To this effect, they went to the extreme measure in 1550 of importing orphan children from Lisbon, in order to establish a connection between the two groups of children and thus accelerate the learning of each other's language.[1] This move can hardly be considered lack of foresight, leaving things to chance, or short-term orientation.

The Jesuits were expelled in 1759 from the Portuguese kingdom, including Brazil, on the grounds that they were too Scholastic and power prone, which they were. The Marques de Pombal, Portugal's prime minister (1750–77), saw the Jesuit Indian missions as an obstacle to Portuguese interests in general, and to those of his own family in particular—such as in the Amazon, where the Marques had sent his brother to foster trade, to which the Indian-prone

Jesuits were seen as a nuisance.[2] Enlightenment had reached Portugal, and the Jesuits represented the vestiges of the old regime. By the time they left Brazil, the Jesuits were running eighteen secondary schools, thirty-six missions, and twenty-five residences. In all, they may have taught and baptized over one hundred thousand Indians, besides helping the Portuguese to protect basic Catholic virtues from too much temptation.

For all their primary educational virtues, the Jesuit intellect was closer to the Inquisitorial than to the inquisitive mind. By and large, science and engineering did not flourish in Brazil, except perhaps through invaders. Such was the case of the French Huguenot settlement near Rio de Janeiro (1555–60) and even more so of the 1612 French founding of San Luis on the island of the same name in the state of Maranhão. French Capuchin brothers there produced two significant texts describing the ecology of the region. Also illustrative of the cultural renewal brought about by foreign invaders was the 1637–44 period of governorship of Johan Mauritius of Nassau-Siegen, centered in Recife and Olinda. In those seven years, the Flemish invaders imported the printing press, drained lakes, founded libraries and museums, brought the first painters, and established the first astronomical observatory (by Georg Marcgraf) in the Southern Hemisphere. In addition, the investigations of Wilhelm Pies, or Piso, granted him the recognition of having founded tropical medicine.

Nonetheless, contact with foreigners and the ensuing flow of information was severely suppressed by the Portuguese after the discovery of gold, toward the end of the seventeenth century. Even descriptive works that might reveal information or attract the attention of foreigners were suppressed, such as that of Rector and Jesuit Provincial André João Antonil, whose book on the opulence of Brazil was available to the public for only eleven days. All copies were confiscated and not heard of again, possibly because the book mentioned the locations of mines.

Education tottered along until the royal family (under British protection and accompanied by fourteen thousand courtiers), fleeing the Napoleonic invasion, took up residence in Rio de Janeiro in 1808. Initially, the king, Dom João, did what most peeved kings would do and embarked on punitive expansionism. He took over French Guyana to the north and what is now Uruguay to the south. This bellicose stance drained the finances of the young empire, and Dom João was begged to leave Brazil by those who had stayed in Portugal, and to take back his Portuguese kingdom when it was safe enough to do so. He returned to Portugal in 1821 with only four thousand courtiers.

The ten thousand net addition, mostly to Rio de Janeiro, and the decade-long sojourn of all fourteen thousand courtier-tourists contributed heftily to raise local cultural and managerial standards, as is manifest in the inauguration of the School of Surgery and Anatomy and naval academy (both in 1808), the public library (1810), several technical schools, the postal service, the Bank of Brazil, and many administrative units, as well as the arrival of the first printing press. Perhaps as important during this period was the rejection of previous regulations that forbade the practice of manufacturing activities in Brazil.

These installations took place only four decades after the United States declared independence. Both lands could have engaged in an expansionary growth path, but only the USA did so. Vianna Moog believes that coal made the difference. In fact, Brazil discovered coal only in the 1820s, three decades after the United States—and then only at the opposite end of the country, too far south to be useful.[3] It was not good coal either, in the sense that its heat content was only about half that of the North American, Cardiff, or German coal.[4] The availability of coal was one factor contributing to the U.S. inward expansion, while the application of steam power also played a definitive role. Lack of high-grade coal, however, does not explain why Brazil did not find ways of making better use of other available sources of power. Perhaps it is for the same reason that Brazil established law schools before engineering schools.

Yet sugar production, the productive mainstay of the country, remained pitifully dependent on animal traction in 1854, when 80 percent of the sugar mills in Pernambuco depended on oxen as the power source for rotating the mills.[5]

Brazil's heavy reliance on animal traction was in sharp contrast even to Antigua, "which boasted 36 sugar mills powered by wind out of its 134 in 1705, with the number steadily increasing into the 1800s."[6] While not imperative that Brazil should also have used windmills—tiny Antigua did so because of its flat terrain, lack of sufficient land to devote to pastures, and strong winds during the milling season—this illustration nonetheless shows how technological adaptation to the availability of local resources can make or break the competitiveness of an industry.[7]

The affluent of early eighteenth-century Brazil were fond of the "enrich your-self" motto;[8] but if literature was to be sold, an eye must be kept on the market and allowance made for the sentimentality of romanticism. In its Indianist form, from Francisco Varnhagem to José de Alencar (1829–77), Brazilian fictional romanticism espoused a conservative outlook of the *bon sauvage*, whose heroism—in a backdrop of luxuriant jungle—would be mirrored in the Creole. The Creoles would eventually expel the Portuguese, allowing Brazil to be run by the locals, free and faithful to themselves. Alencar's lyricism, particularly in *Iracema*, contributed much to form a Brazilian identity in which the role of the Indian is considerably greater than in Argentina, although the share of the Indian population relative to Argentina's total population, still today, is about three times larger than Brazil's.

Gradually, the Indian left the scene, which was taken over by the *sertanejo*, the man of the hinterland, portrayed as the bastion of Brazil's nationhood at a time when the coastal cities of Brazil were under the strong influence of immigrants.

The printing press did more than allow literature to find readers; it also allowed the printing of technical manuals. One periodical advocated the adoption of a higher-yield variety of sugarcane brought from French Guyana and distributed to sugar mill owners. Though it signaled an advance, the printing press on its own would not be of much help if the population could not read. Still in 1889, 85 percent of the population was illiterate, and engineering knowledge was scant and too dispersed to be able to spread by contagion.

Probably more important than the printing press for the development of science and engineering in Brazil was the 1810 commercial treaty that the British imposed on the Portuguese crown in exchange for protection from Napoleon.[9] Indeed, although the treaty privileged the entrance of British goods in Brazil over those of other provenance, it also indirectly allowed the renewal and decentralization of international exchanges that the Portuguese crown had hampered since the discovery of gold in the late seventeenth century.

One of the main beneficiaries of the new flow of people and the opening of manufacturing activities was iron production. The first iron mill, Real Fábrica do Morro do Pilar, opened in Minas Gerais in 1812, with a German *meister-smelter*. Swedish and British expertise was also sought until 1875, when the

School of Mines of Ouro Preto (Escola de Minas de Ouro Preto, or EMOP) was founded and ultimately diminished Brazil's dependence on a foreign workforce. Nonetheless, large-scale domestic smelting only came about as a result of shortages during World War I. In 1917 a spin-off group of EMOP alumni and professors would design and operate the largest blast furnace of Latin America, capable of producing twenty-five tons of iron ore per day. Four years later, this group would merge with another company to form Companhia Siderúrgica Belgo-Mineira. Staffed by a substantial cadre of EMOP graduates, this entity would account for half of all Brazilian production of steel ingots well into the 1920s. But before this union of talent, training, and production deepened—as in the case of Embraer, embodying the symbiosis between an aeronautical school and an aircraft manufacturing enterprise—a lot would have to happen, not least of all the economic development that would lead to the domestic demand for steel.

Moreover, the expansion of agriculture and the foot-dragging abolishment of slavery (which took roughly seventeen years, from 1871 until 1888), would attract a large influx of immigrants, causing the cities to bulge and requiring substantial investments in civil engineering—both to house people and to improve sanitation and transportation services. The added development would increase the demand for electricity as well as spur the deployment of modern machinery and lighting, furthering the need for civil engineering works at a time that steel and concrete had recently been developed (in Monier, France, in 1868).

The first railway in Brazil was built in Rio de Janeiro in 1854, running a length of 14.5 kilometers. It was primarily coffee-driven expansion that allowed 2,300 kilometers of new railways to be laid between 1876 and 1910. By 1885, the port of Santos accounted for 40 percent of all Brazilian coffee exports, and close to one quarter of the total Brazilian railway grid of 9,500 kilometers was found in that port's state of São Paulo. Still, progress was slow. In the same period since the inception of railroads, the United States laid 5.3 times more railroad tracks than Brazil.

The growth of coffee exports required investments in railways and also attracted immigrants, who needed to be housed and fed. The drive to build railways demanded civil engineers, and by 1874 the Escola Central de Engenharia,

Brazil's first and foremost school of engineering, was demilitarized and transformed into the Escola Politécnica de Rio de Janeiro. Yet the expansion of existing engineering schools was not enough. Demand for engineers was now countrywide and growing fast, propelling the opening of new engineering schools: five were opened in the 1890s, two in São Paulo, and one each in Recife, Porto Alegre, and Salvador. Their students joined forces with civil engineers of the likes of Antonio Pinto Rebouças (1839–74), who designed the Curitiba-Paranaguá railway, a particularly significant feat of engineering. Within a half a century after slavery tottered to a close, Brazilian civil engineers were pioneering the design of tests of concrete resistance, leading to at least one being known worldwide by the name "Brazilian test."[10]

Coffee exports paid for investments in transportation, which contributed to the rise in population in the cities, sometimes dramatically. São Paulo's population grew ninefold in the thirty-year span from 1890 until 1920, when it reached 579,000. Growth was also fueled by immigration. By 1905 over half of the resident population in São Paulo had been born abroad.

Rapid urbanization required more than just steel and cement; efforts were diverted to medicine, with the privately run Instituto Pasteur (1903), followed by the publicly run School of Hygiene and Public Health (1913). Rio de Janeiro's sanitary conditions came under stress, and the Instituto Soroterápico, later the Oswaldo Cruz Foundation, was created at Manguinhos in 1900 to deal with bacteriological research and disease prevention.

This was not a peaceful era in Brazilian politics, either. It was the period of the first republic (1889–1930), when education was secularized (1891) and a naval revolt threatened its sanctity (1893). It was also a time when the New Republic, eager to signal its power, suppressed the over-twenty-thousand-strong messianic movement at Canudos (1897), giving rise to one of Brazil's nation-building epics, by Euclydes da Cunha, *Rebellion in the Backlands*. It was a confusing time, when a public compulsory vaccination campaign triggered a revolt in Rio de Janeiro (1904). A group of army lieutenants led the Copacabana Fort revolt in Rio de Janeiro (1922), effectively launching the Tenentismo movement that would wane only in 1927, but not before producing a communist leader, Luis Carlos Prestes, who would be a major political protagonist in the decades to come.

This was also the time of the Semana Modernista (Modern Art Week, established in 1922), when an arts, letters, and musical movement gravitating around São Paulo galvanized Brazil, breaking with romanticism and formalist styles and freeing expressiveness in ways that came to characterize Brazil. Modern Art Week, held at the São Paulo Municipal Theater, is heralded as a cultural watershed in Brazil. It displayed the strength of the vanguard in burying the old lyricism and symbolism of the Parnassian variety. The movement also exhibited a nonxenophobic nationalist stance in which even the language and its grammar were allowed to be freed from their European roots, giving birth to a new Brazilian expression.

Modernist or not, those who needed to earn a living in cinema and radio could not afford to ignore the market; nor could they afford to tarnish their reputations by catering to it. Brazil was and still is a very class-conscious society, leading one of Brazil's best-known classical composers, Francisco Mignone, to sign his more popular compositions such as tangos, waltzes, and *maxixes*—folk music not necessarily approved by society—with the penname Chico Bororó. Guerra-Peixe, another of Brazil's foremost composers, omitted mention from his curriculum vitae of many of his better-known sambas and *choros*.

Nonetheless, Mignone, who graduated with Mario de Andrade at the São Paulo Conservatory of Drama and Music, would become a staunch supporter of modernism, as Guerra-Peixe was, even contributing to the preservation of the regional music of Pernambuco.[11] Yet it was a young Villa-Lobos, an impressionist at best, who participated in Modern Art Week as the only local guest composer in 1922 and would later become rightly associated with Brazil's musical modernism.

The work of Machado de Assis is generally recognized as among the high points in Brazilian literature. Dead for over a decade before the onset of Modern Art Week, he is not modernist, but timeless. *Dom Casmurro* is widely regarded as his most mature piece, a romance about an upper-class family that we need not get into the details of but whose character, José Dias, is the expression of socially parasitic behavior. I will come back to this work in Chapter 15 when analyzing the managerial implications of the Brazilian self-portrait that these characters help depict.

ELITES AND POPULISM

Voting was not compulsory during the Old Republic (1889–1930), nor was it secret. Moreover, when outcomes were contested, they were sorted out by the legislative body, where the status quo would rule in its own favor. All this contributed to the demoralization of the democratic process and led to a generalized apathy among voters, resulting in less than a 4 percent turnout of the electorate until 1923, with troughs of 1.4 percent in 1906, 1918, and 1919. Turnout for Getúlio Vargas increased to almost 13.5 percent in 1945.[12]

The crash of 1929 halved coffee revenues in pounds sterling within three months. The electoral defeat of Getúlio Vargas to a conservative candidate in 1930 sparked successive contestations, and a coup later that year brought about by the Tenentista movement proved to be the end of what became known as the Old Republic. Getúlio Vargas took office after all in 1930 and remained a central character in Brazilian politics until his suicide in the presidential palace in 1954, while still president. His populist administrations did not signify a rupture with the past but did usher in significant changes. Coffee remained key, while cotton rose in importance and was exported mainly to Germany, leading to an association with Hitler. The new social organization would be more nationalist and more corporatist, and Vargas would govern with an eye toward the poor—whose ranks included internal migrants into the cities. For them, Vargas bolstered a set of labor-legislation innovations, such as eight-hour workdays and paid holidays, for which workers employed in the formal sector remain grateful to this day. His industrialist stance led him to focus on the development of infrastructure projects such as electricity generation, liquid fuel production, and the industrialization of basic materials such as steel, caustic soda, and glass. Yet Brazil remained politically conservative. Secret voting was granted only in the 1934 constitution, which also allowed voting by women who were civil servants.

Vargas's populist style included massive mobilization of workers, entrepreneurs, the middle class, and even communists in support of specific projects. He was a staunch supporter of a state monopoly over oil, which became law in 1953 and later yielded Petrobrás, today one of Brazil's most technologically prominent companies. It would take another fifty-odd years, until 2006, for Brazil to become self-sufficient in oil, which is in itself a major feat when considering that Petrobrás began with such a dearth of know-how and is currently the Brazilian corporation with the most patents, drilling for oil 150 miles offshore to depths of five miles below the ocean surface and a further three miles through, rock, sand, and salt. Among Brazilian corporations, Petrobrás holds the most patents registered in both Brazil and the USA.

Despite Vargas's interest in the development of industry, Brazil's vocation remained largely agricultural and its people poor. Basic science, frequently elitist in poor countries, seems to be anathema to populist movements and was never in the forefront during this period in Brazil. Even Perón roughed up his Nobel laureates.

Technology, with its more practical applications, received more support. This is the time of the creation of the Technological Research Institute (Instituto de Pesquisas Tecnológicas, or IPT), which acted as a technological think tank with testing capacity for the ever-increasing demand for practical solutions by industry and government. This is how the IPT became involved in water-provision solutions for cities, power plant design, meteorology, and geology of strategic minerals. In 1942 it attended to over seven thousand requests for technical assistance.

This was also the period of the provision of midlevel technological training through the National Office of Industrial Apprenticeship (Serviço Nacional de Aprendizagem Industrial, or SENAI). A São Paulo entrepreneur, Roberto Simonsen, was behind the initiative, which was later extended to many states and still provides midlevel professional training to about two million students per year.

Nonetheless, São Paulo's elite was more cosmopolitan than the population in the rest of the country, and their offspring needed better local university education. The University of São Paulo (USP) was founded in 1934 on an inquisitive and liberal philosophy. In this it was exceptional, for at the time the country was moving toward a more authoritarian and immediatist style. USP managed to attract several top-notch scientists, among whom the Italian bias seems to have been strong. USP also attracted social scientists of the caliber of Roger Bastide and Claude Lévi-Strauss. The latter was then in his early thirties and went on to become a member of the Collège de France and one of the world's most-cited academics.

But at the federal level the story was different. In 1937, Carlos Chagas Filho presented a proposal to Minister of Education Capanema for a Brazilian agency for science promotion modeled after the Centre National de la Recherche

Scientifique (CNRS) of France. His efforts were to no avail. Vargas, driven by immediate results, could not clearly see the benefits of longer-term investment in science.[13]

The private sector was somewhat more enlightened. Brazil is a large country, and its business enterprises could be far reaching. Given this framework, in 1947 Canadian Light & Power called upon Karl Terzaghi, Harvard University professor of soil mechanics, in search of a solution to the mudslides that were threatening an electrical power station near Santos. This serendipitous incident, and the generosity with which Professor Terzaghi shared his knowledge, laid the groundwork for Brazil's later excellence in the field, with a long-running connection to Harvard's soil mechanics department. The need for docks also loomed large in Brazil, and dock builder Docas de Santos rose to prominence. Its main shareholders had a fondness for scientific philanthropy, which is how the Gaffrée-Guinle Foundation came to fund mostly health-related research in Brazil over many decades.

An even more significant long-term connection with a top American university was wrought through the development of Brazilian aeronautical industrial capacity. Earnest efforts began during World War II, and in 1946 the Center for Aeronautics Technology was created within the Ministry of Aeronautics under the guidance of MIT professor of aeronautics Richard Smith, who also recommended establishing a training institute. Informal training began in 1947, and as it grew it gave place to the Aeronautical Technological Institute (Instituto Tecnológico de Aeronáutica, or ITA) in 1950 at São Jose dos Campos. Embraer was founded by the government in 1969 and privatized in 1994. Its overall initial strategic vision was to build small planes with engines that could be serviced worldwide. This early world outlook facilitated the international expansion of Embraer, which became a world leader in midsized passenger jet planes by 2003 and is today an aerospace conglomerate with customers in nearly sixty countries.

The interesting aspect of the stories of aircraft builder Embraer and steel manufacturer Belgo-Mineira is that both drew substantially on a well-trained workforce provided by public funding. Neither would exist without the workforce prepared by the state. A similar case is found in Embrapa, a topnotch agricultural research unit created in the 1970s. Among its many accomplishments is the adaptation of the soybean to the milder Brazilian climate, enabling Brazil, thirty years later, to become a world leader in soy exports.

THE SEARCH FOR IDENTITY

Brazil was colonized by the Portuguese in a phase of Iberian affirmation that demanded either the expulsion or the forced conversion of religious minorities to Catholicism. The South American colony provided a social safety valve for the Portuguese convulsion, taking in the unwanted and to which it later forcefully added the Negro while poorly dealing with the native Indian. Brazil reached the twentieth century still absorbing large masses of immigrants, who arrived at time when slavery had only recently been put to an uneasy rest. Such a cauldron of iniquities was unlikely to lie docile in the national psyche, and Brazil—as much as any colonized land—has been dealing with the legacy ever since.[14]

This quest for identity is not only a prerogative of the cultured elite. It is also apparent in the lyrics of the samba schools sung in homage to the pharaohs, African deities, and distant kings and queens as well as in the feverish adoption of rap rhythms in the peripheries of the larger Brazilian cities.[15] While more or less romanticized, Brazilian efforts to construe an identity have had to contend with the lack of a ready-made self-image common to Europeans. Darcy Ribeiro, one of Brazil's foremost anthropologists, frames this quest for identity as an assertive differentiation from the nothingness of the non-African Negro, the somewhat white of the partly European, or the harassed *mestiço* of native origin.[16]

While identity may be crucial for attaining self-worth, the construction of a behavioral code is no less important, particularly for explaining Brazilian attitudes about any number of business activities, including exporting software—a subject we will return to in Chapter 10. These products suffer discrimination from the world market when supplied by countries without traditionally high levels of education or with limited track records in the given fields.

Charles Melman attributes to the original violence of the conquest a disease at the symbolic level, which is responsible for the recurrent episodes of violence within a population deprived of an operational framework.[17] Deprived of a symbolic pact, colonized peoples can only interact through a dynamic relationship of master and slave, in which the master rules unbridled. According to Melman, the absence of a symbolic pact also renders a peculiar type of pseudoparanoic hysteria, the main clinical symptoms of which would be envy, inflexibility, susceptibility, and lack of trust and of pride.[18]

Italian psychoanalyst Contardo Calligaris believes that the social (and psychological) dynamics of Brazilians can be best explained by the dichotomy between the conquistador, or colonist, who arrived to give the land a new language, and the settler, who arrived to make a name for himself.[19] The former arrived to exercise his power away from the father. The latter, a wretch in his land of origin, arrived in search of a future. The colonist arrived in search of fruition in a land that was—and, Calligaris contends, still is—free from parental interdiction. The settler in fact desires the interdiction, thus limiting fruition in order to become a subject.[20] Calligaris' conquistador is unbounded, rapacious, and, upon wreaking devastation, ready to move on to other virgin lands—for the Brazilian image passed on to him by his predecessors no longer offers the opportunity for *jouissance*, causing him to declare, "Brazil is no (longer) good."

Calligaris' settler, in contrast, longs for order, for interdiction, and for opportunity, which he was deprived of in his home country and which he does not find in Brazil.[21] Doubly thieved—and orphaned—the settler also cries, "Brazil is no good." The Brazilian settler and the Brazilian Negro both cry for the lost father, both suffer pain in the negation of their name, and both suffer the loss of the opportunity of becoming.

Neither Calligaris' conquistador nor his settler can find satisfaction. The former because, knowing no restraint in his pursuit of pleasure, he suffers in his craving for an elusive full *jouissance*.[22] The latter because, deprived at his parental home, he risked his language, his identity, and himself in pursuit of a promise left unfulfilled. Neither can love Brazil, the country that nurtures them in spite of their disillusionment.

Calligaris concludes his analysis in what he calls the apparent lack of "onetegration" in Brazil. Onetegration, as opposed to integration, highlights the need to become one unit and to accept a national meaning, while integration presumes the accommodation of differing points of view. Becoming one would enable Brazilians to speak in a single voice rather than to regard Brazil as if they were foreigners.[23]

Also in search of oneness, both Melman and French psychoanalyst Roland Chemama point to the need for a pact at the symbolic level to relieve Brazil from its current fragmentation.[24] This fragmentation, and the ensuing battle between conquistador and settler, weakens Brazil's psychological immunology, rendering it not only vulnerable to foreign penetration (witness the perceived glamour of foreign tastes associated with globalization) but also unable to amass the psychological strength even to launch a software export campaign, a subject of Chapter 10.[25]

Fragmentation also has repercussions on the administration of justice.[26] In 1990, São Paulo, the country's most developed state, had fifty times fewer judges than was recommended, and in all of Brazil, 250,000 arrest warrants stood unfulfilled. Impunity is rampant.[27]

AN UNPOPULAR SYMBOLIC PACT

Yet, rather than accepting the void of a symbolic pact in Brazil, we adopt one that we do not like. Calligaris points to the lack of "onetegration," although an ethical approach to the problem clouds the fact that a culture, a pact, or a common code may already exist. It may be one that Brazilians dislike but that nonetheless works, though not necessarily for the majority. In Calligaris' terminology, this may be the code of the unbridled conquistador. The code may even be adopted by the settler when in a position of power, for its relative impunity teaches that the end justifies the means while creating a culture of cynicism, sadly epitomized in the following example of "Gerson's Law."

Gerson was a well-known soccer player who was recruited by a Brazilian advertising agency as the ad man for a certain brand of cigarettes sold in Brazil, which Gerson would promote as both longer and cheaper than other brands. His sound bite closed with a phrase underscored by a facial expression that conveyed to viewers that only a fool would not prefer that brand—as he allegedly did—implying that people should strive to be like him, who liked to take advantage of everything and, perhaps, everyone.

Although effective, the widely commented ad campaign provoked an ethical backlash that harmed the player's image and forced the advertising agency director, Caio Domingues, to devote much of the remainder of his professional career to the attempt to undo the damage and explain what he really meant.[28] The fact that what became known as Gerson's Law would have such an impact on public opinion testified to how intimately the population recognized its jurisdiction. This phenomenon is also seen in the quip that doubles as a title by Brazilian anthropologist Roberto DaMatta: "Do you know who you are speaking to?"—a not uncommon response to an authority's request by anyone operating within a minor sphere of power, alluding to access to protection by a higher-ranking authority.[29]

While the ethical backlash on Gerson showed that not all hope of the prevalence of ethics was lost in Brazil, it also revealed how deeply the rule of Calligaris' conquistador cut in Brazilian society, producing a degraded level of citizenship, in which the masses are still subject to the unbridled *jouissance* of the powerful.

The event that yielded Gerson's law also highlighted the way in which an otherwise condemnable symbolic pact could be used to provoke individual reactions, in this case to purchase an advertised product. The leap from the collective representation to the reactions of individual Brazilian agents is not easy to theorize about, but it is one that advertisers have learned to exploit— and Brazilians are among the best in the field.[30] Such advertising prowess helps to confirm the existence of at least some collective myth that can be harnessed to trigger desired individual behavior, at least where the buying impulse is concerned.

Therefore, while the proof of a causal link between Brazilian imagery and individual responses may remain elusive, for the purpose of my argument it suffices to verify a solid-enough link to support the advertising profession, which brings us back to the beginning.

Melman pointed out that Brazil's social and psychoanalytical genesis may show symptoms of pseudoparanoic hysteria along with a lack of trust. Lack of trust is frequently mistaken for cynicism and remains in the realm of beliefs, whereas cynicism is often an attitudinal response to disappointment, involving experience and affection.[31]

Whether by lack of trust Melman meant cynicism is hard to ascertain. But cynicism is rampant in Brazil, as can be inferred by the voting intentions in October 2002 of many supporters of an indicted candidate for governor of the state of São Paulo. In the possibility of voting for a candidate identified as dishonest, voters must have recognized an opportunity for vicariously realizing the malfeasance that they themselves did not have the chance to incur.[32] The prevailing cynicism in politics may well be the attitudinal response to recurring disillusionment.

Brazilians are born into a cradle of neglect, to a world of unfulfilled promises, and with no unifying authority to appeal to. This start in life can hardly provide the basis of a strong sense of national self-worth, which explains one popular assessment that the majority of Brazilians are born to be henpecked to death. An Adlerian inferiority complex is the likely result, blurring the path to achieving the individual's fictional finalism.

This assessment may help to understand the Brazilian susceptibility, of which several well-known public cases can be cited. In 2002 a spokesperson for then president Fernando Henrique Cardoso complained about the misrepresentation of Rio de Janeiro by no less an offender than Bart Simpson. In response, Fox's Bart challenged the Brazilian president to a celebrity boxing match. Fortunately, that was the end of the story. In another case, a tired American Airlines pilot lifted his middle finger to Brazilian immigration authorities who were applying new procedures, causing delays. The issue absorbed the national press's attention for several days in 2004 and elicited untold numbers of knee-jerk nationalistic reactions. In a more recent example, President Lula threatened to expel a *New York Times* correspondent for printing what a political opponent had written: "What everybody knows is that Lula loves to drink more than he should." In all three cases, Brazilian authorities overreacted and played the fool, displaying precisely the susceptibility that, according to Melman, results from the lack of a symbolic pact.

SUMMING UP: BRAZIL

Initially, Brazil was not settled, it was kept. To keep it out of foreigners' hands, a few Portuguese were scattered along the coast, closest to Portugal, and for their upkeep they devoted their energies to making sugar. To those early settlers, the sighting of sail masts off the coast signaled a threat, for they were likely to belong to foreign invaders. The sea was a source of trouble, not of opportunity. Hence, the heirs of navigators became the rough-hewn *bandeirantes* that populated the hinterland. When they hit gold, they hit a lot of it, leading to a gold rush in the eighteenth century at a time when Portugal's trading business in Asia was being contested by the Dutch. Brazil gained salience, and the Portuguese royalty took refuge in Brazil as Napoleon threatened the

Portuguese crown. Fourteen thousand courtiers moved to Brazil, and as they arrived they must have looked like Martha's Vineyard vacationers landing in the Bronx. It probably took a lot of retrofitting to house them, and doing so implied a significant impulse forward for Brazilian development, let alone what it did to promote the preservation of territorial integrity.

Yet the royal relocation thwarted any incipient political renewal. As Latin America was experimenting with republicanism, perhaps equivalent on the developmental continuum to the adolescent leaving the parental home, the Brazilian royal parents followed suit and moved into the children's new house. Brazil became the seat of the empire, and political development was halted— evident in the fact that Brazil was the last nation in the region to abolish slavery and in the marked prominence of ascription and inherited wealth. Proximity to the ruling authority ensured privileges, and entrepreneurialism and achievement would be procrastinated. Lobbying for power became second nature, and personalization of relationships paved the way to favors and deference. It is hard to imagine an outcome further removed from the North American ethos that galvanized Sarmiento in Argentina, than the Brazilian way of getting along, until republicanism took over in 1889.

Nonetheless, it would take another half a century until Brazil began modernizing, which it did under the protection of a despotic Vargas, financed by Perón. Despotism and modernity walked hand in hand. Leadership became inclusive and protective of the poor, and state-run large enterprises took hold, as in oil and steel. Bouts of democratic rule would on occasion transfer the engines of development to consumer goods, such as cars in the 1950s, but by and large Brazil would remain in the stronghold of centralized authoritarianism of the positivist kind, under an elite that argued that it knew better, such as during the military regime that lasted from 1964 until 1985.

Brazil's evolution differed from that of most other Latin American republics—it was slower at developing politically—but it shares with most the lack of a symbolic pact that would allow the citizenry to be at ease with itself. This translates into a lack of self-esteem that numbs the necessary aggressiveness to actively pursue markets for its intellectual products and other offshoots of its masterful skills of improvisation.

CHAPTER 9

HOW CULTURE
SHAPED OPTIONS IN
THE NEW WORLD

T HE IMPORTANCE OF THE Pilgrims' landing in North
America is well established, yet the difference between
how these newcomers and those in Latin America related to the indigenous
populations—and what they would later do to heal the initial severance—
merits further discussion. I will discuss in this chapter the origins and the
significance of the American Thanksgiving celebration, because there is no
parallel commemoration in Latin America and because it represents deliberate
socially integrative policies in the United States that Latin Americans have not
developed. Those integrative efforts also give salience to different attitudes regarding the poor, relieving poverty, and the meaning of individualism to both
North Americans and Latin Americans. I then illustrate how these cultural
expressions differ in social integration policies as a result of different conceptions of the individual in society. Last, I will review the differences and similarities between both peoples.

Let me initially illustrate these points with a couple of transitional stories
that span the New World from Brazil to North America.

In 1510 a Portuguese explorer named Diogo Álvarez landed in Brazil and
would have been killed by the Tupi Indians had he not fallen into favor with

Paraguaçú, an Indian princess. Because of Álvarez's dexterity with the musket, he was called Caramurú (man of fire) by the much-impressed Indians. Caramurú and Paraguaçú lived together for some time, until Álvarez was offered a trip back on a French ship. He took Paraguaçú with him, and once in France he had the Indian princess baptized and married her. Accounts have her as splendid and obviously unique in Europe. After some time, Caramurú and Paraguaçú returned to Brazil, where they allegedly lived happily ever after.[1] Caramurú is quite famous in Brazil today, where, quite fittingly, a popular fireworks company bears his name.

In another tale, Anayansi was presented to Balboa, discoverer of the Pacific Ocean, by Careta, her father and native chief of Darien, now part of Panama. The most accepted version tells of Balboa's pacification by Anayansi, rendering him a more benevolent conquistador than he might otherwise have been. Anayansi became an interpreter between natives and Spaniards, and her name is today a positive national metaphor for a cultural bridge. So strong is this association that the name "Anayansi" is given to parks, corporations, theaters, and schools and is the first name of many women in Panama.[2]

La Malinche was a captive woman among the Mayas who was presented to the invaders upon the natives' defeat at Tabasco in 1519. Her proficiency with languages made Malinche a valued interpreter and companion of Cortés, with whom she had a child before succumbing to smallpox.

In a final example, Pocahontas was the daughter of an Algonquian chief in North America. Her tribe had captured Captain John Smith, and her father would have had him executed were it not for interference by Pocahontas. She continued with several public displays of loyalty and loving selflessness in favor of Smith and his compatriots, although he sailed for England without her. Conflicting versions of the story notwithstanding, much of what has made it through time and that has been taken for true is, in essence, as sketched out above, and this is also the version picked up by the rosier account of the legend in the 1995 Walt Disney movie *Pocahontas*. The veracity of the details is less important than what they tell of British immigrant attitudes toward the indigenous population. Even if untrue in essence, what counts is that the tale has survived, and that in itself is historical evidence of the molding of the era's separatist attitudes.[3] Even in the case of La Malinche, whom present-day Mexicans tend to despise as a traitor, the role of go-between remains a cherished one; in none of the preceding accounts, except that of Pocahontas, is the invader portrayed as segregationist. The cost of unification is the price being paid today for the past's divisiveness.

UNIFYING A DISPARATE PEOPLE

Self-reliance of the individual fuels the U.S. economic system and has been held as a virtue at least since Ralph Waldo Emerson wrote a poem by that title in 1841.[4] It is a cultural trait that runs so deeply in the people's psyche that most North Americans consider it a point of honor to take care of themselves and their own lot, usually meaning the nuclear family. This entrenched individualism, propped by the self-interest advocated by Adam Smith, results in an economic system based on private enterprise that is largely unfettered by government. People earn what they can in turn afford. Yet the nationally unifying side of the North American credo had to be constructed, because the nation was but a collection of disparate immigrants. The effort to stitch together a national quilt is still very much in the making, but unlike Argentina and Brazil, in the United States it is the object of a deliberate effort, as in the creation of Thanksgiving Day.

A RALLYING POINT FOR AMERICANS

The Thanksgiving holiday dates back to 1621, one year after the Puritans arrived in Massachusetts. The first winter had wiped out half of the settlers, and their Indian neighbors offered to teach the remaining ones how to plant corn and other crops. With this help, by the next fall the Pilgrims and their Indian guests celebrated a plentiful harvest. Another year later, Virginia's native Americans ran out of patience and raided Jamestown, slaughtering 350 settlers. Understandably, the settlers' willingness to give thanks must have suffered a setback, and interest in the celebration waned.

What was initially an intimate celebration may have disappeared altogether if it had not also become a political instrument to promote social cohesion. President George Washington believed that the holiday would reinforce a sense of unity and cooperation toward a national endeavor in the disparate young society. Washington revived the celebration of Thanksgiving more than a century after its humble beginnings, asking Congress in 1789 to make it a national holiday. The holiday was observed but lost its thrust over the years, falling into oblivion until the Civil War. Pioneering Massachusetts feminist and journal editor Sara Josepha Hale then persuaded President Abraham Lincoln of the unifying power of reviving an ecumenical, humanitarian holiday such as Thanksgiving. Lincoln obliged, and the Thanksgiving holiday was observed for a few more years before being forgotten once again. It was then President Franklin Delano Roosevelt's turn to revive the holiday at a time when the country's social fabric was being torn apart by the Depression at home and threatened by fascism abroad. In 1941, the year the United States entered World War II, Roosevelt asked his fellow citizens to honor the holiday and Congress decreed the fourth Thursday in November as Thanksgiving Day. This is how, despite its comings and goings, to this day the celebration of friendship, endurance, cooperation, and plenty consists of a feast including at least some of the indigenous foods enjoyed at that first celebration: roast turkey, cranberry sauce, potatoes, and pumpkin pie.

While there may be disagreement over my telling of the story, my intention is not to alienate North Americans from their holiday but rather to illustrate how the United States managed to construct a national identity by means of a unifying celebration. This example of the building of tradition constitutes a deliberate effort to unite Americans in a common celebration devoid of adherence to any origin beyond that which they have in common: the fact of being there, having emigrated to the United States of America.

There is no equivalent to the Thanksgiving holiday in either Argentina or Brazil. National holidays in both countries tend to gravitate around celebrations of Catholic saint's days and independence of the colonial governments. The latter commemorations do not celebrate the efforts of later waves of immigrants, many of whom hailed from the very countries from which the locals wished to celebrate independence. Perhaps only Sarmiento's public educational efforts in Argentina can be construed as aiming to consolidate the social fabric of a young nation, and it is not by chance that he sought the solutions in the United States, a country that was struggling with many of the same problems as Argentina. But even Sarmiento's underlying efforts and vocal message were divisive, for they positioned "civilized" urbanites against the "barbarous" gauchos of the hinterland.

PAYING FOR THE AMERICAN WAY OF LIFE

Rituals aside, social cohesion must have some foundation if it is to last. Most Americans live comfortably on what they earn, and many even set aside some amount for leaner times or retirement. Yet a substantial number of people in the United States do not have the benefit of a public safety net.

In 2003, 35.9 million Americans lived below the poverty line while 45 million were without health care insurance. Families below the poverty line in the United States may receive limited health and social security benefits in addition to welfare payments to help them meet the basic needs of food, clothing, and shelter. The most common form of welfare payment is Aid to Families with Dependent Children (AFDC), or its successor, Temporary Assistance to Needy Families (TANF).

Federal disbursements through assistance programs amounted to 11 percent of the 1999 federal budget. It is a significant improvement, actually double the share of the federal budget allotment in the 1960s,[5] but this amount has been declining as a share of GDP for the last twenty-five years. U.S. assistance to the needy comes up short when compared to the welfare efforts undertaken in Europe as from the late nineteenth century. Traditionally, people in the United States did not feel obligated to offer welfare support. Immigrants would arrive with remembrances of hardship, hope of improvement, and opportunity in the way of farmland. When agricultural produce was no longer the primary objective, rapid industrialization offered plenty of urban job opportunities.

However, the Depression was a rude awakening. We already saw how President Hoover tiptoed around the solutions to the issue, hoping that the citizens' resourcefulness would have them pulling themselves out of the rut by their own bootstraps. But Americans could not wait that long and voted for President Franklin Roosevelt to sort out the matter. Within days, Roosevelt was providing work for hundreds of thousands in major public works. These were temporary relief programs; only the Social Security system became a permanent institution, and still it is not enough. Why? Because America's prevailing self-reliance ethos frowns upon transfers to the poor.

Many middle-class Americans criticize the U.S. welfare system, particularly for the outlay of cash directed to the AFDC/TANF programs. Critics argue that such payments encourage cross-generational apathy and single-parent families, as payments are based on the number of children in a household, irrespective of the parents' marriage status. Most experts would argue that the welfare system should not be dismantled without empowering the poorest families with the tools for social mobility, such as education and health insurance.

However, the national heritage of self-reliance has won the struggle in the last two decades. Since 1996, welfare payments in the United States have been less generous and more restricted, precisely because of the prevailing belief that social programs tend to trap the poor in dependency and deny them the incentive to take control of their lives. Just how much transfer of resources to the poor can U.S. citizens tolerate, and why? These are relevant questions, for American transfers of social benefits to households—including Social Security—are, as a share of GDP, only half the size of those in Europe, and the allotments are less generous and reach a smaller share of the needy.

There are important institutional factors that prevented U.S. society from matching the European reforms of the nineteenth and twentieth centuries. For one, federally mandated curbs centralized redistributive initiatives in the United States. Moreover, the U.S. court system has consistently blocked redistributive attempts, which are perceived by many as assaults on private property.[6] In contrast, Europe's political system tends to be more highly centralized and keener on proportional representation than the U.S. system. Despite a long democratic tradition, proportional representation is lagging in the United States, and this hinders the growth of smaller political parties that could educate the population on alternative views and eventually build a base of support. Various Socialist parties in Europe have arisen from just such grassroots origins. The European courts, as opposed to the U.S. system, have evolved from overthrown monarchies in relatively recent revolutionary times and tend to see the public collective interest under a kinder light. Despite the institutional factors, the question that still begs an answer is: Why do Americans embrace institutions that hinder significant redistributive attempts?

DOES THE "OTHER" DESERVE HELP?

Another important factor is at play. Scholars have recently suggested that the perceived stinginess in caring for the poor in the United States may stem from Americans' perception of the poor as lazy, while Europeans and Latin Americans tend to view the poor as unfortunate.[7] The problem might lie in the fact that in the United States, where the bulk of the poor are of African descent, redistribution in favor of the poor would mean favoring the Other. Race is the single most significant factor in statistically accounting for redistribution in the USA, and the lack of an extensive welfare state is a reflection of the country's troubled race relations.[8]

American humanism leads U.S. society to take care of its needy, yet its individualism and proclivity to self-reliance limit the extent to which welfare assistance can effectively accomplish this task. The poor are given the message to take care of themselves, because individuals are equal to one another not only regarding rights but also regarding obligations—not least among which is the obligation for their own upkeep.

Leveling the playing field is the objective of the egalitarians. Individualists, on the other hand, believe more strongly in the power of self-reliance and advocate policies oriented to dispelling the sense of powerlessness, along with incentives to ignite ambition. U.S. society has oscillated between the two poles, egalitarian and individualist, but in the last two decades the pendulum seems to have swung harder on the individualist side.

SAME WORDS, DIFFERENT MEANINGS

What is the relationship between individualism and egalitarianism? American individualists can hardly be called nonegalitarian, as they would claim to also abide by the "all men are created equal" credo put forth in the nation's Declaration of Independence.

The North American concept of individuality calls for equality of the sort that grants each person the same value as the next.[9] In Tocqueville's wake, Americans concede that individualism is a democratic concept that entails equality of conditions. Individualism connotes the other side of the coin from egalitarianism.

The Latin American concept of individuality, on the other hand, reflects the Italian Renaissance notion of recognition of a person's inner worth.[10] It is rooted in the idea of intrinsic uniqueness shaped on the difference between individuals.[11]

The Latin American notion of the individual's uniqueness may have deep roots in Catholicism, as expressed in the cherished concepts of soul and protection by guardian angels—or "masters," among the followers of Alain Kardec—but this notion has been considerably secularized. Modern associations of the individual's inner worth recognize the person's dignity, referring not to the dignity of social position but rather to an internal coherence of values that determines the notion of an individual's self-worth, or amour propre. This may mean that a monetarily unsuccessful individual who is guided by his or her own values, even if at odds with those of society, may be more highly regarded than someone who has accumulated wealth by devious means and impassively tolerates insults. Che Guevara immediately comes to mind as an example of the former, while cohorts of corrupt Latin American politicians might illustrate the latter.

The individual's notion of self-worth, as expressed in his or her sense of dignity, is different from the Spanish concept of *honra*, over which five thousand Spanish males died in duels during the seventeenth century.[12] Yet the concepts are interrelated. Possession or lack of honor ought to be determined by an individual's intimate self-assessment, although that assessment can be publicly challenged, even on petty matters. Not responding to the challenge, as in the case of a duel, would undermine the individual's social standing, shattering his or her self-respect and thus depriving the individual of that which makes him or her unique.

Where the stress of individuality lies in the individual's uniqueness—and associated personal dignity—and where the utilitarian ethos is despised, individuals may tend to express their uniqueness by courting tragedy. Passion is the sparkling sheen that announces freedom of choice, for passion defies rationality.[13] If in addition to being passionate a person's decision or action also courts tragedy, then such behavior crowns the individual's selflessness, for it is then apparent that not a trace of utilitarianism factored into the individual's decision, as may be observed in the "moment of truth" in the bullfight.[14] The bullfighter's behavior meets both requirements: the expression of uniqueness and the supreme defiance of pragmatism.

This categorization allows an explanation of such disparate Latin American behaviors as bullfighting, the invasion of the Falklands by Argentina, the Cuban acceptance of Russian missiles in 1962, and Che Guevara's totemic standing, as well as economic ones such as the successful Argentine international debt renegotiation of 2005. It also questions the efficacy of extrinsic managerial pecuniary incentives, for the most admired persons are not after money.

The bullfighter risks his life in compliance with a choreography that requires him to leap over the horns of the bull in order to stab him through the heart, thus dispensing the beast with an immediate, honorable death at the risk of having his genitalia gored.

Fidel Castro and Che Guevara shared the common goal of the triumph of Cuba's revolution, and to Latin Americans both personas epitomize the same admirable trait: obstinate defiance against a much more powerful adversary, the USA. Their expressions of defiance were practiced to the verge of courting tragedy, as in the case of Castro and the Cuban missile crisis. Rather than backing down, Castro was prepared to have the Russians fire the first shots, which would have led to the obliteration of Cuba and much else.

Che Guevara is reported to have preferred death rather than exile in a foreign embassy, should the Cuban Revolution fail. "Search for my body among the dead," he told KGB's deputy head, General Leonov, and subsequently proved his assertion by dying in combat in Bolivia.[15] Che Guevara's handsome looks added some luster to his subsequent elevation to a totemic figure, standing for unrepentant rebelliousness across the world. But El Che was unlikely to have earned such global recognition had he not first secured the admiration of a generation of Latin Americans, precisely for his attitude, his unyielding pursuit of dignity, and his history of courting tragedy against all odds.

If Latin Americans, and Argentines specifically, were not perceived as passionate beyond redemption, President Néstor Kirchner might not have been so successful at renegotiating Argentina's international debt in 2005, during which creditors suffered a 70 percent haircut. Indeed, *The Economist* perceived the knife dueler's stance adopted by Argentina, aligned with its cultural background as epitomized by Martin Fierro.[16]

Important to distill from these illustrations is that Latin Americans value behavior that seeks to prove the individual's uniqueness through the application of dexterity for no practical purpose beyond the satisfaction brought by public recognition. The deed must by definition be challenging, the performance exacting and elegantly carried out, and the pecuniary compensation absent or not seen as a motive.

If, collectively, this behavior is what Latin Americans applaud, then pecuniary incentives will not carry the same weight in Latin America as they do in

the United States. Such incentives would thus need to be even higher in order
to elicit the same response from the Latin American worker as in the USA.
Furthermore, since it is the public that grants the recognition desired by the
actor, individuals will want to downplay their expertise or dexterity in order
to stress the higher significance of group collaboration in the achievement of
goals. Under this ethos, individual meritocratic incentives lose attractiveness,
the group gains prominence, and promotion by seniority is favored over individual performance, for all are necessary to the benefit of the whole.[17]

In any case, the term *individual* carries different meanings to the Anglo-
American and Latin American cultures, and this difference has important
management implications. In an Anglo-American work scenario, executives
may openly challenge the judgment of subordinates, who, as individuals,
are expected to be capable of holding their own ground and expressing their
views, for a worker is deemed to be the boss's equal. On the other hand, Latin
American subordinates are likely to take offense at having their judgments
challenged, particularly if done in public. Depending on the circumstances,
a challenge to a Latin American subordinate is likely to elicit a response that
may be interpreted as exaggerated by the Anglo-American executive.[18] The notion of uniqueness as reflected in the Latin American male will be explored in
Chapters 12 and 13 in interpreting, respectively, leadership attributes and the
literary character Martin Fierro.

The importance of the Latin American notion of the individual cannot
be overrated. The concept is at the core of the personalism that permeates relationships among Latin Americans, to whom loyalty can be established only
among people with a shared notion of the soul and of dignity, because loyalty
demands reciprocity. Thus, the notion of individuality and the amour propre
it implies affects even the degree of trust achievable in relationships, for only
among close and trusted friends are people reassured that their individuality
will not be challenged. A Latin American will less readily trust those who are
not next of kin or close friends than will a North American. It is among their
closest circle that Latin Americans feel at ease, for that is where their individuality is most readily recognized, where one can adopt nonritualized postures
and be accepted without censure.

Outside of this close (and closed) circle, however, the Latin American individual resorts to elaborate ways of interacting and addressing others, a ritual

aimed at ensuring that the counterpart's individuality is being recognized. A salesperson, for example, will frequently allude to the customer's differential status as a way of putting the customer at ease, for he or she thus acknowledges the customer's individuality.[19] Personalism is the device by which an individual can navigate, unencumbered by the trappings of ritualized behavior and distrust. It is through this device that the Latin American establishes the protocol of the meeting of souls that lowers the barriers of distrust and ultimately builds effectiveness.[20] In Chapter 14 I will examine the role of personalism as a hedge against excessive hierarchy in the Brazilian work environment.

This personalization of relationships by means of recognizing individuality, as understood by Latin Americans, is also what allows Latin Americans to accept the unequal distribution of power, for they are initiated into that hierarchy early on. Every Latin American is born into an elaborate array of social networks. Some of those networks may involve close contact with extreme poverty, but the individual's networked resourcefulness, through personalized relationships, may help to break down social confinement. While difficult for the majority, this status quo is culturally accepted. As a result, Latin Americans may appear to both accept rules and yet readily maneuver them to their advantage without any qualms.

Even to non-Puritans, such behavior may seem duplicitous, and it is portrayed as such in most North American films depicting Latin Americans. However, what seems to be a double-edged ethical standard is in fact an effective barrier to entry. An invitation to lunch with a Latin American family, for example, does not grant a stranger the level of access it may imply in the United States. Only the uninitiated will be surprised.

Latin Americans are similarly confused by northerners, who, being so private, might be expected to live locked up in their homes. Still, although Americans may bolt their doors, they leave their yards unfenced, in sharp contrast to the walled-off, impenetrable houses common throughout Latin America. Still, American yards are not public spaces open to all; that is, although unfenced, they are not collective. Similar restrictions apply in the USA to the infringement on a host's time, who may seek to hedge against undue exposure by imposing time limits on guests at a dinner party, say, 7 P.M. to 10 P.M. Such a controlled structure for a social event would be offensive by Latin American standards, and I venture to guess by Mediterranean standards, too, for the Greek concept

of *filotimo* is expected to be unrestricted within the host's bounds of afford-
ability.[21] But, of course, time is money to the kin of Benjamin Franklin, even
when it is not money but energy or effort that is being conserved, while to a
Latin American time may mean no more than an opportunity to build a relationship, especially when invited to dinner.

Thus, there is no duplicity in this behavior; at worst, there is ambiguity for
the uninitiated. The Latin American individual may practice strong collectivist
behavior within the close circle of extended family and friends while still behaving aggressively in the marketplace, and this latter may be perceived with
a longer-term orientation than that which characterizes the U.S. marketplace.
Stressing the orientation and emphasis of behavior within family and work
environments, authors such as Triandis talk of both horizontal and vertical
collectivism and individualism, which I will address in Chapter 11.

THE ENACTMENT OF DIFFERENCES

So far in this chapter I have addressed cultural heterogeneity in Latin America
and North America and the different approaches of each region to dealing with
cultural differences. Having discussed the perception of individuality in both
regions, let us now deal with the enactment of those differences.

The economic expansion of the United States would end up having international policy consequences. I will not review these here but I mention them
so as not to overlook the foundations, exaggerated or real, of Latin America's
resentment of its North American brothers.

As the United States came to be viewed by the world as an international power
capable of confronting enemies in Europe, as in World War I, its power in the
Caribbean region was unquestionable. This position frequently led to forceful
intervention in what were seen as the internal affairs of otherwise independent
countries. For instance, the USA supervised elections, against the hosts' wishes,
in Panama in 1908 and 1912, and in Santo Domingo in 1913 and again from
1916, when the USA took over the administration of the country for seven years.
Something similar happened in Haiti for two decades after the U.S. invasion in
1915. In Panama, after the forceful removal of General Noriega in 1989, the USA
ran the country through indirect rule for two years. In addition to occasionally
landing troops for periods of a couple of weeks, the USA sent covert agents to
Cuba in 1906, to Honduras in 1924, to Guatemala in 1954, and again to Cuba in

1961 in the invasion of the Bay of Pigs. While this intervention failed, Cuba has remained under a U.S. commercial embargo ever since.

Particularly after the building of the Panama Canal, an expense the USA would not have incurred if not for the region's strategic importance, the need to move U.S. naval forces between the Pacific and Atlantic Oceans required that the USA secure Atlantic access to the canal, free from European intervention. The rationale for U.S. intervention in Latin America was enthusiastically espoused by the renowned Harvard professor and first editor of *Foreign Affairs*, Archibald Cary Coolidge, at the turn of the last century.[22] From the U.S. perspective, intervention in the region was warranted to preempt trouble, and thus began its international police role in the region, as sanctioned by President Roosevelt's message to Congress of December 6, 1904.

Some of the larger Latin American countries, like Argentina, Brazil, and Chile, and others not so large, like Uruguay, still today look largely to Europe for inspiration, but the choices of mentors were severely curtailed in the early twenty-first century by the cultural limitations imposed by long dictatorships in the European countries that Latin America had the most affinity with: Italy, Portugal, and Spain. The loss of these father figures made the intrusive U.S. stepfather figure even more bruising.

Fact-finding, sure-footed Anglo-American traits have long been held in opposition to the Latin American flamboyant proclivity to base actions on impressions, without even the perseverance to embody imagination in something deliverable. As the early Latin Americanist Clarence Haring would illustrate, Latin Americans would prioritize the embellishment of their cities with parks and fountains over practical pursuits, such as traffic signals. This tendency would even spill over to libraries, which, Haring observed, would stand a greater chance of being beautified before being stocked and staffed. The same ostentatious cultural traits would lure Latin America's medical doctors to pursue novel techniques rather than preventative laboratory work or public health and sanitation work. This same lack of concern over public issues would explain Latin Americans' historical disinterest in combating endemic graft.

Curiously enough, these impressions, as espoused by Haring, cannot be held to be completely adversarial to Latin Americans. Still, many of the negative traits he concedes as depicting North Americans were deemed only temporary—such as the brusqueness of American manners and verbal intercourse, considered to be a frontier trait. North Americans abroad were criticized by Haring for their loud manners, their excessive drinking, their aloofness from the locals, and their frequent refusal to learn Spanish or Portuguese.[23]

However, what seemed to Haring in the early twentieth century to be only a spillover of a frontier spirit appears to have lasted into the present century. Indeed, what was perceived as the loud behavior of American executives abroad continued to be a matter of concern in the first quarter of 2006, at least as perceived by the *Wall Street Journal*'s Career supplement[24] and by Harvard Business School's *Harvard Management Update*.[25]

Some of this may be closer to an issue of social class than to differences in culture. While not often mentioned, the truth is that New World schooling, north and south, does not excel in the teaching of languages; thus when U.S. corporations venture south, they depend on English-speaking locals in order to communicate. In Latin America these persons tend to come from the upper classes, the only ones able to pay privately for what the public educational system does not provide. Given the privileged pool of students, English instruction in Latin America imparts attitudes and "table manners" that may be different from those of visiting American executives; thus a clash is inevitable, and it is not merely cultural. The disparaging appraisal of Benjamin Franklin's pragmatic mind by Uruguayan essayist José Enrique Rodó in *Ariel* (1900)—"a prudent usefulness, in whose bosom will never raise the emotions of holiness or heroism"—is echoed a century later by Brazilian Harvard law professor and close collaborator of Brazil's President Lula, Roberto Mangabeira Unger: "Pragmatism has become the philosophy of the age by shrinking."[26]

As with any piece of literature that reaches a vast audience, Rodó's *Ariel* in itself may be taken as representative of wide belief in the ideas it espoused. Those ideas were attuned to the regenerationist movement that overtook Spain after its disastrous 1898 defeat to America.[27] Written as a rallying cry to Latin American youth, *Ariel* resonates with all the differences of attitude that still separate the United States from Latin America.[28] Rodó was no uncouth anti-American. He did admire the North American "spirit of political freedom" and its determination to "get things done," as well as its "pagan joy in health, in skill, and in strength."[29] But Rodó, as well as his readers over a century, would not have any of the American deification of practicality as espoused in an aphoristic culture, epitomized by Benjamin Franklin.

These differences can be hard to bridge, and indeed they have been. A century after Rodó's pronouncements one still feels similar expressions of mutual rejection going on. Haring seemed to believe that it was only a matter of time until these differences were ironed out. Nonetheless, in a remarkably candid and possibly unfair concession, Haring asserted that U.S. citizens in South America do not represent, in general, the best that the United States has to offer in terms of "intelligence, breeding, or personality."[30]

Haring attributed the relative lack of a surplus of "good men" to send abroad to the attractiveness of business at home—allegedly greater than what the European attractiveness would mean to its own people, freeing many top minds there to enter into diplomacy, for example. However, two European wars during the twentieth century do not seem to have helped bridge the "attractiveness gap." If anything, the previous century has led Latin America to fall into an orbit closer to the United States and farther away from Europe.

This has led the majority of Latin American emigrants to try their luck in the USA. Tellingly, the stress of their adaptation there has produced higher rates of attempted suicide than those among other immigrants, and higher than those suffered by their nationals left at home. The stress arises from the dichotomies of the two cultures, as is succinctly expressed in this excerpt: "The traditional cultural stories of the macho, the patriarch, the man of gallantry have become unbearable, unfruitful, and untenable for both men and women . . . caught between two cultures, too many Latino men continue not to know how to respond to the changes around them."[31] While bad enough for the parents, it is worse for the most vulnerable. Suicide attempts among the daughters of Hispanic immigrants to the USA are higher than the average; one in five attempt suicide, apparently due to the stress of coping with adolescence in a country culturally so diverse from what they experience in their Hispanic American homes.[32]

The issue is not, however, the result of Latin American versus North American culture, but is more likely associated with different conceptions regarding the organization of the self within society. A joint study of Boston and Istanbul Universities pointed out that mental health may be under the greatest stress when persons of an individualist society are placed within a collectivist one, and vice versa.[33]

SHALL WE ALSO TALK ABOUT THE SIMILARITIES?

Information about the American people has increased considerably in Latin America over the last fifty years. Not only has American literature been more accurately translated and more abundantly published, but American pop music has also become better known, even reflecting Latin American tunes.[34] But perhaps most important of all, American cinema has had a huge role in disseminating a wider understanding of people in the United States.

This closer cultural exposure has helped Latin Americans become aware of regional cultures in the United States, perhaps to the point of detecting the subtle and not-so-subtle differences between the U.S. North and South and of identifying a greater affinity between the cultures of Latin America and the U.S. South.

The resemblance is likely to stem from the patriarchal family arrangements that predominate in both regions and that characterize what sociologist Göran Therborn has defined as interstitial family arrangements: those resulting from a social plantocracy born of the Afro-Creole culture that, in turn, resulted from the dependence on slaves to operate plantations.[35] Such arrangements, which reinforced paternalism, spilled across tobacco and cotton plantations in the USA's Old South and beyond, wherever sugar was planted—be it in British Jamaica; Spanish Cuba and Puerto Rico, as well as parts of Colombia and Venezuela; or even Portuguese Brazil. Central America was largely spared. Indeed, except for the capital of former British Honduras, its capital cities lie systematically along the Pacific rather than the Atlantic Coast. While Negro populations were also enslaved in these former colonies, the plantation system that would require a large influx of slave labor was less prominent in Central America than in North and South America, as the sugar exports to Europe would have had to traverse the mountain ranges of Central America.

The sheer size of the imported African populations, vis-à-vis the local conquistadors, was bound to leave a profound imprint—not only cultural but one that would also indelibly mark the forms of social organization in the New World; a case in point is the legendary sexual rapaciousness of the relatively wealthy heirs of the conquistadors. Where the whiter the color of one's skin would entail access to better living standards, the drive to ensure a lighter skin color in offspring through interracial sex would favor the white male in the dispute for black or mulatto women. Thus the vulgar Cuban saying, "there is no sweet tamarind fruit as there is no virgin mulatto woman," will resonate among Brazilians and Puerto Ricans and elsewhere where ruling-class white males were brought into contact with black slaves in the nineteenth century.[36] That this phenomenon occurred across the Americas is supported by the African American descendants of the USA's consummate Southern gentleman, Thomas Jefferson.[37] Similarly, literary pieces such as Puerto Rican Julia de Burgos's poem, "Ay, ay, ay de la Grifa Negra," which ends by calling for an American fraternity in miscegenation, also resonate across many Latin American countries.[38]

Southerners in the USA believe more strongly than Northerners that external factors control their lives; they also, not coincidentally, die as victims of tornados more frequently than Northerners, presumably taking into account that tornados are less prevalent in the North. Traits of fatalism are everywhere more prevalent in the South than in the North of the United States—and that is something Latin Americans can relate to.[39] For instance, Brazilian Northeasterners—culturally and historically linked to U.S. Southerners—might express a similar pattern of fatalistic responses in the face of natural disasters, and probably more of them suffer from prolonged droughts than Brazilian Southerners would put up with when facing comparable weather adversities; but for lack of Brazilian research evidence this is a matter of conjecture.[40]

Also, U.S. Southerners are more prone than Northerners to believe that praying heals. The *Southern Journal of Medicine* published research arguing that, while too little attention was dedicated to understanding the relationship between spirituality and health, there seemed to be a positive association between the two.[41] In this, too, Southerners in the USA approximate Latin Americans.

Dueling throughout the Americas is no longer a legally admissible way of resolving disputes, but it was a high-profile practice until relatively recently— for instance, between Jorge Battle and Manuel Flores Mora in Uruguay in 1972. Incidentally, Uruguay only timidly repealed in 1992 its decriminalization law of 1920 that had sanctioned dueling.[42] A man in the USA's Old South would lose social standing if he were to refer the settlement of a personal dispute to the courts. Such was the advice a mother would give a son, as seems to have been the case with President Andrew Jackson's mother: "Andy . . . never . . . sue anybody for slander or assault and battery. Always settle them cases yourself."[43] But dueling was not restricted to politicians in the U.S. South; it was rampant.

Dueling has to do with *timi,* or the thymus, described by Plato as that area of the human soul beyond rationality and even desire. The custom became prevalent on the European coast of the Mediterranean, where it came to represent a peculiarly prickly concept of personal honor. The duel was imported to North America by French cavaliers and was known all along the East Coast, particularly in South Carolina and Virginia. Its practice defied public prosecution and was kept alive in the United States, while killing many men, until the 1860s.[44] The "Yankeefication" of the South, after the Civil War, helped to accelerate the demise of dueling, which was widely practiced in Argentina, Uruguay, and southern Brazil until much later—as we will see in the case of the Argentine literary character, Martin Fierro, in Chapter 14.

As already mentioned, literature and films from the United States have contributed immensely to the portrayal of North Americans in Latin America and to the publicizing of similar traits within the two societies. The hierarchical and ascriptive society of the U.S. South is quite familiar to Latin Americans. Paternalism, for example, is rampant in both cultures, having been deeply ingrained in the Old South ever since the colonial times of the Virginia Company.[45] Social oligarchic relationships in Scott Fitzgerald's *The Great Gatsby,* or social networks alluded to in Tennessee Williams's *A Streetcar Named Desire,* are immediately appealing to Latin Americans—as are other such references en passant, as seen, for example, in the line by George C. Scott as General Patton in the eponymous film justifying the selection of a particular aide from a longer list: "I pulled your name off the list because I know your family."

General Patton was no Yankee. In fact, he was born an American Southerner and raised in California in a well-to-do family. He married well, into a rich family in the pharmaceutical industry, and enjoyed playing polo. Patton could do without the army wage, but not without the excitement the military offered. Except for the clout of the pharmaceutical industry, General Patton could easily be from a patrician Argentine family. The fit would be even better if we removed him from his environment and referred only to his passion for polo and his inclination to select aides according to family name.

What is wrong with this method of selection? It worked for General Patton. There is nothing inherently wrong in choosing to work with whom we trust and feel comfortable. We might not get the most skilled collaborator, but we are likely to achieve a solid work team more quickly. This is precisely the nature of work alliances in most patriarchal societies. I will come back to this subject, because U.S. managerial textbooks put great emphasis on the meritocratic underpinning of personnel selection, while it may well be that the Latin American penchant for hiring "who you know" works just as well, as in the case of General Patton when selecting his personal aides. This preference also shows up in the tendency of southern European corporations to emphasize hiring from within rather than from the market. This custom also seems to be routine in Latin American corporations, although research evidence is still lacking.[46]

The social organization that I am referring to in both Latin America and the Old South had strong economic underpinnings, of which the slave-run plantation was only the form, in that it was the technology of the era. The essence of their points in common was a competitive export-oriented agriculture that would require a minimum of economic management to succeed. Tariffs in the United States were a matter for the North to worry about in order to protect its nascent industry. Cotton exporters in the Old South could, like sugar exporters in Brazil, generate the foreign exchange necessary to buy the European goods they needed and which import taxes would only make more expensive.

Mississippi's secession in 1861 resulted in Jefferson Davis becoming president of the Confederate States of America. In his first inaugural address he argued that the South was "an agricultural people, whose chief interest is the export of a commodity [cotton] required in every manufacturing country." He was also interested in "free trade" with manufacturing nations such as Britain and France, and in low taxes. Replacing "cotton" with "sugarcane," Jefferson Davis would sound like a typical Northeastern Brazilian leader of that era. Indeed, about one thousand Confederates migrated to Brazil upon losing the Civil War to the Yankees. They founded the village of Americana in the southern state of São Paulo and initially continued to plant cotton, but later transferred to sugarcane.

The ways in which Southern U.S. culture continues to express itself politically have given rise to such splinter factions in the major parties as the Dixiecrats. Though Democrats by birth, the Dixiecrats' conservative outlook has, over time, led them to join ranks with Republicans. In a significant demonstration of force in 1948, the Dixiecrats almost blocked the reelection of President

Truman by carrying Alabama, Mississippi, Louisiana, and South Carolina. Louisiana's Governor Huey Long also showed many of the characteristics of Latin American populist leaders. In Brazil, the political equivalent of the Dixiecrats is seen in such prominent Northeastern families as the Sarneys in the state of Maranhão or the Magalhães in the state of Bahia. In Argentina, their structural equivalent might be the Rodriguez Saa family of the province of San Luis.

All of these Latin American families are traditional national forces to be contended with. Like the Dixiecrats, their appeal is mostly regional, but their control of their regions gives them a national expression—perhaps not of sufficient weight to be elected president by direct vote but powerful enough to lurk in the background and perhaps rise to top office by chance, as happened to Vice President José Sarney, who was catapulted into the Brazilian presidency in 1985 upon the sudden death of President-elect Tancredo Neves. José Sarney's daughter, Roseana, aspired to the office of president in 2002, but her inclination was curtailed when she, or rather, her husband, was caught with his hands in the cookie jar. Antonio Carlos Magalhães was a long-leading senator whose son's presidential ambitions were cut short by his untimely death in 1998. In 2001, a particularly rough political year for Argentina, Rodriguez Saa became president of Argentina for a mere week, but president he was.

In the end, Latin Americans and North Americans, particularly Southerners, are more similar than we might care to admit. This acknowledgment, along with the USA's own cultural discrepancies between its North and South, helps explain the travails and political disconnects suffered between the U.S. government and its Latin American neighbors. (See the section in Chapter 6 on the lessons from the Little Rock crisis regarding the implications of cultural differences for management.) The bottom line is that Latin America will be better served by trusting its own cultural instincts.

SUMMING UP: OPTIONS SHAPED BY CULTURE

This chapter levels the ground on a series of topics in need of clarification before we move on to cases.

In the first place, the age-old story of the rapport between newcomers and natives was retold here as well as pointing out the segregationist stance among the Pilgrims regarding their Indian hosts, which was greater than in Latin

America among the Spanish and Portuguese, whose mixed origins helped them integrate more readily with unfamiliar peoples. The inherited attitudes of the Pilgrims shaped a containment stance toward the Negro slave and, later, reinforced the resistance to transfers of support that would, from the givers' perspective, reward laziness and licentiousness. The Thanksgiving Day celebration is a carefully crafted attempt to assuage segregationist attitudes that were expressly manifested even a century after the Civil War, as seen in the Little Rock crisis.

In the second place, the North American notion of individualism gravitates around what all people have in common, visible in the attitudes expressed in "equal under the law" and "equal opportunity." The Latin American notion of individualism, in contrast, is expressed in a person's uniqueness under the eyes of God. Furthermore, the sanctity of that uniqueness is expressed in free will, which—in order to be free—must be denuded of all traces of utilitarianism. This may explain why the Latin American's uniqueness is sometimes expressed in flights of fancy or even by aimlessly courting tragedy, rather than through applied work—for in work there is gain, and where there is pursuit of gain there is no freedom. Latin Americans therefore reject American pragmatism, as espoused by Benjamin Franklin's aphoristic conditioning of behavior for gain. The implications for organizational behavior in all of this are enormous, for the behavioral traits discussed in this chapter show that pecuniary incentives ought to be less effective among those who pursue transcendence rather than gain, and that individual merit will lose luster in a society in which recognition must be collective.

In the third place, despite all of the differences, there are similarities between Latin Americans and North Americans, specifically with U.S. Southerners. The similarities stem from the oligarchic undertones of the American South, as befitting its plantation-system origins, and are diversely expressed in both regions' literature, their fatalistic attitudes, and their tendency toward kinship-based selection for staffing and promotion.

CHAPTER 10

DIVERGENT DEVELOPMENTAL PATHS

THIS CHAPTER ILLUSTRATES the various developmental paths taken by the United States, Argentina, and Brazil, highlighting their cultural underpinnings. Looking at the cultural-impact issue from a developmental perspective, I will first illustrate why different developmental stances emerged in North America and Latin America, particularly as an expression of the cultures of the original settlers: Iberia and England.

I argue that Argentina's concentration of landholdings led to the political and economic systems favoring absentee farmers. The concept of rural mortgage credit was thus never adequately developed, thereby choking investment in agriculture and limiting the scale of the agricultural machinery market, which in turn constrained the development of a domestic machinery industry. This sequence of events would bring technological development to a halt, unless sponsored by the state—often not the wisest of referees. This dynamic was at play when Argentina invested in jet plane technology and emulated a car industry under Perón.

In the Brazilian case, I show how a land originally colonized to keep it out of foreigners' hands inherited an inward-looking culture that, coupled with land- and power-concentration proclivities, produced an ineffective judiciary and a middle class that is unsure of its worth and meek when competing abroad for acceptance of intellectual products, such as software. In particular, the focus of this chapter is to reveal the workings of cultural manifestations regarding perceptions of individuality, power, and risk.

North America and Latin America are far from monolithic. Yet, for the purposes of this chapter, I will gloss over regional differences. I will regard the USA's North and South as two coexisting, rich cultures, while assuming that the northern one is hegemonic and thus extends its management mantle over all of Latin America. While these assumptions are difficult to prove, they are even more difficult to argue with, because people are being managed in Brazil and Argentina as if they were in Ohio.

HOW DID CULTURAL LEGACY DETERMINE ECONOMIC OUTCOME?

While both Argentina and Canada became the wheat baskets of the world (together supplying 60 percent of the commodity) in the early twentieth century, only Canada sustained its development. The reasons for Argentina's faltering may stem from a single root: Argentina favored a land-ownership pattern similar to the *latifundio* (large estate) encouraged during the Spanish Reconquista. Brazil followed a similar path. The Portuguese crown distributed the colony's territory among more than a dozen hereditary captainships, to be developed by the beneficiaries. Fewer than a handful of them bothered to do anything about it.

The Canadians and the Americans used basically two land-allocation tools: a ceiling on land prices regulated by a gradual release of public lands to the market, and immigration policy. The first tool enabled farmers to buy land at low prices. The second effectively encouraged preference for northern European immigrants, who were more familiar with family farming than southern Europeans were.

Southern Italians and Spaniards, having evolved from the power-concentrating Spanish regime in Europe, provided the bulk of immigration to Argentina from 1857 to 1924: 48 percent and 32 percent, respectively. In contrast, only 20 percent of Canadian farmers and one-third of the U.S. population prior to 1790 had been born outside the English-speaking world.

The gradual annexation and distribution of farmland encouraged the development of the railway system in both Canada and the United States. The domestically financed U.S. railroad companies had great incentives to lay tracks increasingly westward as quickly as possible, thus opening the territory by making it accessible and linking existing cities. The British-financed Argentine railways, on the other hand, adopted a lower-risk strategy and focused on laying tracks on lands that were already economically feasible. The resulting Argentine railroad grid is thus much denser in the vicinity of Buenos Aires. The cautious Argentine expansion policy limited risk to the railroad companies but also limited the productivity of land farthest from the main exporting port.[1]

Large land allotments prevented poor immigrants from owning land in Argentina. By 1911, only 35 percent of Argentine farmers owned their land, as opposed to 90 percent of Canadian and U.S. farmers. In the United States, land ownership also stimulated farm credit that utilized the estate as collateral, while credit in Argentina went to absentee landlords and was concentrated in the cities, resulting, for example, in the architecturally beautiful northern neighborhood of Buenos Aires, where the wealthy landowners made their homes from the late nineteenth century.

In North America, numerous small landholdings and the availability of railway transport increased the competitiveness of the small farmer. Access to credit enabled Canadian and U.S. farmers to equip their farms and increase productivity, while also tying them to the land over generations. Immigrants to Argentina did not own the land they worked; consequently, they were less bound to it and were seasonally tempted to return home to Europe at harvest time, which followed Argentina's. Tenant farming, nonsimultaneous harvest seasons, and proximity of the population mass to the port are all contributing factors in explaining why Argentina showed the lowest retention rate of immigrants of all the New World countries; only 2 million stayed in Argentina of the 4.5 million who emigrated there from 1890 to 1914.[2]

In Canada and the USA, owning the farmland facilitated mortgage credit, and scarce labor led to mechanization that the credit enabled. Argentine tenant farmers, operating on three- to four-year lease contracts, were not keen on investing in mechanized agriculture with their own capital. Sowing was done principally by hand, and plowing was superficial.

As in the United States and Canada, Argentina also produced talented nineteenth-century inventors who sought to solve local problems. Esperanza, Argentina's first agricultural colony, began operating in 1856 in the province of Santa Fé. Twenty-two years later, colony resident Nicolás Schneider produced the first plow. At about the same time, Bartolomé Long, at Colonia Gessler, produced the first Argentine harvester. During the early twentieth century, Argentina saw the birth of an agricultural machinery industry bearing the names of Rosso at Leone, Istilart at Tres Arroyos, and Senor at San Vicente. In 1929 Alfredo Rotania produced the world's first self-propelled harvester; Miguel Druetta's redesign of the harvester three years later remains in use still today.

During World War I, Argentines Carlos Mainero and Ginaro Minervino took the first steps toward the mechanized harvesting of sunflowers. Even as late as 1950, Roque Vasalli, Santiago Giubergia, and others were still innovating and transformed the harvesting devices that were previously towed over land into self-propelled harvesters. Vasalli and Giubergia were again world pioneers in mechanizing the harvesting of maize. Argentina continued creating agricultural machinery, principally during World War II, when it could not import it. But, again, the disincentives inherent in the nation's farming style prevented the large-scale development of machinery necessary to succeed in the world market.

During World War II and the Perón years, Argentina embarked on significant moves that would prove its technological capacity, if not its business acumen. The Pulqui project developed and tested the Pulqui jet plane immediately after World War II. Argentina was the eighth country in the world to fly jet planes and the first in Latin America to do so. During those years, Argentina built its first diesel-electric locomotive, using Fiat diesel engines, and it also designed and built its first automobile. Much of this effort was centralized in Industrias Aeronáuticas y Mecánicas del Estado (IAME), a state holding company consisting of ten factories, including a metallurgical factory, that manufactured jet planes, locomotives, tractors, cars, motorcycles, parachutes, and propellers.

Yet, despite the creativity, land distribution and exploitation patterns in Argentina favored an agricultural system that was labor intensive rather than machinery intensive. As a result, Canadian farmers in Saskatchewan, for example, invested 4.3 times more per farm unit than did Argentine farmers in 1914–16. The technological choices available to Argentine farmers did not foster productivity increases on the scale of the Canadian system, and without the ability to develop an industrial base that would sustain its growth in a post-agricultural phase, Argentina eventually lost competitiveness as a producer of wheat and other commodities.[3]

IN BRAZIL, CULTURE SHAPES EXPORTING ATTITUDES

I have already mentioned that Brazil's land-allocation policies, similar to Argentina's, favored labor-intensive agricultural production to the detriment of the mechanization of agriculture. Another factor specific to Brazil, however, was the far greater extent to which Brazilian agriculture depended on slavery. Together, large landholdings and slavery contributed to depress Brazilian demand for ingenuity in solving mechanical obstacles to agricultural productivity. I turn now to the modern phenomenon of software development for a present-day illustration of the self-defeating and long-lasting repercussions of Brazil's initial concentration of power.

This section offers a cultural explanation of the factors that constrained software exports in Brazil. One obvious explanation stems from the discrimination imposed by foreign markets regarding products or services originating in countries, like Brazil, without a proven track record in exporting reliable "intellectual products."[4] That cultural barrier, daunting enough on its own, is unfortunately coupled with a homegrown cultural barrier to software exports.

Despite prowess in the domestic software field, the dearth of Brazilian software exports can be attributed to Brazilian business attitudes toward foreign markets that can be traced back to the genesis of Brazilian culture. Reasons such as Brazilian underexposure to foreign cultures are sometimes put forward to explain the deep-rooted inward-looking cultural attitudes that hamper the necessary audacity to penetrate foreign markets, in which a reticence to accept Brazilian technology products make the climb so much steeper than necessary.

THREE SUCCESSFUL CASES WITH LITTLE
EXPORT STRATEGY AND NO PUBLIC HELP

A small information technology (IT) company based in Fortaleza, capital of one of the poorest Northeastern Brazilian states, was introduced to a Swiss "angel" investor through a chance acquaintance at the beach. The investor and the techies from Fortaleza partnered, and their enterprise now offers IT-based urban bus fleet management in Northern Italian cities, with expectations to expand imminently into Eastern Europe.

The second-largest private bank in Brazil, headquartered in São Paulo, had the good fortune to hire a Portuguese international banker who had fled the Portuguese revolution of 1974, taking exile in Brazil. This gentleman's Portuguese business friends, while visiting him in Brazil a few years later, became acquainted with the Brazilian bank's impressive banking software and hardware and asked to have it installed in Portugal, once the need for exile had ended. As it happened, the Brazilian bank's holding company also owned the computer manufacturing plant and software developing firm. The bank subsequently exported hardware and software to Portugal for the next two decades and ultimately purchased a Spanish retail automation company in 2005.

A small and talented software company in São Paulo was tired of selling its man-hours to develop Internet banking for large banks and frustrated to see that inferior products were being launched for millions on NASDAQ by U.S. companies, prior to the 2000 crash. At a cocktail party, partners of the São Paulo company bumped into a worldly Syrian national with investment banking connections, who, for a share of the company, restructured it to sell Internet banking products abroad rather than ill-paid services in Brazil.

The differences in the three cases are striking: the companies have neither size, competencies, ownership structures, or "weltanschauung" in common. Yet they occupy space here because of what they do share: all are Brazilian companies with software development competencies, and all saw and followed through on an opportunity to go international. They also share another fact in common: at the inception of their international adventure lies, not a strategy, but a serendipitous encounter with a foreigner.

These three companies would probably not have contemplated international ventures had they not encountered someone willing to lead them out of Brazil. The interesting point for reflection here is why serendipity played such a significant role in the development of international strategy for these companies. Clearly, if the companies had thought out their strategies beforehand they would not have had to rely on chance in order to expand their markets abroad. It would appear that even the chance bridging role of a foreigner is crucial to the export thrust of an inward-looking country.

Three cases do not constitute a rule, and many other cases might be brought forward to counter my argument; but a pattern emerges. Perhaps Brazilian companies, often young ventures headed by technologists-turned-businessmen, need a helping hand to venture and succeed abroad. Perhaps there is a unique dynamic in the interactions between IT entrepreneurs and foreigners that breaks through formalities and provides the entrepreneurs the freedom to dare. Perhaps the known metastereotypes of foreigners regarding Brazilian technical prowess inhibit that comfort zone from arising easily.[5] And, finally, perhaps the typical "strictly business" relationship is not the type that Brazilian IT entrepreneurs feel comfortable with. After all, it is a long-known trait of Brazilian culture that emotional or affectionate relationships take precedence over the routine of work.[6] If so, no amount of trade fairs, generic or specific, would suffice to promote Brazilian exports to the degree that Brazilian software prowess deserves.

I believe these cases are significant because they illustrate a way of conducting business that is firmly grounded in a culture. Were it not for a guiding foreign hand, perhaps none of the cited companies would have ventured abroad; or, perhaps a longer hibernation would have been required. Ignoring this national trait will blunt the effectiveness of any export policy, particularly of intellectual products. I will now move on to illustrate the nature of the forces that frame Brazilian attitudes toward foreigners and business ventures abroad.

GETTING TO THE ROOT OF AN ANTIEXPORT BIAS

It appears that Brazilian software developers would rather wait to be invited to venture abroad, for then they would be relieved of the responsibility to deliver on an advertised or proposed promise. On the other hand, when accepting an invitation to provide services, that responsibility shifts to the inviting party; hence, when invited to collaborate in an international partnership, the Brazilian IT developers may feel relieved of the burden of performing up to standards of excellence that they judge themselves unworthy of, a perception that also inhibits salesmanship. Knowing that the cost of failure would be borne more heavily by their hosts, the IT developers thus feel more at ease to collaborate in the joint venture.[7]

While technically correct, this explanation is anchored in the premise that Brazilians perceive their technical standards—or marketing capabilities, or whatever else is needed to succeed abroad—to be substandard to those that prevail in a world that they might not see as their own.

It is not clear to me that fear of venturing abroad is a personality trait of Brazilians alone or of software developers specifically, but I intimately feel that for a people, as a society, who come from so far behind educationally, failing in the realm of intellectual products would be, for the selected few educated enough to venture, far worse than for a soccer team to lose a game abroad, having already won so many.

Yet let us examine where this fear may have its roots. Fear of the unfamiliar, of the unknown, is paramount in new ventures. So it was for Columbus, who himself would occasionally fall prey to the fear of encountering a hitherto unknown bestiary in the New World.[8] Is this a reasonable fear for a Brazilian software developer? Surely not; yet the images that give rise to fear and trigger the flight response may only have changed form, while still lurking—particularly those images that may lead to loss of face among peers.

What representation of the world prevails in the Brazilian imagery? One thing stands out: the world remains deeply unfamiliar to the common Brazilian, and perhaps even to the nucleus that provides the segment of software developers.

Television screens undoubtedly convey a substantial amount of information into the Brazilian home, but less so of the type of information that shows how things are made. It is in the nature of television that products are consistently glamorized, as if wrought by the hand of God. Knowledge of the routines followed to ensure quality and efficacy in the production and delivery of those goods is reserved for closer contact, to which Brazilians are substantially underexposed. For instance, only six U.S. nationals were employed in all of the Brazilian software industry in 2000.[9] Furthermore, at least some of these may have been employed for their proficiency in English rather than their software background. Also, the number of minutes of international calls placed from Brazil in 2000, standardized by GDP, ranks as low as India's. China's are 60 percent higher.[10] This portrayal of Brazilian isolation is reproduced in another index of personal contact with the foreign world: international travel. Here, per unit of GDP, Brazilians again fare poorly, poorer even than the Chinese. India sees twice as many international travelers as Brazil does, and Israel turns out to be the country that is most exposed to international travel and travelers, at a rate six times higher than Brazilians.[11]

Brazilians, once again, are singularly closed up on themselves: the total number of international air passengers is only 5.6 percent of the country's population. Moreover, foreign travelers in Brazil are too few to make a meaningful impact in a country so vast. Furthermore, the share of foreigners residing in Brazil has declined for the better part of the twentieth century, depriving

Brazilians of a low-cost opportunity for exposure to foreign ways. For instance, while in the 1940s a student in a Brazilian school could reasonably expect to have a foreign-born classmate, nowadays a Brazilian would need to meet two hundred residents before encountering a foreigner (see Figure 10.1, right-hand scale).

Essentially a rural nation until well into the second half of the twentieth century, almost 80 percent of Brazil's population was living in cities by the year 2000 (see Figure 10.1, left-hand scale). The newly urbanized transferred their rural customs to the cities, diluting the value of cosmopolitanism.[12] It is possible that the Brazilian population at large was, at the turn of the twentieth century, a more closed society than it had been one hundred years earlier.

If there are fewer non-Brazilians living in Brazil than a century ago, if those that live in cities cherish rural values, if Brazilians do not travel or speak over the phone to foreigners, and if Brazilians are unschooled in foreign languages, it is quite likely that the foreign world largely remains a closed book to the bulk of the nation's population. Worse, it is also quite likely that commercial ventures abroad give rise to a deeper fear than is warranted.

However, there would be no fear if there were no desire to succeed abroad, not the type of success that Brazil is already known for—soccer, music, commodities, and Carnival—but the highly eroticized desire to succeed with technology products. What is cherished is the true success that would arise from international recognition, for example, for a Brazilian software product that

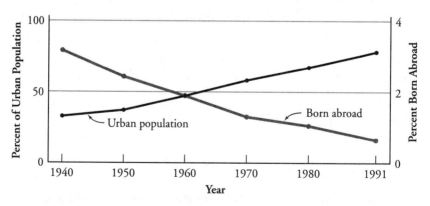

FIGURE 10.1. Urban and foreign-born shares (%) of Brazil's total population
SOURCE: IBGE census data, 2001.

not only meets the standards of its neighbors but also reaches the pinnacle of success: worldwide acceptance.

This tension, brought about by the desire to succeed and the fear of not being good enough, may well be at the root of Brazilians' reluctance to venture abroad commercially except by invitation. This requires further interpretation, for, while unfamiliarity may breed fear, fear can nowadays be easily dispelled with more information. The fear of not being good enough has deeper roots, such as in the inferiority complex alluded to in the Chapter 8 section, "The Search for Identity."

The ineffectiveness of the Brazilian judiciary may also play an important part in the nation's lack of exports.[13] The larger banks and other drivers of the economy have the most to lose from the malfeasance of an independent software provider; thus they may prefer not to outsource software development. By developing software in-house, the banking industry inhibits the development of small technology companies and deprives technologists of the independence necessary to seek new markets and develop new products, thus neglecting the software export opportunity. That a poor judiciary promotes vertical integration is already being verified in the Russian Federation.[14] The cost of vertical integration may exceed that of the risks avoided by holding software development companies captive. The latter miss out on the opportunity to market their services to competing clients, thereby arresting the dissemination of technology across the local market and artificially rendering demand too small to merit further technology development.[15]

Whether the lack of exports of technology products is due to a national lack of self-esteem, the ineffectiveness of the judiciary, the "country of origin effect,"[16] or the vertical integration of enterprises cannot be fully ascertained here; it is conceivably the result of the interaction of all four factors.

I chose to illustrate this phenomenon with the three preceding cases, small to medium-sized entities from opposite corners of Brazil, a country whose people are prone to establishing personal, affectionate bonds yet have limited opportunities to interact with foreigners and to personally shape an adequate representation of the world. It is in this country that the three very competent software developing companies highlighted in the examples had to be personally invited to export their services by means of chance encounters with foreigners who offered the promise of success abroad—very much in the same way it took a Genoese to lead the Spanish, and the English, to the New World. If this diagnosis is right, exhibiting Brazilian software at trade fairs will do little good in terms of promoting sales. Developing software for the sectors that are already exporting or for existing buying patterns may prove more effective.

The implications of this analysis would also affect the export potential of other intellectual products such as biotechnology, engineering, and architectural design. All of these represent intellectual pursuits in a nation unsure of its own international worth and often discriminated against for its wavering confidence; these products cannot be as easily appreciated abroad as, for example, coffee beans in 132-pound bags or an Embraer aircraft in flight.

Once we have recognized the powerful cultural reasons behind the lack of exports of solutions—and of business administration—we can better understand why the Brazilian technology firms highlighted here did not develop export strategies prior to their unexpected entries into the export market. They did not do so because their self-perceptions as entrepreneurs and as Brazilians prevented them from taking the next step into the world arena. Strategizing would have been a waste of time. These software entrepreneurs were behaving rationally by allocating their scarce resources domestically and neglecting export strategy. Yet they were reacting to an incorrect cultural assumption: that they were incapable of exporting because they were not good enough. Breaking this irrational cultural casing is crucial to the success of other Brazilian technology exports besides software, such as engineering design and biotechnology.

SUMMING UP: DOOMED SINCE THE RECONQUISTA?

It was not a lack of Argentine creative capacity that thwarted the nation's transition to a full-fledged industrial society. The technological capacity was there and was put to work, including during the Perón years. Moreover, nothing except culture could have driven Argentina to a latifundio-based agriculture system rather than one based on smaller plots distributed to a greater number of farmers. The concentration of power so typical of Spain during the Reconquista, and of Southern Italy under Spanish rule, was reproduced in the Spanish New World, lock, stock, and barrel. The intolerance and power orientation of early Argentina reflected a proclivity to a style of political organization stemming from monarchic absolutism and religious control. The religious persecution known to Spain and Portugal as the Inquisition was later manifested in direct-action movements against minorities in Argentina, such as the indigenous population and gauchos during much of the nineteenth century, and against unions during several episodes in the twentieth century.

Nonetheless, by World War II, Argentina had managed to produce a technically educated elite capable of mobilizing the country's resources into a lasting industrialization. Argentina is the only Latin American country to have produced three Nobel laureates in science, and basic research could well have blossomed into independent technology. However, the backlash from Argentina's historically deprived segment of the population, as represented by the Peróns, presented Argentina with its first redistribution attempt and the allure of nation building, albeit an intolerant nation. By the time Juan Domingo Perón was ousted in 1955, Argentina was as fractured as it had been a century earlier under the presidency of Domingo Faustino Sarmiento, and the nation's market for industrialized goods remained restricted to internal consumption.

The developmental path of the United States took a widely different course. The USA was colonized by family farmers who worked small plots producing goods for competitive markets and who demanded railroad transportation. The plots could be turned into collateral for bank loans, which fueled demand for labor-saving innovation and agricultural machinery and sifted out the most efficient producers, leading to later concentrations of land that in turn spurred demand for heavier machinery. The resulting products, backed by strong financing, would be accepted abroad, even where the power of the machines offered was in excess of what was needed, stifling the demand for local machinery in such places as Argentina or Brazil.

Brazil's picture is slightly different but closer to that of Argentina than to the U.S. model. Brazil was originally settled by Portuguese with an eye to keeping foreigners out. Sugar plantations signified a way to pay for colonization, which was never as automatic as Argentina's because Brazil's great escarpment facing the Atlantic limited penetration and deprived the coast of plentiful natural harbors. Sugar plantations were established closest to Europe in locations where hydropower solutions were poor, resulting in a labor-intensive sugarcane industry. African slaves and the indigenous population provided the cheapest labor solution, and slavery predominated in the northern half of Brazil, where the sugar plantations were concentrated. Cheap labor discouraged the labor-saving mechanization that helped trigger North American research and investment in agriculture.

A slave society was unlikely to attract European immigrants. Nine-tenths of the Europeans that sought South America as their new home chose the southernmost countries of Argentina and Uruguay, and Chile to some extent, and those that chose Brazil headed mostly to its lower half where slavery was less prominent, predominantly in or south of São Paulo. By the time of the great immigration waves of the nineteenth century, São Paulo had become Brazil's magnet, largely on account of the riches brought by coffee exports. Yet coffee gave rise to even less industrial demand than sugar, its technical requirements being largely limited to picking and bagging the beans. Industrial demand was secondary and was mostly concentrated on railways and steel production. Demand for industrialization was triggered only by the demand to substitute imports in times of scarcity, such as during the Depression years.

This is how Brazil missed out on the need to develop industrial solutions of its own. With no demand for larger solutions, universities focused on engineering for infrastructure: civil engineering was king. This was challenging enough, but it met only local demand that required extensive familiarity with local problems. In general, civil engineers tend to look down toward the ground, an orientation that did not help to motivate Brazilian inventiveness to address problems of a larger scope.

When the need for software development peaked in the United States, Brazilian software engineers were inexorably mired in the pathos of a country that was too inward looking to competitively exploit the expansion of its intellectual products to foreign markets. Brazilians never contemplated the possibility, nor had foreigners become used to seeing Brazilians as purveyors of solutions. The "country of origin effect," a strong discriminating factor, would be too pervasively established abroad to be overcome by a generation of engineers who were both unsure of their own worth and heirs to a culture that had always viewed the rest of the world as a threat, since the times of the first Portuguese settlers. This is most likely why Brazil's software developers have needed an intervening foreign hand to initiate the internationalization of their companies.

PART FOUR

CROSS-CULTURAL MANAGEMENT: THE TOOLBOX

C ROSS-CULTURAL MANAGEMENT is an omnibus discipline resulting from the postwar expansion of multinationals and their concern for effective management of their businesses across the world. It is an area of intellectual pursuit that grew in response to a real-world demand: people across the globe seem to be different in predictable ways; thus, understanding what makes them tick should promote managerial goals.

The cross-cultural management field grew in only half a century of academic effort scattered over ten or so fields of study within the humanities, social sciences, and management. It should come as no surprise that some of the first statistical efforts were developed within multinationals, notably by Geert Hofstede at IBM.[1] Business consultant Fons Trompenaars is another prominent name in the field.[2] Nor should it surprise us that both Hofstede and Trompenaars are Dutch, for, historically, the Dutch have excelled in the realm of cross-cultural management. Of foremost importance, cross-cultural management requires respectful awareness of one's host culture, a quality that has been cultivated by the Dutch since their navigational apex in the seventeenth century. Sensitivity is another competitive advantage of Dutch society in nurturing the growth of knowledge around cross-cultural management.

The Dutch were traders, not empire builders, and they were typically not infused with the intolerant brand of proselytist Catholicism that characterized the Portuguese and Spanish. The Dutch were not in the business of changing other people's minds, but they were adept at negotiating prices and terms. They excelled at building trust and long-term understanding. Where they got into the business of taking command, they were not as effective or as sensitive, such as in Indonesia or Surinam, or in pockets of Brazil.

Thus not only is the field of cross-cultural management interesting, but the "making of" the field is in itself an area of intellectual pursuit that no one has yet stepped into.

CHAPTER 11

WHO'S WHO ON THE PLAYING FIELD

Comparisons are odorous.

Shakespeare, in Much Ado About Nothing

WHATEVER THE IMPULSE for seeking fruitful examples of cross-cultural management, the fact remains that the field is relatively new and still underdeveloped in its theory and methodology. This gap is typical of the nascent stages of an emerging field and of the specialization of human knowledge. Yet if we take a step back and allow ourselves to benefit from the relevant work done in this field by cultural anthropologists, we can find a trail of light.

In the 1940s and 1950s, Ruth Benedict, Margaret Mead, and Geoffrey Gorer focused on "national character" and on the array of "values, beliefs, and practices" that compose a national culture.[1] The evidencing of underlying values helped to understand the differences between nations but did nothing to explain how those differences came about, how those societies evolved, or why they came into conflict, whether between or within societies.

The issue of conflict begets other considerations as well. Perhaps one of the most important issues at stake is the moral evaluation of values. When eliciting, grouping, and comparing people's values, one holds certain ethical theories in the background that, as much as moral theories, are merely the expressions of preferences.[2] Preferences constitute only one source among many determinants of moral choice and the ensuing behavior expressed in that choice, whether approaching international expansion by means of warfare or by means of business negotiations.[3]

Clyde Kluckhohn thus sought to involve the moral dimension of values by seeking to elicit not only what individuals preferred but also what they considered most important.[4] People's preferences are less an indication of reality than what they believe ought to be. The trouble is, the list of values that people consider important quickly becomes intractable for practical purposes.

Among the overlong lists of questionable value that resulted, we can safely count Rokeach's conceptual typology of thirty-six values, eighteen of which are instrumental values. Among these we have values such as ambition, broadmindedness, and honesty. Beyond these, Rokeach offered another eighteen purpose-oriented values, such as world peace and inner harmony.[5] At this point, the values became repetitive and their practical application limited. The result was chaotic. Industrial psychologists were disappointed by the limited practical relevance of long lists of interests-values-preferences for personnel selection.[6]

Academic work in the field of management rises from the demand of its practice just an arm's length away, making it sensitive to the client's needs. But little of the work on values-interests-preferences was carried out by management-oriented academics. If it had been, cultural taxonomists would have shown greater sensitivity to how much information the brain can reasonably be hoped to make sense of. As it happens, the brain cannot reliably process more than about seven variables at once.[7] To be at all useful, classification of cultures must meet that constraint.

By the 1970s, industrial psychologists had turned their attention again to values, this time narrowing their focus to work values. Dov Elizur and Abraham Sagie produced an extensive list that was collapsible into a three-pronged classification of values: material, affective, and cognitive.[8] In the late 1990s, Shalom Schwartz came up with a more manageable list of seven values categories: harmony, egalitarianism, intellectual autonomy, affective autonomy, mastery, hierarchy, and conservatism, which he later termed embeddedness.[9] By the time we reach Schwartz's product, we have already been through a variety of statistically based approaches that, with less theoretical background, aimed at identifying clusters of cultural dimensions. The most famous of these is Geert Hofstede's work, whose publications were among the most quoted in Europe.[10]

We will deal with Hofstede's contribution in greater detail in the next section. For now, suffice it to say that his work, as well as that of Shalom Schwartz, fits into the functionalist line of thought, in which the presumption is that social norms and values provide the glue to societies (and organizations), and therefore it is legitimate to adopt a universalist stance that allows all societies to be classified according to the same set of traits.[11]

However, cultural variations within countries may be as large if not larger than those that occur across countries. Certain groups have more in common with groups from other nations than with the local mind-set. This is the focus of the work of Mattei Dogan on European democracies.[12] Her work repositions differences into emphases rather than kinds. The differences between British and German urban cultures register only a few percentage points, for example, and a French social democrat may have more in common with a German social democrat than with a French conservative. Also of interest, regarding the geographical dispersion of political culture within a given country, is the work of Robert Putnam, particularly in interpreting differences in associativeness, political participation, and government efficacy between Northern and Southern Italy, briefly recounted in the Summing Up section of Chapter 5.[13]

These classic works in political culture paved the way to the understanding that a variety of cultures coexists in every country and that differences stem from the degree to which the culture of one group predominates over others. This stance allows us to focus on the collective attitudes that shape national character, which opens the door to cross-cultural comparisons—the managerial implications of which we will explore at a later stage.

FROM MACRO TO MICRO AND BACK

Around the 1950s, the field of political science, influenced by the behavioral revolution, offered the first breaths of a new approach to organizational settings. Academics shifted their focus from the formal dimensions of institutions to behavior within institutions. Political culture—and the collective behavior of individuals within an organizational setting—would be the focus, offering as a bonus, so to speak, the chance to bridge the micro-macro gap in political theory. As of the 1970s, this approach fell into disfavor, "routinely dismissed as static, conservative, tautological, irrelevant, and worse," and also because "ignoring power relations could not explain change."[14]

The cross-cultural management field, being relatively devoid of theoretical orientation, failed to look beyond the boundaries of its own immediate business interests. This shortsightedness may explain why the work of cultural anthropologist Mary Douglas has only recently begun to be referenced in cross-cultural management.[15]

Douglas came up with an interesting proposition, consolidated in her 1978 work, *Cultural Bias*, that people in most societies resort to four states of mind in order to comprehend the natural, the social, and the supernatural worlds.[16] These states could be called individualism, hierarchy, fatalism, and egalitarianism, representing areas delimited by the strength of rules or boundaries and the sense of belonging. This proposition can be represented by a two-dimensional space in which coordinates tend toward higher-rule density and the abscissa a direction that represents greater collectivism or sense of belonging. Within this plane, the individual is faced with two basic cosmological questions: Who am I? How must I behave?

The first question addresses one's identity/belonging to a group: Do I belong to a group through which I derive my identity, or am I alone? The second addresses the extent to which a person is free to negotiate: Must I abide by many rules of behavior, or am I free to make my own?

Regarding the identity question, belonging to a group requires assuming a continuum between extremes: from individualism, or low group, to collectivism, or high group. Those living on the low-group end of the spectrum face a world of competition, opportunities, and individual rewards. Those in the high-group world, however, do not experience simply the opposite. People in this group are overly concerned with boundaries, exclusion, norms, safety, fairness, and sharing.

The rules/power dimension can also be seen as a continuum, where at the lower end we have people who feel that nature is an opportunity rather than a constraint, to whom risk is just one factor in the process of development, and who believe that competition will ensure efficiency and fairness. At the higher end we will find people who feel overburdened by rules to the point of apathy, who see risk as a constraining threat, and who live in fear of nature.

This is how Douglas and her followers came to offer an answer to age-old questions that had bedeviled social scientists with a political or organizational bent. Her grid dimensions address the issue of power/ranking, and her individuality vectors address the issue of status/group.

Extending the grid analysis, we can organize both vectors on a Cartesian plane, in which the rules/power dimension is the y-axis and the groups dimension is the x-axis. Focusing first on the southwest quadrant allows us to observe the combination of both dimensions (see Figure 11.1), typifying a cultural bias. The low-group/low-grid combination will define individualism, in which people are unconstrained either by rules or by the group. This is the world of individuals capable of establishing or breaking free of their own networks.

Moving clockwise and maintaining a similar level of low-group values, we gradually reach the highly regulated environment of fatalism, in which roles are ascribed by clear-cut definitions (such as age or sex) or by position or lineage.[17] Here, individuals perceive the world as a threat to be avoided, at best, by sticking to the status quo.

Still maintaining the high-rule level but releasing the group variable, we move clockwise again to the northeast quadrant of hierarchy, in which the prevalence of rules remains high but people are increasingly tightly knit into

	Low Group	High Group
High Grid	**B—Fatalism** Destiny determines Nature is indomitable Risk averse	**C—Hierarchy** Group organizes Bureaucracy determines Autonomy is discouraged
Low Grid	Realm of competition Individual achievement is cherished Market oriented, innovative, risk takers **A—Individualism**	Bound to shared code Outsiders are disliked Tradition oriented **D—Egalitarianism**

FIGURE 11.1. Mary Douglas's group/grid plane

SOURCE: Based on D. Douglas Caulkins, "Is Mary Douglas's Grid/Group Analysis Useful for Cross-Cultural Research?" *Cross-Cultural Research* 33, no. 1 (Feb. 1999): 111.

groups.[18] This is the area in which the Weberian bureaucracy—or patriarchal environment—predominates. Decision making is top down, the environment is perceived as aggressive, yet its aggressiveness may be contained collectively. Safety is found in belonging to a group. Life takes place within highly ordered groups that provide meaning.

The final (southeast) quadrant, egalitarianism, leads us to a world of tight-knit groups with few rules or hierarchy. People are still very concerned with themes of inclusion and exclusion, but they reject the strong hierarchy of the Weberian/patriarchal realm and are unconcerned with nature, which is seen as ephemeral and whimsical. Deviant behavior or mistakes lead to scapegoating in this realm.

MEASURING THE UNMEASURABLE

Even if our intent were not to develop a predictive capacity on a complex subject matter, we should at least attempt to assess the existing cultural gaps. Knowing which of the dimensions presents the largest differences will help determine the extent of managerial input. I will first review the pioneering efforts of Hofstede to measure differences, given a limited set of tools, followed by those of Trompenaars and Schwartz. While they also focused on categorizing values, the bulk of their efforts went into surveying values and defining statistical clusters. Schwartz innovated further by seeking to interview niches of cultural repositories, such as educational services, rather than confining the analysis to management circles. After presenting these three contributions, I will offer a critique.

GEERT HOFSTEDE: THE MAKING OF THE LARGEST SURVEY

Working at IBM in the late 1960s, Hofstede created the largest-ever cross-cultural management survey. It comprised over 117,000 paper-and-pencil questionnaires and one hundred standardized questions, each initially applied to subsidiaries in forty countries. Ten more countries were added later along with three more regions: eastern and western Africa, as well as the Arab-speaking countries. Hofstede limited the analysis to subsidiaries that supplied at least fifty questionnaires. Altogether, fifty-three countries/regions were initially processed. A second task was completed in 1972, adding more country cases until the database included seventy-two international IBM subsidiaries comprising thirty-two occupations. Altogether, the questionnaires required the handling of information in twenty languages.

Beyond the daunting issues of the sample's size and format (writing tools, languages, delivery, and retrieval, among others), what was the theory that framed the questions? Hofstede addressed this question as follows: "Inspired by Kluckhohn[19] and Rokeach[20] I defined a value as 'a broad tendency to prefer certain states of affairs over others.' The term *values* is generally reserved for mental programs that are relatively unspecific; attitudes and beliefs refer to more specific mental programs."[21]

Furthermore, where did the focus of the questionnaire come from? What dimensions was Hofstede hoping to unearth? He responds: "The common issues Inkeles and Levinson[22] identified in the anthropological, sociological, and psychological literature at that time were: 1. Relation to authority; 2. Conception of self, in particular: (a) the relationship between the individual and the society; (b) the individual's concept of masculinity and femininity; 3. Ways of dealing with conflict, including the control of aggression and the expression versus inhibition of feelings."[23]

The surveys aimed at eliciting personal values regarding work environments. Hofstede believed that people's socialization in family, in school, and later in organizations helps to develop mental programs through which people respond to challenges. Since those programs reflect culture—which is controlled by occupation, education, age, and other factors—the data would reveal country cultures as corroborated by answers given by the IBM subsidiaries. Factor analysis initially revealed only three cultural dimensions, but that changed to four after data were controlled by national income, wherein high power distance and collectivism emerged as distinct dimensions. In all, the statistical treatment of the data explained 49 percent of the variance.[24] Functional equivalence was Hofstede's key for making comparisons: "One should compare like with like."[25]

One may rightly wonder whether country data is an adequate source for cultural references. After all, many countries, large and small, are not culturally homogeneous, and some cultures spill over national boundaries. Hofstede was cautious about this as well. Country-based data is only a convenient proxy. Survey data, frequently obtained from a restricted segment of the population, such as the employees of a corporation, was required to be validated by information from other sources, like census data, which is usually only available at the country level.[26]

Hofstede's concern about the possible bias of his own ethnocentrism led him to work further on values that would better reflect Asian culture. This effort revealed a fifth dimension that he initially called "Confucian dynamism," which captures the extent to which people have a future-oriented perspective rather than one focused on the present. This dimension later evolved into long-term orientation (LTO), to account for the fact that it applies to many countries that had no contact with Confucianism, such as Brazil.

Could Hofstede have added more cultural dimensions? Yes, but would the results have been more manageable? Probably not. Hofstede was operating from within a company that paid for results. Whatever he came up with needed to be sound and have relevant practical applications, and five categories seemed about right.[27]

Hofstede's Five Dimensions of Culture

Because of Hofstede's standing in cross-cultural management, and because some of his cultural dimensions appear in the works of subsequent authors, I will only briefly describe each of his five dimensions. See Table 11.1 for a summary of each dimension and a selection of countries that, according to Hofstede's research, best represent the enactment of each dimension.

Power Distance   This dimension deals with the extent to which a society is vertically stratified and the manner in which it attributes different levels of importance and status to members of the different strata. Feudal Europe or the caste system of India provide extreme examples of this stratification. In Western societies, stratification is less extreme but is frequently obvious, as in the case of Brazil, where skin color can be directly associated with an economic strata. Yet this dimension also includes the level of acceptance at which stratification occurs or is considered functional to the working of society. The power distance dimension thus deals with the extent to which the less powerful members of society accept that power is unequally distributed.

Individualism and Collectivism   In individualistic cultures, the social (and business) organization promotes an orientation toward individual benefit as a precondition of the functioning of the system of reward for effort. Thus, individualistic societies may display few ties beyond those of the nuclear family, whereas in collectivist societies people belong to strong, cohesive inner groups that are expected to ensure the benefit of all. Loyalty to one's inner

TABLE 11.1 Values reflecting Hofstede's cultural dimensions

High power distance (Arab world, China, Brazil, Ecuador, Indonesia, Malaysia, Mexico, Venezuela)	**Low power distance** (Australia, Canada, Germany, Netherlands, Scandinavia, USA)
• Hierarchy is necessary • Inequality is acceptable • Bosses remain aloof • Everyone has a place • People depend on a leader • Privileges are rights of the powerful • Power displays confirm rank • Change is resented	• Hierarchy is merely functional • Inequality begets correction • Rank is achieved • Bosses are accessible • Leaders serve the rank and file • Privileges are earned • Power displays are discouraged • Change is functional
High individualism (Australia, Austria, France, Germany, Italy, Scandinavia, USA, UK)	**High collectivism** (Chile, China, Colombia, Brazil, Indonesia, Mexico, Portugal)
• Self-orientation renders efficiency • People are responsible for themselves • Decisiveness is rewarded • Individual achievement is the ideal • Privacy is a right • Rewards are individualized	• Collective orientation provides harmony • The group takes care of all • Group decision making is best • Group's success comes first • Membership provides identity • Privacy comes after group needs • Group protects in exchange for loyalty • Social rewards for performance and excellence
High uncertainty avoidance (Argentina, Belgium, Chile, Japan, Portugal, Uruguay)	**Low uncertainty avoidance** (Australia, Canada, Scandinavia, UK, USA)
• Conflict is threatening • Low tolerance for deviations from the norm • Heavy reliance on technical advice • Consensus seeking is paramount	• Conflict breeds opportunities • Innovation thrives on deviations • Information is everywhere • Consensus deenergizes
High masculinity (Austria, China, Colombia, Germany, Ireland, Italy, Japan, UK, USA)	**Low masculinity** (Chile, Costa Rica, Netherlands, Scandinavia, Portugal, Uruguay)
• Clear definitions of gender roles • Men are assertive, decisive, and dominant • Work is a priority • Growth, success, and money are paramount	• Gender roles are loose • Quality of life takes precedence • Failure begets assistance
High long-term orientation (China, Brazil, India, Japan, Taiwan)	**Low long-term orientation** (Australia, Canada, Germany, Scandinavia)
• Everything depends on everything, as do deadlines • Long-term networking is seen as a "capital reserve" • Mutual obligations are assets to both parties • Networking combines obligations and sentiment	• Timeliness implies respect • Deadlines are to be honored • Favors received are receivables to others • Reciprocity refers to the short-term exchange of favors

NOTE: Selected countries demonstrate indices with greater than 20 percent distance from the average for each dimension.

SOURCE: Based on Hofstede's data, http://www.geert-hofstede.com (accessed Mar. 7, 2006).

group exists in both types of cultures, but self-sacrifice for group benefit will go further in collective societies.

We can quickly find some familiarity in Mary Douglas's grid theory and the work of Harry Triandis, who rightly saw greater depth in Hofstede's working concepts of individualism and collectivism.[28] To Triandis, people are neither purely collectivist nor purely individualist. They may behave one way or another depending on their attitudes toward the group and toward the webs of authority. Triandis thus came up with the notion of horizontal and vertical classifications of collectivism and individualism, breaking these latter two cultural traits into four. People can behave with deference to the group to the point of abiding by its rules, even when the rules lead them to discomfort; those would be the vertical collectivists. On the other hand, when people defer to the group but are more prone to contest its authority, they are horizontal collectivists. Similarly, we have the people who want to do their own thing to the point of not even being interested in competing or acquiring status; those would be the horizontal individualists. If, however, people who are individualists also wish to achieve distinction and higher echelons in the hierarchy, they would be deemed vertical individualists. As we can see, this simplified version of Triandis' work is not much of a departure from Mary Douglas's grid/group theoretical framework. Nonetheless, Triandis' work has percolated into other important research, such as the work on leadership by the GLOBE project, which I will review in my discussion on leadership in Chapter 12.

Uncertainty Avoidance   This dimension refers to the extent to which the culture accommodates risk and ambiguity. Members of cultures with high uncertainty avoidance feel threatened by uncertain, ambiguous, or otherwise unknown situations. This is expressed in a need for formality, predictability, and clear rules. In societies with less need to avoid uncertainty there tends to be less job-related stress, greater willingness to try out innovation, and fewer penalties for failing when departing from standard procedures.

Masculinity and Femininity   This dimension addresses the extent to which a society allocates occupations along gender lines. In "masculine" societies, men are seen to be assertive, tough, and concerned with material success, whereas women tend to advocate qualities such as modesty, tenderness, and issues related to the quality of life. At the extreme, this means that "tougher" jobs like jet pilots will be reserved for men, while women will be teachers and caretakers. The penetration of more men in command jobs will permeate the society with masculine values. This is why masculine cultures prefer achievement and competition over reserve, modesty, or concern for the social and environmental costs of that success.

Long-Term Orientation This dimension deals with the extent to which society invests in long-term projects and relationships, delaying immediate reciprocity in view of future compensation. Pride in virtue and the quality of the network are valued components in the network-building effort. In this sense, the effort put into building reciprocity networks is seen as an inclination to build assets for the group. Networking, or *guanxi* in Chinese, is less a component of the collectivist dimension than it is of the long-term orientation dimension, because networks become a functional asset of the organization with a view to future reciprocity.

Collectivism or Long-Term Orientation?

Yeh and Lawrence have argued that, statistically, long-term orientation in fact indicates the presence of collectivism and therefore adds little to the explanatory power of the model.[29]

The literature on Chinese business practices emphasizes the significant effort that the Chinese put into *guanxi* and networking, the effectiveness of which often astonishes foreigners while also creating a significant barrier to entry. The pervasiveness of *guanxi* actually facilitates the flow of business for foreigners by overriding the lack of objectivity of Chinese procedures and institutions.[30] This provokes the unsettling question: Could long-term orientation be merely another version of power distance or even collectivism?

Nonetheless, international research on joint ventures in China—the country with the highest rating of long-term orientation—suggests that the most significant reason for cultural clashes lies in differing time horizons and perspectives regarding status among partners, rather than in differing attitudes toward individualism.[31] Operating with an awareness of differences in the time horizon is crucial to the success of a joint venture with a Chinese partner. This would suggest that differences in long-term orientation may cause problems in international joint ventures, while the same is not necessarily true for perceived differences in power distance, individualism, and masculinity/femininity.[32]

FONS TROMPENAARS

Trompenaars's work is less methodologically neat than Hofstede's, at least in the academic sense that would lay the method open to scrutiny and eventual replication. This is largely because his work is commercial and disclosure of its methods is mostly reserved for clients. But Fons Trompenaars is no amateur. He studied economics at the Free University of Amsterdam and subsequently earned his PhD at the University of Pennsylvania's Wharton School. Trompenaars also worked for Royal Dutch Shell in many countries and has consulted worldwide for numerous companies. Charles Hampden-Turner, his long-time collaborator, has no less of a distinguished academic and consulting career. The practical managerial relevance of their work has added to their well-deserved reputations, resulting in the sale of half of their consulting practice to the KPMG network. Rather than setting out to impress academics, Trompenaars and Hampden-Turner focused on international managers and their instrumentation.[33]

Trompenaars's work draws significantly on Kluckhohn and Strodtbeck's cultural orientation model.[34] The efficacy of the latter as a model for interpreting cross-cultural management is compromised by the loose boundaries of its orientations, possibly its main shortcoming.

Trompenaars's Seven Dimensions

Trompenaars argues that each culture seeks to solve three basic dilemmas: relationships with others, the handling of time, and relationship with the environment. In response to those dilemmas, Trompenaars assumes that, based on its values, every society has developed cultural dimensions that form along seven orientations (see Table 11.2).

Universalism Versus Particularism   Universalist cultures create rules to guide the behavior of their people, and these are not subject to exception—particularly not to exceptions grounded in relationships such as family ties or patronage. For example, giving false testimony in court to bail out a friend who struck a pedestrian at a crosswalk while driving intoxicated would be inadmissible in a universalistic society. Such societies are more prone to legitimate their citizens' duties to respect the rule of law even beyond national borders. Such was the presumed justification of the U.S. intervention in Panama in order to remove

TABLE 11.2 Values reflecting Trompenaars's cultural dimensions

Orientation	Investigation
Universalism versus particularism	Do rules take precedence over relationships?
Individualism versus communitarianism	Do we function in a group or as individuals?
Affective versus neutral cultures	Do we expect emotional displays?
Specific versus diffuse cultures	How far do we get involved?
Achievement versus ascription	Is status the result of achievement?
Time perception	Planning for the future, time management, and organization of tasks: Are these sequential or synchronic?
Relation to nature	Where lies the locus of our control and of our relationship with nature?

SOURCE: Vincent Merk, *Communication Across Cultures: From Cultural Awareness to Reconciliation of the Dilemmas,* Eindhoven University of Technology, Faculty of Technology Management, July 2003, p. 3.

a corrupt General Noriega in 1988, or the U.S. invasion of Somalia only four years later in Operation Restore Hope, ostensibly to live up to its name.

Particularist cultures prize relationships over rules, which they view as general guidelines subject to interpretation aimed at respecting the sprit rather than the letter of the law. Thus, using the earlier example, giving false testimony in court to help a good friend who made the mistake of driving under the influence of alcohol and had the misfortune of running over a pedestrian is less reprehensible than it would be in a universalist society.

Examples of universalist societies are the United States, Germany, and the United Kingdom, while Venezuela, Brazil, and China are examples of particularist societies.

Individualism Versus Communitarianism Trompenaars's categories of individualist and collectivist societies are similar to those of Hofstede.

Affective Versus Neutral Cultures In affective cultures, people expect a display of emotions and feel puzzled when feelings are not expressed; they may tend to overlook subtle signs of emotions offered by people from less expressive societies. People in neutral societies, in contrast, are socialized into believing that overt displays of emotions are wrong; they may be overwhelmed by such displays by people from more affective cultures.

Examples of neutral societies are Sweden, Japan, and the United Kingdom, while Italy, Brazil, the Netherlands, and Mexico illustrate affective societies.

Specific Versus Diffuse Cultures   Members of specific cultures tend to comprehend reality in components, one segment at a time. Reality is then reconstructed in the same way, and explanations, which tend to be inductive, also respond to this pattern as well, turning interactions into purposeful and economical events that may be disconnected from other interactions. People from specific cultures concentrate on hard facts, contracts, and evidence. Similarly, private life is separated from one's public life, and few considerations that are valid for one may be used to interpret the other. While members of specific cultures may exhibit significant public lives that are open to interaction, their private lives are more judiciously guarded.

People from diffusely oriented cultures comprehend reality more holistically; all dimensions tend to be interrelated, and the structure of relationships may carry more weight than the constituting elements of reality. Explanations tend to be deductive and, because relationships are cherished, style is as important as substance and tends to involve demeanor, ambiance, and bonding geared toward acceptance. The public sphere is relatively small vis-à-vis the private sphere, but its size is unimportant, as trust and bonding form the basis of relationships; without these, foreigners will not be accepted to either realm. On the other hand, once accepted, no doors will remain closed.

France and Germany provide examples of specific cultures. Latins in general, not only Latin Americans, tend to conform to the diffuse orientation.

Achievement Versus Ascription   In an achievement-oriented culture, status is conferred upon recognition of achievement, and individuals must continually prove their worth as long as they are able. Individuals in ascription-oriented societies, in contrast, may be born into status by virtue of the legal system, beauty, or wealth. Take the British House of Lords: 41 percent of its members are former members of Parliament, members of the European Parliament, or councilors. While this means that many stood for election at least once, many never did, and those that did stand for election will never need to again. Furthermore, the House of Lords is dominated by males; less than 10 percent of its members are women.

The USA is an example of an achievement-oriented culture, and much of Europe is as well, except where royal traditions might lurk behind the scene.

Few achievement-oriented societies are found in Latin America; perhaps
Argentina and Uruguay—the most European of all—come closest, but even
in those countries class-ridden paternalism predominates.

Perception of Time[35] Every society has an intimate concept of time that
reveals how it relates to the future and how it manages its activities and other
important business attitudes. Past-oriented cultures revere ancestors, cherish
collective experiences, and frequently exhibit a cyclical nature that entails
the repetition of events. This orientation detracts from a sense of urgency in
taking advantage of opportunities, because the common perception is that
conditions may repeat themselves. Present-oriented societies do not attach
much significance either to the past or the future; immediate gratification
tends to be emphasized.

Many underdeveloped countries, typically those with predominantly
young populations, display a significant immediate-gratification orientation.
Culturally, they may be said to live only in the present. Yet that stance, like
the phenomenon of urban violence, may be as much a function of the society's
age bracket as of actual neglect of the past and future. It is quite likely that as
these populations age they will mellow and move metaphorically out of jeans
and into trousers, denouncing the values associated with Jack Kerouac and the
Beat generation, for example—an evolvement that I am not fully convinced
will be an improvement.

Relationship to Nature People's attitudes toward the environment may
be classified as internalistic or externalistic, according to where people
perceive their control locus to be. People in internalistic cultures perceive
nature as controllable and subject to human influence. They feel inclined to
act resolutely in relation to natural phenomena and believe they can work
nature to their advantage as well as limit their exposure to its whims. This
cultural assumption that nature can be conquered or controlled prompted
many in the United States to blame President Bush for not doing enough in
the case of hurricane Katrina, for example, either by acting peremptorily to
strengthen infrastructure in advance of the storm or by acting swiftly after
it occurred to diminish the pain brought about by the losses. On the other
hand, externalistic cultures perceive that the locus of control is beyond them;
they see themselves as part of nature and are inclined to seek harmony with
nature rather than oppose it.

SHALOM SCHWARTZ'S APPROACH

Professor Shalom Schwartz, of the University of Jerusalem, set out to improve research design both conceptually and methodologically.[36] Schwartz stressed the cultural dimension of the analysis over individual attitudes, and he used school teachers and students as survey subjects rather than business employees— for, as he rightly argues, school is at the core of the process of transmission of society's web of attitudes, such as conceptions of prosperity and security.

By focusing on schools, Schwartz also managed to separate the effect of subcultures within countries; he collected data from Arab and Jewish schools in Israel, from French- and Anglo-Canadian schools, and from French cultures both within and outside of France.

Schwartz argues that the first basic issue confronting all societies is the nature of the relationship of the individual to the group. This can be conceptualized as a continuous axis bearing individualism and collectivism at opposite ends. At the collectivist end of the continuum we would have the people who view the individual from the perspective of the group's survival. This pole stresses issues regarding duties to the group, group identity, and group belonging, all referring to security, conformity, and tradition. These are status quo–oriented dimensions, which are important to close-knit societies that prize harmony. Schwartz chooses to call this pole embeddedness, while in earlier approaches he named it conservatism.

At the opposite end of this continuum we have autonomous individuals who prize the realization of independent pursuits and stress their own attributes such as motives and emotions, and who live in a society that encourages individuals to develop these pursuits and give them practical meaning. This pole comprises two types of autonomy: intellectual, focusing on such issues as curiosity and creativity; and affective or hedonistic, focusing on such issues as pleasure and diversity.

To Schwartz, a second basic issue is the survival of the structure of a society, which entails sanctioning the behavior that sustains it. Certain behavior is considered socially responsible and must be maintained, which may imply tolerating unequal distribution of power and resources, for example. The capacity to tolerate inequities is associated with the hierarchy pole in the Schwartz taxonomy. This pole stresses social recognition of authority in the allocation of resources. Behavior based on perceiving one another as moral equals and being oriented to ensuring the welfare of others, as well as one's own, is associated with the egalitarianism pole of this dimension. An egalitarian orientation subordinates the self to the advancement of the community.

Schwartz's third basic issue has to do with the way society relates to the natural and social world. Mastery portrays values that legitimize control of the natural environment, while harmony refers to a more reciprocal relationship. The mastery pole indicates a proclivity to favor change and growth, with traits such as self-assertion expressed in ambition, success, audacity, and competence. This may manifest itself in megaprojects such as land reclamation from the ocean, as seen in Tokyo's airport and in Hong Kong and Singapore, or in digging a tunnel under the English Channel. It may also be expressed by leading a world revolution, in the case of Russia, or by seeking to export democratic values, in the case of the United States. The opposite end of this dimension prizes harmony, seeking to blend in to the environment, which is to be protected.

Schwartz then attached all six cultural dimensions to opposing poles of vectors: autonomy versus embeddedness, harmony versus mastery, and egalitarianism versus hierarchy. In addition, he divided autonomy into two subdimensions: intellectual and affective autonomy.

Because teachers play an explicit role in socialization, as an occupational group they characterize the reproduction of national values. Thus primary and high school teachers and their students were sought as respondents to Schwartz's survey in sixty-seven nations. Schwartz then assigned the dimensions to individual vectors on a graph (see Figure 11.2). Vectors for highly correlated dimensions point in the same direction, while vectors for highly negatively correlated dimensions have the same axis orientation but in opposite directions. For uncorrelated dimensions, the vectors are perpendicular to each other. The origin of the vectors is akin to the resulting center of gravity of the observations (representing nations), meaning that nations that are close to the origin have average values for the dimensions crossing at the origin.[37] The graph illustrates that nations score higher in a given dimension the farther away from the origin the vectors fall, as represented by the crossing of the dimensions. For readability, I have chosen to represent clusters of nations rather than individual ones. Thus the francophone countries are highest in intellectual autonomy, whereas Sub-Saharan Africa generally scored lower in this dimension and higher in

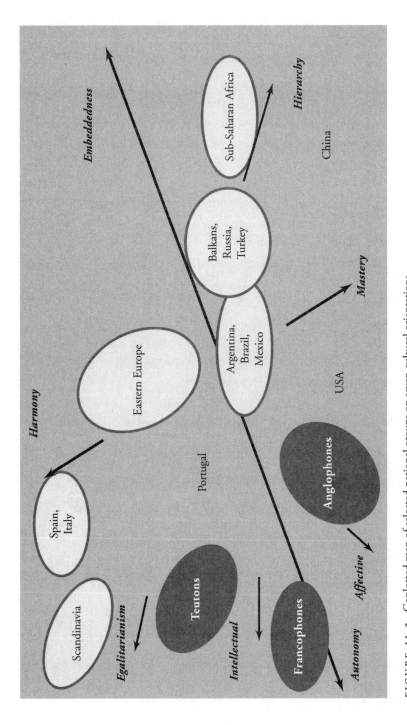

FIGURE 11.2. Coplotted map of selected national groups on seven cultural orientations

SOURCE: Author's rendition of original mapping and interpretations by Shalom H. Schwartz (Hebrew University of Jerusalem) in *Comparing Cultures: Dimensions of Culture in a Comparative Perspective*, ed. Henk Vinken, Joseph Soeters, and Peter Ester (Leiden/Boston: Brill, 2004).

embeddedness and hierarchy. Scandinavians are higher in egalitarianism; Mediterranean Spain and Italy, in harmony; and the USA, in mastery.

China is the virtual opposite of Italy and Spain in almost all values except embeddedness and affective autonomy.

Schwartz's work also suggests clusters of cultural affinities. In some cases, these clusters show geographical proximity, and the cultural cohesion they represent was key to the early diffusion of religions. For instance, Western Europe is clustered in the upper left of the quadrant, where egalitarianism, autonomy, and harmony are prized. Eastern Europeans cluster in the upper center, where harmony is prized. Africans cluster in the lower right, prizing embeddedness and hierarchy, while English-speaking countries cluster in the lower left, prizing autonomy and mastery.

It would not be unwarranted to suggest that the presence of Latin America so close to the centers of all of the dimensions cannot be a matter of chance. It could be that the cultural proximity among the Latin American countries results from the blending of cultures into a system of attitudes characteristic of the Iberian New World, permeated by Mediterranean values, thereby allowing for the graphic proximity of Portugal (as well as Greece, Croatia, and Romania, not shown). A similar interpretation could be made for other cultural blends, such as the Balkan States and Turkey, which also appear close to the dimensions' crossings.

Note that other similarly "blended" nations, the United States and Australia (the latter not shown), also appear closer to the center of the dimensions.

RECONCILING THE MODELS

Mary Douglas offered the most with the least—two dimensions rendering four cultural biases. Her dimensions focused on two fundamental questions: the issue of belonging and the issue of rules of behavior.

A society's options regarding both of these issues gave rise to choices among four cultural biases on the low-to-high continuum: fatalism, hierarchy, egalitarianism, and individualism. Douglas's informed proposition has the attractiveness of elegance and even addresses many of the issues (dimensions) that concern Hofstede, Trompenaars, and Schwartz. However, it does not tell us how peoples come into those choices—or cultural biases—nor why these choices evolve.

Even allowing for the fact that the models use different terminology, the concepts necessarily overlapped to a great extent. Hierarchy is central to all four of the models highlighted in this chapter. Even with the more subtle wording used by Trompenaars, one can see that a society that ascribes status presupposes a prevailing high power distance, which is what Hofstede describes as the extent to which a society will accept differences in power and status. All of the models cover the issues of individualism and collectivism in roughly the same way. Trompenaars, more focused on individual interaction than the other three, developed the societal dimensions of universalism-particularism and affective-neutral. Schwartz verged on these categories by separating the autonomy dimension into the two subdimensions of emotional and intellectual. Neither of Trompenaars's two surplus dimensions can be folded into those of individualism and collectivism without significant loss. Yet both of these dimensions address the way that people deal with each other in societies, which are largely characterized as individualist or collectivist.

Douglas's treatment of fatalism as a cultural bias—as both a condition and a process leading to the condition—can be partly translated as a cultural bias evolving from a people's relationship with time and the ensuing uncertainty. Essentially, in Hofstede's approach, the attitude toward uncertainty involves time and change. A fatalist attitude, à la Douglas, will paralyze change and render, in Hofstede's words, high uncertainty avoidance. Douglas's fatalism also involves Trompenaars's issue of nature and time, and Schwartz's concept of mastery (or lack of it). It involves repeated frustration regarding change, implying a perception of time to be unveiled and, to some extent, the role of nature in shaping that fatalism. It may be that natural events are seen as so overwhelming that they instill in society a belief that people are at the mercy of nature.

Hofstede's masculinity-femininity dimension has no correspondence in Douglas's cultural biases and only a partial correspondence with Trompenaars's achievement-ascription bias or Schwartz's autonomy bias (see Table 11.3). Trompenaars's ascription approach to status can involve the status ascribed to women on account of their gender, which is central to Hofstede's dimension, while the latter also involves the achievement orientation of males in society. Nonetheless, those interpretations have little correspondence with Douglas's four cultural biases.

TABLE 11.3   Correspondences between the cross-cultural models

Douglas	Hofstede	Trompenaars	Schwartz
Hierarchy	High power distance	Ascription	Hierarchy
Individualism	Individualism	Individualism	Autonomy
Fatalism	Uncertainty avoidance	Time perception and relationship to nature	Harmony Mastery
Egalitarianism	Collectivism	Collectivism Ascription Diffuse	Egalitarianism Embeddedness
No correspondence	Masculinity	Achievement Specific	Autonomy Mastery
No correspondence	No correspondence	Affective-neutral	Intellectual and emotional autonomy
No correspondence	No correspondence	Universalism-particularism	No correspondence

Trompenaars's specific-versus-diffuse dimension also has no comparable dimension in either Douglas's or Hofstede's models, and only a limited comparison, through autonomy, to Schwartz's model. This dimension does add to the typification of cultural styles of peoples and could be applicable in business meetings and negotiations, although it did not elicit the interest of the other three models and is left somewhat orphaned in the correspondences noted in Table 11.3.

It is unlikely that the Trompenaars, the Schwartz, or even the shorter Hofstede model could be collapsed into Douglas's model with no loss of information. But the fact that the more complex Trompenaars and Schwartz models can be shown to stem from Douglas's confers to the latter some preeminence, in the sense that her model may help to determine how the other two come into play and when to use them.

Which Model to Use?

Trompenaars's model would appear to provide more guidance on leading face-to-face encounters. On the other hand, Hofstede's model is more appropriate to macroscreening in preparation for international expansion. Even then, one would want to keep in mind that Hofstede's model may be of greater relevance to the more modern, urban type of industry akin to the narrow source of his data: IBM. Schwartz's database is still being built but is nonetheless the strongest, mostly on account of the thoroughness behind the method, not least due to the choice of schoolteachers and students as the source of data. Yet, on the whole, Hofstede's model has been submitted to more extensive validation by the academic community, considering also that access to Trompenaars's methodology was mostly restricted to subscribers to his consulting services. Note, however, that Hofstede's indices are becoming outdated, as is obvious in the cases of countries that no longer exist or that evolved later into market economies, like those of the former Soviet Union. Also, we will see in the next section how statistical outcomes based on surveys may not be as correct as the mathematics of the methods might imply.

Shalom Schwartz's graphic representations help to highlight the geographical as well as cultural clustering of countries. Proximity seems to hold at least one key to the explanation of cultural diversity in that it promotes the diffusion of practices, norms, and values—including those crystallized as the institutions that give them permanence. Thus Schwartz's clustering shows striking similarities not only with Hofstede's statistical clustering but also with Samuel Huntington's, which took a nonstatistical route.[38] Huntington's approach should serve as inspiration for us to use more nonstatistical data to portray our societies more fully. This is what we will tackle in the following chapters on Argentina and Brazil, after critiquing the methods used to elicit the data—for covering the world with statistical surveys is frightfully expensive and time consuming, and does not always tell us more than we already knew. Moreover, the way surveys are conducted may even lead to distortions of the images of nations.

Questioning Questionnaires

We have seen the amount of effort, time, and talent that goes into comparative international surveys. Yet, revealing as they are, surveys still have shortcomings, particularly for Latin Americans. It must be assumed that survey questions elicit different responses depending on the respondent's cultural background. The variations in the responses will then be taken to portray the cultural orientation of the respondent and to determine the cultural clusters to which respondents belong. This allows the researcher to happily write his or her report, with the confidence of one who operates in an environment that is academically sanctioned by a strong number of precursors.

But what would happen if respondents interpreted questions differently in different countries? We would be in trouble, as indeed we already are. I do not mean whether people in different countries will respond differently to the same questionnaire in English. It has already been ascertained that asking nonnative English speakers to respond to questionnaires in English dilutes the survey's expression of cultural differences.[39] Rather, I am discussing (1) whether the selection of questions, even when correctly translated, allows the respondent to react in a way that can be attributed exclusively to his or her culture and not to other environmental issues, and (2) whether the respondent's cultural proclivities can in fact be ascertained by the questionnaire, given its lack of questions on issues that might be central to a given culture.

For instance, the findings of Hofstede's seminal work—that people manifest a preference to work according to rules and that they prefer not to change jobs, even if they feel tense or nervous at work—are taken to mean that people prefer to avoid uncertainty, in the sense that people feel uncomfortable with ambiguity.[40]

Based on this definition, Brazil came to be considered among the countries in the world with the greatest orientation toward uncertainty avoidance. Yet this orientation would also entail discomfort with ambiguity. However, neither is true. Not only is the entrepreneurial orientation of Brazilians high by most measures, but Brazilians also display an enormous tolerance for ambiguity—both in their literature, as seen in Jorge Amado's classic work, *Dona Flor and Her Two Husbands,* and in their culture, as was indicated during one recent summer when a transsexual was a serious contender for Rio de Janeiro's Summer Muse. Brazilian ambiguity is also expressed by the pervasiveness of syncretism in religious affiliation. Animist beliefs are strong in cultures with such large African roots, perhaps explaining why the beliefs of the nineteenth-century French philosopher and spiritualist Alain Kardec are more prevalent today in Brazil than they ever were in France. These beliefs, held in the world's largest Catholic nation, can at times defy rationalism and affect the course of the administration of justice.

Take, for instance, the outcome of one manslaughter trial. *Psychography* is the channeling, through a medium's handwriting, of the spirit of an otherwise dead person. To believers, the handwriting of the medium expresses the spirit of the deceased. So far, so good. But in May 2006 in southern Brazil, testimony of the spirit of a manslaughter victim was used to refute the allegations of the prosecution, which did not challenge the psychographed document accepted by the court. The seven-person jury returned with an acquittal of the defendant by a 5-to-2 vote, because the deceased had communicated that the defendant was not the person who had mandated his death.[41] Since then, a major national newspaper has reported three more cases and informed about an association of Kardecist magistrates with seven hundred members, and another with a further two hundred.[42]

The pervasiveness of such beliefs is testimony to the acceptance of the paranormal in the daily lives of Brazilians, to whom rationality is just one of the options. It follows that the same would be true in Brazilian business, though not many would be as candid as one of the founders of Natura, Brazil's leader in the national cosmetics industry. This successful entrepreneur admitted, in a management publication addressed to young entrepreneurs, to have consulted a medium at the time of founding the company.[43]

Uncertainty is a fact of life, in the sense that it arises from the knowledge that some unpleasant events may happen but cannot be foretold. On the other hand, risk is restricted to describing those events, unpleasant or not, for which occurrences can be gauged to some extent, and they are usually expressed in percentage terms or probabilities.

Surveys would all look straightforward, fair, and exact if they were applied across cultures under uniform circumstances. Yet underdevelopment has many facets, and they all combine to render environments with greater uncertainty than in developed countries. Changes in the underdeveloped macroeconomic environment may be so sudden and so drastic as to wipe a corporation out of business. Learning to anticipate and to cope with these changes is an art that few businesses have managed well.[44] Also, perhaps because they are concentrated in the more volatile tropical climates, underdeveloped countries tend to experience more natural disasters such as droughts, typhoons, and tsunamis than are prevalent elsewhere, and when these occur, safety nets are poor and insufficient. Brazilians must contend not only with natural uncertainties but also with manmade ones. There are fewer deaths due to malpractice in the United States than in Brazil, for example, and per capita consumption of anesthetics is much lower in Brazil. Thus, besides the uncertainty associated with surgery in Brazil, people there also have to put up with more pain. Presumably, there is also a greater chance of being killed by a stray bullet in Rio de Janeiro than in New York, let alone Tokyo.

Naturally, people in underdeveloped countries develop coping strategies for dealing with heightened uncertainty in their daily lives, but coping is not preferring. People simply cannot avoid a high level of uncertainty and may already have reached their limits by the time they are ready to answer a survey. The desire to reduce exposure to uncertainty, where feasible, would lead to the stated preference by Brazilians of knowing in advance what is expected of them at work. Hence their expression of preferring to work according to rules. North Americans subjected to the same diet of uncertainty would most likely answer in the same way.

Yet it is possible that people who state their preferences for knowing and abiding by work procedures are only matching the emphasis that their culture places on the written word. This is particularly true regarding the rules and procedures embedded in the foundations of civil law. The Latin dictum, *nulla poena sine lege* (no penalty unless prescribed by law) sums up the foundation of modern law in constitutional states and found a place in the Napoleonic code, which inspires much of the legal system of Latin American countries and which emphasizes clearly and accessibly written legislation. Therefore, in Latin America, where cultural conditioning has led people to expect rules to be written down, when a worker expresses a preference on a survey to work according to a procedures manual, it should not be interpreted to indicate that he or she is more averse to uncertainty than a U.S. worker who may prefer to complete tasks without a manual. Such expressions of national culture, as written law, permeate the organization through its deepest cultural levels by means of tacit assumptions and unspoken rules.[45] Ignoring those unspoken rules would mean neglecting the significance of culture in the very research geared toward unearthing its relevance.

Also, we have to consider the issue of length of formal training of the workforce. I have informally interviewed several human resource directors in Brazil, and many expressed their preferences that employees adhere to rules in order to avoid the consequences of ill-conceived initiatives, as are likely to result among a workforce with only a few years of schooling. Other HR directors stated that employees prefer to know the delimitations of their duties because getting into trouble is avoided further down the line. Disposition to work by the book in Latin America may be more revealing of the society's high power distance orientation than of a high aversion to uncertainty.

In fact, MIT professor Richard Smith and his team have argued precisely that: in the case of China, they found preliminary evidence that Chinese employees work within sanctioned practices in deference to powerful and distant bosses who would not appreciate being consulted on minor decisions that people should know how to handle.[46] Therefore, one could safely conclude that working by the book or frequently consulting peers—which amount to the same attempt to absolve oneself of a potential wrong decision—may indicate aversion to the certainty of being punished upon making a mistake more readily than it indicates a generalized aversion to uncertainty.

We then have to deal with the interpretation of other questions, such as the attitudes inferred in the preference for job stability. The formation of expectations in this area may not be traceable to a survey alone. For instance, expectations regarding job stability require familiarity with growth prospects in the sector or skill segment in which people work and in the growth of the economy as a whole, besides a host of other variables whose variation is poorly captured by a survey.[47] Take Uruguay, for example: anyone born there in the mid-twentieth century would be lucky to find a job by age twenty-five and would be unlikely to find more than a couple of job prospects during the span of his or her work life. To a Uruguayan in the 1970s, it must have been unfathomable to risk leaving a job with leading IBM, for example, in search of a better job. There were no comparable alternative jobs in Uruguay at that time. If uncertainty were to be measured by society members' determination to hold on to their jobs at the leading information technology company, then Uruguayans were deserving of their score of 100, indicating the highest-possible index of uncertainty avoidance, which is how they were portrayed in the Hofstede survey. But are Uruguayans as averse to uncertainty as they were made to appear? That remains to be proven, particularly because so many of Uruguay's citizens emigrated due to their nation's nonexistent job market.[48] In Uruguay, at least in the 1970s, holding on to one's job, even a job that made one feel nervous or tense at work, was more likely a reflection of meager alternatives than a display of uncertainty avoidance.

Similarly, "frequently feeling nervous at work" is a very slippery concept in itself, besides being highly correlated with punishment and job expectations, because in high power distance societies, punishment may not be proportional to mistakes. Tension and nervousness regarding job stability would only strengthen the willingness to work according to established procedures, if only to have recourse to a modicum of defense when penalized. This may explain why multinational employees from Brazil and Argentina appear to feel less secure than North Americans when it comes to speaking out on the job.[49] Only one in five students in a leading executive MBA program responded that they always felt comfortable in speaking their minds at work. These respondents were high-potential senior executives who had been released from work to attend the course at their companies' recommendation and expense. Those who do not enjoy similar support from their supervisors tend to be considerably less comfortable in speaking their minds.

One would also want to temper these views with the natural environments that constitute different peoples' realities. For instance, Hofstede's masculinity definition correlates strongly with Schwartz's mastery values. Both stress independence, success seeking, daring, and ambition among people who prefer to choose their own goals. This may find expression in Trompenaars's locus of self-control and relationship to nature. To correctly appraise a respondent's attitude to the surrounding natural environment, one would have to compare replies of different respondents to the same environment. But when people respond to questionnaires, the environment they have in mind is their own, and that varies across countries. For instance, nature in the rain forest can be deadlier than in the meadows of the British Cotswolds. Most of the planet's poisonous snakes, spiders, and insects inhabit the underdeveloped tropical countries. Nature, understandably, tends to be regarded as hostile in such places and perhaps even overwhelmingly enough to ever dream of combating it, except by contention. This does not mean that the people that merely slash and burn have a lower disposition to change the environment in which they live. For instance, Israeli Jews are portrayed as having an external locus of decision and a mastery attitude toward their environment. Clearly, the Israeli Jews have irrigated desert areas and turned them into reasonably fertile orchards, but today's Israeli Jews, by virtue of being mostly immigrants to their land, did not develop their culture in the deserts they now occupy, at least not in the better part of the last five thousand years.

The preceding discussion—questioning surveys on issues of power distance, aversion to uncertainty, nature, and job stability, among others—is another way of arguing that a survey is not like a thermometer that one can go hopping around the world with, placing it under people's armpits to discern useful information about average body temperatures and the dispersion of their temperatures.

Also, the questions in surveys may reflect the culture of the surveyor more than the answers provided by the respondents. Respondents must try to fit as neatly as possible into the constraints of the survey, sometimes resulting in answers that are contrived or at any rate less revealing than answers might be from respondents who share the same culture as the surveyor. This phenomenon has already been put forward in the case of ability assessment tests in the culturally diverse United States. The question-answer disconnect is probably even more pronounced in the case of surveys across cultures that are markedly different from that of the surveyor.[50] Surveys do not travel well. Entire areas of importance may be omitted from surveys. When Hofstede realized this, he extended his survey to include the dimension of long-term orientation, in order to accommodate Chinese as well as Brazilian respondents.

Still, not all that was left out of the surveys has to do with long-term orientation. Latin Americans, for instance, seem more inclined than North Americans and northern Europeans to believe in the importance of nonrational components of human thought. There is more magic in the daily lives of Latin Americans; a hunch will be followed through with less resistance in Latin America than in the USA, for example. This is why no white Anglo-Saxon Protestant offspring could possibly have come up with the blend of magic into life apparent in *One Hundred Years of Solitude*; it was Colombia's Gabriel García Márquez that did so. Magic is so widely associated with Latin America that in the American soap opera, *Medium*, it is a Hispanic American, Miguel Sandoval (playing district attorney Manuel Devalos), who hires a medium (Patricia Arquette, Emmy award winner, 2005) to help him sort out police cases with little to go on beyond the evidence of a crime. Apparently, it would have been too alien to an American audience to entrust the administration of justice to a medium hired by an American district attorney. This may be why the district attorney doing the hiring is a Latino, and why the hiring of a medium is revealed only to the viewers. Positivism is not yet dead in America.

However, if reliance on nonrational components of thought is so prevalent in Latin America, why is it that surveys offer no window for its revelation? Perhaps it is because few Latin Americans have been involved in crafting the surveys. If carefully designed to truly target respondents' cultures, surveys allowing for the nonrational might reveal insights into the role of charisma in leadership among Latin Americans; into attitudes toward uncertainty proper, not the type defined by high power distance; or into feminine orientation, with its overtones of intuition.

If Latin Americans believe that it is important to rectify the missing elements in international surveys that measure culture, they should develop new surveys and seek to have them answered across the world. That it has not yet been done is largely due to three obstacles: time, money, and lack of international networks.

None of these is easy to overcome. Redrafting the questions in order to reflect cultural attitudes that would more closely portray Latin Americans in their own diversity would, in itself, be a daunting undertaking—not least because, in Latin America social psychology is not as fully developed as psychoanalysis. While possible, garnering first-rate support for crafting questions is more difficult in Latin America than in developed countries.

Research funding is also typically short term and unlikely to sustain a research group over the period required to develop such a survey, build the network necessary to support it, analyze the results, and see them published. The Wharton School–based GLOBE leadership project took fourteen years, while research funding cycles in Latin America are seldom longer than a year.

If Latin American surveyors were to choose the Hofstede piggybacking route, that is, surfing over the extensive network of a large multinational such as IBM, they would be disappointed to learn that local multinationals will not carry them far from headquarters. This route is currently being tested by a sample drawn from a Brazilian multinational, restricted to seventeen cities in Brazil and three foreign capitals, those of Argentina, Chile, and Paraguay.[51] This Southern Cone conforms to one of the first markets that an expansionist

Brazilian company would target, precisely because it offers the closest and most familiar markets for Brazilian goods. In fact, the Southern Cone countries, including Uruguay, make up one of the culturally least diverse regions that one could select in Latin America, to the point of conforming to a Latin American subcultural cluster.[52] In order to compare that data pool to a more diverse one, one option is to use a proven questionnaire, although it would not serve the purpose of breaking new ground and asking fresh questions that are relevant to local cultures.

Subcultural clusters also occur within countries the size of Brazil, and it may be worth investigating the managerial nature of the various cultures.[53] Still, they are unlikely to reveal more than we already know. Which brings us to a different methodological issue: Should cross-cultural research continue to emphasize question-based surveys and the measurement of cultural clusters? Perhaps it is time to shift research away from surveys and toward evaluations of responses to images.[54] Yet has not the attempt to measure distracted us from a broader attempt to understand? It is precisely the unsatisfactory state of affairs in clustering country cultures that has led me to suggest alternative ways of portraying a country's culture (see Chapters 14 and 15).

SUMMING UP: CROSS-CULTURAL DIFFERENCES WILL REMAIN IMPORTANT

If globalization, which largely entails the spread of Western culture throughout the world, were successful in also spreading values and attitudes, then we would see an increasing emphasis at least in individualism. Indeed, affluence— with the accompanying spread of the English language, increased travel, and greater exposure to Westernized mass media—should help the shift to happen. Psychology professor Kuo-Shu Yang has suggested that it may already be happening.[55] Yang believes that the advantage of collectivist values are obvious when available resources are at a minimum but that collectivism becomes less attractive as society develops, which is when individualist values become more functional due to modernization. However, Yang also points out that in areas such as the choice of leisure activities, the cultural component and the significance of social class will remain large in determining the degree of individualism pursued. Thus, in Latin American societies, where the social class differences are very significant, individualism will be pursued primarily within the thinner ranks of the most affluent classes.[56]

While one can perceive a trend toward convergence in the higher strata of societies, there is no indication that it will make smooth progress. The rapid modernization of the elite will alienate this trend from the slower-paced adaptation of the majority. In countries where the elite dictate the quick-paced Westernization process, this may even lead to social strife. Indeed, history provides ample examples of significant regressions of accelerated Westernization, notably Iran. Latin America, with its many electoral successes of grassroots candidates in the twenty-first century, is perhaps another, albeit subdued, example.

In any case, even without regressions, the trend toward market-oriented, competitive, and autonomous individual development is not fast, as the Little Rock crisis of 1957 made evident in the United States; a full century after defeating the Confederates, the Yankees were again obliged to send in troops to enforce a Supreme Court ruling (see Chapter 6). It is probably safe to say that societies will show increasing signs of adaptation to Western business values, but at least for the time horizons valid for business decisions, cultural values will remain largely the same and management will be well served by adapting to them.

I believe that the United States, being a more permeable empire than Britain ever was, will also be changed in the process of globalization and will not insist on some of its more universalistic and internationally abrasive attitudes, thus slowing the pace of a unilateral worldwide cultural convergence, which in any case would not be entirely American.

I also believe that we should suspend moral judgment on the outcomes of this evolution and instead view it as a passage in the flow of history that we are all a part of. In so doing, Latin Americans need not fully embrace all aspects of current U.S. society or its values, not least because significant chunks of it do not fit, and cannot be made to fit, their cultural expectations.

PART FIVE

MEASURING THE IMPACT OF CULTURE ON MANAGEMENT

HAVING HERETOFORE REVIEWED the contributing factors to cross-cultural management, in this section I will analyze the ways in which cultural differences affect management. I begin with a brief contemporary analysis of leadership issues pertaining to the European roots of the New World; next, I discuss how corporations allocate talent as they grow and what implications this has for the management of subsidiaries. I will also introduce an exploratory survey capturing the opinions of subordinates regarding the ideal leader, showing that a preference for foreign-appointed managers is highly unlikely. I then move on to suggest alternative ways of seizing the cultural dimensions that are valued in Argentina and Brazil. Next, I turn to strategic dimensions of management such as control, feedback, teamwork, mergers and acquisitions, and aversion to uncertainty—all of which are contingent on culture and which, when overlooked, are sure to cause losses in management effectiveness and therefore in productivity. Lastly, I close the section with a final chapter reviewing the book's main contributions to the debate on culture-based management.

HOW DOES CULTURAL HERITAGE MANIFEST
ITSELF IN MANAGEMENT?

The Iberian world displayed an unusual degree of audacity in its innovation during the fifteenth and sixteenth centuries. Sailing where no Europeans had ventured before was an occupation suitable only for risk takers. Iberians were at the forefront in adapting ships, sails, and charts; mapping sea currents and winds; and improving navigation techniques—in short, developing information-seeking strategies with the single purpose of achieving higher performance. This is hardly what would be expected of a population that is averse to uncertainty.

Iberia's capacity to contribute to a grandiose plan exhausted itself by the eighteenth century, however, when the region began to import rather than export concepts and methods.[1] From that point on, Iberian descendants would have to accept that they inhabited a world not defined by either Spain or Portugal. Portugal's empire was now more reminiscent of a mosaic than of the overarching system of its former days of glory. Iberia also lost its creativity; Goya was the only genius offered up during this period.

Managerial theory sprouted its tentative roots in the late nineteenth and early twentieth centuries. It is thus a relatively recent phenomenon and was developed mostly in countries with strong industrial leads. At that time, South America was still struggling with the collapse of the Iberian ideal and the deepening of social rupture, noted a century earlier as much by Sarmiento in Argentina as by Simón Bolivar in Venezuela.[2]

Under these circumstances, the dissemination of managerial theory was merely overflow. South America took to it as it once had taken to the concept of habeas corpus, downloaded from British merchant ships in the nineteenth century: unwholeheartedly. Neither system—not the British habeas corpus nor North American managerial techniques—have taken sure root in the lower half of the New World, where leadership styles descended from absolute monarchies; where experience with the Inquisition may have accentuated a culture of cunning, self-protective reserve; and where trust must be painstakingly earned because it is never granted.

Cultural differences between the USA and Latin America can be downplayed, but not denied. That managerial techniques conceived in the United States will more closely reflect U.S. culture than Latin American culture is also obvious. Still, the mere existence of cultural differences does not mean that they will be imposed, although there is plenty of evidence indicating they will cause trouble.[3] There is also evidence that cultural managerial values are not necessarily transferred en masse by U.S. multinationals to their subsidiaries[4]—at least such was the consensus when U.S. accounting firms set up shop in Holland. In particular, low power distance and individualism may be left at home.[5] Personnel management in multinationals is by and large left to the locals, perhaps explaining why hiring practices in Greek firms demonstrate little variance from those of multinationals in Greece.[6] But we do not know for sure what happens in Latin America.[7] It could well be that cultural differences in Hofstede's masculinity dimension between the USA and Latin America could prove beneficial to the association, in that the aggressive stance of one partner may be tempered by the relationship orientation of the other.[8]

However, evidence also indicates that discrepancies in genuine uncertainty avoidance and long-term orientation are likely to be disruptive to joint ventures.[9] Why this is so is more difficult to nail down. It could be that issues regarding the power distance and collectivism dimensions adhere more closely to the personnel management field and that an agreement can be made to leave those problems to the locals to resolve. Yet uncertainty avoidance and long-term orientation also have to do with the amount of risk and the temporal dimension that the partners envisage facing together, and those difficulties are likely to appear only after they start working together, when it is too late.

For better or for worse, cultural differences are there to be reckoned with. The challenge is to raise awareness in order to work those differences to an advantage. The cultural chasm that leads to different accents in leadership styles, teamwork, feedback, and risk taking is not necessarily altogether bad. What is unproductive is pretending that the differences do not exist and failing to recognize that the cultural grounding of Latin Americans will invite the development of more appropriate managerial techniques for that region, ultimately enhancing productivity and contributing to higher growth.

CHAPTER 12

LEADERSHIP

O F A LEADER WE EXPECT the ability to integrate the vision of the group, with the greater purpose of aligning the efforts of subordinates, even beyond or despite their individual interests. Because the leader triggers the integrative vision, we call this style of leadership charismatic. And because we also expect leaders to channel and transform nonaligned expectations into one, we also call this style of leadership charismatic-transformational.[1]

Charismatic-transformational leadership does presuppose the existence of a group, but its strength lies more in the personality of the leader. This contrasts with the transactional leader, who is expected to perceive and manage the expectations of the group, negotiating expectations for rewards in order to achieve the most for the group. This process transfers some control to the group at the expense of the leader's power.[2]

Furthermore, one could argue that a transactional leader must first be recognized as a leader prior to securing the legitimacy to transact on anyone's behalf. In order to avoid a tautology, it becomes necessary to offer clues as to how leaders are recognized. The leadership-grooming process implies a recognizable set of predetermined leadership qualities. Fortunately, these seem to be open to scrutiny, as they are generally registered in people's minds through the process of socialization. In this way, the recounting of stories, films, and details of life situations provides our minds with information that we learn to categorize, thus enabling the shortcuts with which we simplify and make sense of the complexity of the data we receive. Indeed, people process information by categorizing perceptions. They constantly match perceived personality attributes to cultural ideals of leadership qualities.[3] We must also allow for some fuzziness in the categorization process. Classification becomes indistinct when the mind cannot readily differentiate all members from all nonmembers of a category, that is, effective leaders from ineffective ones. This is when culture, as a learned experience, is resorted to with greater emphasis in order to sort out the men from the boys.

We should expect the desired leadership traits to vary with function and culture. For instance, the traits expected of a religious leader would be different from those of a business leader. Also, given the greater emphasis on charisma and personal charm expected of a leader in societies of a collectivist culture, we should expect transformational leadership to be more effective in such societies as well as in those with relatively high power distance, such as Brazil, where obedience is more easily offered. Still, in high power distance societies, managers will be expected to lead in a more detached manner, while subordinates will work more by the book than in low power distance societies. This may appear contrary to sanctioned approaches in cross-cultural management literature, but it is quite likely that in high power distance societies one does not make decisions by constantly consulting with the boss but rather by adhering to patterns of procedures that ensure acceptance and avoid reprimand.[4] If any risk aversion is implied in this path, it would be the aversion to the risk of being reprimanded; particularly because reprimands in high power distance societies may be substantial.

Also, other cultural dimensions may bring to bear demands on leadership style. Take, for example, high power distance societies with a relatively strong feminine orientation, such as Brazil. The favored leadership style there will still be transformational, but the effective leader will be expected to consult his or her subordinates more frequently than in societies with lower feminine orientations. Very much along the same lines, an aversion to uncertainty orientation is likely to limit the impetuosity of a transformational leader. Yet masculine societies have more trouble with consultative leaders.

Societies that are more egalitarian and collectivist will expect leaders to adopt personal styles similar to those of their subordinates. Riding a bike to work, for example, would be acceptable in the Netherlands but not in Mexico. An Argentine general manager in Mexico shared with me that for three years he ate lunch at a more expensive restaurant than he would have wished because that was what was expected of him by both his employees and his clients.

LEADERSHIP AND CULTURE: PROJECT GLOBE

The Global Leadership and Organizational Behavior Effectiveness (GLOBE) project is the 1991 brainchild of Wharton professor Robert House. Funded in 1993, the project focused on leadership and organizational issues and evolved into a network of 170 researchers in some sixty cultures spread across the world. The project has inspired the spin-off of dozens of stimulating papers on leadership and, so far, two hefty books.[5]

Because top leadership carries the burden of companywide decisions, such as formulating strategy or overall allocation of resources, managers in this echelon may tend to downplay the role of compassion vis-à-vis lower-level managers. But these latter have a strong sense of the effectiveness of top leaders and of the mix of attributes that signal the best among them. Accordingly, the GLOBE project carried out a worldwide survey seeking to assess the universal leadership attributes as perceived by middle managers.

That work points to the worldwide acceptance among middle managers in charismatic-transformational leadership roles, the main characteristics of which entail team orientation and a participatory nature as well as integrity, communication abilities, and coaching skills.[6] The same study also provides guidance regarding negative attributes, or those that hinder effective leadership, such as being a loner, ruthlessness, dictatorial tendencies, irritability, and nonexplicitness.[7]

The GLOBE project identified six attributes of effective leadership as perceived by middle managers (see Figure 12.1).

According to the GLOBE project, charisma is everyone's champion, only slightly more for middle managers in the United States than for Brazilians

Charismatic	Visionary, inspirational, self-sacrificial, integrity
Team oriented	Integrator, consultative, team builder, collaborative, diplomatic
Self-protective	Self-centered, status conscious, conflict inducer, face saver
Participative	Delegator, egalitarian
Humane	Generous, compassionate
Autonomous	Individualistic, independent, unique

FIGURE 12.1. Universally endorsed leadership attributes according to GLOBE

and Argentines taking part in the GLOBE project. While its expression may vary even among this narrow sample of countries, charisma is paramount to all business leadership styles.

BUSINESS LEADERSHIP IN THE EUROPEAN CONTEXT

The GLOBE project showed evidence of clustering in twenty-one European countries regarding leadership attributes.[8] Statistical clustering methods detected at least two clusters in Europe, one in the northwestern quadrant, and another in the southeastern quadrant. Within the northwestern cluster, we have the usual suspects: England, Ireland, the Netherlands, Sweden, Finland, Denmark, Germany, Austria, and Switzerland. A trained historian or cultural anthropologist would have reached similar conclusions without the survey simply based on the shared cultural legacy of these countries, facilitated by topography and readily expressed in terms of their languages and religions. This is why the GLOBE project authors were led to conclude that splitting up the leadership data between west and east revealed that "the northwest cluster seems to represent typically Western attitudes."[9]

The other European countries in the GLOBE project are a matter apart. The statistical clustering method produces some strange bedfellows. France, Italy, Spain, and Portugal are closely linked in terms of religion, language, and geography. Yet Hungary, the Czech Republic, Slovenia, Poland, Greece, Russia, Georgia, and Albania, while culturally similar to one another, show less commonality with Latin American countries, although perhaps not enough to register statistically.

Still, there are statistical similarities between the Latin European countries and the rest of GLOBE's southeast cluster (not shown in Figure 12.2) that need to be accounted for. GLOBE authors argue that diplomacy is more valued in Europe's southern and eastern cultures (Latin or not) than in the northwest. Perhaps Schwartz would have called this harmony, since approximately the same countries cluster together in his work as well.

However, GLOBE authors attribute this clustering to the political intricacies of management in centrally planned economies, despite the fact that none of the European Latin countries fell into this category—at least not the type of planned economies that occurred in the Eastern Bloc. Moreover, Latin European countries share with the other southeastern countries a proclivity for high power distance. Whether this tendency is related to Catholicism of the Roman or the Orthodox variety might be a matter of interesting discussion. I believe that the greater emphasis given to diplomacy in southeastern GLOBE countries is due to the fact that the stakes in power disputes are much greater in high power distance cultures; hence, diplomacy—or Schwartz's harmony—pays a larger dividend.

But differences between *Romania continua* (contiguous countries exhibiting Romance languages) and others in the western-southeastern cluster are prominently noted in the Latin European heritage of today's Latin American population. From the Latin American perspective, therefore, it would have been more useful to isolate the results of the Latin European countries from those of the rest of GLOBE's southwest and eastern clusters. To correct this disadvantage, I considered each of the attributes using GLOBE's published data on the rankings for England and Latin Europeans.

By comparing the averages of the rankings of desired leadership attributes of Spain, Portugal, and Italy with those of England, we derive the current differences in the desired leadership characteristics of the countries that provided the lion's share of immigrants to the New World.

Figure 12.2 illustrates variances in the leadership cluster of western Latin European countries vis-à-vis England. The greatest differences surface where one would expect them to, regarding gender, power, future orientation, collectivism, and uncertainty avoidance.

One can hardly imagine what the prevailing leadership attributes may have been in the countries that populated the New World at the time they did.

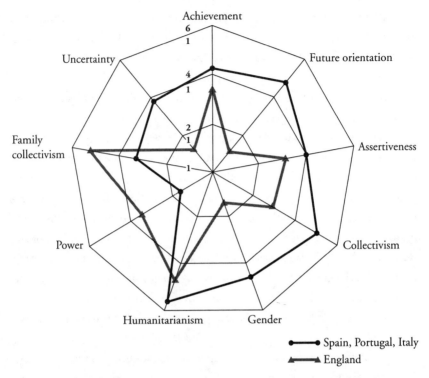

FIGURE 12.2. Attributes ranked by the two clusters that provided the most immigrants to North and South America

SOURCE: Paul L. Koopman, Deanne N. Den Hartog, and Edvard Konrad, "National Culture and Leadership Profiles in Europe: Some Results from the GLOBE Study," *European Journal of Work and Organizational Psychology* 8, no. 4 (1999): 503–20.

What we now have at hand are the stated differences in beliefs of those same countries regarding leadership attributes. That is remarkable in itself; for five hundred years since the discovery of the New World, despite centuries of formal training, experience, and convergence derived from much greater exposure to communication and travel, these Latin European countries still stand apart from England when it comes to desired leadership attributes. For instance, only in achievement, assertiveness, and humane orientation does the ranking of England—the country that supplied the bulk of the USA's immigrants—approach the average rankings of Spain, Portugal, and Italy—the countries of origin of the three main immigration flows to Brazil and Argentina.

BUSINESS LEADERSHIP IN LATIN AMERICA

This section turns to the importance of paternalism in Latin America, its impact on populism, and how the latter, in turn, influences the expression of charisma. Once the concept of charisma is elaborated and imprinted in people's minds, it acquires permanence and influences their images of acceptable leadership styles. I will examine why foreign managers may falter in their efforts to direct local subordinates, despite the appointees' best efforts, suggesting that it may be for the same reason that Perón would fail in the USA: because, despite Perón's charisma, his style is not what North Americans would chose to follow.

Paternalism is surely in the DNA of Latin American leadership styles. It is defined as a hierarchy within a group, by means of which advancement and protection are expected in exchange for loyalty, usually to a father-figure, or patriarch. The domineering apex of the hierarchy is exercised paternalistically, as within a family, and in fact forms an extended family. Such conditions can conceivably result in varying degrees of indentured service—including household slaves, for example. While "almost family," household slaves were not equal to cousins; cousins, in turn, were nearly the same as brothers. Strict primogeniture was never a predominant Iberian trait, enabling the emergence of a larger network of relatives and associates bound by a diffuse goal of family advancement as well as by a strong sense of broad reciprocity.

This social arrangement, which permeated all spheres of life, was not restricted geographically and encompassed urban as well as rural lifestyles, although it was strongest where less contact across borders occurred, such as on inland haciendas, or plantations. Its legitimacy would not be questioned in other organizations, including government or even ecclesiastical circles.

It perhaps takes another Latin American to fathom the pervasiveness of the patriarchal social contract that embraced even extramarital arrangements and their resulting offspring, so commonplace that Spanish law would recognize several levels of illegitimacy.[10]

Populism may be seen as the urban political expression of paternalism. It is a long-held form of making politics in Latin America, where individuals traditionally belonged first and foremost to a family, through which they were bound to a patron.

There was little chance of survival beyond these kinship relationships mired in Mediterranean origins and as expressed in the interconnections of the Mafia in New York City, for example. Besides, Mediterranean paternalism was at the root of the loyalty networks that enabled the success of the "company," the basic mercantile economic unit through which, at minimum, two partners would engage in productive activities.[11] Usually, one partner would provide the capital and the other, the mercantile know-how or other essential knowledge, such as navigational experience.

These partnerships would endure long periods without profit. Vasco da Gama took more than two years to discover the cape route to Calicut and was sustained by patriarchal networks. These binding relationships naturally had regional ties, and a person's geographical origin would suffice as an entry to the fold when closer kinship could not be established. Thus, because merchants from Seville and Burgos felt they could trust each other more than outsiders, it was the Lucchese network in São Paulo (with the Martinellis at the apex) that artist Fulvio Pennacchi would turn to when in need of a backer for his craft.[12]

Patriarchal networks fit like a glove in a new and hostile world, where everyone depended on the rest for survival and where networks were needed that were tight enough to ensure survival but also loose enough to incorporate members of the clan arriving on boats from distant ports. Thus paternalism acquired legitimacy, and its permeable frontier shaped its urban political dimension: populism.

Despite its fiery language, populism has traditionally been a reformist rather than a revolutionary movement. It sought reform without threatening the basic fabric of society, which remained firmly grounded in concentrated private property, even when espousing modest redistribution attempts. Populism's strength derived from the longing of the dispossessed for protection and inclusion. Inclusion was to be brought about through the general betterment of the working class and the integration of the poor into society. Charismatic populist leaders invariably capitalize on the poor's need to belong. This was the case of the "shirtless" under Perón, of Brazilians under Vargas, of Mexicans under Cárdenas, or more recently, of Venezuelans under Chavez and Bolivians under Morales. Some populist leaders had enormous followings yet never made it to the presidency, such as Peru's Victor Raúl Haya de la Torre or Colombia's Jorge Eliécer Gaitán. Others achieved the presidency several times but failed to complete their mandate, such as Ecuador's José María Velasco Ibarra.

All of these leaders offered understanding, protection, and dignity to the masses—in the thymus sense so stressed by Fukuyama[13] and by Bourdieu when referring to honor in Mediterranean males.[14] All achieved great followings in Latin America by offering much more than what children could expect from a father, or even a mother, as Evita Perón occasionally described herself.

It is interesting to note that in family-owned Brazilian businesses the figure of the owner is frequently referred to as the "father," and the staff is considered part of the "family."[15] Management theory, being mostly North American and thus bound to the concept of individual self-reliance, fails to allow for this paternalistic style of leadership. While ubiquitous in Latin America, paternalism is frowned upon by modern managers there, despite the population's deep association with it. Aycan points out a similar relevance of paternalistic relationships in the Middle Eastern and Asian business environments.[16]

Populist leaders in Latin America have historically attracted—and still attract—massive followings. One may question the wisdom, modernity, or even fairness of the moral pact in a populist political setting, but one thing is certain: populist movements reveal a desire by the populace to surrender individuality—an inclination that is unknown in North America, where much of the thinking on corporate leadership takes place.

If the tradeoff of individuality and freedom for protection, as revealed by Latin American workers' allegiance to populist leaders, is anything to go by, expecting a Latin American employee to commit to a corporation merely for money is bound to lead to disappointment. When confronted with a mercenary style of leadership, in which the boss demands allegiance in exchange for a wage, Latin American workers are likely to feel shortchanged. Their response will be to accept the money but to reciprocate less than is expected or desired. From a business point of view, the worker displays lack of engagement. From the worker's point of view, he or she has been betrayed; for, by limiting his or her own engagement to the agreed wage, the boss has shown a lack of interest in and protection of the worker, "no matter what." While this may seem exaggerated to the trained North American manager, it is not to Brazilians. So much so that downsizing in Brazil, though not in the United States, is perceived as a moral defeat of the boss.[17]

It would appear that a Latin American employee, once basic needs are satisfied, expects a much greater allegiance from the boss than a fair pay arrangement would imply. No amount of team-building exercises will undo the original sin of limiting the employee's expectations for protection to a salary. Excluding the worker's mother from the company's family health coverage only confirms the foreignness of the administrative culture in countries where the family unit frequently involves an elderly mother or grandmother, if not a grandfather as well.

HOW CULTURE AFFECTS ENACTMENT OF THE DIMENSIONS

Charisma, it seems, is king. Nobody expects a leader, even a business leader, to be completely lacking in charisma. The issue we need to look into is what is recognized as charisma in different cultures, or even how charisma functions within one culture in varying roles, such as education, religion, or public administration. But let us focus here on business leadership.

Cross-cultural sensitivity may be less exciting than charisma, but it also can make or break a business relationship. The personalization of business relationships is a treacherous intercultural field. The business leader in a U.S. multinational in Brazil or Argentina must be ready to break with leadership standards that might be acceptable in the United States, such as objective business relationships, in order to fine tune his or her leadership style in the new environment. Like some of the best actors, managers would do better if they relied on intuition rather than rationale.[18] But relying on intuition is not generally recommended in a culture such as the United States, so conditioned by aphorisms such as "look before you leap" or "watch your step."

In cultures where intuition is downplayed and where the stakes are usually high, business leaders will tend to transfer command of their behavior to their trusty analytical prowess, putting intuition aside.[19] However, rational thinking may not always lead to better results and may ignore important alternatives. Perhaps we think we behave like fools when we are in love, yet that is when we are at our best in persuading the other of the honesty of our feelings. Let our behavior be run by our minds, and the love spell will be broken.

The best leaders do not seem to know how they "do it," nor can their subordinates explain why they follow them. Professor Rob Goffee of the London Business School claims that good leaders have good situation-sensing skills, that they show they care, and that they have an excellent sense of timing and context.[20] Although it might be difficult to recognize that leadership skills cannot be explained or taught, we can recognize that these qualities are contingent on culture.

THE VICEROY IS THE WRONG MAN IN THE WRONG PLACE

I have argued that the prevailing views on leadership in Latin America are different from those in the United States and that those differences are culturally based and therefore stable, perhaps even over centuries, with roots in an area of Europe that remains culturally distinct from the European region that gave birth to the USA. I will now argue that not only are leadership styles different, but also the natural selection of expatriate managers sent to Latin America, or of local managers selected there, may worsen matters in terms of leadership effectiveness.

The prevailing foreign managerial style may be selecting the wrong people for leadership positions in multinationals in Latin America. If the U.S. leadership paradigm is out of synch with the Latin American one, an executive in the United States seeking someone to lead a multinational's operation in Latin America is likely to select and promote the one who best matches the North American paradigm, not the other way around.

Anthropologists have pondered the issue many times, to the point of utilizing it in their basic training.[21] Faced with selecting an informant to explain cultural nuances in a society under study, the anthropologist would do well to ask what type of insertion the candidate has within his or her own community that drove him or her to play the role of informant. For instance, upon entering an Amazonian Yanomami tribe, the much-vilified anthropologist Chagnon was accused of using as key informants "outcasts in their own society, people he could bribe more easily."[22]

This is not to be construed to mean that multinationals perversely select and groom leaders that their community would not itself choose to follow. But it does mean that in the process of selecting a local leader to represent a multinational in Latin America, the "weeding out" process, at best, favors the bias of the person doing the selecting. The leadership outcome is usually so uninspiring that seldom does a Latin American executive of a multinational succeed as a leader of any other type of local organization.[23]

A LEADER FOR EACH PHASE

As if this were not enough, another trend is at work that compounds matters: mature U.S. business organizations—the type more likely to expand internationally—tend to select disciplined rather than creative minds to oversee Latin American operations. The artistic mind, in the typology conceived by Canadian social psychologist Patricia Pitcher, would be an individual who is emotionally intelligent, visionary, creative, and eager to arrange a team of collaborators capable of innovating and venturing into challenging opportunities.[24] Such people have people-oriented minds, they thrive on contact, and they readily become personal. Yet artist leaders also need the collaboration of controlling talents, which Pitcher called technocrats, and dependable people who could be trusted to run the operation; these Pitcher called craftsmen.

Pitcher is not alone in believing that a modern corporation requires a mix of talents that covers a broad spectrum of personalities. Her concept of a modern company is one that embraces "all kinds of perspectives . . . even the cerebral, analytical, and uncompromising." However, Pitcher also maintains that while the artists and craftspeople possess an innate ability to live with that diversity, the technocrat has a harder time. This is why the technocrat, once in power, tends to shoo the rest away.

It may well be that the technocrat is most vital in the mature stage of a corporation, when the latter cannot as easily accommodate the emotional outbursts or indiscipline that might characterize artists, or the lack of worldliness that might characterize craftspeople.[25] We can picture what might happen in a corporation entering the painful growth phase of discarding its artists and craftspeople by examining a similar situation that is more readily at hand, as seen in the 2004 film *Ray*, directed by Taylor Hackford.

Ray Charles, the blind musician, had met up with Jeff Brown, a good man who was willing to help out. In the early days, Jeff was Ray's factotum. He would guide Ray, book his shows, count the money, carry the luggage, and provide him with an ample supply of thin-wristed ladies, which Ray so appreciated. Ray and his band continued on, loosely, among friends, spinning the webs of loyalty that unite those who have been in the trenches together. As Ray's success increased, he felt the need for a collaborator who was more attuned than Jeff to the wiles of the entertainment industry. Ray settled for Joe Adams, who took over management. Joe arrived with his own way of doing things, his own Taylorist disciplinary standards, and he soon clashed with the band members, who were used to the casual style of leadership under the venerable Jeff Brown.

The clash of managerial styles is portrayed in the scene in which Fathead, a prominent band member, forcefully expresses his dislike for the managerial style of Joe Adams, which included applying fines to players who arrived late to rehearsals. Fathead wishes to clear matters with the boss, Ray Charles. Feeling that Joe Adams has overstepped his own authority, Jeff Brown also joins Fathead in the complaint. All three, Joe, Fathead, and Jeff enter Ray's office. The scene has two parts: first, in which Fathead is dismissed from the meeting, reserving the managerial decision to be handled by Joe and Jeff, but arbitrated by Ray. Second, after Ray has established that he is aware that Jeff, his longtime collaborator, has been milking the business, Jeff is angry and saddened because he feels his old-time boss has abandoned him, particularly by paying Adams more than himself. Feeling irreparably betrayed, Jeff Brown leaves and Joe Adams assumes complete control.[26]

FATHEAD NEWMAN: Ray, this fool, Joe Adams, is trying to fine me for being late.

RAY CHARLES: What time did you get here?

FATHEAD NEWMAN: What? Just now. The band's still setting up. Jeff never—

JOE ADAMS: I'm not Jeff.

FATHEAD NEWMAN: That's a fact, Jack.

(Jeff ushers Fathead away and takes command as leader of the band.)

JEFF BROWN: Ray, you said the band was my thing.

RAY CHARLES: That's right, I did.

JEFF BROWN: Fathead, you go on back to rehearsal.

FATHEAD NEWMAN: Ray! You know how it is, you've been there.

JEFF BROWN: Fathead, go on now. I'll take care of this. Ray, you want to tell me what's going on man?

JOE ADAMS: I'm not doing anything I haven't been asked to do. Ray's running a business. He shouldn't have to waste time hearing why people were late.

JEFF BROWN: I'm not talking to you, Joe. I'm talking to Ray.

Notice how Fathead, addressing Ray, appeals to the old group ethics: "You know how it is, you've been there." Ray doesn't reply, and Jeff, feeling he is losing his grip on the band, asks Fathead to leave and demands that Ray clarify the lines of command. Joe interrupts, arguing that Ray is "running a business."

(Same sequence, after Ray accuses Jeff of stealing and asks Joe Adams to leave him alone with Jeff.)

RAY CHARLES: How could you do that? We've been through so much. We were like brothers.

JEFF BROWN: Ray—if we were like brothers, why are you paying Joe more than you're paying me?

RAY CHARLES: Damn all that. You broke my heart.

JEFF BROWN: Well you know what, Ray? You broke mine a long goddamn time ago.

RAY CHARLES: Well, there it is.

(Jeff walks away.)

JEFF BROWN: You know something, Ray? You're gonna get yours one day. And I pray to God he has mercy on your soul, you son of a bitch!

Now notice how Ray appeals to family bonds to reprimand Jeff for stealing from him. Jeff also appeals to family ethics to justify his behavior, invoking a standard by which everyone would receive according to their needs, which would possibly be too Marxist for this film—or perhaps according to seniority, which would be very African, very Mediterranean, and consequently very Latin American. It seems to have never entered Jeff's mind that a market-oriented professional management would demand that people be paid according to what is necessary to retain them; that would be too market oriented, too "American" for the old-school band, although by then it is being run like a business.

The scene illustrates a managerial cultural clash, in this case, between subcultures in the USA. Unrefined Jeff is sidestepped as the creative, loyalty-bound startup band morphs into the new-era, professionally managed band. Fathead and others may be disoriented in the turnaround, but now, presumably, the band will be more dependable. Will meeting on time for rehearsals happen at the expense of creativity? Not yet, as Ray was still there to guarantee the musical quality. But the threat was instilled.

Perhaps Pitcher would have said that Joe Adams, in the artistic environment, represents the technocrat character, while Jeff represents the craftsman and Ray, the artist. In this case, the craftsman lost his job. Of interest here, however, is that we can observe a similar phenomenon in the management of multinationals in developing countries. What matters is that many—perhaps most—of the multinational companies that set up shop in Latin America do so to seek access to markets for older products that have hit a slow-growth phase in the United States or elsewhere. These are mature organizations, and the artists that may have initiated them are long gone. Organizations that expand internationally are likely to be managed by technocrats.

International expansion in Latin America is not for the high-fliers—unless they are very young—nor for artists seeking challenges. It seems that the technocrats, given their disciplined minds, are catapulted to positions of leadership they were not born to and sent off to manage Latin Americans. Despite their shortcomings, in Latin America they are the bosses, stifling the creativity of the artists beneath them, if any get hired at all. Headquarters does not like surprises and will seek dependable individuals who will have to learn how to cope with small and thin markets overburdened with government regulations. That is all.

Whether it is an American expatriate or a local who is selected for the job of top manager in Brazil or Argentina, the decision is largely made with an eye to the bottom line, not to diversification, innovation, or international expansion from Latin America—challenges that might attract the artist mentality. The appointed subsidiary leader in Latin America will operate within stringent headcount and financial restrictions that are in place with a view to a global strategy that was not designed by the hired leader. Those selected for these down-to-earth jobs will be highly paid and command a lot of attention while they are in the job, but they are unlikely to be leaders of the type befitting the local workforce. This is why, upon retirement, they rarely find a fit in local organizations, despite their vast experience. Not only do the executives' pay scales and profiles as multinational gofers deter local organizations from wooing these potential candidates, but the crucial issue of leadership style also acts as a key obstacle.

A group of my students conducted a study that revealed the degree of executive career crossover between Brazilian and multinational corporations. It is very low, indeed. Out of one hundred top managers of foreign subsidiaries in Brazil, only sixteen had not been employed in a multinational corporation immediately before being promoted to the subsidiary's top position.[27]

MATCHING LEADERS TO FOLLOWERS

It appears that the leadership styles of foreign-appointed heads of subsidiaries are inadequate to lead organizations in emerging markets. The mismatch has profound implications for productivity and foreign direct investment in these markets. As the outsourcing of manufacturing and service jobs proceeds toward lower-cost, more patriarchal, and more collectivist societies with broader perceptions of time, further problems will arise from the uneven matching of foreign-appointed leaders with workers in emerging markets.

The Behrens Leadership Survey

To test whether national culture makes a difference in pairing business leaders with workers, I took an unchartered route to complement previous work such as the Wharton-based GLOBE project.[28] Survey-based work may have succeeded in eliciting universally desirable qualities of leaders, such as charisma, but it has not shown what such qualities mean to different cultures nor, therefore, which leadership style is most effective, and where. In taking this avenue, I also attempted to redirect, in favor of the worker's point of view, the usual research focus on the leader.

Assuming that national culture determines the acceptability of business leadership styles, we should be ready to accept that leadership that is more attuned to national styles will render better responsiveness among workers, will stimulate engagement, and will foster productivity. At job-entry levels, this cannot be reliably tested, for there are too many extraneous factors affecting the decision of taking a job or not, and the entrants have too little experience to be able to compare business leaders. But, at the middle-management level, people have developed a fair idea of the significance and effectiveness of business leadership and should be able to make informed comparisons.

Through a Web-based questionnaire, my research team asked principally EMBA alumni, both Brazilian and foreign, to rate on a five-point Likert scale a given set of business leaders according to their acceptability as leaders.[29] We illustrated their styles in six-second muted videos played on YouTube.com. The leaders, all white males in their fifties through sixties, were each purported to deliver an equivalent flow of rewards to shareholders and workers. The characteristics being rated were the leaders' appearance and demeanor, not their efficacy in achieving results, as they were all expected to deliver the same results, nor the quality of their judgment, for their arguments could not be heard.

The conditions of the selection may seem too stringent to be meaningful; however, we already know that students exposed to silent videos of unfamiliar lecturers have rated the effectiveness of a given lecturer almost as highly as students who had studied a whole semester under the same lecturer.[30] This suggests that there is a cognitive level at which experienced businesspeople, for example, process imperfect information to the degree possible.[31] Empathy with a leader is one cognitive area where this fuzzy logic stance plays a most relevant role.[32]

The 147 anonymous replies, largely from middle managers (73 from Brazil), came from basically two networks: EMBA alumni of the Brazilian business school IBMEC São Paulo, and alumni of London Business School, who supplied half of the 74 non-Brazilian responses. Many of the remaining foreign replies came from members of EMONET, the professional and academic network on emotional intelligence supported by the Academy of Management listserver, and at least eight came from the University of Chicago Graduate School of Business. Both categories of respondents, Brazilian and foreign, worked principally in banking, law, and consulting companies. Representatives of manufacturing companies were almost entirely absent. Over two-thirds of respondents were males in their mid to late thirties. We excluded the replies of those who acknowledged recognizing any of the leaders in the videos, and were left with 130 valid replies.

Upon viewing the muted videos of the business leaders, two sets of IBMEC EMBA students, one with six students and the other with twenty, were asked to freely associate their impressions of the leaders using single words, and to choose an animal that best fit each leader's style (see Table 12.1). The students' impressions were then reviewed by a social psychologist for possible deviations of their perceptions, given the variety of quality and image backdrops. No such deviation was detected. Incidentally, this test was repeated in Buenos Aires with ten participants at an executive workshop, and again with thirty-five salespersons from the pharmaceutical company Schering during a Fundação Instituto de Administração (FIA) course in July 2008, and rendered similar results.[33]

Results of the Survey

The most favorable responses of all the alumni, Brazilian and foreign, clustered around the slim, bearded owl-type leader of a Brazilian engineering design company with seven hundred employees, in which close to four hundred are

TABLE 12.1 Summary of comments by the Behrens survey's focal groups

Leader's organization	Most frequent words inspired by the leader's style among Brazilian EMBA students	Animal the students associated with the leaders	Why this animal?
Brazilian engineering design company	Magistrate, balanced, knowledgeable, sure, professor, able, fair	Owl	Wisdom
American low-fare domestic airline company	Hard, fair, penetrating	Eagle	Big picture
Brazilian agro-industry	Protective, reliable, avuncular, fair, likable	Cow	Serves caringly
Large international American retailer	Tough, straightforward, focused, reliable, difficult	Lion	Rules
American packaged-food distributor in Brazil	Unreliable, used-car salesperson, self-protective, careerist, me-first	Vulture	Scavenger
British and New Zealander activist-entrepreneur	Inflexible, reliable, unobtrusive, nonthreatening	Beaver	Predictably industrious

owner-employees, underscoring what was already known publicly: that people want to work for this leader. Almost two-thirds of the foreigners and 51 percent of the Brazilians regarded this candidate favorably. His gestures calmly conveyed a priestly, fair, and knowledgeable impression of reliability, as befits knowledge-based industries (see Table 12.2).

When asked whether that leader would also be amenable to their coworkers, the more egalitarian non-Brazilian alumni mostly held their ground. The Brazilians, however, tilted toward the Brazilian cow-type leader of a large agribusiness corporation, who conveyed a calm, paternalistic, and more protective image. The tilt was sizable; while the non-Brazilian alumni's initial preference for the owl-type leader dropped by only 10 percent, the Brazilians' preference for this leader dropped by 43 percent. Their shift to the cow-type leader is a concession to a patriarchal, nonegalitarian society where a leader who is best for the alumni of an elite business school may not be deemed to be the most appreciated by the rest of the working population.

The two American-style leaders were deemed acceptable to almost everyone and aroused the lowest rejection. The eagle-type leader—the star American—was the head of a domestic U.S. airline company who had innovated low-fare services. The other American, the lion-type leader, was the head of one of the world's largest retail chains. His measured hand gestures underscored his facial expressions—appearing to stress stringency and constraint. Perhaps on account of this perceived inflexibility, Brazilian unfavorable response to the lion-type leader amounted to 28 percent.

The least-appreciated business leader of all, to both foreign and Brazilian alumni, but particularly to the latter, was the vulture type. He was the Brazilian head of a U.S. packaged-food retailer in Brazil selling about $160 million a year. He was perceived to be as trustworthy as a used-car salesman, and over two-thirds of the respondents had a strongly unfavorable perception of this leader. A full 43 percent of the Brazilian replies opted for the alternative, "I

TABLE 12.2 Summary of the critical replies to the survey questions

With which business leader would you feel most comfortable at work?			Which business leader do you think the majority of your coworkers would prefer to work with?		
Top choice	% of replies within cultural cluster		Top choice	% of replies within cultural cluster	
	Foreign	Brazilian		Foreign	Brazilian
Owl	**33.3**	27.7	Owl	**30.0**	15.9
Eagle	18.3	18.8	Eagle	15.0	25.0
Cow	10.0	18.5	Cow	20.0	**31.7**
Lion	3.3	20.3	Lion	6.7	16.9
Vulture	0.0	6.2	Vulture	0.0	4.6
Beaver	10.0	15.4	Beaver	18.3	14.5
Bottom choice			Bottom choice		
Owl	3.3	16.9	Owl	3.3	14.3
Eagle	11.7	10.9	Eagle	5.0	10.9
Cow	10.0	15.4	Cow	11.7	17.5
Lion	11.7	4.7	Lion	10.0	7.7
Vulture	26.7	**44.6**	Vulture	**25.0**	**30.8**
Beaver	**31.7**	38.5	Beaver	18.3	30.6
Total replies	60	65	Total replies	60	65

NOTE: Bold numbers indicate highest share attained by replies within the cultural cluster.

would rather not risk work under his command." This robust negative rating would seem to convey a marked dissatisfaction with a boss who is deprived of the qualities expected by subordinates, Brazilian or not. It may be that this young executive, trying too hard to be accepted by the foreign bosses, ends up disenfranchised by his colleagues, locally and abroad. Apparently, the foreign-appointed local boss is about as convincing as a leader of locals as a drag queen is to a man.

Of course, these are only first impressions regarding a single case in a controlled setting. Exceptions can be readily named—for instance, Antonio Maciel Neto moved from the presidency at Ford Latin America to that of Suzano Papel e Celulose, the publicly listed Brazilian paper mill. This move came after Maciel Neto's successful stints with two Brazilian publicly listed companies and two unlisted ones, at the federal government and a public oil company. But the likes of Maciel Neto are also hard to come by, which is why the news of his move from Ford to Suzano made headlines—because it was news, in the sense that "the mailman who bit the dog" is news.

A sixth videotaped leader, who was British, spoke for six seconds without any facial expression whatsoever. That was deemed reliable, predictable, and fair, and he was designated the beaver-type leader. Yet this style was uninspiring to most—except to some who mostly turned out to be active in the IT industry—thus the beaver-type leader made too little of a dent in the choices as to be an effective alternative. With the benefit of hindsight, it did not seem to be a satisfactory choice to include this leader in the same set as the others, but he was the only European leader of whom we had a satisfactory video.

This piece of research was an exploratory step toward eliciting views on business leadership styles from the "other end of the gun." The leader who, in the real world, was chosen by his colleagues to lead the company was the calm-inspiring, owl-type leader, the one overwhelmingly preferred by foreigners and Brazilians alike. The foreign-appointed leader of a U.S. multinational, the vulture type, failed flatly in eliciting intuitive approval. Not even top world business leaders, such as the eagle and lion types, while amenable, became the first choice of Brazilian followers, and, in any case, such leaders are in too short supply to provide a solution for staffing leadership openings in emerging Latin American markets. The leader perceived as paternalistic was the most acceptable to the putative majority of Brazilians.

The effectiveness of leaders of knowledge-based industries may be less sensitive to national boundaries, and these were the top choices of both cultural clusters; yet, when it comes to leading the majority of workers in Brazil, the preferred leadership style, that of the cow-type leader, is the most attractive nationally of all the choices, conveying a sense of patriarchal, protective, and caring leadership—as might be expected in the case of Brazil.

SUMMING UP: LEADERSHIP SURVEYS IN LATIN AMERICA

Charisma carries the trophy in leadership issues, business and otherwise. Yet charisma is not the only attribute that followers seek in a leader. The GLOBE project tells us that quite clearly. Furthermore, GLOBE data show that we can expect differences in leaders in the various cultures we are most concerned with. We suspected this already; after all, one can hardly conceive of a candidate like Argentine General Perón ever carrying a presidential election in the USA. What we did not know is how the enactment of charisma may affect the efficacy of a leader in a culture different from his or her own.

Because the enactment of charisma is culturally contingent, the policy of choosing people from one culture to lead business in another culture may be problematic. This is why we asked people of different cultures to express their preferences for working under different types of leaders, as perceived in a test construed to gauge the charisma of the sample leaders. Exploratory as this test may have been, it succeeded in illustrating the expected choices: first, everyone preferred to work with the leader who, in real life, has been chosen by his followers to lead them; second, the average workers, although not the elite, within a culture appeared to side with the leader best cut out to lead them—and those chosen were not foreigners. Third, local leaders chosen by foreigners to lead locals may be the worst type of leadership choice.

Representatives of Brazil's sizable agribusiness or retail sectors, eminently Brazilian and thus less permeable to the Davos culture of EMBA students at elite schools, were totally absent in the survey. This might explain the high commonality of preferences in choosing the owl-type leader. A broader coverage, encompassing more typically Brazilian sectors, is likely to increase the Brazilian adherence to the patriarchal cow-type leader—with occasional authoritarian overtones that perhaps render the image closer to that of a bull than a cow. In a further extension of this approach, one would also want to test the acceptability of a broader range of leader types, including women and alternative ethnic groups, as well as a more homogeneous set of video qualities. If the research were sufficiently funded, one would want to consider hiring actors to perform the leadership clips, for it is possible that executives will become increasingly shy of exposing themselves to a public vote.

For leadership grooming, business schools in Latin America may benefit from studying leadership styles in authentic national organizations such as soccer clubs, political parties, or samba schools. Another possibility is to study business sectors where northern managerial techniques have not yet penetrated, with the overall aim of discerning local decision-making styles as well as indigenous approaches to the process of selection, leading, evaluation, and rewards—particularly regarding team performance. It would also be important in any research endeavor to unearth the acceptable mechanisms for control of activities.

In Brazil, a likely arena for these studies would be, for example, the road and air transportation industries. In those environments, the web of personal relationships and allegiances—so prevalent in Latin American interaction—is even more pronounced and less subject to the intervention of foreign management techniques. The research agenda should seek to understand the implicit or moral contract established between the owner-boss and the employees of targeted national industries, and then strive to emulate that bond in a corporate setting and to model it in business schools. Determining what business practices are being applied in settings such as the transportation industry would require training anthropologists to spot telling signs or training business management students in anthropological techniques. The first alternative is perhaps more fruitful.

Whether leadership qualities are innate or acquired is immaterial to our discussion. It is obvious even in informal settings who the leaders are, especially in environments where there are few formal obstacles to prevent them from rising to relevance. Anybody who has set foot in a shantytown can attest that the young residents quickly learn the tricks necessary to attain objectives, teamwork among them. The problem lies in how to get the youngsters from where they are to positions where they can use their acute skills to make a positive difference.

Nonetheless, this research on matching leaders to followers makes some simple observations, such as the paucity of executive crossover between national and multinational organizations in Brazil. I argue that this is largely an issue of fit, which is corroborated by the responses of survey participants in the research project I conducted regarding leadership.

In all, the survey is a litmus test on leadership that has conveyed the importance of correct matching of leadership styles to national and corporate cultures. Yet if local leaders of multinationals continue to be chosen from among those who resemble their foreign owners, the selections are likely to be frustrating to the local workers and ultimately disappointing in terms of limited worker engagement, reduced productivity, and poor returns for investors.

This trend could also have political implications. For lack of an alternative and sufficient wisdom, as the U.S. managerial credo makes further inroads into domestic Latin American companies, national styles of social interaction will lose even more ground, creating additional frustration and disappointment. Some of this discontent has been manifested in the last decade of electoral outcomes in many Latin American countries. People are being managed as foreigners in their own lands, and they are telling us they do not like it.

Local leadership potential abounds, but it must be honed and directed in order to generate business and run day-to-day operations. If training occurs in environments where the management style does not reflect the local culture, we are unlikely to reap the best results from our local talent. People will not fit in comfortably, and the potential for alienation will be great.

CHAPTER 13

LITERARY PORTRAIT OF
A CULTURE: ARGENTINA

We should look at ourselves through our own eyes.

Noam Chomsky

I F WE, AS LATIN AMERICANS, are to look at ourselves with our own eyes, we need to be daring enough to break with the northern pattern and to seek solutions for ourselves with the tools that we already have at our disposal. This approach may not render neat statistical surveys, nor will it render internationally comparable results, but it should prove more useful for knowing ourselves than looking into a mirror that is known to distort our image.

Tools that are sound and readily available to apply to Latin American culture in a way that will help us understand how we relate to each other and to work—that sounds like a tall order. But, in fact, there is a lot out there. Much of it is solid and informative, but ancillary, such as the work of social scientists—which is bound to be contested by one school of thought or another. What we need is to use our social sciences training to shape instruments that portray us as the vast majority of people see us, for it is those shared images that both facilitate and constrain our interaction. To this end, widely accepted art, particularly literature and cinema, can be very useful. To the cultural portraits they help build, we can then add the interpretative structures proffered by the social sciences.

We need stories that focus on archetype-like constructs. These help define what people expect in order to form the landscape, the shared backdrop that orchestrates our behavior and facilitates communication and teamwork.

JUNGIAN STEPPING STONE

This topic deserves a short digression. Archetype is central to Jungian psychology, which argues that there are three levels of psyche: one conscious (the ego) and two unconscious (the personal and the collective). The personal unconscious would be that generally known as Freudian, referring to our repressed, personally acquired memories; the second, the collective unconscious, refers to the human congenital mental structure shared by all. This collective unconscious is what gives expression to preexisting forms that are repeated in various cultures and that Jung referred to as archetypes.[1]

Archetypes can unconsciously guide behavior on the strength of instinct, particularly when reality fits an archetype, as perhaps it does in the image/role of the South American gaucho, the Western cowboy, or the Mexican vaquero. For instance, the roughness embodied in the roles of the gaucho, cowboy, and vaquero is inherent to their function. What is not inherent to them is a propensity to band together, as seen in the gaucho *montoneras*, or mounted raiders.

The universal banding together of young males for intergroup aggression or warfare matches the Jungian archetype, if not the primordial image,[2] inasmuch as those aggressive expressions are mediated by archetypes that are biologically transmitted to the descendants of the triumphant males. This warring behavior is pervasive enough to characterize a universal psychological law.[3]

The mere existence of *montoneras* is not enough to characterize the gaucho as a Jungian archetype. But the fact that they existed, and that cowboys and vaqueros would also pack together for purposes of aggression, as depicted in endless accounts of American films of the Western genre, suggests that in the functional role of the gaucho we may encounter a pattern of behavior that is common enough across cultures as to reveal an underlying archetype. Whether the gaucho can be construed with the force of an archetype is not central to my argument; what is central is that the received gaucho story carries significant weight in Argentina as to provide a backdrop for the behavior of males in Argentina. This may be interpreted by some to reveal an underlying archetype, bolstered by

the legendary figures of the American West and Mexican haciendas, but I will
leave such musings to those who are better equipped to expound on them.

CAN LITERATURE REVEAL MANAGERIAL
TRAITS OF A PEOPLE?

Literature is unreliable as a documentary source, but it is useful as a bellwether
of market demand. It cannot substitute journalistic or historical sources for
evidence of past attitudes or styles, yet when a novel is widely accepted, it may
appropriately answer relevant questions, such as, What does it say about its
readers at the time? What does it say about the historical setting, about the
web of people's attitudes? In this way, the novel is revealing both as a glimpse
of the world at a given historical juncture and regarding the needs it may have
fulfilled among its readers.

As James Smith Allen has reflected, "Because literature was recreated by
historical audiences, the world view expressed by the novel may well involve
the beliefs of the readers themselves, who were the most enthusiastic about a
particular work."[4]

A widely accepted novel reveals a collective bond, whether unconscious or
crafted, between author and reader, and it is also telling of public demand. In
accepting this dialectical relationship between the novel and its audience as a
system pregnant with sociological information, we concede that a novel's complexity cannot be reduced to its plot, nor its ideology to what the novel's characters may be asked to voice. Wolfgang Iser takes this point further, giving the
reader an active writing role in the reading of accepted fiction, for it is the reader
who reads meaning into the author's allusions in the text.[5]

Moving the onus of significance from the text to the literary system re-
moves the focus from the author or publisher and places it on the public, with
its own system of beliefs and needs and its own interpretation of the work. We
can thus retrieve information from the past as reflected in its literary activity—
writing, publishing, reading, and literary criticism—as well as through literary
pieces themselves. By endorsing an approach to history via the literary system,
we can also draw sociological meaning from art, for fiction reveals a collective
mentality.[6]

It is this "public's imagery" that Beatriz Sarlo attempted to reveal in her
interpretation of serial romantic literature published weekly in Buenos Aires,

mostly between 1917 and 1925.[7] The focus of her comments can be taken to be a genre, described as containing "certain mythic structure, formed in a core of narrative meaning found in those works that can be readily discernible as related and pertaining to a group."[8] The romance genre, in particular, provides the arena in which to reveal "mythical, allegorical, and symbolist forms" that pervade the literary tradition of a country. The American Western genre is defined by a symbolic landscape, a frontier between civilization and wilderness, and a lonely hero.[9] In Argentina, this landscape was the Pampa, the frontier that was described in similar terms by Sarmiento with his reference to "civilization or barbarism," and the lonely hero turns out to be Martin Fierro. That literary mark in the country's history offers a rich source of meaning that allows society to reexamine itself even after the myths have faded away. Sarlo put it this way: "When the myths of a traditional society have lost their stronghold on the present, with their literary footprints one can build an ideal model on whose terms society can reflect upon itself."[10] It is on this strength of the meaning of a traditional myth that I will base my attempt to interpret the leadership relevance of Martin Fierro.

WHAT CAN MARTIN FIERRO TELL US ABOUT ARGENTINA?

No society can be reduced to one iconic figure. Yet the prevalence of Martin Fierro in Argentina calls for further reflection. What did—or, indeed, does— Martin Fierro mean to Argentines?

In Chapters 6 and 7 I have drawn attention to the fact that both the U.S. and Argentine societies have produced similar functional heroic characters. While in America he is called a cowboy, in Argentina (as well as in Uruguay and southern Brazil) this character is generically referred to as a gaucho.[11]

Experimental psychology begins to empirically test Jungian archetype theory by seeking to elucidate whether innate human mental structures establish function and inherent knowledge. If this were so, folk heroes would find immediate general appeal as the expressions of a people's collective functional desire for a hero with shared characteristics. The existence of innate structures would underscore the strength of archetype theory, in that it would provide a scientific basis to explain the recurrence of myths and folktales in different cultural settings.[12] In Argentina this heroic character is epitomized by Martin Fierro.

In 1872, shortly after the time when Sarmiento was asking President Mitre to "spare no gaucho blood in wiping this barbarian out of Argentina," José Hernández produced the epic rhymed poem, "Martin Fierro," the main character of which was Hernández's own homage to a style of being Argentine at a time when Europeans were being invited to populate the hinterland. And, yes, José Hernández was a Rosas sympathizer (see Chapter 7 for the implications of this alliance).

The gaucho was the frontiersman in an unfenced, cattle-rearing Argentina. The skills then in high demand in the rural zone were horse riding and shifting cattle herds from one place to another. "Gaucho" was the generic name of the individuals who provided these services, very much like the cowboy of the American West, except that in Argentina the frontier also meant greater integration with Indians. The gaucho's mixed ancestry testifies to this miscegenation while also distancing him from the more European-centered urban landscapes and styles. Urban disdain for the gaucho was frequently expressed in allusions to his barbarism. Indeed, roughness was a gaucho trait, paramount to building skills that spanned physical strength, courage, and decisiveness. These attributes and others, such as excelling in horse riding, matched the requirements of life in the hinterland of Argentina as opposed to its cities.[13] Civilization, in Sarmiento's sense, had little use for the gaucho, particularly because the gaucho's upbringing and sheer inclination made him more likely to fall prey to the sway of regional caudillos of a despotic bent, such as Rosas, than to the arguments of the educated urban elite. Yet the urban elite made use of the gaucho, too, whether in wars against the Indians or in campaigns to secure the frontiers. Gauchos were drafted in great numbers, occasionally forcibly so, causing substantial grief to their families.

José Hernández crafted his poem to tell the story of a fictional gaucho, Martin Fierro, who, although married and a father, was drafted to a remote outpost to secure the frontier. While there, he was forced to work for the commander of the frontier garrison, and when he finally managed to desert the army to return home he finds no family and his house destroyed. Subsequently, an errant Martin Fierro finds some consolation in rural bars, where he will promptly respond to challenges, or lead them. In a knife fight he kills a man and is forced to remain at large. A death occurs in another duel, and there are hints of other deaths. Fierro becomes a fugitive of justice as well as a deserter of the army. Cruz, one of the assailants in a raid to capture him, switches sides in admiration of the courage with which Fierro fights for his freedom. Both Fierro and Cruz retreat to an Indian camp, far from civilization. This reversal of loyalties and protection of the underdog against authority had already caught Darwin's attention.[14]

The preceding is a perhaps unfair rendition of a poem that promptly met widespread acceptance in 1872, selling nearly fifty thousand copies in bookstores and rural bars. Those who could not read knew the poem through recitings at bars, where the regional dialect in rhyme, in which the poem was written, was occasionally accompanied by guitar players. Seven years later, Hernández wrote a closing poem, allowing Cruz to die in an epidemic and reintegrating Fierro to the frontier. Fierro returns, finds his estranged children, and enters into a showdown with the brother of the first man he had killed in a duel. This showdown no longer takes the form of a knife fight but rather that of a challenge in the rhyming, poetic improvisation called *payada*. In this sense, Fierro defeats both black brothers, the first in a duel, through superior fighting resources, and the second by means of a *payada*, allegedly through superior intellectual resources.

In subsequent editions, both poems, "La Ida" and "La Vuelta" ("The Departure" and "The Return"), were published together. In "The Return," Hernández's Fierro is a gaucho with cleaner fingernails. In a way, Fierro became wiser and mutated into something of a Sarmientine gaucho, as a mocking Borges would have it. Yet, to Martin Fierro's sympathizers, this made no difference at the time. Fierro was a hero who did not deserve to die in an Indian campsite, which was the sentiment that gave rise to the poem's sequel.

For all its merits, it is hard to believe that "Martin Fierro" would have met with the acceptance it did were it not for the fact that it played to the uneasiness with which Argentina, and Buenos Aires in particular, were becoming cosmopolitan. This meant blending in the myriad foreigners arriving to its shores and fencing the landscape to improve cattle herds and make way for agriculture. The resulting impetus was to retire the gaucho, a deeply disturbing notion to the new cauldron of people. The poem's main character, Martin Fierro, offered coalescence to a society in transition and in search of an identity. Yet much of the political significance of "Martin Fierro" came later, under the orgiastic pen of Leopoldo Lugones, who elevated the poem to its current prominence as the epitome of Argentine nationality. By Lugones' time, however, the gaucho had lost its subversive potential.

In its own time, half a century before Lugones, "Martin Fierro" espoused the indictment of the elite, those who would outlaw a family man, subject him to the ignominy of forced labor, and offer him no justice. That Fierro turned into an arrogant brigand could be attributed to his deprivation of dignity by elitist authorities. What were subsumed were Martin Fierro's virtues: love of freedom, a man's recourse to dignity and courage, which is to be defended with one's life if necessary. In that sense, Hernández's poem offered the *criollo* a local version of the medieval Spanish literary tradition, complete with a wandering cavalier and duel.

By Lugones' time, Martin Fierro had been cleaned up; only his virtues remained vivid in the imagery of Argentina. By then there were no gauchos left. The land had been fenced with barbed wire and the nomadic gaucho had been emasculated into a peon. This is how, from an urban perspective, someone who was essentially a transgressor, a killer, a fugitive of justice, a drunkard, and a hoodlum became a national hero.

THE MAKING OF A LEGEND AND A BRAND

The fact that Martin Fierro became a national identitary figure conferred nationwide acceptability to the twentieth-century gaucho that he had lacked in Sarmiento's time. Although the gaucho has been downgraded into a peon, cattle ranching and its derivatives—including tanneries, leather goods, and barbecue houses—are prominent on the urban scene still today. Martin Fierro helped the gaucho become a brand with marketing appeal. *Nobleza Gaucha (Gaucho Nobility)* was Argentina's first film success (1915). Shown in over twenty theaters simultaneously as well as abroad, its musical script was sold separately and by 1922 it had inspired a tango by the renowned composer Francisco Canaro. A popular yerba maté was also packaged under the same brand name. *Nobleza Gaucha* was remade in 1937, and *Martin Fierro*, the film, came in 1968. The gaucho is even the protagonist of a widely read comic strip, "Inodoro Pereyra." Pereyra is aided by a firmly grounded wife, Eulogia, and faithfully accompanied by his dog, Mendieta. Inodoro plays the frontiersman forever struggling to secure traditions from foreign onslaught. For example, Inodoro Pereyra receives a weakened Clar (*sic*) Kent, who flees when he mistakes for kryptonite Inodoro's green-colored tea. Thus, the sipping of yerba maté, a quintessentially national tradition and a legacy of the Guaraní Indians, could send the Yankee Superman flying.[15]

As the gaucho was becoming a brand, several authors were turning him into a legend. We have seen how Sarmiento victimized the gaucho in *Facundo* (1845) and elsewhere—although even in Sarmiento we found redeeming features of the gaucho. We have also seen how José Hernández cast the gaucho under a kinder light in "Martin Fierro" (1872 and 1879). Half a century later, Argentina's best writers were still gravitating around the gaucho, helping to frame a legend focused on Martin Fierro. Leopoldo Lugones (National Literary Award, 1926) excelled in his regionalist writings, as in *El Payador* (1916), effectively canonizing Martin Fierro.[16] Jorge Luis Borges' first literary steps were also regionalist in their essence and met with immediate acclaim. Ricardo Güiraldes, only a few years Borges' senior, had a more laborious path toward recognition, meeting overwhelming acclaim only with a revised gaucho protagonist, *Don Segundo Sombra* (1926).[17]

Don Segundo Sombra, a strong, wise gaucho, is a mentor to young Fabio. Kiplingesque in its allusions to *Kim, Don Segundo Sombra* offers a savvier gaucho whom experience has taught to be selective in meeting unwarranted challenges. There is no lack of courage in *Don Segundo Sombra,* but rather a renewed respect for life, grounded in Güiraldes' own firsthand experience with Hinduism and other related oriental spiritual avenues.

Yvonne Bordelois has suggested variations of the perspectives of both Güiraldes and Borges regarding Martin Fierro's initial duel with Moreno, which leads to Moreno's death and to Fierro becoming a fugitive of justice. That passage in "Martin Fierro" is uniquely brutal, both in its racism and its cruelty.[18] It is a passage that Borges suggests should be read with horror rather than applauded. In Güiraldes' *Don Segundo Sombra*, the protagonist dismisses rather than accepts a similar challenge. To Borges, more adept at portraying knife fights that are all the more dramatic for their brevity, the dismissal of an invitation to a duel by Don Segundo Sombra, which so captivates the young Fabio, is both unrealistic and frustrating. Borges would later tell of lending the book *Don Segundo Sombra* to an urban swaggerer (*guapo*) who, in frustration, returned the novel to Borges, for he saw little action in it.[19]

Borges rewrote the duel passage in his own *El Sur* (*The South,* 1953), in which Dahlman, an Anglo-Argentine librarian like Borges, moves to "the South," where he accepts a challenge to an impossible duel in which he predictably dies. In Borges' view, Dahlman threw down the gauntlet in a challenge to the environment merely by penetrating a barbaric region that operated by a different set of rules.[20]

We thus have three literary renditions of similar challenges: in the first version, Martin Fierro, amid racial slurs, horrendously knives an opponent whose languid corpse he throws against a fence, to bleed to death. In the second version, Don Segundo Sombra dismisses the challenge made by a drunken gaucho. And in the third version, Borges sends a semiforeigner to a probable death, the outcome of which is accelerated by the acceptance of a challenge. Only in Don Segundo Sombra's comparable episode are no knives drawn, although, later, in Chapter 23, they will be.

Despite the continuous redrawing of the image of the gaucho, a collective Argentine mentality remains focused on some image of the gaucho whose traits we can attempt to name. What values did Martin Fierro portray that earned him such great acceptance in the 1870s and 1880s and that are still cherished a century and a half later? (See Table 13.1 for a rendition of those attributes.)

One must admit that, despite the literary effort invested in turning Martin Fierro into a hero, he is hardly the type likely to help build a fair, trusting society. Much of what is found in "Martin Fierro," particularly characters such as the old man Viejo Vizcacha, stem from the Spanish picaresque tradition of

TABLE 13.1 Author's classification of gaucho adjectives present in Bordelois's *Un Triángulo Crucial*

Character Traits	The Gaucho
Posture, Appearance	Proud, strong, noble, free, bonded with nature, functionally dressed, armed
Attitude	Challenging, masculine, rough, chivalrous, susceptible, luxurious, resolute
Behavior	Violent, revengeful, loyal, spiteful, courageous, adventurous, generous, insubordinate, friendly
Social navigation	Freedom seeking, independent, superstitious, individualist, clannish
Inspires	Respect, fear, nostalgia, support for the underdog

SOURCE: Ivonne Bordelois, *Un Triángulo Crucial: Borges, Güiraldes y Lugones* (A Crucial Triangle: Borges, Güiraldes and Lugones) (Buenos Aires: Eudeba, 1999), 94–95.

Lazarillo de Tormes (Burgos, 1554?), for example. However, whereas in that genre the protagonist endures humiliation, the Argentine protagonist becomes megalomaniacal, finding no obstacle to his sagacity. Failure, when it happens, can be conveniently blamed on a third party.[21]

COULD ALTERNATIVE ARCHETYPES HAVE PREVAILED?

We have seen that the gaucho was promoted to an iconic figure through a literary canonization by Lugones, supported by Borges, and complemented by Güiraldes. All three led a literary movement that contributed to shape the image of the gaucho with values that became identitary values for Argentines inasmuch as they represent an Argentine archetype.

However, by the turn of the nineteenth century, and despite the wide acceptance of the poem "Martin Fierro," the gaucho was still synonymous with a brute.[22] Somewhere along the line, the gaucho image was turned on its head. The gaucho continued to be a brute, but his brutality was now commendable, even turned into an art, where a defiant life was played in staccato. The reification of the gaucho can be attributed largely to the nationalist Lugones, the same Lugones who sided with the political right to oust from the presidency of Argentina the son of an illiterate Basque immigrant, President Yrigoyen (see Chapter 7).

President Yrigoyen was far from a gaucho. It could well be that the twentieth-century cultural history of Argentina was written mostly by the victors on Lugones' side, leaving little chance for the surfacing of alternative iconic styles. It is also possible that Argentines, left to their own devices, would once more choose to vote into office a man like Yrigoyen, whose reclusive style earned him the nickname of Pelado, an allusion to a large armadillo that hides in deeply dug burrows. However, that has not happened.

Borges' politics were as sinuous as those of Lugones, but his artistic flirting with knife fights may have many roots. His focus can be attributed to his military family tradition or to a catharsis, dramatizing his victory over the school bullies who repeatedly beat the frail Borges to the ground, but not to his sinuous politics; after all, Borges despised Lugones and was a supporter of Yrigoyen at the time Yrigoyen was ousted. But the truth is that Borges' writing did not contribute to projecting a more palatable gaucho. That was the work of the proverbially gentle Güiraldes, through Don Segundo Sombra.

But the acceptance of Güiraldes' gaucho style seems to have been short lived, and Güiraldes himself died young, in 1927, only a year after the publication of *Don Segundo Sombra*. Prior to this publication, Güiraldes had met with little recognition and thus had limited influence in spearheading an alternative gaucho style.

The fact that Don Segundo Sombra has faded away without becoming a symbol, as Martin Fierro did, and that Argentines have had, not many, but nonetheless a few chances to vote in the last century without ever again favoring a leader so far removed from the gaucho style as Yrigoyen was, may mean that the coarse gaucho Martin Fierro was destined to become the archetypical Argentine after all.

In terms of the archetypical behavior, the aforementioned resolution and susceptibility led to violent outcomes, hence the frequent literary allusions to knife fights that end in the death of one of the contenders. The gaucho is also spiteful, holding long-lived grudges, and as cunning as an animal waiting to pounce. Living on the edge of a knife, the gaucho is highly attuned to nature, its magic and its flow. Always on the move, he can only hold on to little and will gladly share what he has with those he trusts. That trust is not offered but rather earned through respect, as in Cruz's respect for Martin Fierro's courage when fighting for his life. That trust bonds men into dyads—three is one too many—but looser and shorter-lived alliances may lead to the Facundo Quiroga type of group formation, as seen in the *montoneras*. Although nature and the gaucho's lifestyle offer him little structural support, the gaucho is a free man, uncomfortable with hierarchy. Sarmiento has said about Facundo that he is a volcano waiting to explode.[23]

THE GAUCHO'S DRIFT TO THE URBAN SCENE

Don Segundo Sombra became a film in 1969, a year after *Martin Fierro*, and the gaucho legend continues very much alive. But gauchos are nowhere to be seen except on screen. These gauchos reflect the imagery of Argentines; yet what gaucho values have actually filtered through to the Argentine people of the twenty-first century, and for how much longer will these be present?

For gaucho values to disappear completely, the functional gaucho would need to cease to exist. That will not happen readily, for Argentina's rural life will remain strong for a long time to come. The diet of the typical Argentine in 2005 included almost four times as much beef as that of a European and almost 50 percent more than the diet of an American.[24] Despite eating so much meat, Argentina cannot consume all of the beef it produces and is also one of the world's prominent exporters of prime beef. Argentina still depends on agriculture for over 50 percent of its merchandise exports. It is unlikely that the significance of agriculture will fall soon enough to depreciate the values inherited from a time when agriculture was more central. Rural sector imagery will continue to play a major role in Argentine culture, though not necessarily in the image of the gaucho. Some drift has already occurred.

Beatriz Sarlo believes that Jorge Luis Borges preyed on the cherishable attributes of Martin Fierro and transferred those virtues to the urban landscape in the attitudes of the urban swaggerer (*guapo*).[25] While this may have been a winning literary strategy, seeking a new setting for an old archetypical figure, it in fact piggybacks on the widespread acceptance of the original archetype. A modern consequence of this is the success of urban detective stories, such as those of Ricardo Piglia, which nonetheless bow to Argentina's rich history and blend of literary genres.[26]

Yet for management purposes it makes little difference whether Argentine attitudes toward leadership derive from a long-dead gaucho or an urban *guapo*. What concerns us is that twentieth-century trends seem to have extended the life of the array of values originally associated with the gaucho, and that these values will thrive well into the twenty-first century. This should settle the issue of the duration of the gaucho archetype: it appears that it will be with us for a long time to come. The pattern of Argentine male behavior that this archetype induces is a mixed blessing, however, because while it facilitates teamwork by providing a tacit shared understanding, it also constrains a departure from the script. Argentine leadership style boils down to a highly choreographed tango. I will apply this approach to some examples.

THE LEADERSHIP ENACTMENT OF THE ARCHETYPE

This spiteful penchant for adventure, this degree of independence—including independence of mind as to the opinions or rights of others—and this disposition for resolutely joining forces on short notice to take revenge at knifepoint could have led Argentina to take the Falkland (Malvinas) Islands from British hands in 1982. From the point of view of an analysis of leaders and followers, it is not relevant to delve into the domestic and international scenarios that led to that war. What interests us here is the fact that those scenarios expressed themselves in the way they did, in a brief, dramatic showdown with the resulting demise of the challenger, as in a knife fight. This was a "war of honor unsupported by economic interest."[27]

Just about everything was wrong with the invasion of the Falklands (Malvinas), but the Argentines went ahead with an ill-planned adventure nonetheless. In hindsight, it seems that the move was a miscalculation on the part of the Argentine armed forces, as would befit an adventure.[28] Yet it was not only the repressive Argentine government that backed the invasion; although led by the government, it was collective enough to merit reflection. In many ways, this war was a gaucho—even a *montonera*—movement, at least in the lack of preparedness and planning that characterized the Argentine advance on the islands. Moreover, the invasion mostly involved holding civilians at gunpoint, symbolic of the actions of a *montonera*. Lastly, it was also a war of honor, to retrieve the islands that were seen as snatched away by Britain over a century earlier. Honor was involved to such a degree that, twenty years later, more Argentine veterans of the scuffle may have committed suicide than died fighting on the islands they set out to retrieve.[29] This tragic outcome could mean that the veterans, once rapturous in a flight of folly for self-respect, could never adjust back to the grim reality of defeat in an unheroic existence. So unfitting of a gaucho, to lose all except his life! Suicide settles matters, in order for the gaucho ethic to prevail.

Of course, the business world is less dramatic. But it is this autonomous, individualistic, unique, and independent nature expressed by the Argentine war leaders that portrays precisely the elements characterizing Argentine business leaders in the GLOBE project. Alas, in that study, it is the Argentine business leaders who stand out in the autonomy dimension as the most autonomous—even more so than those of Europe, as portrayed by England, Spain, Italy, and Portugal, or those in the rest of the Americas, as portrayed by the United States, Brazil, and Mexico. The Argentine leader is seen as being "out there," leading on his own, asking no questions, as if the pack had no alternative but to follow.[30]

I came across an Argentine general manager who convincingly illustrated the stereotype, which is nowhere less appropriate than in neighboring Brazil.

The Brazilian directors of a multinational, who were accustomed to being consulted on major decisions, were left constantly wondering what was going on in the Argentine manager's mind, who—to compound matters—was not particularly well versed on Brazilian issues. He asked no questions, or when he did ask he cut the answers short, and he made every decision on his own. Against the explicit advice of collaborators, he made important appointments that soon proved obviously wrong. He also took too long to recognize turf wars when they happened, and he was perceived to impart disciplinary sanctions unfairly.

In another situation, the only Argentine in an MBA course in São Paulo also stood out from the others when responding to the autonomy dimension of the GLOBE project. All of the Brazilian students stressed issues such as team integration more than the Argentine manager. But it was in the autonomy dimension, where leadership traits stress attributes such as independence, individuality, and uniqueness, where the student from Argentina scored way above his Brazilian colleagues.[31]

Was not this Argentine MBA student simply expressing the leadership attributes of a gaucho? Of course, suicide following dishonor is not acceptable in Western business ethics. Aspects of the gaucho style are remnants of another era. However, its flair survives and is transmitted through the Martin Fierro that lives in all Argentine males, because the poem was mandatory reading when they were at school, as a shared history. This shared history provides the backdrop that both builds expectations and facilitates communication, while also constraining options. An Argentine leader will have a lot of explaining to do if he wishes to take a stance different than what Martin Fierro would do under comparable circumstances. Indeed, the gaucho legacy is not always ineffective. The resolute, defiant gaucho stance may pay off, particularly as in a bluff. Take, for example, the case of the Argentine foreign debt renegotiation led by President Néstor Kirchner in 2005. Over 75 percent of international creditors accepted a substantial haircut in lieu of the president's "or else" clause, and the renegotiation was widely seen as a victory for President Kirchner. A year earlier, the parallelism between the president's dogged stance and a knife duel had been noted by a journalist of *The Economist*.[32]

Could a Brazilian president have been as successful as Kirchner? It is unlikely, for Brazilians lack the "stubbornly resolute" image of the Argentine, as portrayed in Martin Fierro and as enacted in the war over the Falklands. Most certainly, Brazilians would never have invaded the Malvinas. This is a strong assertion, but one that is backed by Brazilian diplomatic behavior regarding the dispute over fluvial islands with Paraguay. That dispute was with a much weaker neighbor over islands in the boundary river Paraná, which only emerge during the dry season. Brazilians proposed to submerge the islands in the largest-ever man-made reservoir that would be the result of the proposed world's largest hydropower dam, Itaipú. The dam was built, the resulting hydropower was split with Paraguay, and the disputed islands were never to be seen again. If the contrasting stances regarding the resolution of a dispute over islands do not show a difference in the character of these two people— Argentines and Brazilians—what does?[33]

Would an Argentine leader thus be effective only when leading other Argentines or bluffing? Certainly not. Provided the Argentine-style leader is capable of developing and communicating a vision, this style may be very effective in change management situations when strong and quick-paced autonomous leadership may be more in demand. In other situations of a more routine nature, an Argentine-style leader of non-Argentines may need more coaching and monitoring in order not to alienate his or her followers, particularly in Brazil.

LIMITATIONS OF THE LITERARY APPROACH

Literature and other cultural expressions, such as cinema, may help us better understand the social constraints that shape behavior, such as that of the main character in "Martin Fierro." This analysis may even help us understand the aftermath of situations that, like the war over the Falklands or the debt renegotiation, were not part of the Martin Fierro story. Veterans of the short-lived war were asked to surrender and back down. In Martin Fierro's terms, they lost face—they were dishonored—and they could not live with that. Yet it is just that dramatic style that, in business, lends such persuasive strength to a bluff, as in President Kirchner's debt renegotiation of 2005.

There is also the question of how well a nineteenth-century iconic figure can condition today's behavior. Theodore Zeldin concedes that it is impossible to represent a people through individual characters, which was cause for frustration in his own book *The French*, in which he resolves that there is no such thing as "the French" but that there are sixty million minorities of

Frenchmen.[34] Zeldin's challenge is hard to contest. My aim, however, was not to characterize Argentines but rather the iconic figure of Martin Fierro. In doing so, I attempted to point out his essential traits, for those seemed to be the reflected image that Lugones believed to be so relevant to the male population of Argentina as to be emulated. Otherwise, it would be difficult to understand why Martin Fierro continues to permeate Argentine urban literature during the twentieth century. Martin Fierro's traits meet a functional necessity, which is what legitimizes the icon.

The suggested literary approach leaves many modern questions unanswered, even significant ones such as the role of women in business today or even whether a myth can capture all the diversity in a people; and it may not satisfactorily answer those questions, considering the behavior of contemporary males. In order to attain broader literary guidance we would need to widen the literary scope considerably. I believe I have made the point that within the reach of Latin American scholars there are alternatives to the expensive statistical route that has served us so poorly.

SUMMING UP: IS LITERARY ANALYSIS RELEVANT TO THE REST OF THE WORLD?

Looking at ourselves with our own eyes, seeking meaning in our cultural expressions, ought to provide something others can make use of as well. In this section, I attempt to translate what we have learned of the gaucho Martin Fierro as an iconic expression of Argentines to suggest ways in which research into the cross-cultural field could be enriched by using what we readily have at hand, like literature, rather than stubbornly treading a comparative statistical path that is too expensive for our research muscle, which has allowed little expression to the Latin American behavioral style and whose capacity to enlighten matters seems to have reached diminishing returns.

I have argued that the archetypical attitudes of a gaucho are that he has a challenging stance, typical of a man who will hold his ground. He is also assertive, as becomes an irrepressible masculinity, also apparent in his chivalry. Not all is charming, however; the gaucho is cunningly spiteful and will take revenge at the appropriate moment. He is also susceptible, responding in kind to any perceived challenge, even before determining whether a challenge was intended. Consequently, his response is resolute, perhaps to the point of leaving little wiggle room for reconciliation. All is life or death with the gaucho. We have also seen that these traits have migrated to the urban scene to dress the swaggerer (*guapo*), who is "all mouth and trousers." Yes, the gaucho is high on the masculine side of Hofstede's dimensions, particularly on account of his assertiveness and resolute stance.

Obviously, the gaucho is far from averse to uncertainty. He bets his life in just about any move he makes, whether against an animal or another human being. He literally lives on a knife's edge. Thus, in Hofstede's dimensions, the gaucho does not shun uncertainty; much to the contrary, he blends into it.

Because of the gaucho's penchant for freedom and independence and because of his travails with hierarchy, an Argentine's patience with high power distance ought to be rather low. Through Martin Fierro we have also become acquainted with the gaucho's fierce disposition to fight alone. What was Martin Fierro fighting for? Not for justice, nor for the independence of colonialists, nor for anything of the sort. He was fighting for dignity, for self-respect. Martin Fierro was not an individualist in the American sense: equal in the eyes of the law. He is an individual in the Latin American sense; he believes he is unique. He will not hesitate in being unfair, and he will use any trick necessary to ensure his survival. To his peers, his maneuverings will not be seen as character flaws but rather as expressions of his resourcefulness—as in Maradona's convocation of the "hand of God" in scoring a goal against England.[35] These traits are far from egalitarian.

Martin Fierro is a Latin American individualist in the sense that he claims his right to uniqueness, and he differs from the North American individual in that his unbounded freedom allows for little patience with structure and hierarchy. There is a significant difference from North to South in the meaning of individualism, as already discussed in Chapter 9. To a North American, individualism connotes equality; to a Latin American, it connotes uniqueness. Gauchos may even temporarily group together for aggressive purposes, and the result may be called a *montonera* attack, but his freedom orientation will limit the life even of the *montonera*. There is no such thing as an old gaucho, let alone any reference to a rest home for gauchos. Like MacArthur's old soldiers, the gaucho fades away alone; he is not a collectivist.

There is no role for women either. The gaucho has no string to lead him out of the labyrinth of his own psychological enclosure. He can rely only on his knife. Women are eclipsed and excluded from Martin Fierro.[36] There is no couple; when there is, the stage is reserved for the man, who shares it with no one. Without a mother to guide the child to the gaucho's soft underbelly, the child is prone to develop tyrannical, omnipotent traits to overcome his own vulnerability. Kill first or be killed. All men are the gaucho's Minotaur.[37] The gaucho does not fit well into the four-dimensional Hofstede grid except at its extremes of high individualism, low power distance, high masculinity, and low aversion to uncertainty.

CHAPTER 14

LITERARY PORTRAIT OF A CULTURE: BRAZIL

B RAZIL IS LARGE by just about any measure. In terms of area, it is three times larger than Argentina, four times larger than Mexico, and as large as the United States before the purchase of Alaska. Because Brazil is so big, it is also diverse, be it from the point of view of climate, scenery, or the population dispersion.

Brazil has no sole literary icon like Martin Fierro. Perhaps this is due to its greater diversity stemming from its size. Perhaps it is also because Brazil retained an imperial figurehead until about the time Martin Fierro was being disseminated, freeing Brazil from the need for a construed national coalescing icon beyond that provided by an emperor, or the recent memory of one. Despite Brazil's lack of a unique national literary icon, we will see in this chapter that considerable effort has been devoted to the issue of Brazilian national character, and that Brazilian literature provides us with significant clues to national traits.

Because so many Brazilians have contributed work to the subject, we may well reflect on what sets Brazilians apart in so many ways. In addition, potential managers of Brazilians, foreign or not, are well advised to study how and to what degree Brazilians are different, in order to understand why management of people in Brazil should follow a course of its own. For, in their uniqueness, Brazilians reveal what makes them tick—what leads them to engagement, what prompts them to trust others and to respond to incentives aimed at individuals, how they work in teams, and how they respond to different leadership styles. In this chapter, I will address some of these issues within the scope of a literary approach to Brazilian temperament and the ways it can be appraised by means of characters of novels that have won wide acceptance among Brazilians. I will then close the chapter with an application of the literary evidence of Brazilian character traits.

BRAZILIAN ROOTS

If the initial endowment, of people and environment, may provide a significant imprint to a culture, even shaping its initial evolution, as time goes by, one should expect culture to evolve relatively independently from the initial formula, breaking away from path dependence.

At first, the environment must have been a strong determinant of attitudes, at least through self-selection: Brazil was only for the most persevering. While British colonizers in North America encountered a gentle two hundred miles of Atlantic plains just beyond the shore, Brazil, in contrast, presented a steep massif (great escarpment), often up to a mile high and seldom more than three miles from the beach—sometimes much closer. The same escarpment is responsible for the scarcity of navigable rivers flowing west to east in Brazil and for the scarcity of natural harbors.

Penetration into Brazil was to be done vertically. Climbing was prominent in the colonizers' first experience in the New World. Also, the heat and humidity made a lasting first impression, prompting one member of the Magalhães expedition, Antonio Pigafetta, to record nothing else besides the excessive heat during their stay in Rio de Janeiro.[1]

Soon enough, the *mestiço* Portuguese blended with the native women and later with the Negro women, and their offspring blended with all. Subsequently, the great migrations from southern Europe during the nineteenth century offset somewhat the impact of the non-European stock, but not by much, giving rise to the Brazilian blend of today—more "European" toward the temperate southern zones and up to 50 percent native Indian in the North, with African inputs stronger along the middle Atlantic coast of Brazil, where the plantation economy was predominant. Due to both the various blends and the wide geographical dispersion, there is no such thing today as a uniform Brazilian people in terms of shape and color. On cultural terms it may be less so, although harder to assess.

WHY THE DIFFERENCES?

Gilberto Freyre believes that the Portuguese on the eve of colonizing Brazil were emerging from centuries of adventure, either by influence of the English and French crusaders resting on their way to the Holy Land, or by their own explorations and commerce with Asia and Africa. Also, Jewish traders were plentiful in Lisbon, as were many other peoples engaged in trade and money-lending. None of these activities would endorse slow-paced agriculture or the manual arts, nor would they produce the most useful stock for colonizing Brazil.

The search for adventure had not permeated the whole of Portugal. The traditional old-world Portuguese love of agriculture was kept alive by the likes of the Duarte Coelhos and the Albuquerques, along with much of the North Atlantic region. These inhabitants were reputed, by the good-natured port dwellers, to be dim-witted but hardworking, honest and loyal, religious—also content, in a provincial way—and musically oriented.[2] Much of Brazil's original settlers and sugarcane developers derived from northern Portugal.

Furthermore, as the Portuguese advanced into Brazil, they did so after centuries of contact with dark-skinned people of a higher standing and learning, namely, the Moors. A cultural familiarity with the "enchanted Moorish lady" (*a moura encantada*) may have oriented the collective unconscious of the Portuguese settlers in Brazil as well as their attitudes toward the native American women.[3] Moreover, intimacy with the Moorish social organization had familiarized the Portuguese with the Moorish concept of beauty in plump, dark-skinned women and with concubinage, if not with outright polygamy,[4] in addition to the concept of household slaves—kept, perhaps, like a poor relative would be. This is how one of the aforementioned Albuquerques would come to live in Brazil with a native lady whom he had baptized with the half-Christian name of Maria do Espírito Santo Arco-Verde (roughly translated as "Mary of the Green Bow Holy Spirit"), with whom he had eight of the total twenty-four children he is known to have fathered.

The Portuguese might have picked up greater literacy rates and a more scientific inclination than they did, but their limited intellectual pursuits were compensated for by their commercial acumen and trading skills, which introduced Europe to a sizable number of staples such as tea, sugar, and rice, along with the parasol and the umbrella, the palanquin, porcelain, and oriental rugs, which were first found on European soil in only the best shops of Lisbon during the sixteenth and seventeenth centuries. It was also the Portuguese who introduced cotton—and underclothes—and the habit of daily bathing into Europe, both of which substantially improved European hygiene. Intellectual pursuits are not everything; the Portuguese had what it took to make them rich: commercial acumen and an audacity that was second to none in Europe. The Portuguese, after all, became traders over the course of exploring the African coast for almost ninety years. At the time, that required almost four generations of courageous exploring stamina.

If the Spanish discovered the New World, then it was the Portuguese who inaugurated modern international trade. Its yield justified the risks and remained high enough as to delay the colonization of Brazil until Dutch commercial expansion eroded the attractiveness of Asian trade to the Portuguese.

Those were the times, and thus were expressions of the Portuguese adventurers. What, then, is the lasting Portuguese legacy in Brazil in terms of characteristics of the Brazilian people? Fernando de Azevedo has suggested that certain traits of the Brazilian character, such as sadness, unhurriedness, and sensuality are African in origin, just as the traits of nomadism and a spirit of adventure are aboriginal in origin.[5] Yet what traits can be considered natural of a people when observed under abnormal circumstances? Joaquim Nabuco has stated that there was nothing inherently sad about the Negro, nor the native, except for their enslavement. Humberto de Campos would have nothing of the alleged sadness of the Brazilian, for the Portuguese was jovial and communicative and the aboriginal was no less festive—indeed, his feasts might last days, if not weeks. Moreover, the native's alleged taciturnity, according to Campos, is the trait of a hunter.[6] Campos, following Nabuco's stance, believed that the aborigines' only sadness stemmed from confronting their own destiny and from the sense of inferiority that the situation imposed.

Paulo Prado came up with what he believed were two of the main characteristics of the Brazilian people: sensuality and envy. Sensuality borne out of the passion with which the Portuguese mixed with the Indians, and envy on account of the unquenchable greed for gold that brought the Portuguese to Brazilian shores.[7] Afonso Arinos de Melo Franco advanced five traits that he believed to be typically Afro-Indian and that were assimilated by the Portuguese in the New World, presumably making them Brazilian: (1) dissipation and lack of foresight, (2) lack of appreciation for the land, (3) salvation through chance, (4) love of ostentation, and (5) disrespect for the legal order.[8] To these items, Fernando de Azevedo advances another two traits: the predominance of the emotional, the irrational, and the mystical in the Brazilian thought process—and perhaps a consequence of these: a fatalistic attitude that Azevedo attributes to the awesome natural forces that the Brazilian had to contend with.

Let us first deal with Azevedo's claim to an overwhelming Brazilian sensibility, along with his claim that this does not induce intelligence.[9] For sensibility, not intelligence, would be the factor responsible for the perceived syncopated nature of Brazilian behavior, imbued as it is with an irregular rhythm and marked by indolence and bouts of impetuous behavior in response to emotions or necessity. These traits would trigger the sudden transformation of the *sertanejo* (hinterland dweller) from listlessness to the resourcefulness and relentlessness of a Titan, as suggested by Euclydes da Cunha.[10]

For whatever reason, Azevedo believed it was not logic that excited the Brazilian. Logic would require penetration, vigor, perseverance, and exactitude, of which, Azevedo argued, the Brazilian has less of than what he generously has to offer: grace, brilliancy, and humorous spins.

Returning to Franco's five traits, at least since the time of Miranda Reis we have known that those traits attributed to the Brazilian people may have been the expression of a stage of development rather than of an immutable character of the people.[11] For instance, lack of foresight may derive from the lack of purpose in planning to a people forced to live from hand to mouth; moreover, lack of appreciation for the land is a confirmed trait of a nomadic people, which disappears as quickly as sedentarism takes over, when enabled by agricultural progress. Salvation through chance is a more resistant trait, although not necessarily a Brazilian one—or at least not descriptive of the whole nation, but rather of segments of many nations—particularly among the less educated, as is frequently expressed through adherence to gambling.[12]

Let us not lose sight of the fact that salvation through chance, if indeed it is sufficiently evident in Brazil to deserve attention, should receive less attention than that devoted to quite a few other countries. In fact, Brazil's gambling expenditure on a per capita basis in 2000 was one hundred times less than the expenditure in either Japan or Australia. Canada's and the USA's expenditures were forty times greater than Brazil's, and Portugal's was twice as high, and still the average Portuguese gambled only about $10 in 2000.[13]

Seeking salvation through chance instead of devoting efforts to science and engineering is another matter, but it is also the expression of an attitude toward rationality that has fallen out of favor, but is not necessarily wrong. Azevedo believes that the Brazilian thought process is unusually permeated by a mythical or emotional dimension, coloring Brazilian argumentation with a nonrational sense that is harder for the uninitiated to accept.[14]

The Weberian disenchantment with Western life may have freed inquisitive minds for a spurt of creativity previously unknown and which has been expressed in considerable material progress since. However, disenchantment also allowed for the disappearance of the socially integrative aspects of a shared cosmogony that allowed all of the involved parties to understand their role in life. This may also explain the disrespect for the legal order pointed out by Mello Franco. His last point, love of ostentation, is another matter entirely. It is a question of taste, the Brazilian style being more Levantine or Mediterranean than the more reserved northern European style.

LACK OF TRUST

Tristão de Ataíde emphasizes the reserve of the Brazilian.[15] Sergio Buarque de Holanda adds that the distrust that characterizes the Brazilian temperament may also have its origins in the low population density that led people to live in isolation from each other, more exposed to banditry, in particular, but also to the seduction of traveling strangers. But if this were an explanation for lack of trust, no people should be more distrusting and reserved than the Panamanians, or perhaps the many inhabitants of the Caribbean islands. Because of their positions along the route between the Golden Pacific and Europe, both of these groups constantly encountered strangers and pirates of many nationalities, but one does not hear that "lack of trust" is any the more remarkable among them.

Knowing that adversity may be too fierce, or their saints too weak, may have taught Brazilians not to overly expose themselves. This is what Fernando de Azevedo believes is the origin of the Brazilian reserve, or distrust. This trait is expressed as a limitation to what otherwise would be considered a cult to hospitality: "but this hospitality, far from being open and without reserve, is almost always accompanied by vigilant attention and at times by severe discretion."[16]

Nonetheless, it is this personalism of relationships that, despite its limitations to the appearance of a developed nation, helps transmit to the Brazilian people one of their most attractive traits: their amiability. Azevedo, along with Holanda, one of Brazil's best-known social analysts, stresses cordiality as one of the most salient traits of Brazilians. Indeed, the celebration of Brazilian cordiality gives rise to the highest lyricism.[17] While the measured Protestant may queasily shrink away from the Brazilians' flowery style of the lyrics of hospitality, the truth is that the Brazilian people have shunned Jacobinism and systematic abuse of any other people, except through slavery.

Vianna Moog has offered a toned-down alternative interpretation for the proverbial Brazilian amiability, that it may be self-serving and reflect mostly a coping strategy within a hostile environment. According to Moog, there is a gradient of Brazilian amiability; highest where survival is most difficult, such as in the northern rain forest, and less pronounced in the South, where people of the plains can get by despite being more abrasive to each other.[18] Moog's creative proposition may explain the gradient in amiability, but it does not explain why Brazilians would be more amiable than other peoples who have an even tougher time in keeping death at bay. In all, until proven wrong, we ought to take Brazilian amiability at face value, if only because it is so pleasant, whatever the reasons that prompted it.

This same temperament shaped Brazilian religious practice, which never had the angularity of Puritanism or even the rigidity of Catholic dogma. Rather, Brazilian religiosity became very domesticated, blending the religion of its many peoples in a syncretic voluptuous mysticism that helps and protects rather than hectors or punishes. This is why, according to Gilberto Freyre, Brazil's temples were always busy with family celebrations of baptism, marriages, and feasts, paying homage to saints who are faithful friends while the Virgin Mary doubles as a sort of godmother to the children.

This domesticated Catholicism, which forgives its contingent of saints for failing to deliver, underscores Brazilian fatalism. The Brazilian people are quick to resign themselves to the powerlessness even of the saints and deities that come to their help. The saints' shortcomings make them more fraternal, giving rise to a "friendship in the trenches" style of relationship, galvanized by a joint capitulation under the adversity of forces that are too strong, too hostile. Thus, the crushing power of adversity did not render a man in revolt, but rather a docile man capable of bitterless submission, confident that his turn will arrive. This is the Brazilian version of the Portuguese Sebastianism introduced in Chapter 4.[19] The Brazilian version, as adopted by Padre Antonio Vieira or as manifested at Canudos (1896–97),[20] may also drive the devotion to Padre Cícero at Juazeiro.[21]

ARE BRAZILIANS INDIVIDUALISTIC?

Fernando de Azevedo also believes Brazilians are exceedingly individualistic.[22] The sarcastic allegory frequently attributed to the Brazilian journalist Otto Lara Rezende (1922–92) is that Brazilians would only cooperate with one another when facing a common enemy, like cancer. Sergio Buarque de Holanda (1902–82) believed that, in a land where authority was imposed by barons and chieftains, no durable collective agreement could be reached, except as extracted from people through coercion. Mílton Rodrigues Silva also believed that because physical labor tends to equalize people, and labor is resented, Brazilians would only work together when threatened by adversity, such as in exploratory incursions like those of the *bandeirantes* or when protecting the land under the threat of an Indian attack.[23] Even then, Rodrigues Silva believed, such cooperation would be obtained only under unquestioned authority, such as that of a chieftain or military officer. To these authors, collaboration would appear to be a second-best necessity to a people who would, under any other circumstances, prefer to act individually.[24]

Nonetheless, difficulty in political cohesion should not be taken as evidence of extreme individualism, particularly in a country so vast and with such poor communications. Argentina faced similar individualistic pressures during the same phase of the nineteenth century, when it lost to chieftains' fractiousness half of the territory it had inherited under the Buenos Aires viceroyalty. In the Brazilian case, the more common slavery relationships made hierarchy paramount, which—coupled with the personalism derived from patron-client relationships inherited from Iberia—may have made interregional alliances even more fractious than in Argentina. Nonetheless, Brazil managed to hold its ground more than Argentina did. Thus, if political fractiousness is a token of individualism, Argentines would doubtlessly be more individualistic than Brazilians, which perhaps is correct; but if Brazilians are also held to be individualistic, then we will need a richer parameter with which to compare them to other peoples, for fractiousness may derive not only from the existence of self-serving individualist chieftains but from poor communications. It may well be that to a collectivist-oriented Brazilian, even minor deviations of behavior appear all too evidently as individualism, thus to be censored.

IDENTITARY CHARACTERS IN BRAZILIAN LITERATURE

Many of the literary characters that have shaped Brazilians' self-images were produced at a time when the country, after abolition, was reasserting the value of work. Octavio Ianni believes that this is the social factor driving the creation of literary characters demonizing idleness and luxuriousness.[25] Nonetheless, charming idle roguery was already the theme of *Memories of a Militia Sergeant* (*Memórias de um Sargento de Milícias*) by Manuel Antônio de Almeida, published in Rio de Janeiro in 1854 three decades before the abolition of slavery.[26] Yet the fact that idleness and luxuriousness demanded demonization at all is in itself telling of the pervasiveness of their widespread acceptance. Moreover, many characters were given a second chance at life with the advent of cinema, when their celluloid versions appeared in the 1960s.[27]

Jeca Tatú is a character brought to life by Monteiro Lobato in 1914. Initially, the author intended to portray the stultifying existence of the hillbilly in the São Paulo hinterland. Lobato subsequently toned down his approach in an attempt to dignify the lives of the characters.

Macunaíma was brought to life by Mario de Andrade in 1928. Both urban and rural, Macunaíma is also Negro, white, and Indian. The protagonist's intentional metamorphosis—à la Holy Trinity, three in one—facilitated his adoption as a national character, not least because the innocently playful character of unburdened luxuriousness is driven by the intention to retrieve his lost talisman. Playfulness has also been considered a Brazilian trait by a well-known Brazilian psychoanalyst, Betty Milan.[28]

Mario de Andrade called Macunaíma a hero with no character and no national borders ("parageographical"), thus attributing to Macunaíma a transcendence extending even beyond Brazil. The book was turned into a four-hour play that was performed nearly a thousand times. A shorter version was widely performed in Brazil and abroad, and in 1969 it was made into a movie by Joaquim Pedro de Andrade, allegedly to discuss the hero—who, according to Andrade, was too individualistic.[29]

Modern or not, to Darcy Ribeiro, Macunaíma is the Brazilian hero to many, not least because he represents the plight of resistance to an identitary fragmentation of the Brazilian nationality under the onslaught of foreignness, as represented by the giant Piaimã.[30]

José Dias is a household character in the novel *Dom Casmurro,* by Machado de Assis. José Dias lies his way into the household, securing sustenance in exchange for petty services. All three protagonists—Jeca Tatú, Macunaíma, and José Dias—portray a national character that existed well before their authors brought them to life; otherwise, it might be difficult to explain the broad acceptance the characters instantly received upon arriving on the scene.

The work of Machado de Assis is considered the epitome of Brazilian literature. Both Monteiro Lobato and Mario de Andrade became widely known in literary and artistic circles. Monteiro Lobato was also a significant entrepreneur, art critic, and polemist. He was behind the political movement "O Petróleo é Nosso" (It's Our Oil), which led to the foundation of the national oil company, Petrobrás. All three authors, each in his own era, circulated in the apex of Brazilian literature, and their works earn them wide acceptance still today, when their characters are readily recognized even beyond literary circles.

The significance of these literary successes is partially based on society's recognition of itself in the characters. The attributes of all three characters illustrate that Brazilians readily identify unwholesome characters acting with impunity, helping to crystallize a negative Brazilian imagery of itself. Socially, these images allow for the triumph of procrastination, deceit, and opportunistic behavior, and collectively they breed lack of trust.[31]

We can appreciate in all three of these characters a collection of traits that creates in the reader a tension between an inclination to help and a guarded reserve to avoid being taken for a fool, as would be the case if one fell for the alluring attractiveness of Macunaíma's innocent roguish behavior, or the pleading meekness of José Dias (see Table 14.1).

This fear of being constantly preyed upon is deeply ingrained in the culture and is expressed in humor, epitomized by the "false friend" (*o amigo da onça*). This fictional character was created by Péricles de Andrade Maranhão and occupied the back page of the weekly *O Cruzeiro* for over two decades from the 1940s.[32] Today the magazine is recognized as a period piece, and the comic strip that it carried was so popular that fans would furtively read it at newspaper stands before replacing the magazine, unpaid. To make this slightly

TABLE 14.1 Deconstruction of traits of selected Brazilian literary characters

Author Traits expressed in	Monteiro Lobato: Jeca Tatú	Machado de Assis: José Dias	Mario de Andrade: Macunaíma	Summary
Posture, appearance	Squatting, humble, disrespected, somber	Humble, unassuming, weak	Colorful, irreverent, childlike	Amiable, disarming
Attitude	Apathetic, aspiring to tutelage, fatalistic, unhappy, mute	Plain, disguised, fortune seeker	Irresponsible, lazy, affable, luxurious, mystical	Adventurous
Behavior	Spontaneous, indolent, naïve, reserved	Averse to work, rogue, scoundrel	Nomadic, artful, playful, seductive, relaxed	Roguery
Social navigation	Negotiates favors, personalizes relationships, anarchic	Inconsistent, parasitic, dissimulated, conniving, shortsighted	Astute, deceitful, opportunistic, anarchic, dreamer	Preys upon others to preempt being preyed upon
Inspires	Piety, assistentialism	Commiseration, guarded reserve	Distrust, contention	Guarded protection, distrust

NOTE: Author's classification of traits based on Seixas's deconstruction of the character Jeca Tatú by Monteiro Lobato, also the author's own deconstruction of the character Macunaíma by Mario de Andrade; on Bosi; and on Vianna Moog's deconstruction of José Dias, the scoundrel character in Machado de Assis' *Dom Casmurro*.

SOURCES: Jacy Alves de Seixas, "Tênue Fronteiras de Memórias e Esquecimentos: A Imagem do Brasileiro Jeca-macunaímico," in Horácio Gutiérrez, Márcia R. C. Naxara, and Maria Aparecida de S. Lopes (eds.), *Fronteiras: Paisagens, Personagens, Identidade* (São Paulo: Olho D'Água, 2003); Alfredo Bosi, *Historia Concisa da Literatura Brasileira* (São Paulo: Editora Cultrix, 1994); Vianna Moog, *Bandeirantes e Pioneiros, Paralelos Entre Duas Culturas* (Rio de Janeiro: Editora Civilização Brasileira, 1964).

more difficult, the magazine's editors began publishing the comic strip on different pages every issue.

It is this proclivity to take advantage of others, in large and small ways, that breeds lack of trust and limits the growth of companies to the confines of the family network and the personalism inherent in such networks. In nepotism, this is taken to blatant extremes. For instance, in 2005 the speaker of the Brazilian House of Representatives admitted in Brasília to seeking employment for relatives in government and that he saw no evil in the practice, alleging that his relatives were all competent and that rules against nepotism were the refuge of officials with incompetent relatives.

Yet, alongside the distrust that admittedly hinders the growth of companies beyond closed, trusting networks, such as families, we would need to explain the success of the Baron of Mauá, who overcame this latent pervasive distrust. His nineteenth-century businesses included iron, railways, shipbuilding, public utilities, and banking and spanned from Argentina to the Amazon and London, at a time when a reply by letter would take over two months to arrive. Also during the twentieth century, a large, informal gambling network called *jogo do bicho* (the animal game), most prominent in Rio de Janeiro, spread along lines of trust, not necessarily family lines.

Therefore, let us not capitulate complacently to facile explanations for Brazilians seeking the comfort of small business. There are current examples of large Brazilian corporations that have broken the bonds of family networks, and other business networks both formal and informal have found a way to grow, despite earlier poor communications and what appears to be a low level of societal trust. We need to understand this better.

DISTILLATION OF THE BRAZILIAN MANAGERIAL ENVIRONMENT

So far in this chapter I have covered over a century and a half of efforts in order to reflect on the style of Brazilian development as shaped by the environment and its people. Through the perceptions of several authors I have attempted to portray a Brazilian style of interpersonal relationships that shapes the managerial environment. Some of these traits can be seen under an unfavorable light.

Yet I contend that the traits portrayed by identitary characters in the literature are a reflection of the environment in which the people must live and work. What appears as a drawback, such as an inherent high level of distrust, may only be the result of a culture shaped by past experience; in other words, it may be functional in the current environment. If, with time, a more positive set of experiences should emerge, those negative traits may recede.

Let us now backtrack to the summary of traits found in the three characters of Brazilian literature that I have selected: Jeca Tatú, José Dias, and Macunaíma. They are traits that seek to disarm through roguery, which conveys a sense of adventure and also breeds distrust. Altogether, those traits express a proclivity for survival through evasion and a tendency to vie for protection, as through personalism, when evasion is not possible. This is the natural response of those who feel too weak to cope with the threat. It is not an exclusively Brazilian attitude.[33]

Brazilian traits similarly express evasion; they reflect the coping strategy of an oppressed people. All three of these literary characters seek to deflect aggression and survive, whether through their appearance (disarming), attitude (adventurous), behavior (roguish), or social navigation (preying). They all show a disinclination for teaming up, unless it was with their families. Macunaíma travels through Brazil with his two brothers, José Dias is a loner leeching off a family, and Jeca Tatú is mostly homebound. This is what confers to the Brazilian the individualistic trait perceived by many analysts and commentators.

These traits and coping strategies manifest themselves in a management environment as one might expect: in evasion. An English manager of one of Brazil's leading banks once asked me, "Alfredo, have you ever tried to lead Brazilians?" Shrugging his shoulders, he replied to himself, "It is like trying to lead a bunch of cats. Each one wanders his own way, doing his own thing, without confronting you." Still, this English gentleman was no samba school leader born to lead thousands of costumed followers dancing to the beat of hundreds of drums.[34]

Knowledgeable Brazilian authors have summarized Brazilian traits in the working environment, beginning first and foremost with the notion of hierarchy, defined as involving power concentration and passive acceptance of inequality.[35] Spyer Prates and Tanure de Barros offered ten traits, supported by a survey of 2,500 managers.[36] These traits are largely encompassed by the five traits offered by Borges de Freitas.[37] For clarity of my argument, I have blended both classifications into one that involves hierarchy, lack of trust, personalism, roguery, and adventure (see Figure 14.1). Lack of trust was not offered in either of the classifications but stems from the consequence of the meaning of "roguery" in Borges de Freitas and from "impunity" in the Spyer Prates–Tanure de Barros classification.[38]

In fact, I believe that all of the traits in both classifications stem from negative experiences with exaggerated expressions of the first category: hierarchy.[39] The others all depict evasion strategies that ensure survival. Passive acquiescence is a form of loyalty under tolerable duress, when exit is either too hard or perceived to be an exaggerated alternative.[40]

This is why dependency, loyalty, impunity, conflict avoidance, and passivity figure so prominently in the responses of the managers surveyed by Spyer Prates and Tanure de Barros. At least two-thirds of the respondents agreed that those were prominent cultural traits present in Brazilian corporations. Yet all of the traits proposed by Tanure de Barros and Spyer Prates can be reduced to reinforcers of hierarchy. They all rely on personalism to ensure conformity. *Malandragem* (roguery) is only a survival strategy for the weak.[41] Those at the top of the hierarchy scale need not resort to roguery because they have access to impunity. The wise and weak will be passive in order to avoid conflict, or literally evade through adventure—whether in reality or by means of daydreaming or engaging in other such distortions of reality.[42]

Perhaps Moog was right after all, and the proverbial Brazilian amiability is yet another side of the same strategy: to disarm, to neutralize, because the character already has too much to worry about in a naturally hostile environment.[43]

Hierarchy	Concentration of power, discrimination, formalism
Lack of trust	Controls, passivity, by the book
Personalism	Personal bonds prevail over structure, paternalism, loyal
Roguery	Ambiguity, *jeitinho*, pious lies, conciliatory, disarming
Adventure	Dreamer; averse to discipline, method, and perseverance

FIGURE 14.1. A sketch of the Brazilian managerial environment

SOURCE: Author, based on Alexandre Borges de Freitas, "Tracos Brasileiros para uma Analise Organizacional" (38–54), and Marco Aurélio Spyer Prates and Betania Tanure de Barros (55–69), in *Cultural Organizacional e Cultura Brasileira*, ed. Fernando C. Motta Prestes and Miguel P. Caldas (São Paulo: Atlas, 1997).

Take also the Brazilian proclivity to teamwork (once distrust has been dispelled). Once bonded, the team demands absolute loyalty. Finger-pointing within the team is tantamount to treason. Management can hardly discern what goes on within the Brazilian team, let alone evaluate individual contributions, because the team is impermeable to management. The team will seek to deliver what is demanded, perhaps only as a strategy to be left alone. What we could attribute to a high-powered proclivity for teamwork may in fact be the result of the same strategy: to evade hierarchy by seeking the realm of egalitarianism within a homogeneous team.

This analysis leads us to believe that in an environment where power distance is less threatening, less bruising, Brazilian workers would gradually abandon the socially deleterious traits that characterize their organizational behavior. Trust would be more readily granted, and emotional, affective autonomy would remove the need for personalism. Roguery would not be celebrated, and perseverance would triumph over adventure.

This is what was perceived by the human resources director migrating to a high-tech Brazilian company from a multinational. At the Brazilian-run corporation, naturally democratic for the most part on account of the homogeneous, high training level of much of the staff, relationships tended to be open, free, and happy as well as productive. This should come as no surprise, for being Brazilian should not mean happiness at the expense of effectiveness.[44]

The central issue of this book is precisely illustrated by the earlier example in this section that calls for curbing the pattern of exaggerated hierarchical command in Brazilian business. It is possible to be Brazilian and effective, providing that Brazilians are managed as Brazilians and not as a generic entity. The central argument of this section is that it is easier to change the environment of a corporation than that of the overarching culture in which the corporation operates, as in the case of the Brazilian high-tech company. It is perhaps a piecemeal solution, but it is one that ought to increase corporations' competitiveness and gradually spread by means of emulation to the rest of the economy.

Struggling for piecemeal solutions rather than a comprehensive managerial revolution is even better attuned to what appears to be a Latin American proclivity to operate through guerrilla tactics rather than tin-soldier armies. As with the high-tech corporation above, or the Natura case discussed next, these cases are very good news; they show that providing a nurturing working environment would help dispel the current reliance on excessive controls. The working environment would allow for greater creativity, more innovation, and a greater sense of belonging and personal realization, the lack of which are deeply troubling to Brazilians.[45]

CAN MANAGEMENT BE DIFFERENT AND BETTER?

Let us now take a closer look at the Brazilian cosmetics corporation, Natura, which developed an organizational culture around Brazilian cultural traits.[46]

Attuned to the nation's well-known penchant for beauty and sensuality, the Brazilian cosmetics industry is sizable. Its world ranking is slightly above that of the country's GDP, and the cosmetics and fragrances sector has grown at about three times the Brazilian rate of GDP growth over the last decade. In 2004 this sector employed, directly, close to 2.5 million people, or 2.7 percent of the economically active population.

The two largest Brazilian companies in this sector are O Boticário and Natura. Both have expanded internationally to sell products that are synonymous with the country's image, unshackled by the barriers faced by the software sector. In 2004 these two companies were listed among the top one hundred companies in *Who's Who of Cosmetics*.[47] O Boticário's foreign revenue is 2 percent of its total revenue, which in 2004 amounted to $188 million, placing it in fifty-eighth position in the world ranking. Launched in 1977, O Boticário sells through its own shops as well as a franchise chain, and it achieved a significant differential in 2005 upon being honored with the National Retail Foundation award in the United States.[48]

Natura's roots can be traced back to 1944, but as such Natura was founded in 1969 and built its direct-sales network into a significant entry barrier to its Brazilian market niche. Natura has been present in Argentina, Bolivia, Chile, and Peru for over a decade. Still, its international revenue is just 2.8 percent of its total revenue, which in 2004 amounted to $870 million, ranking thirty-first in the world.

Avon, the American cosmetics powerhouse, started in Brazil in 1959 and chose to focus on the Prahaladesque fortune at the bottom of Brazil's pyramid, where it built the world's largest direct-sales network. O Boticário competes with Natura productwise and positions its products with discounts of up to 20 percent of Natura's price range. That O Boticário is not a rival of Natura as yet is largely because of its relatively smaller size. Due to both size and sales strategy, Natura's immediate rival is Avon—the one Brazilian, the other American. Do they differ in their managerial characteristics, and does this show in their effectiveness? Apparently the answer is affirmative on both counts (see Table 14.2).

Tanure and Duarte have studied Natura in depth and believe that its managerial style has incorporated three significant characteristics of Brazilian culture: power concentration, an emphasis on personal relationships, and flexibility.[49]

One of Natura's founders is Luiz Seabra, who, attuned to Brazilian culture, stressed from the outset his belief in building long-lasting relationships: "Seabra . . . called every manager and director on their birthdays, he knew the names of the cleaning personnel in his office and avoided formality in his interactions with people. His personal conduct had become a source of many of the stories and myths that almost defined the soul of the company."[50] Seabra is one of three copresidents of Natura, the only three in the company to have individual offices. The others operate in open-space architecture with little distinction as to hierarchy. The direct-selling method was chosen in order to share profits with the workforce and better integrate them into the company.

Sharing profits implies sharing efforts. Natura's sales representatives are required to purchase the Natura products that they resell. This reduces the need for working capital at Natura and did away with the frustrating process of collecting from sales representatives. In addition, if sales representatives can come up with some initial capital, they have more chance of selling to Natura's target consumer. The relational dogma fits the strategy.

Natura's sales force is managed through sales promoters who are meant to act as friends and counselors to the sales team, besides promoting adherence to Natura's mission and vision. Because building lasting relationships is part of this mission, the sales force is rewarded not only for profits but also for client retention and seniority, thus incorporating into the recognition spectrum a significant element of Brazilian relational and personalistic culture. Incidentally, in a separate but comparable industry in Central America, personalization also seems to be the root of success of the Grupo San Nicolás in El Salvador.[51]

Greeting team members on their birthdays may be just a ritual, but it is telling of the attitude emphasized by high management. With this attitude,

TABLE 14.2 Comparison of two managerial paradigms

	Natura: Brazilian-style management	Avon: American-style management
Sales volume (in US$ billion)	1.91	1.74
Net sales (in US$ million)	957	826
Number of units sold (in millions)	215	704
World ranking	31	6
Target market segment	Classes B and C	Classes D and E
Average family yearly income	US$7,800	US$3,600
Size of distribution network (number of persons)	357,000	980,000
Number of products in catalogue	Close to 500	Close to 5,000
Staff development	Sales-oriented courses	Sales-oriented courses
Recognition based on	Performance Seniority Client retention	Performance
Incentives	30% above sales	30% of sales
Sales support	Products paid for in advance Support materials provided	Product advanced by Avon Support materials, if bought
Hierarchy	Open-space office layout, except for presidents Informal addressing One cafeteria for all No reserved parking spaces	Space allocated by status Addressing is formal One cafeteria for all Parking reserved for bosses
Relationship building	Personal birthday greetings by presidents Encouragement along the chain Performance targets suggested by lower echelons	No such thing Sales reps feel paramount Targets set top-down
Call center	Outsourced	Outsourced
E-sales	Incipient	Incipient

SOURCES: All figures on the companies are for 2005 and were extracted from several publicly available marketing publications. Other Natura data were assembled from information in Betânia Tanure and Roberto Gonzalez Duarte, "Leveraging Competitiveness upon National Cultural Traits: The Management of People in Brazilian Companies," *International Journal of Human Resource Management* 16, no. 12 (Dec. 2005): 2201–17. Some Avon data were kindly provided by a former high management and marketing executive with Avon, who prefers to remain anonymous.

Natura is willing to invest in an average of a thousand phone calls per day. Apparently, all of these aspects of a Brazilian style of management lead to Natura having the lowest turnover rate among Brazil's direct-sales companies.[52] Company loyalty, however, does not prevent Natura sales representatives from also selling Avon products, and vice versa. The practice is frowned upon by both companies, but it is part and parcel of the entrepreneurial spirit of the sales representatives, which Natura also encourages by asking its representatives to first buy the products they are meant to sell. After all, selling expensive products may stimulate greater sales effort overall. Natura representatives often feel inclined even to sell Avon products rather than leaving a home without closing a sale. Even better if they can close sales for both companies.

While the owners of Natura are still in charge, they are also called on to help reach accord in decision making, besides granting unusual autonomy to all, even regarding significant decisions such as product returns or purchasing enterprise resource planning (ERP) systems.[53] This flexibility to accommodate the unforeseen is granted down the line. Call-center operators can decide to accept return purchases on the spot. Power, according to Tanure and Duarte, has been redefined in that it has been channeled in the pursuit of a shared mission.

Avon would appear to be the direct opposite of Natura. Although a subsidiary of a U.S. corporation, Avon displays little of the alleged American egalitarianism. Hierarchical attitudes are pervasive. Its army of sales representatives is close to three times larger than Natura's, and individuals earn proportional commissions as at Natura, only on much lower overall sales based on a much broader catalogue. In all probability, modern human resource management, as well as making sales and managing receivables, are much more cumbersome, and painful, at Avon.

Yet if Natura's competitive advantage in Brazil resides in its closer harmony with Brazilian culture, would not this same factor be an obstacle to Natura's international expansion? So far, Natura has expanded along similar lines in culturally close countries within its own South American region. But in 2006, Natura wet its feet in no less of a formidable market than Paris, with an open concept store. Even if the shop takes off, how effectively will Natura be able to export its corporate culture to a society where it may be less effective? This remains to be seen.

It appears that Avon has the edge over Natura when it comes to international expansion. At any rate, technology may force some convergence between the two. Both companies have outsourced call-center services and now also sell through their websites. Although dedicated call-center operators may be properly trained to represent Natura well, does their standing within corporatewide efforts turn call-center operators into the poorer cousins of an otherwise close-knit Natura family? How does this orphaned call center fit into the corporate mission and the truthful relationships Natura seeks to promote? Why would anyone want to be a call-center operator dedicated to Natura and not also be an employee of Natura? If lower-cost services were Natura's only motivation for outsourcing one of its corporate components, the inconsistency of the rationale would act as a wedge in the relationship-based commitment that Natura wishes to promote and claims to espouse. Moreover, outsourcing call-center services is more attuned with Avon's more impersonal sales stance; at Avon, this decision causes no tension. But it is a source of tension at Natura, and it may come back to haunt the company.

Internet sales, or e-sales, also pose less of a distraction at Avon, which focuses on lower-ticket sales. Among these, shipping costs appear to be almost prohibitive. Indeed, a low-cost item sold over the Web may carry a 33 percent increase when including delivery costs, even for Natura.[54] This difference may not be significant to Natura's customers, but it may knock the wind out of the sails of Natura's sales force. The growth of e-sales is likely to add more stress to Natura's strategy than to Avon's, largely because it may not be an issue for Avon, given that Avon's market niche appears to be mostly below the segment of households with computers linked to the Internet.

Despite the potential culture clash brought on by international expansion, and the tensions caused by technology and nonexclusive representatives, Natura offers a very interesting case of a successful attempt to reflect local culture in a managerial style. Teamwork proclivities are reinforced by open-space architecture, one cafeteria for all, no reserved parking spaces, and openness to discussion. Relationships and teamwork are also reinforced by a compensation system that rewards seniority and client retention rather than more narrowly defined performance, as at Avon. Strengthening personal relationships is celebrated, as reflected in management's custom of calling people on their birthdays.

In all, Natura seems to show how a piecemeal managerial solution may be turned into a competitive advantage without attempting to change national culture. Natura surpassed Avon in 2005 in both gross and net sales. It would seem that focusing on the bottom of the pyramid is not enough, but that managing Brazilian style is also a crucial strategy.

Natura offers a successful case of grounding managerial techniques in Brazilian cultural values. It is possible to be different and better. The Natura case implies accepting a "halfway strategy," that is, implementing experimental revisions infused with a radical pragmatism à la Mangabeira Unger that envisions a dignified alternative to the stultifying mediocrity that curtails any departure from the received dogma.

This incremental approach will allow corporations to participate in the unbridling of creativity necessary for dismantling the conventional wisdom. This "radical pragmatism" will free workers from the bondage of unnecessary hierarchies, allowing them to evolve and to engage in the construction of corporations and themselves. This calls for downplaying the foreign stereotypes of roles within corporations and offers a path to the emancipation of the worker as well as an alternative to subterfuge in the face of exaggerated hierarchy and demands for submission. This call is not far from Mangabeira Unger's bid for a radicalized pragmatism to supersede shortsighted pragmatism—that unsavory product of fatalistic and alienating capitulation.[55] There is nothing wrong with pragmatism per se, except in the stultifying acceptance of routine on which it rests, which saps all initiative and results in defusing all heroism and alienating people from their chance to flourish.

SUMMING UP: THE APPLICATION OF A BRAZILIAN LITERARY PORTRAIT

Brazil is a country without heroes. An emperor figurehead may have provided enough coalescence to ensure territorial integrity and a sufficient guiding reference to preclude the need to create a unifying iconic figure like that of Martin Fierro for the Argentines. Nonetheless, Brazilian literature suggests the rapid acceptance of organizationally deleterious characters that readers recognize as real and ubiquitous. I contend that these characters gain acceptance not necessarily because of their negative characteristics but because they espouse a survival strategy that is legitimized by the majority.

While not adhering loyally to an unfair social structure, rather than voicing disapproval and being vanquished by the asymmetry of forces, Brazilians have traditionally been constrained to passively accept unfairness and attempt to work out personal solutions to their unfair predicaments. Personalization of relationships, the *jeitinho*, adventure, or plain roguery are evasive attitudes resulting from perceived weakness, given the exaggerated hierarchy. This is why I contend that less threatening workplaces may provide the conditions for Brazilian workers to realize at work the display of engagement they develop elsewhere, like in samba schools, where Carnival aficionados are known to work for months, often without pay. By supporting at the workplace the expression of national cultural traits, such as personalized relationships, the Brazilian cosmetics company Natura may be closer to providing the type of work environment that may allow Brazilian workers to flourish. That is underscored by the success of El Salvador's Grupo San Nicolás, which achieves high performance by individualizing relationships with its staff.

Still, literary accounts insist over and over again on an exaggerated authoritarianism as a recurrent trait of Brazilian leaders. This reflects the paternalistic nature of leadership as historically practiced, but the representation of authority in this manner may tend to encourage continued exploitation. Restraint has mostly been pursued through unions and legal arrangements, which are an expression of the political forces. In management, we should be more creative than that. Paternalistic leadership—as exercised by a royal figurehead whose authority was bestowed upon him by "divine right" and sanctioned by the church—is medieval and calls for medieval inspiration. Then, we had the *corregidores* to mediate disputes. I suggest we should resort to a similar instrument today, for it would be attuned with present-day culture. In colonial times, the *corregidores* were rotated in order to inhibit favoritism; today, a similar function could be performed by retired personnel chosen by employees. These contemporary go-betweens would have the necessary independence besides the advantage of knowing the organizational culture. With mounting cultural adhesion, similar innovations could be blended into paternalistically run organizations.

WORKING TOGETHER: COMMUNICATION, PERCEPTIONS OF TIME, WORKING IN TEAMS, AND INCENTIVES

T HIS CHAPTER FOCUSES on differences in communication styles, perceptions of time, teamwork appraisal, and compensation. It begins with two issues that are crucial to working in teams: effective communication and shared notions of time. The chapter then addresses the nature of teams in U.S. and Brazilian cultures and the ways in which the differences require specific arrangements—both for evaluating individuals' contributions to team performance and for designing compensation arrangements that meet workers' expectations without hampering their engagement with the broader corporation.

COMMUNICATION AND TIME

Communication is one of the most subtle and interesting areas of cross-cultural management. Unfortunately, its lessons are most relevant in the early stages of new interaction between cultures. This offers little opportunity to learn by doing. Thus it pays to learn in advance, or to move on to another culture and try to get it right the next time.

Communication Styles

The cultural preference for communication styles is manifested not only in terms of the volume of speech but also of its rhythm and pitch. For instance, nurturing cultures prefer slow, mellow tones and respect for the interlocutor—as, for instance, interrupting one's own speech when others wish to speak. On the other hand, interruptions are actually a display of interest in Italy, Spain, and most of the Latin New World, but not in England, Canada, or the United States. Also, diction and one's choice of words is essential to charismatic leadership. In egalitarian cultures, speaking as though to the man on the street is a valuable skill in public speaking, whereas in high power distance cultures, speaking to make oneself understood may be less of a goal than communicating one's status and breadth of knowledge. In Latin America, city politicians have been known to speak to uneducated peasants in ways that leave them confounded but impressed with the speaker's eloquent style. After all, Catholic Mass in Latin America was celebrated in Latin until only a generation ago. This does not mean that making oneself clear is not desirable in Latin America, but that people should not refrain from using all the body language and additional emphases that are expected in that culture.

Edward T. Hall, born in 1914, was awarded his PhD in anthropology from Columbia University in 1942. He is considered to be one of the founders of intercultural communication studies. One of his main contributions was to propose that, across cultures, communication may vary in the extent that it is independent from the context in which it takes place.[1]

In any culture, the range of contextualization of speech varies from low context to high context. Low-context speech is the kind that conveys a meaning that is minimally related to the circumstances or their history. Examples of very low-context speech are most instructions, such as "pass the salt." The tone in which it is stated may vary, moreover, perhaps even implying that "you never pass the salt" and that therefore "it is hard to live under the same roof with you." The tone, then, adds context to the instruction, and being attuned to the variations and interpretations of tone helps the overall effectiveness of communication. Yet context is not merely a matter of tone. Communication may entail allusions to shared history, thus conveying a meaning far richer than apparent in the plain interpretation of what is being said or read.

Communication is not only about what is being said, but also about where and how. The higher the complexity of the implied meaning arising from the physical setting—for example, the color of flowers being presented—the higher the context is said to be. Fine poetry, such as "Leda and the Swan" by William Butler Yeats, is frequently high context and is an acquired taste, as are foreign cultures.

Take that poem's third stanza: "A shudder in the loins engenders there/ The broken wall, the burning roof and tower/ And Agamemnon dead"—Yeats's eighteen-word allusion to the Trojan War through the birth of Helen, fathered by Zeus upon raping Leda. Helen would later marry Menelaus, brother of Agamemnon and the most powerful king in the region. Menelaus had received Helen from her father upon the condition, binding on all contenders for Helen, that none would wage war for her once her father had made the decision to give her to whom he would chose. Yet the beautiful Helen, as attractive and passionate as could only have been born from such a rapturous encounter between Leda and Zeus, would fall for Paris, elope with him, and spark the Trojan War. Yeats, in his eighteen words, the sum of which is obviously much greater than its parts, effectively conveyed my one-hundred-word condensation of *The Iliad*. Such can be the power of high-context communication.

In contrast, low-context communication focuses more attention on the literal meaning of words and less on their context.

Low- and high-context communication are not exclusive domains of any given culture. People in all cultures use both styles in their daily lives. Sometimes we speak in high-context mode, using allusions, perhaps in order to spare the feelings of others. At other times, we may resort to a lower context, such as in the command, "turn left." But we are all capable of operating on a continuum between high and low context, and we choose the most appropriate styles depending on the circumstances, without implying that either end of the spectrum is better than the other. For instance, while we may choose a high-context style of communication in a family setting, we may switch to low context when a guest appears, helping the guest to fit in to the conversation (see Figure 15.1).

The choice of communication style is not related to the degree of its efficacy but rather to the desire to be understood. It is frequently said that individualist cultures prefer low-context communications that allow a greater chance of being understood. While this association does exist, it is not readily apparent that communication is more effective in low-context cultures. Cultures made up of many recent immigrants may resort to lower-context communication in order to reach a lower common denominator that will facilitate effective communication. More stable cultures, particularly older, more collectivist,

High-context
- Asian
- Arab
- Mediterranean
- Latin American
- Northern European
- Australian
- North American
- Scandinavian
- Teutons

Low-context

FIGURE 15.1. Selected countries by high- and low-context communication styles
NOTE: Note that high-context cultures tend to overlap with collectivist or embeddedness cultures, and low-context cultures with individualist or autonomous cultures.

and more homogeneous ones, may prefer higher-context communication in which more meaning is conveyed with the same number of words, while still ensuring that appearances are preserved in contentious situations. Although high context is less clear to strangers, it is nonetheless effective among people to whom it is directed.

Cultures that communicate in high context also keep well informed about what is important in their lives, with particular emphasis on people. High-context cultures keep tabs on networks involving family, work associates, friends, and even clients and the families of clients. This extensive and rich backdrop is perceived as giving meaning to exchanges. Conversations may take longer, but they are more rewarding.

People in low-context cultures allow little interference of "extraneous" information because they compartmentalize life more neatly. Detailed information is required in order to transmit meaning in any communication, yet low-context cultures manage to maintain a concise style of communicating in most contexts.

People from high-context-communication cultures may want to curtail their use of allusions when meeting people from low-context cultures, as they may not be fully understood.

High- and low-context cultures differ greatly in their ways of relating and, to a lesser but still significant extent, in their views of reality. The further apart they are on the context scale, the more difficult is the communication between them. People with opposite communication styles are best advised not to attempt to meet in the middle. Lowering the context to even below that of the low-context culture is their best chance for effective communication. Picture these difficulties as similar to those that would be experienced by human resources professionals (high context) when communicating with finance officers (low context).

Common sense may lose ground when dealing with unfamiliar issues or circumstances. Therefore, it pays to revert to the most appropriate media for communication when difficulties arise. Just as one would seek an adequate context level when communicating, the appropriate media is equally important. High-context cultures require rich media, which e-mail is not. The richest media is face-to-face contact, and it should be given priority when communicating with people from high-context cultures.

Jenai Wu and David Laws report on an e-mail exchange between Argentines and Russians involved in designing a joint software product.[2] The team members chose to communicate by e-mail despite working in close proximity to each other, and they were ultimately unable to switch to face-to-face contact when difficulties arose and began to increase with each new exchange of e-mail. "Cold" media, such as e-mail, hinder the affective aspect of interactions that can defuse tense situations. In international settings in which cross-cultural teams communicate frequently by e-mail, the risk of misunderstanding always lurks in the background. Absent the possibility of face-to-face exchanges, members should at least rely on phone conversations when doubts surface, rather than allowing negative stereotypes to cloud the collaboration.

Perceptions of Time

The term "polychronic time use" was originated by Hall in 1959,[3] in contrast to monochronic (sequential) time that is essentially economic and is characterized as exhaustible, linear, tangible, and segmentable.[4] This economic approach is behind expressions such as "time is money" or "there is not enough time" or "do this after that." To people from monochronic cultures, time appears to flow as from a limited container, which is to be drawn from judiciously and continuously until time has run out. Not applying time to work is seen as a waste. A sense of urgency prevails because a single, exhaustible span is all the time the individual has to perform a task. Time becomes money, and idleness becomes an affront to God. Reality is the work of a Lego master; pieces can be perceived and the whole disassembled into its component parts, to be reassembled without regard to the setting in which this occurs.

Polychronic (synchronic) time use, in contrast, allows for several actions to be carried out simultaneously. Rather than perceiving time sequentially as a line, polychronic cultures see it as a broad swath within which more can be accomplished, including making time for friends. Time is not exhaustible because it is also perceived as a circular flow. Like the seasons, opportunities come and go, hence the lower sense of urgency among polychronic cultures. Synchronic cultures may well offer the best fit to uncertainty, for their flexible attitude toward time allows the unscheduled shifting of activities in order to accommodate supply disruptions, for example. Plans are of less importance in such societies, as non-task-related issues may interfere at any juncture. The ability to switch from one task to another is desirable when supply management is erratic and the just-in-time inventory system turns out not to work as well.

Early time management studies were biased against polychronic time use because it seemed to ascribe more than twenty-four hours to a day, when considering all the multitasking that went on. Attempting to do more than one thing at a time was seen as appropriate only when under pressure, when people were "forced" to accommodate interruptions to tasks. The fact that customers were being attended to while the bread was baking was perhaps not taken into consideration. More recently, polychronic time use and the people who practice it have received more appreciation.[5] This includes women, among whom polychronic use of time has traditionally been more prevalent.[6]

Revisiting Context and Time

Hall united the concepts of context, communication, and time perception. He also examined perceptions of space, but we will not get into those here.[7] I have already mentioned the correlation between context and time perception, in that high-context cultures tend to be polychronic in the use of their time. Both traits are seen more frequently among collectivist cultures than among individualist ones. I now add that the individualist cultures tend to be more present and future oriented, while collectivist ones tend to hold the past in greater esteem. It helps to see the whole in order to perceive what are merely different angles of looking at cultures. Collectivist cultures tend to be older and more stable. They revere the past (they are not as future oriented) and honor relationships with those with whom they build shared networks and a common understanding, which is expressed in a rich communication (high context). This induces them to have a long-term orientation and to perceive time as a circular flow, in which much can be accomplished simultaneously (polychronic), but without the sense of urgency of the individualist cultures.

TEAMWORK AND INCENTIVES

Rewarding teams is not a fad; its success is increasingly lauded in such diverse sectors as those of Kodak, Boeing, AlliedSignal, Federal Express, and Texas Instruments.[8] A common obstacle to introducing a system of rewards aligned with team performance is the difficulty of envisaging a fair and effective individual payment system in agreement with collaborative performance. This problem is exacerbated in collectivist cultures such as Brazil, where reflection on such matters is perhaps not prioritized.

Individuality and Teamwork

Teamwork is praised but poorly rewarded. Particularly in developing countries, personnel management techniques derive from a time of little specialization in industrial production. Individuals were as interchangeable as parts, and individual performance was relatively easy to measure. As specialization increased, production and delivery became increasingly dependent on the specialized, timely input of people whose work interacted with that of others on the spot. Production became increasingly collective, but payment remained individual and progressively divorced from joint performance.

Deciding to phase in a reward system for team performance is one important step; deciding how far to take it is an entirely different question. In American steel plants, for example, it may make sense to go full throttle and adopt Japanese human resource management techniques—emphasizing job stability, workforce training, and profit sharing—rather than limiting teamwork to specific problem solving, as is the current tendency in that industry.[9]

An individual reward system based on team performance may be more difficult to implement in a collectivist culture such as Brazil than in an individualist one such as the United States, due to the varying degree to which individual members of work teams retain their identities within the team. In the United States, the work ethos remains individual; teams are composed of individuals that happen to be working together on a task. Brazilian workers, on the other hand, invest a greater degree of their individual identities; the group undergoes a process of fusion and gains an identity and an ethic of its own. An effective Brazilian work team expects unrestricted allegiance to the group; anything less is disloyal.

Still, individuals in work teams in foreign-managed corporations in Brazil possess names and payroll codes just as anywhere else. The ill-advised U.S.-trained manager may mistakenly project such clerical assignations of individuality onto individualization of the work accomplished. Although the transference is not warranted, it tends to guide the current practice of team performance evaluation in Brazil.

U.S. multinationals in Brazil regularly apply teamwork performance measures, despite the fact that their application in Brazil is more complex than in the United States. If managers in Latin America were to follow the foreign practice of individualizing team performance, they would run the risk of subverting the tacit egalitarian arrangement of Brazilian work teams that says all workers deserve equal pay. While apparently fair on the surface, the practical outcome of this attitude is the ongoing support of free riders, which is demoralizing to the team and ultimately damaging to overall productivity.

Loyal to its collectivist background, the Taiwanese multinational Trend Micro favors teamwork-based bonus distribution, as it does in Asia, to stimulate its sales in Latin America. The multinational encountered no trouble in rolling out its team sales incentive system in Latin America, but it had to scrap it in the individualist United States.

The losses to managerial efficiency owing to poor team-based performance may not be as frightful as is commonly assumed. Multinationals employ an increasing number of local staff who, even if unwittingly, succeed in adapting human resources procedures to local cultures. This may have some bearing on why researchers found no significant differences in hiring practices between domestic and multinational companies operating in Greece.[10] Yet the reward systems currently practiced in Brazil to account for individual contributions to team performance do not seem to have been borne out of research, as might benefit the situation.

The problem does not have an obvious solution. For instance, an excellent team may fail to perform well because its work depends on the unsatisfactory performance of another team. Possible solution: Team rewards could be molded to reflect the degree of the team members' control over their output. In another example, sales teams are frequently rewarded with a variable bonus reflecting a percentage of their total sales. However, the term "total sales" may have a different meaning to salespeople than it does to the financial team. Whereas installment sales are easier on the client and thus often promoted by salespeople, they are not as welcome to the financial team as up-front sales because sales in installments require larger working capital. Possible solution: Introduce into the sales team reward some measure of the financial cost of the sales team's decisions on the corporation.

It may sound obvious, but it is not beside the point to insist that an individual's team-based reward should first and foremost be fair. A sound practice to ensure fairness and ownership of the process would be to involve the interested parties in the design of the reward system. This will (1) ensure that the system reflects actual practice and (2) increase participation by those whose pay and work evaluations depend on the evaluation. In order for this to be acceptable to workers, rewards should be aligned to corporate objectives and kept flexible enough to be adapted to changes in corporate strategy. This requires that the teams have clear, measurable, and attainable goals that are negotiated with team members and clearly communicated.[11]

That is the basic goal. Arriving at it is not easy and is perhaps the last stage of a long process involving an appropriate review and evaluation process. Even then, such an approach would be valid only for corporations in the appropriate organizational stage, those that are satisfied with their readiness and the competitiveness of their compensation strategies.[12] Once these are in order, a corporation should clearly consider who is eligible to participate in the incentive plan, match the funding to the goals, and choose both the timing and the type of reward.[13]

Self-Evaluation by Teams: A Primer

In higher management, the problem of apportioning rewards to individuals working in teams may result from a spillover of poor training in teamwork methods at business schools, or even earlier.[14] We begin to see a concern with preparation for effective teamwork at the business school level, where teamwork is evaluated similarly to that in the business world—with one major difference: in business, rewards are finite, while top grades in a school setting are not. If instructors are to encourage effective teamwork with fewer free riders and with the least amount of expensive faculty intervention for assessment, they will have to encourage self-evaluation within teams.

In one possible scenario, an instructor would assign a certain amount of points to a student team, to be allocated among members according to their perceived performance. In order to force some level of decision making within the team, it would help to assign a number of points not easily divisible by the number of team members. Points earned would count toward students' course evaluations.[15]

Another scenario would be one that encourages a close association between the group's performance and the contribution of each member. Let us assume that each member's contribution to the group amounts to 100 possible points. The number of members of each group may vary. Upon interacting, the group assesses each member and determines his or her contribution to the group. Equal assessment for all is acceptable. The instructor then evaluates the group's product, perhaps awarding it 80 out of a possible 100 points. This is thus interpreted as 80 percent of the possible contribution of each member; in a group of four members, for example, the group will have achieved 80 percent of a possible 400 points, or 320 points. That number of points is distributed among the team members according to their own previous assessment of what they perceived each member would contribute to the outcome. This system has been in practice for over five years and has been tested on over five hundred students.[16] During this time, only about one quarter of the evaluation pool opted to distribute all the points equally among team members.[17]

The challenge of teaching and evaluating team performance does not apply only to academic settings. Those who are close to industry's educational structure feel the pinch as well and have often addressed the issue, for example, by instituting peer evaluation of fellow team members.[18] But the problem of evaluating team performance affects teams everywhere and in all walks of life, including surgical teams, to name just one crucial and life-enhancing application of the discipline of teamwork.[19]

Individual Compensation for Work Done in Teams

Teamwork is likely to become increasingly important, and it is one of the competitive advantages of collective-oriented cultures like Brazil. To make the most of this competitiveness, individuals need to be supported in fulfilling their team orientation by being fairly rewarded. However, the same culture that facilitates teamwork also hinders the assessment of individual contributions within teams. One possible way out is to transfer to the team the responsibility of fairly allocating the collective reward for the team's contribution. If this measure is coupled with voluntary team formation, team leaders who are perceived as unfair would increasingly have trouble attracting collaborators. While perhaps not error free, this route promises greater transparency within and among teams and less call for second-guessing what really goes on inside teams that choose to leave their supervisors in the dark.

CULTURES AND INCENTIVES

Despite many warnings against extrinsic incentives, the jackass fallacy still prevails.[20] When it comes to rewards, managers—especially those trained in the American tradition—think first of cash rewards.[21] It could well be that Brazilian teams, and even Argentine teams, would prefer some of those rewards to come in the form of greater job stability, but nobody seems to have asked them.[22] In not being asked, people are being treated as unimportant, in detriment to their commitment to the job. But perhaps they are not asked because they may come up with answers that seem odd or unexpected. Let us look at a real case illustrating the difference in attitudes of two shop attendants in Washington, DC, and Rio de Janeiro.

A young executive walked into an upscale shoe shop in Washington, DC, and asked for a pair of brown shoes of a certain style. With an earnest smile, the shop attendant kept bringing not brown but black shoes in various lengths and widths, until the customer's precise shoe size was ascertained and the attendant exclaimed, "Well, there you are! What else can I do for you today?"

Pointing to the black shoes, and as if afraid to sound impolite, the young executive stuttered, "Thanks! But do you have them in brown?" "Sorry," he heard from the attendant, "we do not carry those shoes in brown."

Some time later, the same executive walked into a smart shoe shop in Rio de Janeiro and asked the attendant for the same type of shoes, still in brown. Graciously, the attendant let him know that the store did not have those shoes in brown, but that its competitor across the street did.

An American shop attendant is directed to sell. A Brazilian attendant doubtlessly receives the same directive, but the Brazilian apparently sees the customer not as a sales opportunity but more as a fellow pilgrim, to whom one offers directions when asked. Modern and foreign managerial techniques have been in place in Brazilian retailing for decades now and pursue the same objective: to align salespeople with their employer's goal. Yet those incentives do not seem to entice the same response in Brazil as they do in the United States. The question of why the same incentives would result in different effectiveness may be relevant to other collectivist societies that are not firmly oriented toward competition and accumulation.[23]

But the principal-agent misalignment is quite likely to be indicative of a cultural misalignment. Collectivist societies share a notion of "fair price" and may frown upon the notion of "charging what the market will bear." Those that take the latter route are likely to benefit exaggeratedly in collectivist environments, at least for a time.

Humans, we are told in management textbooks, toil for money, and most management motivation strategies rest upon that simple assumption. Extrinsic incentives, such as sales commissions, are designed with this in mind, yet it appears that when evaluating employee performance, American managers prize intrinsic motivation such as commissions or bonuses above all other types.[24] This lack of a match between the incentive system and the appraisal system leads employees to exert themselves where influencing the impressions of their supervisors is involved rather than devoting their efforts to performance. A similar gap in Latin America, where the level of distrust is already high, would tend to thwart efforts toward employee engagement, despite the fact that Latin Americans are motivated more by intrinsic aspirations than extrinsic ones.

Are extrinsic incentives effective at all?[25] They seem to be more effective for salespersons who operate far from the manager's view.[26] But this assumes that people do not like to work and that they would not work if they could get away with it.[27] People who are well off seem to continue toiling for something other than money; perhaps they also toil for recognition, and money is only a poor proxy for recognition. Notice the most recent case in point offered by the Google lads, who resisted giving up control of Google, although their original idea is unlikely to make them wealthier now as fast as other investment opportunities would.

That humans strive for recognition has been recognized at least since Plato's concern over the human soul as represented in the thymus—that area of man's soul beyond rationality and even desire. Hegel attributed man's participation in contests and wars that are devoid of any economic meaning to his avid striving for recognition. Yet it was Marx's materialism that folded religion and "men's striving for recognition" into an ideological superstructure serving economic motivation, which, unbridled, drives human behavior.

What we need to ask ourselves now is whether a late-nineteenth-century-based managerial incentive system, neglecting thymus, is in fact effective and whether it may not be wiser to develop a system that is appropriate to each stage of development, rather than lazily imposing the North American system on all, and, furthermore, to post at all Latin American business schools the credo "in our father's image."

After all, the value-ridden managerial technology embedded in the globalization path renders many people foreigners in their own countries. This feeling of inadequacy deprives people of their basic need for recognition and is at the root of the fundamentalist overtones of the reaction to globalization—whether seen in the protests at Seattle against the World Trade Organization, the terrorism in the Middle East, or the passive resistance of a shoe shop attendant in Rio de Janeiro.[28]

Once we allow for a more creative managerial outlook, we will be able to see more readily why Rio de Janeiro samba schools manage yearly to put on the street quite a few thousand dancers and musicians who have practiced for months and spent relative fortunes on decorations and costumes—all for no money and without MBA advice. Joãozinho Trinta, who has masterminded many of those Carnival feats, argues that he simply allows people to achieve their "desire for realization." Now, if that does not blend Plato's thymus into a managerial incentive system, what does? Yet why are those popular team management skills so notably absent in the region's managerial technology?

SUMMING UP: THYMUS AND PECUNIARY INCENTIVES

We intimately know that people work for more than money. But money is a convenient way of rewarding—so convenient that one would not dream of scrapping it altogether—yet it does not work miracles, either. Resting on the assumption that extrinsic incentives such as commissions or bonuses will align the agent with the principal, as in sales attendants with shop owners, is bound to breed trouble in countries with high power distance such as Brazil and Argentina. In those countries, the ready allegiance is more likely to benefit the underdog, like the passerby who needs help, conceivably perceived by workers as a fellow pilgrim to whom one owes allegiance and support, which will be given at all costs.

Perhaps a system tallying referrals between shops may be more attuned with the local culture. This has a better chance of ensuring that the paramount satisfaction of the customer will be achieved and that the referring shop and its sales attendant will be rewarded for their guidance. While such a system may be most practicable within closely connected business zones, such as shopping centers, the difficulty of implementation should not be sufficient reason for ignoring that extrinsic incentives like sales commissions are missing the point.

CHAPTER 16

STRATEGY AND CONTROL

THIS CHAPTER WILL FOCUS on strategy and control matters that are affected by culture, beginning with the alleged greater uncertainty aversion of Brazilians and Argentines. I will show that surveys have been biased against cultural traits that are inherently Latin American, and that this may have led Brazil and Argentina to be portrayed as uncertainty-averse countries to a greater extent than is warranted. Because responsiveness to uncertainty levels are crucial to investment in research and development (R&D), I will pay more attention to redressing the survey-based rendition of Latin Americans as being unusually risk averse.

I then address control and performance instruments such as anonymous denunciation and feedback. I argue that the Latin American propensity to work in teams fosters engagement that could be jeopardized if workers are subjected to a climate of denunciation, especially in environments such as Latin America that offer little juridical constraints to false denunciation. Widely practiced feedback techniques are brought into question because, as currently applied, they do not reflect the fact that collectivist cultures, particularly high power distance cultures, require specific conditions for applying such tools.

Regarding strategy, I point out that outsourcing and single-purpose companies may not be the most effective avenues in "smaller ponds," where opportunities may not allow for adequate gains in scale and where their implementation will break the solidarity bonds that heighten engagement within the corporation. Because single-purpose companies in North America can be said to be expressions of obsession, I will analyze obsessiveness as represented in the epic novel *Moby-Dick* and in the temperance movement in the United States. I also delve into mergers and acquisitions, where I call attention to the importance of culture in determining the length of the planning horizon as well as the acceptable level of indebtedness of a corporation.

AVERSION TO UNCERTAINTY

According to Hofstede, two-thirds of the countries and regions he surveyed reflect people who are less uncertainty averse than Brazilians were evaluated to be. About 80 percent are less uncertainty averse than the Argentines and the Spaniards. Just about all peoples surveyed are less uncertainty averse than the Portuguese. Can all of these groups be as averse to uncertainty as Hofstede's statistical analysis would lead us to believe?

Let us assume for a moment that the eminent Dutchman is right in believing that the preference by Brazilians and Portuguese to know what is expected from them—as depicted in a book of procedures, for example, and as would express the preference not to be left rudderless—can be taken to be an expression of aversion to uncertainty, as discussed in Chapter 11.

If, as I have argued in this book, the inhabitants of the New World are cultural heirs to their forefathers, the Brazilians would tend to be risk avoiders if their Portuguese forefathers also were. We had no Hofstede in the fifteenth and sixteenth centuries to compare the attitudes of the Portuguese people to those of the rest of the world. But we do know that the Portuguese were daring navigators seeking new trade routes around Africa, sailing where no European had been before. We also know that the Portuguese persevered in their search for a route to India for almost a century, until Vasco da Gama finally succeeded. Furthermore, we know that when the Portuguese discovered the routes, and the riches to be made by trading along them, they set themselves to take advantage of those routes, despite the risks. These were substantial, as can be gauged by the fact that, every year, of the seven ships that sailed to Asia, only four returned.[1] Knowingly facing a casualty rate of that sort is not for the fainthearted. Surely, the Portuguese could not be taken to be uncertainty avoiders nor nonentrepreneurial, at least not in the fifteenth and sixteenth centuries. Perhaps not even through the eighteenth century. By the nineteenth century, Napoleon had wreaked havoc with Europe's minor powers, and Portugal folded even more tightly under the protection of England.

Yet Portugal was always a small fish in a large pond. It is surprising that the Portuguese ever set off in small boats to accomplish what they did. Furthermore, it is surprising that small Portuguese companies still act in much the same way. For instance, Logoplaste, active in plastic containers, piggybacks on the expansion of large multinationals such as Nestlé, producing in loco the needed containers for Nestlé wherever they may go. The Pestana group, active in five-star hotel management, establishes strategic alliances with airlines and tour operators to cater to the needs of tourists at their destinations. In barely a decade since their first foreign direct investment, these two companies have become, respectively, third and fifty-first in European ranking.[2] Portugal, which once took the world in small boats, is now taking it in small companies. If anything, the Portuguese have learned to manage uncertainty, not to avoid it.

We know from Chapter 3 that Spain's history is no less wondrous, and while it suffered the same plight as Portugal under Napoleon, and both experienced long and conservative dictatorships during the twentieth century, Spain made a significant comeback since the 1980s. This is illustrated in the expansion of Spanish multinationals, mainly in Latin America but also elsewhere. By 1992, Spain's cumulative foreign direct investment had exceeded investment by foreigners in Spain. By 2006, *The Economist* was reporting that the country's businessmen were the "new conquistadors."[3] Mauro Guillén, of Wharton, is particularly scornful of such tags because, he argues, they undermine the credibility and forcefulness of Spanish expansion by instead attributing it to something akin to striking gold again, five hundred years later.[4] There are over one thousand Spanish firms investing abroad—a far cry from a handful of "conquistadors." Spain is responsible for only about 2 percent of global GDP. What makes this foreign expansion particularly remarkable is that it is taking place without the usual accoutrement of power, neither protected by state diplomacy nor induced and helped by a particularly strong state-run information system.

This Iberian resourcefulness, which seems to be making a comeback, is in the nature of Latin America's heritage. If Latin Americans were not willing to face uncertainty, they would not rank among the world's most entrepreneurial people, which they do, according to the 2004 Global Entrepreneurship Monitor (GEM) ranking.[5] To GEM, Latin America outranks even Africa and the Middle East as the most entrepreneurial region of the world. North America, as a region, comes in third. It could well be, however, that much of the entrepreneurial activity by Latin Americans comes from people who would rather have jobs in which they could contentedly follow written procedures, and that for lack of such jobs they start businesses of their own. Although they might appear to be entrepreneurial by virtue of being self-employed, in fact it could be the lack of availability of secure jobs that leads them to entrepreneurial undertakings. If that analysis is so, then Latin Americans would be less entrepreneurial than North Americans—who are presumably not driven to entrepreneurship from lack of other options—despite starting up more companies than North Americans. Indeed, GEM also tells us that the ratio of necessity-driven Latin American entrepreneurial activity vis-à-vis North American entrepreneurial activity is 4 to 1. Nonetheless, the share of opportunity-driven entrepreneurs in Latin America was 59 percent in 2004 and had remained remarkably stable for four years.

Without being too partial to Latin Americans, one could claim that, for every person driven to entrepreneurial activities out of necessity, there are two that are driven by opportunity. If this assertion is in error, it is less of one than in stating that Latin Americans are nonentrepreneurial. By extension, Brazilian entrepreneurs would by definition be no more uncertainty averse than the Portuguese navigators and traders were, Hofstede notwithstanding.

Lack of Innovation as an Expression of Uncertainty Avoidance

If Brazilians are entrepreneurial and daring, why would they not be innovators? This is a frequent question, but not a fair one. Both Brazilians and Argentines have shown considerable disposition to innovate in the sciences and in engineering. As noted in Chapter 7, Argentine scientists have been awarded three Nobel Prizes in the sciences and, by the 1960s, had offered significant innovations in agricultural machinery, despite the country's relatively small domestic market. I have also shown that Brazilian engineering, particularly civil engineering, made world-class strides in a field not conducive to exporting and remained mostly confined to its own frontiers until large civil works dwindled in the 1980s. By then, the technical competitiveness of those civil engineering companies was not confined to engineering but had extended to management know-how, without which they could not have managed to execute what until recently was the largest hydropower dam in the world, Itaipú.

What we need to understand is why that creative capacity does not translate into productive technology. That Argentina and Brazil are not alone in this conundrum, should not put the matter to rest. Let us briefly review the issue.

Much of what we call innovation today happened in the manufacturing sector. Yet in Latin America that sector came into being mostly from a process of import substitution. It could hardly be considered innovative. Demand and lobbying power helped raise the import barriers, and a nascent industry developed under state protection, divorced from university research, which was made redundant by technology embedded in the imported machinery. Rather than an expression of risk aversion, this type of development was an expression high power distance.

Another possible explanation may be found in managerial exhaustion. Let us assume that the managerial mind-set focused on operational excellence seeks to minimize risks, and that the mind-set oriented to innovation tends to take risks. It could well be that managers in developing countries, already coping with high levels of uncertainty in making their businesses run, cannot devote as much attention to innovation as managers who operate in more stable and predictable environments.

After all, how much do these countries invest in research and development? Scale determines volume; thus let us compare the R&D effort as a share of GDP. The United States not only invests more in R&D as a share of GDP (1.61 percent at the turn of the twentieth century), but it also differs in the composition of the expenditure: the production sector may contribute close to half of that effort. In Brazil and Argentina, the source of funding is the opposite: the production sectors frequently invest less than one-third of overall investment as a share of GDP, leaving the government to make up the rest. At least in Brazil, this may again be an expression of the lobbying strength of private enterprise, as befits a high power distance business environment.

Why would private entrepreneurs invest in research themselves if they can put pressure on the government to do it for them? This seems to have been the thinking behind the Brazilian Genome Project, when a cooperative of orange growers invested less than 4 percent of the $15 million coughed up by the government of São Paulo. The portion invested by private companies amounts to less than one-half of 1 percent of the yearly exports of frozen orange juice concentrate, an industry that was under threat from the *Xylella fastidiosa* bacterium and that might well be rescued by government-funded research.

Yet investment in research tells only part of the innovation story. We need to understand the efficiency of that investment. Does it result in something that may enhance productivity? If so, one would imagine that whoever put in the research effort would want a share in the proceeds of a practical application. To that purpose, the researcher would want to patent the innovation. Unfortunately the patenting side of the story is even weaker than the investment in research.

Dog-Eat-Dog, and the Safety of the Kennel

If Brazilians and Argentines were uncertainty averse and collectivist, they would seek the comfort of government employment rather than attempt to survive through employment in corporations bound by an individualist and competitive ethos. If, in addition, Brazilian scientists and engineers were nurtured by a meritocratic ethos as happens elsewhere, they would shun family-owned enterprises for being less meritocratic and riskier than the government, at least to the highly trained professional that is not a relative of the owners.

Bernard Rosen reported that, in general, Brazilian boys appear to be pushed to excel in specific activities less than their counterparts in the United States.[6] This is the result of a study conducted in the early 1960s, during the formative years of many of the current Brazilian leaders. Furthermore, the same report argued that Brazilian parents of boys tended to overstate their sons' achievements. This was attributed to boys being nurtured in an overindulgent and overprotective environment, vis-à-vis the North American culture.[7] On a more positive note, the same author reports that Brazilian boys are nurtured in an environment that shuns aggressiveness and stresses conciliation. It would seem that the conditioning of Brazilian males is not primed for a competitive market economy. Indeed, research suggests that among executives of Brazilian corporations, factors such as humility, search of meaning at work, and personal realization at work take precedence over the aggressiveness necessary to focus on results.[8]

Lack of priming for competitiveness may be the result of a sheltered environment, as expressed by high tariffs in addition to overprotective parents. This attitude is revealed in the low interest in intellectual pursuits among the Brazilian entrepreneurial elite. Indeed, Maria Fernanda Teixeira da Costa recorded the responses of twenty-nine top entrepreneurs of Brazilian exporting corporations selected among the corporations responsible for 85 percent of all exports in the country.[9] The companies surveyed are among the largest five hundred Brazilian corporations; two-thirds employed at least five thousand people, and over one-third employed over ten thousand.

The survey purported to explore entrepreneurs' adherence to Martin Seligman's twenty-four strengths of character.[10] Support for "love of learning" came in last among sixteen significant categories. Curiosity ranked fourth. One may feel satisfied that at least curiosity ranks high, but keep in mind that these were exporting entrepreneurs. Curiosity may rank substantially lower, if significant at all, among nonexporting entrepreneurs. That "love of learning" figures so low is in agreement with the Brazilian private sector's demonstrated low proclivity to invest in research and development. Again, the respondents were exporters and therefore active in a more competitive environment than entrepreneurs producing for protected markets. Among nonexporting entrepreneurs, "love of learning" is likely to receive a low to insignificant ranking.

Finding a Fit for Local Researchers

It is questionable whether Latin American researchers would find careers with the subsidiaries of multinationals. By and large, those companies are not in Brazil to develop technology but rather in search of clients for their finished products. Occasionally, U.S.-based multinationals invest in R&D in Latin America, but the flows of that investment are offset by the investments of Latin Americans in R&D in the United States.[11] The net effect of R&D investment flows between North America and Latin America is zero.[12] Managers of multinationals in Brazil are directed to sell and not to buy, least of all to buy technology. This is why multinationals in Brazil offer little hope of employment to highly trained Brazilian scientists and engineers.[13]

At present, four in every five Brazilian scientists and engineers are engaged in research work for the government or for universities. The ratio is precisely the opposite in the United States. The divorce between university-based technological pursuits and private enterprise has delayed the adaptation of imported technologies to the Brazilian reality. For instance, larger radiators and faster fans took decades to be installed in water-cooled bus engines that had been designed for colder climates. French electrical equipment used in the glass industry performed poorly under the wide voltage fluctuations of the Brazilian electricity grid. Swiss spinning machines designed for longer-fiber Egyptian cotton produced substandard cotton threads in Brazil.

Because multinationals will not hire the local talent in sufficiently large numbers, and because national companies are largely family-owned and nurtured within industrial policies that provide an insular environment, Brazilian scientists and engineers find little hope of employment in the private sector. Thus they look largely to the government for research positions and thereby circumvent the competitive environment. This may help explain why, among the Brazilian organizations that can claim at least twenty patents abroad, state-run corporations and two public universities answered for almost half of these up to the year 2000.[14]

FEEDBACK

Employees typically show a significant interest in knowing how they are doing, and managers are equally compelled to report on employees' progress. Just as well, for accurate feedback exchange is crucial to sound management. The trouble is that the feedback process does not work as well in the Latin American environment as it does in the United States. Mistakes tend to occur at three cultural levels, as determined by (1) the asymmetry of individualist-collectivist attitudes, (2) high and low power distance orientations and the associated social status–related implications, perhaps most common in Mexico and Peru, and (3) high- and low-context levels when communicating.

In high power distance cultures, the employee is more likely to ascertain his or her standing in the workplace by asking peers, not the boss. Peers and third parties in general provide a safe alternative to asking a supervisor for feedback, which in high power distance cultures may even be impolite, just as telling the truth may be hazardous. Many have lost their jobs for that sin. High power distance cultures prize allegiance over independence and punish offenders; asking questions to the boss breeds discomfort, particularly if the boss does not know the answers. Thus in Brazil, as in China, workers feel more comfortable asking their colleagues for informal performance appraisals.[15]

Let us examine a well-known case in the United States. Even egalitarian countries like the USA have bureaucratic pockets of high power distance, and the Central Intelligence Agency is one such example. In its mission to serve the nation, the CIA must route its information through government channels, even when the receiving government officials may dislike the information. However, telling the truth has been hazardous for CIA officials, as in the case of Joseph Wilson's refutation of the hypothesis of purchases by Iraq (under Saddam Hussein) of uranium from Niger, as the U.S. government would have it. Disappointed by the report, a high governmental aide illegally leaked the news that Wilson's wife was a covert CIA official, putting her life at risk as well as effectively ending her career.[16] Such are the consequences of not being part of the dominant team in a high power distance culture, or in this case, subculture.

In the more collectivist Latin American culture, the emphasis on teamwork tends to minimize and be suspicious of the individualization of contributions to tasks accomplished collectively. North American feedback techniques that seek to elicit feedback from and about individuals in Latin America strike out on both counts. Not only do these techniques ask the wrong questions to the wrong people, but they also fail to address the nature of teamwork. If, in addition, we consider that the United States is a low-context culture and that Latin America is a higher-context one, where communication requires a greater density of shared codes, any feedback that does take place is sure to be accompanied by a lot of fanfare.

The giving and asking of feedback should be relatively straightforward, but it is not. Culture affects both the ability to tell and be heard and the way employees become apprised of their performance.[17] The more egalitarian the society, the more transparent are its feedback exchanges. Thus it is not surprising that U.S. managerial techniques rely strongly on direct appraisals of individuals' performances, nor that those same techniques fail to perform as well when transplanted to Latin America. We have known this for over two decades, but the message seems not to have penetrated human resources management in Latin America, where business consultants have long earned their livings applying 360-degree evaluations, under the erroneous assumption that the feedback will reveal all.

Both feedback giving and asking must be adapted to the host environment, particularly in Latin America.[18] For instance, a North American tends to seek specific information from a coworker or subordinate, frequently limited to what is necessary to make a prompt professional assessment and not sparing of hard and direct questions. A Latin American respondent, on the other hand, will feel inclined to first get to know a coworker in order to decide how to relate to him or her before answering any questions. Even then, the Latin American's answers will at first be elusive and tentative, as if sending out feelers; yet the North American expects straightforward answers. While the lack of tuning may be uncomfortable under any circumstances, this cultural asymmetry is fatal in a feedback environment. Worse, once the first miscommunication takes place, trust will be eroded.

Yet the feedback process is necessary and ultimately appreciated by those concerned. Besides asking the right questions, we need to ensure that feedback follows more appropriate avenues. This implies enabling lateral and indirect feedback when in high power distance environments.

Denunciation as a Control Mechanism[19]

In the United States, corporations frequently allow anonymous denunciation in order to pinpoint possible deviations from compliance.[20] It is cheap and effective and not wholly unethical in the U.S. environment, where the legal system can enforce severe penalties for false accusations. In Latin America, however, where law enforcement is notoriously weaker and accusers are not always held accountable, there is little beyond self-respect to refrain employees from making false accusations.

Several American multinationals in Brazil and elsewhere in Latin America are offering anonymous hotlines for reporting to headquarters in the USA possible deviations from compliance. These reports are evaluated, and a few are selected for follow-up. This process takes time, and the accused may not even know he or she is under investigation. But in collectivist environments it is hard to keep secrets for long. The person under investigation may perceive, by the attitudes of colleagues and supervisors, that something is wrong, and a climate of anxiety thus takes hold during the weeks or months of investigation. Worse, denunciations are occasionally made for no other reason than envy or other ill-founded motives that may be compounded by a competitive environment that is relatively alien to Latin American culture.

The anonymous denunciation instrument has its benefits to the corporation, not least of which is its low cost.[21] Yet to a Latin American, the ethical grounding of an instrument of control based on anonymous accusations is unethical and nearly unfathomable. This negative reaction may be the result of a collective, unconscious rejection of the unfairness of the Holy Inquisition, which, through its Edicts of Faith, washed away the presumption of innocence and turned denouncement into religious duty.[22]

To Latin Americans, the denial of anonymous denunciation as a means of compliance enforcement also contains the implicit rejection of the utilitarian moral that drives the reward model acceptable to North Americans. Under utilitarianism, all maximizing behavior benefits the individual. To counter the trend implied by utilitarianism, the corporation should seek to align employees' interests with those of the corporation by attempting to curb criminal deviations by employees. This can be accomplished by increasing the penalties for deviation along with the probability of detection. A foreign corporation in Latin America can do little more than fire an offender—a penalty that merely imposes the loss of a wage and provides too little in terms of deterrence, particularly when the stakes are high. From the perspective of the corporation, early detection is beneficial, and denunciation is made easier under cover of anonymity.

The implementation of anonymous denunciation instruments exemplify how cultures differ and how lack of respect for those differences can lead to productivity losses.[23] While a well-meaning corporation would not unfairly sanction an innocent employee victimized by the false allegations of an anonymous denunciation, restraint can do little to assuage the grief of an employee and his or her family and friends during an investigation—and beyond, if the investigation is inconclusive, as many are. Moreover, asking any employee to remain hostage to the corporation's goodwill is a throwback to the times of rule by divine right, when citizens were forced to trust in the restraint of the royal mandatory in the enforcement of his will.

It was precisely the battle of the British people through the centuries that led to restraints on Charles I's powers through the Petition of Right in 1628. The clauses of the petition found their way into the USA's Bill of Rights, where they protect Americans on issues such as arbitrary arrest and imprisonment, nonparliamentary taxation, and martial law.[24] Prior to the petition, the English people had to trust the king not to abuse his powers. In fact, "Trust the King" was the only argument put forward by the British chief of justice Sir Edward Coke when opposing the petition.[25]

The Petition of Right passed, and the rest is history. But a modern instrument of coercion such as anonymous denunciation, which is limited only by the restraint of the power that applies it, is most certainly a throwback in political terms and ethically unacceptable. That it is not seen as such in the United States does not affect its ill fit in Latin America, a region where poor law enforcement and an ineffective judicial system put honest workers at a disadvantage. Those conditions will not improve in the very near future.

Results of a Survey in São Paulo

In order to determine the impact and attitudes of employees regarding anonymous denunciation, I carried out a survey in São Paulo during January–March 2006. The survey had only ten Web-based questions and was administered electronically, and the call for respondents was sent by e-mail to alumni of the Executive MBA program of IBMEC São Paulo, and of the Katz Business School's Global Executive MBA in São Paulo. Altogether, of the 175 respondents, 27 percent worked for fully owned Brazilian corporations, 14 percent for joint ventures with Brazilian corporations, 22 percent for U.S. corporations in Brazil, and 24 percent for European corporations. Two-thirds of all respondents worked for companies with over five hundred employees, one quarter were either the boss or reported to the boss, and two-thirds were male.

Overall, the picture that emerged is that anonymous denunciation is not frequent among the largest Latin American corporations operating in São Paulo, that anonymous denunciation is most resented at the higher corporate echelons, and that a favorable attitude toward anonymous denunciation diminishes when people personally know anyone that has been harmed by the instrument (see Figure 16.1).

Indeed, even the largest Latin American corporations tend not to practice any form of anonymous denunciation, not even through suggestion boxes. The share of U.S. corporations in the same size range that allow for anonymous denunciation is six times higher. European corporations of the same size rate somewhat lower, but still at almost six times the Brazilian level. Large Japanese corporations in Brazil do not practice anonymous denunciation.

Competition is strongest at the top, and that is also where managers tend to become lightning rods for disgruntled employees in a work environment that is generally more patriarchal and authoritarian than in the United States. Only two respondents, both of them four notches below the boss, knew someone who had been unfairly accused. Also, the greater the distance to the top dog, the more diffuse the attitudes toward the instrument appear to become in Brazil, suggesting that those more frequently targeted by anonymous denunciations are precisely the top dog and those in the two rungs immediately below the top.

Interestingly enough, all of the top leaders were willing to admit to some deterioration in the organizational climate by the introduction of anonymous

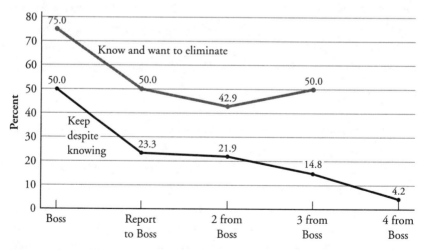

FIGURE 16.1. Percentage in Brazil of persons acquainted with someone accused anonymously, who wish to eliminate or keep anonymous denunciation, by reporting distance to top leader

denunciation instruments, because "all feel under threat." None of them acknowledged any improvement in the organizational climate due to the introduction of instruments that would "allow anyone to denounce bosses and
colleagues." However, it was precisely at the lower echelons that considerable
satisfaction with an improvement in organizational climate was reported regarding the possibility of denouncing colleagues and bosses.

A major factor in determining attitudes toward anonymous denunciation
was whether the respondent was acquainted with anyone who had been accused
unfairly. A full 84 percent of respondents were in favor of some method of
anonymous denunciation, yet familiarity with the consequences of the misuse
of the instrument seemed to have a sobering effect on all. Among respondents
in that category, support for the method drops, at best, to 50 percent among
top leaders, and opinions for keeping the instrument, among those who know
anyone unfairly victimized by the instrument, never rise above 25 percent for
all levels of hierarchy, except for the top leaders—although only two respondents fit this description.

Views among those who wish to eliminate the instrument are stronger once
they know someone unfairly victimized: 75 percent of the top leaders are in
favor of scrapping the instrument, and support for scrapping the instrument
never drops lower than 45 percent.

Puerto Rico is a good example of why instruments designed for use in the
United States may travel poorly. The University of Puerto Rico at San Juan
established an anonymous denunciation scheme in 2004, and by 2005 the
instrument was playing havoc with its organizational climate. Puerto Rico
is a self-governing commonwealth associated with the United States, but its
judicial system, except for federal transgression issues, is Puerto Rican and as
unreliable as elsewhere in Latin America. Because the legal system cannot be
counted on to protect employees' images when wrongly accused, the accuser—
even when accusing unfairly—has the upper hand.[26]

Whether in Puerto Rico, Brazil, or anywhere else in Latin America where
law enforcement is less efficient than in the United States, anonymous denunciations are likely to cause a lot of grief at the workplace, jeopardizing people's
engagement and discouraging innovation and other error-prone initiatives.
As an instrument of managerial control, it is precisely the type of example
of a U.S. managerial tool that should not be applied without adjustments in

Latin America, if at all. Forcing employees in Latin America to be subject to arbitrary accusations goes against what Americans would expect of their own employers in the United States, and Latin Americans know it. Simply put, it reflects poor management and it breeds distrust.

SINGLE-PURPOSE COMPANIES, A CONTEMPORARY MOBY-DICK

Single-purpose companies are deemed more efficient because in *sticking to their knitting* they *stay focused*, both at the *top of the mind* of their clients and on *developing competencies*, which allows companies to *capitalize on scale* while building *competitive advantages* that create barriers to *market entry* in their *market niche*.

In itself, the preceding paragraph seems customized to make top grades on an MBA exam of the 1990s. Yet the single-purpose company was more than a buzzword, and when it arrived in Latin America, managers took to it like to so many other American beats. In deference to this fad, banks in Latin America fired hundreds of matronly *Dona Maria* coffee maids and outsourced coffee services to single-purpose companies that installed coffee vending machines. Yet the *Dona Marias* who had served coffee in São Paulo's corporate cubicles also served up smalltalk and a means of connecting people by breaking the isolation of naturally gregarious employees.

Of course, not only coffee maids were shed; whole information technology (IT) departments followed the same route as the *Dona Marias*. Whether outsourcing has worked as well in Latin America as it did in the United States may be too soon to tell, but the early signs in Brazil's IT field are not so good.

Brazilian software developing companies have not yet acquired the size that would allow them to specialize.[27] This could be the result of small, fragmented markets in the sense that only a handful of business poles exist in Brazil that are large enough to justify specialized software development providers. These conditions are more prevalent in developing countries; it is not a difficult problem to anticipate. This fact alone might have discouraged outsourcing in that field. Yet the elusiveness of success may also be the result of applying in Brazil a strategy developed in the United States for its own peculiar demographic circumstances.

Since the 1980s, U.S. demographic trends were forecasting a shortage of entry-level talent in the mid to late 1990s.[28] By 1990, the news had hit the business press,[29] and a year later academic business journals were publishing studies on the implications of such labor shortages.[30] Outsourcing in the United States was a logical organizational response to the need for more specialized use of increasingly scarce and therefore expensive professionals—of which software development was only a miniversion of a broader national trend.

On the other hand, as from the mid-1990s, Brazil was educating more software developers than it could employ. Consequently, wages for software developers flattened during the decade and then dropped, as did the number of students in undergraduate studies at Brazilian universities.[31] Obviously, the circumstances were different in the USA and in Brazil, but U.S. companies operating in Brazil took no notice of the differences and, under instructions from headquarters, followed the same outsourcing fad that was peaking at home—gutting IT departments in the process.

An alternative for the Brazilian software development sector would have been to develop software for third parties abroad, as the Indian developers did. Why it did not is the topic of Chapter 10. But software outsourcing for the domestic market should not have been the first option for young software developers, just as it should not have been corporate policy to eliminate IT departments. A proof of the mistake is that Indian companies such as Infosys, Satyan, and TCS arrived in 2005 in Brazil and are sweeping up the same software developers that the ill-advised outsourcing companies had dispensed with.[32] A decade of turmoil, low wages, and wasted Brazilian talent is the only result to speak of.

Foreign and local firms operating in Brazil adopted outsourcing software development even at the expense of strengthening their own competitive advantages in mastering a field so critical to their success, and they did not benefit from obtaining a superior independent service. Corporations took this route because of the lack of an independent ability to discern what was best for them in Brazil. In hindsight, outsourcing software development services was an obvious mistake for the majority. However, had the conditions been more favorable for a successful outsourcing strategy—for example, if the market for software development had been less geographically fragmented, or if a labor supply shortage had indicated a more restricted availability of the scarce resource—would outsourcing, with the specialization it depends on, be a sound organizational response in the Brazilian culture? There is no obvious answer, at least not for Brazil, but historically, monomaniacal pursuits of the sort embodied in single-purpose companies have been more of a North American domain than a Latin American one.[33]

Monomania

Take, for instance, Herman Melville's *Moby-Dick* (1851), which can be seen as an epic quest on which generations of Americans have been nurtured, starting with Melville's transcendentalist contemporaries—the same circle of people who befriended the Argentine Sarmiento, as we saw in Chapter 7.

As a literary piece, *Moby-Dick* defies classification. If it were an epic quest, it would fit in with epic traditions of the conflict genre, such as *The Iliad,* or with the search for reason in a life-transforming journey, such as Dante's *Divine Comedy*.[34] Whether *Moby-Dick* fits into either of those epic styles is immaterial to our own quest; what matters is that *Moby-Dick* was, and still is, a fundamental part of American literature and that the central quest of its tale is represented in a "monomaniacal" pursuit.

Whether the white whale that is the focus of Captain Ahab's relentless obsession in the book is a representation of the Self, or whether the captain was maddened by his obsessive hatred and blinded by his craze, are still open questions. What is not, and what is more relevant to our purposes, is the fact that Melville chose to express Captain Ahab's quest as a single-purpose obsession to chase down Moby-Dick, and that American readership has heightened the book's significance, ensuring its tall standing for the last century and a half—even longer than Martin Fierro has stood among the Argentine people.

Moby-Dick Lives

In 1956 John Huston directed the film version of *Moby-Dick,* starring Gregory Peck as Captain Ahab. That feat encapsulated Huston's own obsession with the story. Similarly obsessive American epics have been transferred to the screen in great style, such as Coppola's *Apocalypse Now,* which nominally relates the persecutions carried out by Vietnam War renegade Colonel Kurtz. But the film also retells Joseph Conrad's *Heart of Darkness* in the setting of Vietnam, with imagery particular to that lived by the Vietnam War soldiers: a mysterious tiger emerging from the jungle typifies the environment's natural hostility; a shooting spree on a bridge, when the chain of command has broken down, highlights the senselessness of the war; and the added twist of Playboy bunnies ushering forth from American helicopters expresses the lunacy of it all, as does Colonel Kurtz's bizarre quest—all of this adding to the perception of the Vietnam War as one of America's great ambiguities, very much like Captain Ahab's monomaniacal persecution of Moby-Dick.[35]

Obsessions are singular in their focus, and perhaps not even rare. What stands out is the apparent American disposition to mobilize around pursuits that, to other cultures, appear to be obsessions. Take the temperance movement as an example.[36]

The temperance movement was a British idea that initially discouraged the drinking of spirits in England in the 1830s. By the 1840s its followers began advocating teetotalism: neither beer nor wine was acceptable, nor was offering alcohol to others. By the time the temperance movement reached the United States, an antialcohol obsession took over. The Woman's Crusade (1873–74) sought to destroy all alcoholic beverages and to force the closure of saloons. The Anti-Saloon League was founded in 1893, and two years later it became a nationwide movement. In its twentieth-anniversary convention in Ohio, the Anti-Saloon League proposed what became the eighteenth amendment to the U.S. Constitution, which succeeded in passing in 1916. Both in 1917, the American Medical Association voted to support Prohibition and Oklahoma passed the Bone-Dry Law, making it illegal even to provide wine at Catholic sacraments. That portion of the law was overturned a year later, but Oklahoma would repeal Prohibition only in 1959.

I could continue with examples of American obsessions—ranging from substantive ideas such as political correctness to lesser fixations such as imposing the use of darker clothing colors after Labor Day—but I believe I have made my point. There exists a militant side to the American character that stems from a universalist stance (see Chapter 11), which becomes obstreperous when it is impinged upon foreigners. Lamentably, American obsessions that need not be shared are unnecessarily imposed on Latin Americans as a matter of course by managers trained in the American ethos.

Single-Purpose Stands for Monomania

The preference for single-purpose organizations may be precisely one of those American obsessions. The Latin mind, in contrast, is more disperse. As seen in the preference for polychromic use of time, there seems to be a greater acceptance of a multiplicity of objectives in Latin America. This may be even more pronounced in Brazil, where diffuse objectives such as quality of life may play a stronger role in people's imagery. To Latin Americans, single-purpose companies appear as boring and threatening as Protestant bankers: all efficiency, no meaning.

Unable to fathom the reason for American obsessive behavior regarding deadlines, goals, and time limits for dinner parties, Latin Americans may feel extremely uncomfortable when subjected to what they perceive as stringent and senseless work guidelines.

INTERNATIONAL JOINT VENTURES

This section calls readers' attention to the importance of cultural influences in areas of management not readily recognized as being contingent on culture, such as finance and its supporting base of accounting. The issues become most relevant in international ventures and are especially acute when expansion occurs in countries culturally distant from the country of origin.

International expansion brings risks of its own, largely stemming from asymmetry of information in foreign markets. An important initial decision is whether to establish a wholly owned subsidiary abroad or to merge with an existing partner in the target market. The latter, known as an international joint venture (IJV), is said to lower the risks associated with incomplete local information regarding the institutional framework or distribution channels, for example, and is probably the safest route to take when the cultural distance is greatest between the home country and the foreign country.

Nonetheless, merging with a foreign corporation is bound to mean trouble at some level, and the cultural sort of trouble is what we will focus on. Any new culture will pose challenges, particularly on issues such as adapting to the environment and responding to its threats. Attitudes regarding these challenges are affected mostly by cultural differences in uncertainty avoidance and long-term orientation.

Adaptation to the internal dimension of a corporation has much to do with people's attitudes toward hierarchy, individualism, and assertiveness or masculinity. Still, as difficult as it may be in an international joint venture, the decision can be made early on to leave the management of human resources to the locals. Tanure de Barros and colleagues suggest that this is the corporate activity most often relinquished to local management, principally for the greater flexibility and faster adaptation that tend to result. Finance and control, together with R&D, are more often retained at headquarters, with a host of other activities prone to ad hoc solutions falling in the middle ground, such as purchasing, marketing, and sales.[37] While this arrangement frees up foreign managers to focus on other pertinent matters, it still leaves a lot to be decided jointly. How to finance the endeavor is one such prominent decision.

Until now, finance was believed to be the least troublesome component of all. Finance has evolved into a set of commonly agreed-on decision-making methods, and the application of those shared methods was not expected to generate difficulties in IJVs. But it has, largely due to differing perceptions regarding acceptable levels of uncertainty and length of the planning horizon. For instance, deciding how much debt to take on is related to the corporation's confidence level regarding the maturity length of the investments. Too much debt repayment too soon can bankrupt the company.

How much debt to carry is a crucial strategic decision for any corporation, IJV or not. The textbook approach regarding leverage recommends that a projected stream of earnings must leave enough aside to pay for the debt. How much is enough depends mostly on culture and the perceived damage that failure would cause. Embeddedness- and mastery-oriented cultures, à la Shalom Schwartz, tend to borrow less, relative to profits, than other cultures. Cultures with a strong sense of embeddedness tend to prize harmony with partners and shareholders. They also tend to revere public image and to have autocratic leaders who feel responsible for their employees—who, in turn, are loyal to the leaders. Failing one's followers and partners has a high moral cost in cultures that prize embeddedness. High mastery cultures arrive at similar decisions for different reasons. These are cultures in which success is associated with individual prowess and an orientation toward being in control. Constraining debt covenants are the opposite of what these people stand for, just as bankruptcy represents the loss of control.

Fortunately, these hypotheses have already been tested.[38] The authors of a 2002 study regressed 1996 national average, corporate finance leverage data on Schwartz indices for cultural dimensions. Banks and utilities were excluded from the sample, and American and Japanese corporations were most numerous—but no country in the sample was represented by fewer than fifty corporations. The data were also controlled by the corporation's business activity. As predicted, the coefficients for mastery and embeddedness were both negative and highly significant (higher mastery or embeddedness led to lower debt ratios), and both variables jointly explained 44 percent of the variation. The results were robust inasmuch as they were confirmed for data for different years, for the countries' levels of economic development, for the legal systems that determine the strictness of investor protection, and for the effect of industry, when only mastery was less significant.

Other authors have focused on the longevity of international joint ventures with Dutch participation and have found that the lifespan of IJVs is shorter the greater the disparity regarding Hofstede measures of uncertainty avoidance and long-term orientation between the Netherlands and the target market.[39] These cases strongly suggest that even financial decisions may be contingent on culture.

But there is more. Finance relies on accounting procedures and the reports they generate, and accounting procedures since the time of Sidney J. Gray have been shown to reflect local cultures in many ways, despite the entire convergence pretense in Generally Accepted Accounting Principles (GAAP).[40] Some of the cultural practice dimensions suggested by Gray, such as uniformity of procedures or the professional level of the accounting practitioners, may be ascribed to the rigor of their training. Nonetheless, the perception of what constitutes sufficient rigor in accounting procedures is contingent on culture. Other dimensions suggested by Gray involve straightforward cultural traits, such as conservatism and secrecy. For instance, the level of reserves for bad debts is contingent on culture, as is how much to reveal on a balance sheet.

Globalization will no doubt seek to standardize and harmonize accounting procedures by means of international accords on these matters. Progress may be more rapid among large companies that deploy enterprise resource planning (ERP) systems. Nonetheless, it will be a long time before new accounting procedures filter down to the sources, to the myriad bookkeepers who tally records in developing countries. An accelerated imposition of standard practices may result in legal standards that are out of sync with local practices, which just might lead to a new definition of double-entry accounting.[41]

SUMMING UP: INTERNATIONAL JOINT VENTURES

Finance is contingent on culture, in direct and indirect ways, to an extent that only recently became apparent. Culture's direct influence derives from differences in perceptions of an acceptable level of uncertainty or time horizons, and its indirect influence derives from the accounting work that finance professionals must rely on. Because of the nature of the work of accountants, this group of practitioners tends to look backward more frequently than forward, making the profession an inherently conservative one that is relatively impervious to change. A "big bang" drive to harmonization practices may lead to the appearance of duplicitous standards, defeating the purpose of the ongoing process of convergence. This convergence, however, may take much longer than the quick-footed finance professionals would wish to accept.

CHAPTER 17

THE WAY FORWARD

CULTURE PROVIDES the resourcefulness to deal with nonroutine managerial matters. Training, a procedures manual, and quality control take care of the rest. Or they should.

Yet reality is humbling. Nonroutine decisions take over day-to-day management. Routines must constantly be adapted to accommodate such uncontrollable forces as supply disruptions, slack in demand, delinquent payments, exchange rate volatility, and competitor inroading. Slowly but surely, local culture creeps into the processes of multinationals operating in Latin America. The curse to effective management is that variances in culture are often dismissed as unimportant. On the surface, Latin American culture may not stand out as alarmingly different from U.S. or European culture, yet the cultural disparities are large enough to breed trouble—such as occurred in the United States during the Little Rock crisis in 1957. As highlighted in Chapter 6, even the outcome of the U.S. Civil War in favor of the North did not prevent the living beliefs of a significant number of Southerners from remaining at odds with the nation's desegregation laws nearly one hundred years later. Without a match between a culture's living beliefs and the laws meant to guide its behavior, people's motivation to uphold the law of the land will wane. When there is great disparity, people must be forced into compliance, as witnessed in Little Rock when the U.S. National Guard was called in to uphold a unanimous Supreme Court ruling. Moreover, those who abide by the law only under the threat of its enforcement will adopt strategies to circumvent what they perceive as unfair laws—which triggers the need for further allocation of resources in order to oversee compliance.

The same is true for managerial techniques. When corporate procedures are out of tune with the living beliefs of those being managed, management is apt to react with coercive behavior and micromanaging, resulting in wasted resources, unhappy employees, and lower productivity. It need not always be so, but it takes time for people to change. Turning the formula on its head by adapting managerial techniques to new cultures is the clear solution.

Some will say that convergence of cultures is an ongoing process, and that the present lack of congruence between Latin American culture and North American management techniques will eventually straighten itself out naturally. I cannot disagree more, for the trend toward convergence, while positive, is simply too slow to make a difference. We have seen in Chapter 12 that middle management in southern Europe and northern Europe continue to this day to display different leadership styles. In the United States, it has taken almost a century and a half and a civil war for the country to accommodate on its own continental territory a modicum of convergence that people can live with. A century and a half is a long time to suffer, even when the suffering is being done by someone else. The message to management is that corporations will be better off adapting their policies and instruments to the people being managed, instead of expecting everyone to suddenly dance to their beat.

This book has also pointed out significant cultural differences as expressed in the tales and myths of origin that reproduce themselves in the socialization of our peoples; in doing so, both Americas perpetuate the perceptions of their differences. Such is the case in four tales addressing the early meetings of the white man and the native Indian woman. On the North American side, we have the abandonment of Algonquian Indian princess Pocahontas by the Englishman John Smith. On the Latin American side, we have three nonsegregationist stories that speak to a difference in attitude between North and South regarding the willingness of newcomers to the New World to adapt to cultures.

Latin America is hardly monolithic, but the fact that its nations are different from one another does not make them more similar to the United States. I have illustrated those differences mainly through Brazil and Argentina, yet the argument holds that all Latin Americans differ from North Americans in predictable ways. Still, likenesses can be discerned among Latin Americans and Southerners in the USA. Both regions share fatalistic traits, similar codes of chivalry and honor, and patriarchal political structures. The culture that gives life to a Latin American oligarchic family is only a distant cousin of the Southern Dixiecrat in the United States. And it is not by chance that both the Confederates in the American South and Latin America's Caribbean countries saw the rougher edges of U.S. achievement-oriented expansion.

This book has also stressed the differences in individualism, both conceptually and regarding the manifestations of individualism. I have argued that individualism in the Americas is no more than a cognate. It implies equality under the law to North Americans, but uniqueness to Latin Americans. Moreover, this uniqueness is largely expressed in the freedom from utilitarian choice, as warranted by choices that court tragedy, ranging from bullfighting to Argentina's invasion of the Falkland Islands to Cuba's acceptance of Russian missile bases.

If a relentless pursuit of one's choice, to the point of defying tragedy, is to be the measure of an individual's uniqueness and honor, then compromise will be dishonorable, negotiation will be perceived as capitulation, dissent will be cajoled into submission, and tyranny will be the consequence, even in the workplace. This unyielding stance is so prevalent in Latin America that, as with ideology, people are unaware of the extent of its determination. For instance, although politics ought to be the arena of negotiation, one of Argentina's significant political parties contains the word *intransigent* in its title. Chile's national motto reads "Through Reason or by Force," implying "my way all the way." Brazil's positivist motto shaved off the initial "love" part of the Comtian heritage, leaving us with the last bit, "Order and Progress"—still somewhat softer than Chile's, but barely. Indeed, in Brazil, the "order" directive has often been tyrannically enforced since the positivist motto took root toward the end of the nineteenth century, as it was similarly enforced in Mexico under Porfirio Díaz.

Whether the preceding ideological foundations go far enough in characterizing the exact size and shape of all of Latin America's peculiar political excesses is not the issue. What matters is that this ideological tradition is old and broad, stemming from a Mediterranean concept of honor and self-love that discourages conciliation with others. It is not by chance that none of the Mediterranean countries that provided the core of European immigrants to Latin America have themselves been models of political innovation in the last four hundred years, with the lamentable exception of the innovation of fascism. The ideological bent that gave southern Europe a Mussolini, a Franco, and a Salazar also found its expression in Nasser, Boumedienne, Perón, and Vargas in less developed countries. This is precisely the point I wish to make and that ought to have deep implications for the style of managerial leadership that people in Latin America expect to find and ultimately abide by in business, despite the stated participatory styles rendered by surveys.

I have also discussed the differences in the disposition toward uncertainty, suggesting that the history of the Iberian heritage points not to uncertainty aversion but rather to adventure-seeking characteristics. Centuries of geographical exploration and hazardous trading could not have engendered either a people keen to avoid uncertainty or lovers of routine work. Yet routine work is required in great quantities in order to secure and deploy innovation in productive processes. While I have also pointed out that innovation is not wholly absent in Latin America, it so happens that it is largely divorced from production, as expressed in the region's low number of patent requests. That the lack of patent filings is not an exclusively Latin American problem should not lead us to complacency, because development anywhere is unlikely without the deployment of indigenous innovation in the solution of local problems.

I have also discussed differences in the enactment of masculinity as reflected in the greater dispersion of objectives that characterizes the Latin American. Latin Americans tend to perceive single-purpose concerns as obsessions; they also differ from Anglo-Americans in their attitudes toward time. "Time is money," the epitome of industrious American aphorisms, as attributed to Benjamin Franklin, is yet another expression of what Latin Americans view as North American obsessiveness—similar to Captain Ahab's relentless persecution of a whale in *Moby-Dick*, a literary icon that has seeded the thought formation of so many generations of Americans and that finds a contemporary expression in the portrayal of Colonel Kurtz in Coppola's *Apocalypse Now*. We will no doubt see a similar film depicting the quest for Osama bin Laden in the near future—for evil, in the American psyche, can be individualized and therefore Satanized, as Moby-Dick once was or bin Laden now is, overlooking the significance of the forces that gave rise to bin Laden's large following in the Middle East. Such monothematic obsessions are less frequent in the Latin idiosyncrasy. Thus in Latin America, single-purpose companies are unlikely to remain single purpose for long, and outsourcing is unlikely to spawn the specialization and yield that recommends that strategy in North America.

To a Latin American, time occupies a broad band within which many concurrent activities may be pursued, the building of relationships not least among them. This perception has deep implications, because neither time nor space bears the specialized function in Latin America that these concepts signify to a North American. The Latin American is also likely to expect that the workplace provide the same opportunity as anywhere else for forming friendships and pursuing other nonobvious connections to productivity, and all of these factors combined may, in fact, contribute to the effectiveness of teamwork. Perhaps this is why Joãozinho Trinta, a famous samba school director responsible for numerous top prizes in Rio de Janeiro's Carnival parades, attributes the success of his leadership to "allowing people to become." The current American-tailored workplace is a poor model of this philosophy; in such settings, feedback breeds tension, controls are excessive, and coercion is rampant. Foreign managerial controls, such as anonymous denunciation instruments, only make matters worse, for they exacerbate Latin Americans' inherited discomfort with centuries of Inquisitorial persecution.

I have also discussed how and why Latin Americans have a much stronger proclivity to asymmetrical power relationships at work. This stems from centuries of similar Iberian power relationships that were reproduced in Latin America by means of unequal access to land and other resources. In both Argentina and Brazil, large estates were the norm, as was the practice of sharecropping or leasing parcels from landowners. These relationships were underscored in Brazil through slavery to a greater extent than in Argentina. The fact that slavery was also prominent in the Southern USA only partially redresses the cultural differences between Latin America and the United States. The latter underwent a civil war in order to expand positive law that would reflect the ethos of a universal man rather than one whose rights depended on the color of his skin, whereas in Brazil slavelike relationships lingered on.

Both the relative size of the Negro population in Brazil at the time of emancipation, vis-à-vis that in the United States, and the oral tradition of the slaves' religion ensured that African animist values would percolate into Brazilian Catholicism, rendering it different from, and more malleable than, the form of Catholicism practiced in the USA. This difference in flexibility may also be responsible for the chronic shortage of Brazilian priests, reflected in the inhabitants-per-priest ratios in each region. If Catholicism in Brazil were more malleable, perhaps more Brazilians would take the route of priesthood. As it stands today, Brazilians can be expected to marry, baptize their children, and die according to Catholic rites, and perhaps attend Mass every now and then, but living the life of a priest requires a more rigid acceptance of Catholicism than the Brazilian people can comfortably bear. Americans seem to have an easier time with the restrictions imposed by Catholicism, and Brazil's relative scarcity of priests has been supplemented by an influx of North American evangelical purveyors.

The North American accommodation of Catholic inflexibility is also indicative of the cultural differences that alienate U.S. managerial techniques from Latin Americans. Still, the main religious difference between the two regions is that the United States is predominantly Protestant, as it has been from the start. In being Protestant, North America was the intellectual beneficiary of the Protestant Reformation and was inoculated against the medieval hierarchical institutions of Scholasticism. Thus, North America was better prepared to embrace modernism without having to struggle with religion in order to do so. To modernize, North America never needed to become anticlerical, as Mexico and Uruguay did. Moreover, Protestantism ensured that, if only for the sole purpose of Bible reading, the American population would be literate from the get-go. Reading, whether the Bible or anything else, was never a primary distinction of the Catholic Iberian people. Illiteracy spread well into the twentieth century, when radio and, later, television helped loosen the grip of ignorance over the Latin American population, particularly Brazil's. Nonetheless, inspired by the United States, Argentina, Chile, and Uruguay made significant strides against illiteracy still in the nineteenth century, when

those countries showed a lower illiteracy rate than that of Spain, the country
to which they owed their existence and their educational heritage.

Besides religious differences, the density and diversity of the native populations of Latin America also distinguished it from North America. Several
countries in Latin America blended the richness of very significant portions
of native Indian cultures into their populations and cultures. Some did so actively and forcefully, such as Mexico, particularly after Porfirio Díaz; others
did so in a limited way, such as Brazil in response to the Semana Modernista.
A very few acted forcefully in the opposite direction, like Uruguay, where the
native population was either decimated or pushed across national borders.
Others simply did nothing, like Argentina, despite a native Indian population
proportionally larger than Brazil's.

Further philosophical inputs differed as well. North America imported British legal institutions and the inclination to resist encroachment by the state, as
well as British individualism and its inductive, empirical style of reasoning. On
the other hand, Latin America looked to France for inspiration and adopted
Encyclopedism, with its rationalist bent, which would later lead to a ready acceptance of Comtian positivism. Interestingly enough, Uruguay and Argentina
adopted positivism of the English variety, as espoused by Spencer. Those that
followed the Comtian strain only reinforced their authoritarian background,
as with President Vargas in Brazil at least until the mid-twentieth century, and
Porfirio Díaz in Mexico, as expressed in his slogan *pan o palo* (bread or the
club). Positivism would hold a firm grip for much longer in southern Brazil,
which produced a few of Brazil's military dictators after the coup of 1964.

Large indigenous theocracies; a centralist and hierarchical Catholic church
that backed large, power-concentrating landholdings; and positivism, particularly
of the French variety, all combined to create a powerful synergy that helped send
Latin America on a developmental path significantly different from the North
American one, most notably in the acceptable level of power concentration within
both social and business organizations. The high power concentration among
lay members of society in Latin America, free from the caring constraints of
Iberian Catholicism, led to an administration of justice that made a mockery
of the system that had prevailed under Spain's Catholic kings. Impunity is the
heritage of Latin America, and poor self-esteem is the living consequence among

its people, inhibiting the expansion of intellectual products and services such as software and engineering design.

In contrast, the North American developmental path may have been intolerant at first, but its Protestant bent ensured a highly literate population, a swiftly applied law, and town meetings. Grassroots problem solving and the power of literacy were tangible, and citizenship was a daily practice—while in Latin America the people remained subjects in a flock. This had deep implications for leadership styles, including business ones. Latin American organizations do not flatten well: hierarchy will remain palpable, and people will still expect to be told what to do. Thus the number of people that can be effectively managed reduces to a smaller scale in Latin America than perhaps elsewhere, which suggests that improving small-team management techniques is a worthwhile goal—if accompanied by curbs on the proclivity toward exaggerated authoritarianism for the small-group leaders.

Much of this book has been devoted to rescuing the positive elements of the medieval overtones of the inherited Latin American culture. Yet correcting the current foreign managerial shortcomings may even require reintroducing medieval instruments of administration of justice, such as the *corregidores*. A modern-day equivalent could be selected from among a firm's retired employees and executives, who would help bridge existing gaps in fairness in administering workplace practices. This contingent would be relatively impartial and intimately aware of the organizational culture and of the tacit agreements regarding the acceptable administration of corporate policies, placing such persons in a unique position to decide on quick and fair solutions regarding minor disputes.

Surely the natural endowments of the two Americas also played a significant part in differentiating their development paths. The North American plains generously opened themselves to successive waves of immigrants and their wagons, whereas the South American equivalent of easily accessible plains would be found only in distant Argentina. Brazil shielded its beauties behind the great escarpment, forcing immigrants to climb through the insidiously hostile rain forest before exposing its own high plateaus to avid foreigners. And, of course, there was the gold and silver, which dilated the pupils of greedy adventurers hoping for a quick stroke of luck. Several areas of Spanish America lay riveted with gold and silver, yet initially it appeared to be more abundant on the Pacific Ocean side of the New World. Greed was such a propellant that Argentina and Central America were at first populated on their Pacific shores rather than from the more intermediate Atlantic shores.

It is hard to conjecture whether the English settlers in North America would have been so industrious had they struck gold earlier. When gold was discovered, they behaved very much like the Spanish and Portuguese immigrants, as witnessed by the California Gold Rush. Then, in Protestant America—exactly as had occurred in Catholic America—luck replaced merit as the source of recognition for success. The hymnbook was shoved aside, and physical strength took the reins. Nonetheless, the discovery of gold in the United States occurred late enough for the country to have developed a significant level of industrialization, capable of satisfying domestically the sudden rise in demand for goods that the westward expansion entailed.

American industrialization was supported by superior education, a shortage of manpower, and the convenient proximity of high-quality coal and iron ore mines. At the time, Argentina had neither of these minerals and Brazil had discovered iron ore but very little coal that was worthy of the name, which in any case was located far from the iron ore mines. Nor was an educated labor force close at hand in Brazil. Much to the contrary, slavery depressed inventiveness by discouraging investment in any effort to replace an abundant and inexpensive labor force. Neither Brazil's resources nor its education were sufficient to come up with an invention of the magnitude of the steam engine; but if the steam engine had been invented in Brazil, its power would be measured not in horses but in the number of slaves it would have replaced.

The cultural differences that characterize the New World have been somewhat portrayed by the application of questionnaires aimed at eliciting the different attitudes. The surveys, important as they have been, have assumed that different peoples can abstract from all their history and richness and react in the same way to the same questions. I have suggested that this is a very strong assumption and that, in the effort to elicit numerical cultural indices, researchers have necessarily either downplayed differences that are intractable by surveys, or produced results that distort important attitudes. In the first alternative, surveys have reported that charisma is universally recognized as a necessary quality of leadership, yet the results do not capture the desired enact-

ment of charisma, thus overlooking the difference it may make to Argentines
or Brazilians to be led by a Franklin Delano Roosevelt instead of a Perón or
Vargas, respectively. In the second alternative, the surveys have portrayed Latin
Americans as strongly averse to uncertainty, yet historical and direct evidence,
such as a high disposition for entrepreneurial initiatives, points precisely in the
opposite direction.

Moreover, with the exception of Shalom Schwartz, cross-cultural surveys
have tended to be elitist in their coverage, neglecting the views of the vast majority of the populations. The people surveyed by business-oriented surveys
are unlikely to be the ones who in Bolivia voted for Evo Morales, in Peru for
Ollanta Humala, in Venezuela for Hugo Chavez, or in Brazil for Lula. Yet those
voters are the people whom corporations will hire to carry out their activities,
and to whom they will expect to sell their goods. Those voters will also decide
to protect foreign investment, or not. So far, cross-cultural quantitative surveys in Latin America have not told us more than we already knew about the
elites that speak English and travel abroad. Quantitative surveys, as heretofore
administered, have hit the point of diminishing returns. Some of the measurements they have rendered may be way off the mark, as I have suggested in the
book, either by asking inappropriate questions or by omitting pertinent questions. Not only are the measurements yielded questionable, but also the classification of cultural clusters has not rendered groups that are any different from
what could have been surmised by interpreting information from history and
the social sciences. Latin Americans need to develop their own instruments to
portray themselves and to look inward through their own eyes.

Because the effort of producing better survey results across so many cultures
is frequently beyond the funding accessible to Latin American researchers, an
alternative is to make do with the cultural information readily available. When
judiciously selected and analyzed, literature can provide a wealth of information
at little additional cost. When this becomes insufficient—as when a literary
piece fails to reflect the values of all of the players on the business stage, such
as women—cinema may provide a more modern complementary outlook.

The combination of artistic sources with the analyses of social scientists
and business students is bound to be very revealing, particularly when the
analyses are grounded in actual business and organizational practices and focused on unearthing indigenous organizational strategies, leadership styles,

evaluation of teamwork, and ways of control. This could be done, in Brazil's case, by closely studying the management of quintessentially national organizations in the sports and entertainment industries, such as cinema, music bands, soccer clubs, and samba schools. These organizations deal with cultural expressions and require business-type organizational strategies in order to deliver their products or services. Moreover, in being 100 percent national, their organizational structures provide a natural fit with local cultures. This research strategy must study intentionally for-profit national organizations that may have grown large, such as agribusiness and the passenger transportation industry in Brazil, or agribusiness and engineering consulting companies in Argentina.

In order to achieve some relevance and efficacy, Latin America must revive the nationalist nonxenophobic movements that swept Mexico after the 1910 revolution, and Brazil around the Semana Modernista of 1922. Both revolutionary movements expressed themselves in the arts, performing and nonperforming. Unfortunately, the ideas that lent them sustenance petered out before they could spread to management.

In Latin America, "milk tooth" business schools were set up in the early twentieth century. Brazil's first so-named business school was little more than a school of accounting, and in Mexico, the people were too caught up in a revolution to settle easily for scientific management techniques. Mexicans at that time were weary of scientific management after almost four decades of the authoritarian Porfiriato mandate and the policies of Porfirio Díaz's "scientists." Mexican nationalism and Brazil's modernism came too early to benefit the business schools of those countries, and when the first business schools per se were founded in Latin America, mostly after World War II, catching up was the rallying cry. North American corporations were expanding, and they demanded managers with training similar to that of the managers at headquarters. Latin American business schools thus contented themselves with training students for niches developed for other peoples. At the time, little reflection was given to the implications of introducing North American management methods into Latin American societies, but there is no excuse now.

Much of the management instruction that has taken place in Latin America resembles rote drilling under the direct or indirect tutelage of North American business schools. Some of the foreign managerial practices that were introduced, such as anonymous denunciation, came across as culturally alien to local populations and have thus bred contempt over time. Others require constant reinforcement, binding business and staff to a permanent bondage and to a tutelary relationship, whether through hiring foreign consultants, importing foreign textbooks, or sending students abroad.

In earlier times, only a few patriarchal families from underdeveloped countries managed to command resources large enough to send their offspring to study abroad and learn the tools of the trade "from the horse's mouth." Such was the case of the Macris in Argentina and the Prados in Brazil, as it once was the case of the Berlas in India, the Soongs in China, and the Oeis in Indonesia. Yet even if those foreign-educated offspring had possessed the needed talent to run their inherited businesses into a prosperous future, their impact would still only skim the surface of the problem—namely, that cultures are inherently different and slow to converge, even when there is sufficient evidence that convergence is entirely desirable or already occurring.

This book is, in sum, a libertarian cry to rethink management practices in Latin America, seeking to tailor them to the cultures of its people rather than the other way around. The blend of indigenous and inherited values fluctuates across Latin America. One solution will not fit all. The rethinking effort needs to be homegrown, based first and foremost in respect, and receptive to local values. Across Latin America, a traditional orientation toward social justice often guides people to shun greed and even profit. That attitude is prevalent in much of what is regarded as great in Latin America. It extends from Sarmiento's free public school educational revolution in Argentina, which rendered five Nobel laureates in the twentieth century, to Brazil's state-run oil company, Petrobrás, which holds four times more patents abroad than the leading patent holder among private Brazilian corporations.

The commonwealth orientation among Latin Americans is a residual of the state-led discovery of the New World. It was consolidated by the spread of a medieval Catholicism with a collectivist orientation, which found support in the indigenous communities that were converted as well as in the African populations that were enslaved. But this collectivist cultural cauldron has very deep roots in Mediterranean culture—particularly in the notion of uniqueness of the individual, with its passionate and intransigent overtones—as well as in the role of honor and family in the behavior of individuals.

All of the above suggests that Latin American culture is too old, too deeply ingrained, and even too great to discard. Certainly, attempting to effect change solely through business schools, even with the input of foreign enterprises, is not enough. As old-fashioned as it may sound to the business school circuit, the most promising way forward is to listen to local cultures and to attune management practices to their cues.

NOTES

INTRODUCTION

1. "What's Behind Edward C. Prescott's Nobel Prize?" *Knowledge@Wharton* (Dec. 1, 2004), http://knowledge.wharton.upenn.edu/article.cfm?articleid=1082 (accessed Aug. 22, 2008).

2. Agrícola Souza Bethlem, *Gerência à Brasileira* (São Paulo: McGraw-Hill, 1989), 3–9.

3. Simon Ulrisk Krag and Malene Durjsaa, "Modernization and Management: Business School Teaching Across Countries," *International Journal of Cross Cultural Management* 6, no. 1 (2006): 19–36, esp. 31.

4. Davos, the yearly seat of the World Economic Forum, congregates a transnational elite with a Weltanschauung that Harvard Professor Samuel Huntington has captured as that of the "Davos Man": "these transnationalists have little need for national loyalty, view national boundaries as obstacles that thankfully are vanishing, and see national governments as residues from the past whose only useful function is to facilitate the elite's global operations." Samuel Huntington, "Dead Souls: The Denationalization of the American Elite," *American Future* (Sept. 26, 2005), http://americanfuture.net/?page_id=144 (accessed Aug. 22, 2008).

5. Huntington believes the Davos Men and Women do not represent more than 4 percent of the American population. Ibid.

6. Professor Northrop attributes India's parliamentary success, compared to that of Pakistan, to the lower share of Islamic population in India and to the fact that, upon partition, India retained the larger cities where the more modern-oriented population lives. Even so, Minister of Law Ambedkar told Northrop in 1950 that these modern Indians

represented less than 3 percent of the population. F. S. C. Northrop, *Philosophical Anthropology and Practical Politics* (New York: Macmillan, 1960), 14.

7. Robert Alan LeVine, *An Introduction to the Comparative Study of Psychosocial Adaptation* (New York: Aldine de Gruyter, 1982), 98.

CHAPTER 1

1. Robert Alan LeVine, *An Introduction to the Comparative Study of Psychosocial Adaptation* (New York: Aldine de Gruyter, 1982), 4.

2. Margaret Mead, *Coming of Age in Samoa: A Psychological Study of Primitive Youth for Western Civilization* (Washington, DC: American Museum of Natural History, 1973), 65, 75, 76, 81, 90, 96, 124.

3. P. Christopher Earley, *Face, Harmony, and Social Structure: An Analysis of Organizational Behavior Across Cultures* (New York: Oxford University Press, 1997), 29.

4. Charles Winick, "How People Perceived the Mad Bomber," *Public Opinion Quarterly* 25, no. 1 (Spring 1961): 25–38.

5. When the Mad Bomber was caught, he was found to be a fifty-four-year-old white Catholic man of Lithuanian ancestry.

6. Thomaz Lenartowicz and James P. Johnson, "A Cross-National Assessment of the Values of Latin America Managers: Contrasting Hues or Shades of Gray?" *Journal of International Business Studies* 34, no. 3 (May 2003): 266.

7. Luiz Felipe de Alencastro, *O Trato dos Viventes: Formação do Brasil no Atlântico Sul, Séculos XVI e XVII* (São Paulo: Companhia das Letras, 2000).

8. Samuel P. Huntington, "Keynote Address" (presented at Colorado College's 125th Anniversary Symposium, "Cultures in the 21st Century: Conflicts and Convergences," Feb. 4, 1999).

9. See, for instance, the interesting criticism of the alleged convergence regarding alternative developmental paths in Mauro F. Guillén, *The Limits of Convergence: Globalization and Organizational Change in Argentina, South Korea, and Spain* (Princeton, NJ: Princeton University Press, 2001).

10. For an interesting anthropological appreciation of the Latin American ethos, see John Gillin, "Ethos Components in Modern Latin American Culture," *American Anthropologist* 57, no. 3 (June 1955): 488–500; Michael Herzfeld, "Honor and Shame, Problems in the Comparative Analysis of Moral Systems," *Man* 15, no. 12 (June 1980): 339–59.

11. Book of Ezekiel, 34:23, 37:24–28.

12. Mariano Picón Salas, *A Cultural History of Latin America* (Berkeley: University of California Press, 1968), 40.

13. José Enrique Rodó, *Ariel* (Austin: University of Texas Press, 1988 [1900]).

14. The dismissive Iberian attitude toward experimental work is still very much alive. Recently, a journalist asked the Spanish Catholic priest who directs one of São Paulo's elite schools, why the laboratories were so sparse. The father replied, "It is better that way; lab

classes add little to the students' understanding of the topic and have the disadvantage of taking too much precious time." *Folha de São Paulo* (Apr. 29, 2005): sec. Especial 13.

15. For an early discussion of these issues, see John Gillin, "Modern Latin American Culture," *Social Forces* 25, no. 3 (Mar. 1947): 243–52, esp. 244.

16. José Hermano Saraiva, *Historia Concisa de Portugal* (Lisboa: Europa-América, 1998), 99.

17. These impressions are offered not as a fairness-orientation ranking of societies, but rather to call readers' attention to the difference in what is desirable or meaningful in each society. Nonetheless, it could well be that the Iberian cultural template, for all its inherent unfashionable inefficiency, will end up providing a balsamic alternative to the legitimation crisis that affects the fast-food mass financial derivatives culture, as seen in 2008.

18. Primo de Rivera was Spanish ambassador to Argentina and influenced the Peronist circles that took to corporatism. Perón later sought exile in Madrid, under Franco's care.

19. Leopoldo Zea, "Philosophy and Thought in Latin América," *Latin American Research Review* 3 (1968): 13–16.

20. Eduardo Davel Paes Barreto, João Gualberto M. Vasconcellos, "Gerência e Autoridade nas Empresas Brasileiras: Uma reflexão Histórica e Empírica sobre a Dimensão Paterna nas Relações de Trabalho," in *Cultura Organizacional e Cultura Brasileira*, ed. Fernando Motta and Miguel Caldas (São Paulo: Atlas, 1997), 94–110.

21. Eugene C. McCann, "An Aspect of Management Philosophy in the United States and in Latin America," *American Academy of Management Journal* 7, no. 2 (1964): 149–52.

22. This was perceived by Richard Morse some four decades ago in "The Strange Career of Latin American Studies," *Annals of the American Academy of Political and Social Science* 356, no. 1 (Nov. 1964): 106–12.

PART 2

1. James Lockhart and Stuart B. Schwartz, *Early Latin America: A History of Colonial Spanish America and Brazil* (Cambridge: Cambridge University Press, 1983), 1.

CHAPTER 2

1. D. M. Wilson, *The Anglo-Saxons* (New York: Praeger, 1960), 36. English Christianity was built on Saxon polytheism, and Saxon Gods still live on in the names of the English week: Tuesday derives from Tiv, god of war; Wednesday from Woden or Odin, the highest god in Norse mythology; Thursday from Thunor, god of thunder; and Friday from Frig, goddess of love. Saturday, Sunday, and Monday are named for Saturn, the Sun, and the Moon, also worshiped by the Anglo-Saxons. Christmas replaced the winter Yule fest, and Easter derives from the Saxon goddess for spring, Eostre.

2. Christopher Brooke, *The Saxon and Norman Kings* (London: Batsford, 1963), 171.

3. Frank Barlow, *The Feudal Kingdom of England, 1042–1216* (London and New York: Longmans, Green, 1955), 392.

4. From Giovanni Boccaccio's description of the Black Death in *The Decameron*, trans. M. Rigg (London: David Campbell, 1921): "One citizen avoided another, everybody neglected their neighbors and rarely or never visited their parents and relatives unless from a distance; the ordeal had so withered the hearts of men and women that brother abandoned brother, and the uncle abandoned his nephew and the sister her brother and many times, wives abandoned their husbands, and, what is even more incredible and cruel, mothers and fathers abandoned their children and would refuse to visit them."

5. Josiah Cox Russell, *British Medieval Population* (Albuquerque: University of New Mexico Press, 1948), 367.

6. Ibid., 375.

7. John Kelly, *The Great Mortality* (New York: HarperCollins, 2005), 110.

8. Helen Cooper, *The Canterbury Tales*, 2nd ed. (Oxford: Oxford University Press, 1996), 23.

9. Tampering with the Bible may have been part of the same initiative that would feed "our trespasses" rather than "our debts" into the "Lord's Prayer," as in "forgive our debts," which is how it read since the first century AD. The fact is that the "Lord's Prayer" prayed by Catholics today is not the same "Lord's Prayer" prayed by Protestants, precisely in an issue so central as forgiving debts, or not. See the commentary by Clodomiro Vianna Moog, *Bandeirantes e Pioneiros: Paralelos entre Duas Culturas* (Rio de Janeiro: Civilização Brasileira, 1964), 166ff.

10. The significance of Jack Cade's revolution did not escape Shakespeare's attention, nor that of the modern literary critic: "Although Cade's confident assumption that he speaks on behalf of those who dare not speak for themselves may well be mistaken, it bespeaks a consciousness of collective interests and shared goals that is, for all rights and purposes, a consciousness of class." Thomas Cartelli, "Jack Cade in the Garden: Class Consciousness and Class Conflict in 2 Henry VI," in *Enclosure Acts: Sexuality, Property, and Culture in Early Modern England*, ed. Richard Burt and John Michael Archer (Ithaca, NY: Cornell University Press, 1994), 56.

11. British pragmatism would surface almost five hundred years later, with North Sea oil-pricing during the OPEC-induced oil shortages. Although not formally a member of the oil cartel, Britain would peg the price of its resource to that fixed by OPEC.

12. Almost as if shrugging his shoulders in the face of the recurrent restrictions to his authority, King Charles let them "have it": "'Soit droit fait come il est désiré.' That was the answer they had been hoping for. That was the answer which made the Petition a matter of record and gave it the force of a common law decision." Harold Hulme, *The Life of Sir John Eliot, 1592 to 1632: Struggle for Parliamentary Freedom* (London: Allen & Unwin, 1957), 255.

13. It would take the Swiss another two and a half centuries, until the Helvetic Republic constitution (1798), to tolerate cohabitation of religious faiths.

14. The Whig interpretation of the Glorious Revoulution would have ended the divine right of kings to hereditary succession in 1689. Yet the divine right to a divine mon-

archy lingered on. Gerald Straka, "The Final Phase of Divine Right Theory in England, 1688–1702," *English Historical Review* 77, no. 305 (Oct. 1962): 638–58.

15. Peter Kropotkin, *The Great French Revolution, 1789–1793*, trans. N. F. Dryhurst (New York: Vanguard Printings, 1927).

16. W. C. Costin and J. Steven Watson, *The Law and Working of the Constitution: Documents 1660–1914* (London: A. and C. Black, 1952), 46.

17. Robert M. Adams, *Paths of Fire: An Anthropologist's Inquiry into Western Technology* (Princeton, NJ: Princeton University Press, 1996), 108.

18. John D. Montgomery, *Technology and Civic Life: Making and Implementing Development Decisions* (Cambridge, MA: MIT Press, 1974), 11.

19. George Douglas Howard Cole, *A Short History of the British Working-Class Movement 1789–1947* (London: Allen & Unwin, 1960 [1948]); and E. P. Thompson, *The Making of the English Working Class* (London: Victor Gollancz, 1965), 41.

20. Adams, *Paths of Fire*.

21. H. J. Habakkuk, *American and British Technology in the Nineteenth Century: The Search for Labour-Saving Inventions* (Cambridge: Cambridge University Press, 1962), 190.

CHAPTER 3

1. Over the centuries of cohabitation on the Iberian Peninsula, the cultural exchange may have been larger than the sexual one. The latter, while not overpowering, was substantial, as is revealed by recent mitochondrial DNA analysis. See E. Bosch et al., "Genética e Historia de las Poblaciones del Norte de África y de la Península Ibérica," *Investigación y Ciencia* 317 (Feb. 3, 2003): 62–69, esp. 69.

2. Old Castile and Andalusia had between 20 and 30 inhabitants per square kilometer in 1591, as opposed to a figure of under 15 for New Castile and under 8 for the kingdom of Granada, weakened by a recent, bitter civil war and the expulsion of its Moorish people. This was well below the averages for France (34) or Italy (44) at the time. See James Casey, *Early Modern Spain: A Social History* (London: Routledge, 1999), 22.

3. Ibid., 61.

4. Giovanni Botero, *The Reason of State*, trans. P. J. Waley and D. P. Waley; notes by D. P. Waley (New Haven, CT: Yale University Press, 1956 [1589]), 146.

5. Anglo-Saxon readers should note the informal title of "father" attributed to the Marquis of Ensenada. The association of a leader to a father figure will be a recurrent theme in the paternalistic leadership relations mentioned in this book, as representative of a leadership style most common in Latin America.

6. James Casey, *Early Modern Spain: A Social History* (London: Routledge, 1999), 25.

7. A similar assessment may be found in Peter C. Emmer, "The First Global War: The Dutch Versus Iberia in Asia, Africa and the New World, 1590–1609," *e-Journal of Portuguese History* 1, no. 1 (Summer 2003): 2.

8. Nina Ayala Mallory, *El Greco to Murillo: Spanish Painting in the Golden Age, 1556–1700* (New York: HarperCollins, 1990), 21.

9. Casey, *Early Modern Spain*, 165.

10. Ibid., 166.

11. The *corregidor* was the magistrate who administered justice in a territory in the name of the crown. The period of incumbency was only one year, and by petition of the neighbors it could be extended to two years. It was believed that by frequently shifting *corregidores* the administration of justice could be insulated from corruption and favoritism. Robert S. Chamberlain, "The Corregidor in Castile in the Sixteenth Century and the Residencia as Applied to the Corregidor," *Hispanic American Historical Review* 23, no. 2 (May 1943): 222–57, esp. 230.

12. Casey, *Early Modern Spain*, 166.

13. David Ortiz, Jr., "Redefining Public Education: Contestation, the Press, and Education in Regency Spain, 1885–1902," *Journal of Social History* 35, no. 1 (2001): 73.

14. Ibid., 73.

15. Martin Blinkhorn, "Spain, the Spanish Problem and Imperial Myth," *Journal of Contemporary History* 15, no. 1 (1980): 15–25.

16. Lawrence E. Harrison, *Who Prospers? How Cultural Values Shape Economic and Political Success* (New York: Basic Books, 1992), 53.

17. Timothy Mitchell, *Passional Culture: Emotion, Religion, and Society in Southern Spain* (Philadelphia: University of Pennsylvania Press, 1990), 91.

18. Christina Turner, "Cultural Continuity and Change in Gremio Fiestas in Yucatan," *MACLAS Latin American Essays* (Apr. 1, 2000).

19. Michael S. Werner, ed., *History, Society and Culture*, vol. 2 (Chicago: Fitzroy Dearborn, 1997), 1130.

20. Gary H. Gossen and Miguel Leon-Portilla, eds., *South and Meso-American Native Spirituality: From the Cult of the Feathered Serpent to the Theology of Liberation* (New York: Crossroad, 1993), 164.

21. Ibid.

CHAPTER 4

1. "J. M. Durão Barroso," *El Pais* (Madrid, Feb. 12, 2004): 1.

2. Harold V. Livermore, *A History of Portugal* (Cambridge: Cambridge University Press, 1947), 230.

3. For a review of the role of Jewish connections and international trade during the sixteenth and seventeenth centuries, see Cecil Roth, "The Economic History of the Jews," *Economic History Review* (New Series) 14, no. 1 (1961): 131–35, esp. 134, regarding the sugar trade.

4. It is also surprising that it would be the Dutch to compete against the Portuguese before the French or the English did. See Peter C. Emmer, "The First Global War: The Dutch Versus Iberia in Asia, Africa and the New World, 1590–1609," *e-Journal of Portuguese History* 1, no. 1 (Summer 2003): 3.

5. José Hermano Saraiva, *Historia Concisa de Portugal* (Lisboa: Publicações Europa-America, 2001), 168.

6. L. M. E. Shaw, "The Inquisition and the Portuguese Economy," *Journal of European Economic History* 18, no. 2 (1989): 415–31, esp. 416, where one can find: "The main change between the mid-sixteenth century and the mid-eighteenth century was that the Portuguese merchants had disappeared as a commercial force."

7. See Roth, "Economic History of the Jews," 134.

8. Richard James Hammond, *Portugal and Africa, 1815–1910: A Study in Uneconomic Imperialism* (Stanford, CA: Stanford University Food Research Institute, Stanford University Press, 1966), 100.

9. Wilson Trajano Filho, *Pequenos Mas Honrados: Um Jeito Português de Ser na Metrópole em nas Colônias*, Serie Antropologia, 339 (Brasília: Universidade de Brasília, Departamento de Antropologia, 2003).

CHAPTER 5

1. T. J. Hatton and Jeffrey G. Williamson, *The Age of Mass Migration: Causes and Economic Impact* (Oxford: Oxford University Press, 1998), 9.

2. Ibid., 45, 46.

3. Thomas James Dandelet, *Spanish Rome, 1500–1700* (New Haven, CT: Yale University Press, 2001).

4. Robert D. Putnam, Robert Leonardi, and Raffaella Y. Nonetti, *Making Democracy Work: Civic Traditions in Modern Italy* (Princeton, NJ: Princeton University Press, 1993).

5. Ibid.

CHAPTER 6

1. Ruth Schwartz Cowan, *A Social History of American Technology* (Oxford: Oxford University Press, 1997), 51–52.

2. Megan Marshall, *The Peabody Sisters: Three Women Who Ignited American Romanticism* (Boston: Houghton Mifflin, 2005).

3. H. J. Habakkuk, *American and British Technology in the Nineteenth Century: The Search for Labour-Saving Inventions* (Cambridge: Cambridge University Press, 1962).

4. Frederick Jackson Turner, *The Frontier in American History* (New York: Henry Holt, 1935).

5. Robert Hofstadter, *Anti-Intellectualism in American Life* (New York: Vintage Books, Random House, 1962).

6. Arthur Aiton (1940) sought to compare the North and Latin American frontiers and argued that he found similar traits in both. Frontier people were remarkably individualistic, self-confident, democratic, inventive. Arthur S. Aiton, "Latin American Frontiers," in *Where Cultures Meet: Frontiers in Latin American History*, ed. David Weber and J. Rausch (Wilmington, DE: Scholarly Resources, 1994), 19–25.

7. Sascha O. Becker and Ludger Woessmann, "Was Weber Wrong? A Human Capital Theory of Protestant Economic History," CESIFO Working Paper no. 1987, category 4: Labour Markets (May 2007), http://www.cesifo-group.de/pls/guestci/download/CESifo%20Working%20Papers%202007/CESifo%20Working%20Papers%20May%202007/cesifo1_wp1987.pdf (accessed Oct. 9, 2008).

8. For an analysis of how culture influenced the evolution of railways in America, Britain, and France, see Frank Dobbin, "Why the Economy Reflects the Polity," in *The Sociology of Economic Life*, ed. M Grannover and R. Swedberg (Boulder, CO: Westview Press, 2001).

9. Gerben Bakker, "The Decline of the European Film Industry: Sunk Costs, Market Size, and Market Structure, 1890–1927," London School of Economics, working paper 70/03 (Feb. 2003).

10. U.S. Population Census Bureau, 2004.

11. Telegram from the parents of nine African American students to President Eisenhower, http://www.presidentialtimeline.org/html/record.php?id=128 (accessed Feb. 18, 2008).

12. Ann Williamson, *Black Power on Campus: The University of Illinois, 1965–75* (Chicago: University of Illinois Press, 2003), 26.

13. "College Enrollment and Work Activity of 2007 High School Graduates," *News: Bureau of Labor Statistics* (Apr. 25, 2008), http://www.bls.gov/news.release/pdf/hsgec.pdf (accessed Oct. 9, 2008).

14. "College Students by Age, Sex, Race, and Ethnicity," U.S. Census Bureau (several years), http://www.census.gov (accessed Oct. 13, 2008).

15. Ruth Schwartz Cowan, *A Social History of American Technology* (London: Oxford University Press, 1997), 260–62.

CHAPTER 7

1. William Spence Robertson, "Las Ideas Políticas de Mariano Moreno: Autenticidad del Plan que Le Es Atribuido," book review by Mariano Moreno and Enrique de Gandía in *Hispanic American Historical Review* 28, no. 1 (Feb. 1948): 109–11.

2. "Unitarians" in this sense was not a reference to the Protestant group but to the political group "Unitarios" that would favor a non-Federalist Argentina.

3. William Dusenberry, "Juan Manuel de Rosas as Viewed by Contemporary American Diplomats," *Hispanic American Historical Review* 41, no. 4 (Nov. 1961): 495–514.

4. Andrés Carretero, *Tango, Testigo Social* (Buenos Aires: Ediciones Continente, 1999), 21.

5. Violent pressure groups in support of "nationalism" would surface recurrently. The Liga Patriótica, most active from 1919 to 1930, was among the most notorious of these. See Luis Maria Caterina, *La Liga Patriótica Argentina: Un Grupo de Presión Frente a las Convulsiones Sociales de la Década del '20* (Buenos Aires: Editorial Corregidor, 1995).

6. José Feinmann, *Filosofía y Nación* (Buenos Aires: Editorial Legasa, 1982), 34.

7. Juan Bautista Alberdi, *Fragmento Preliminar al Estudio del Derecho* (Buenos Aires, 1837), 117.

8. Quoted in Nicolas Shumway, *The Invention of Argentina* (Berkeley: University of California Press, 1993), 147.

9. Domingo Faustino Sarmiento, *Facundo: Or, Civilization and Barbarism*, trans. Mary Peabody Mann (New York: Penguin Classics, 1998 [1845]).

10. James R. Scobie, "The Aftermath of Pavón," *Hispanic American Historical Review* 35, no. 2 (May 1955): 159.

11. Barry Velleman, *Mi Estimado Señor, Cartas de Mary Mann a Sarmiento (1865–1881)* (Buenos Aires: Editorial Victoria Ocampo, 2005).

12. Leopoldo Lugones, *Historia de Sarmiento* (Buenos Aires: Editorial Universitaria de Buenos Aires, 1960), 74.

13. José Carlos Nicolau, *Ciência y Técnica en Buenos Aires 1800–1860* (Buenos Aires: Eudeba, 2005), 243–64.

14. Diego Abente, "The War of the Triple Alliance: Three Explanatory Models," *Latin American Research Review* 22, no. 2 (1987): 47–69.

15. Raúl Mandrini and Sara Ortelli, "Uma Frontera Permeable: Los Indígenas Pampeanos y el Mundo Rioplatense en el Siglo XVIII," in *Fronteiras: Paisagens, Identidades*, ed. Horácio Gutiérrez, H. Márcia Naxara, and Maria Aparecida de S. Lopes (São Paulo: Olho Dágua, 2003), 64–65.

16. Félix Luna, *Breve Historia de los Argentinos* (Buenos Aires: Planeta, 1993), 129.

17. In 1980, Adolfo Pérez Esquivel, another Argentine, became a Nobel Peace Prize laureate. The activities that earned him distinction, however, were intended to undo Argentine society's own making, namely, the brutal repression unleashed by the armed forces in the late seventies. Therefore, despite the distinguished individual's own personal merits, courage not least among them, that Nobel award is not precisely a distinguishing one for Argentina.

18. Beatriz Sarlo, *El Imperio de los Sentimientos* (Buenos Aires: Editorial Norma, 2004), 20, 34.

19. David William Foster, Melissa Fitch Lockhart, and Darrell B. Lockhart, *Culture and Customs of Argentina* (Westport, CT: Greenwood Press, 1998), 60.

20. Alberto Spektorowski, "Argentina 1930–1940: Nacionalismo Integral, Justicia Social y Clase Obrera," *Estudios Interdisciplinarios de América Latina y el Caribe* (Hebrew University of Jerusalem) 2, no. 1 (Jan.–June 1991), http://www.tau.ac.il/eial/II_1/spektorowski.htm (accessed Jan. 13, 2008).

21. Leopoldo Lugones, *La Guerra Gaucha* (Buenos Aires: Ediciones Centurio, 1962).

22. Leopoldo Lugones, *El payador* (Buenos Aires: Stockcero, 2004).

23. Nonetheless, between 1917 and 1928, 40 percent of the army officers promoted to general had immigrant ancestry. Immigrants may have been shunned from politics, but they found alternative paths. Boris Fausto and Fernando Devoto, *Brasil e Argentina: Um Ensaio de Historia Comparada (1850–2002)* (São Paulo: Editora 34, 2004), 206.

24. Ibid., 199.

25. Quoting diplomatic archives of Argentina and the United Kingdom, Hamilton Almeida provides ample information on Perón's support for both candidates. See Hamilton Almeida, *Sob os Olhos de Perón* (São Paulo: Record, 2005), 25–30.

26. Mercosur or Mercosul, Spanish and Portuguese names, respectively, for the organization established in 1991 to foster trade, economic, and political cooperation among members. Full members include Argentina, Brazil, Paraguay, and Uruguay; Bolivia, Chile, and Venezuela are associate members.

27. Enfranchisement, however, was in no way Evita's initiative. Enfranchising women—because of the women's religious conservatism—had already been recommended by the Holy See in 1919. Evita herself, far from a feminist by modern standards, would say, "No feminist movement will achieve success and permanence if it does not follow a man's quest." See Marcos Aguinis, *El Atroz Encanto de Ser Argentinos* (Buenos Aires: Planeta, 2005), 124–25.

28. My approach to this issue is functional and I believe that few among Perón's multitude of followers would be able to elaborate any further, although it can be argued that Perón's following represented more than people were aware of at the time. For instance, among the best of many excellent diverging views, Ernesto Laclau would consider that Socialist populism may actually be the heightened instance of class struggle. See Ernesto Laclau, "Por qué Construir un Pueblo es la Tarea Principal de la Política Radical," *CDC* (online) 23, no. 62 (May 2006): 3–38, http://www.scielo.org.ve/scielo.php?script=sci_arttext&pid=S1012-25082006000200002&lng=es&nrm=iso (accessed Sept. 11, 2008).

29. Bishop Antonio Baseotto was dismissed by President Kirchner after he suggested that Kirchner's minister of health should be thrown into the ocean with a rock tied to his neck for having reduced the requirements for women to have abortions.

30. Mário Goloboff, "Entre la Integración y el Rechazo, la Comunidad Judía en Argentina," *Le Monde Diplomatique* 80 (Feb. 2006): 28–29.

CHAPTER 8

1. Fernando de Azevedo, *Brazilian Culture: An Introduction to the Study of Culture in Brazil* (New York: Macmillan, 1950), 144.

2. Keneth Maxwell, *Mais Malandros, Ensaios Tropicais e Outros* (São Paulo: Paz e Terra, 2006), chap. 16.

3. Anthracite coal was discovered in Pennsylvania in 1792, and in Southern Brazil (Santa Catarina), in the 1820s. For background on the U.S. discovery, see http://www.celticfest.org/2008CelticClassic/pdfs/2002_CelticInfluenceonLocalIndustry.pdf; for the Brazilian discovery, see http://www.dnpm.gov.br/ba/conteudo.asp?IDSecao=511 (accessed Oct. 10, 2008).

4. Clodomiro Vianna Moog, *Bandeirantes e Pioneiros: Paralelos entre Duas Culturas* (Rio de Janeiro: Civilização Brasileira, 1964), 50.

5. Shozo Montoyo, *Prelúdio para uma História* (São Paulo: Edusp, 2004), 143.

6. Douglas Heffington, "Antiguan Sugar Mills: An Adaptive Use of Relic Geography," *Focus* (Fall 1993): 7ff.

7. Heffington, "Antiguan Sugar Mills."

8. Alfredo Bosi, *Historia Concisa da Literatura Brasileira* (São Paulo: Cultrix, 1994), 102.

9. The treaty was more than a commercial one in that it also required the acceptance of religious freedom; it discouraged slavery and imposed on Brazil the extraterritoriality of British law. All provisos favored not only the arrival of British goods but also of British subjects, their business, and their ideas.

10. Shozo Motoyama, *Prelúdio para uma Historia: Ciência e Tecnologia no Brasil* (São Paulo: Edusp, 1994), 34.

11. Elizabeth Travassos, *Modernismo e Música Brasileira* (Rio de Janeiro: Zahar Editores, 2000), 10–12.

12. Francisco Vidal Luna and Herbert S. Klein, *Brazil Since 1980* (Cambridge: Cambridge University Press, 2006), 8.

13. Motoyama, *Prelúdio para uma Historia*, 271.

14. Charles Melman, "El Complejo de Colón," *Freud-Lacan,* Casa de la América Latina, Paris (Oct. 22, 1990), http://www.freud-lacan.com/articles/article.php?id_article=00300 (accessed Jan. 13, 2008).

15. Miguel Caldas has speculated on whether the pervasive image of the powerful foreigner is to Brazilians an archetypical construction or an inferiority complex. See "Santo de Casa Não Faz Milagre: O Arquétipo do Estrangeiro na Cultura Brasileira," in *Transformação e Realidade Organizacional, Uma Perspectiva Brasileira*, ed. Miguel Caldas and Thomaz Wood, Jr. (São Paulo: Atlas, 1999), 172–97.

16. Darcy Ribeiro, *O Povo Brasileiro,* 20th ed. (São Paulo: Companhia das Letras, 1995), 131.

17. Melman, "El Complejo de Colón."

18. Carmen Backes, *O Que É Ser Brasileiro?* (São Paulo: Escuta, 2000), 36–37.

19. Contardo Calligaris, *Hello Brasil!* 6th ed. (São Paulo: Escuta, 2000), 17.

20. Raimundo Teixeira Mendes, a Brazilian positivist, was responsible for inserting the motto "Order and Progress" into the Brazilian flag in 1889. In the view of Calligaris (ibid., 20), such a motto could only find justification in the mind of a settler, not a conquistador. Perhaps it was the conquistadors' unconscious that inspired the 1892 (defeated) initiative to remove the interdiction by congressional action, alleging that the motto was in poor taste.

21. Ibid., 29.

22. We are stressing the Brazilian case, but structurally the relationship of the rapacious conquistador with the land is the same wherever he goes. Take, for example, the reply of the nineteenth-century Bolivian dictator Cecílio Melgarejo when asked about his projects for government: "Do not bother me with such things, let me lust," as quoted by Argentine historian García Hamilton in an interview in a Buenos Aires newspaper: "Los

Argentinos Siguen Buscando un Salvador," *La Nación* (Apr. 8, 2006), http://www.lanacion
.com.ar/cultura/nota.asp?nota_id=795684 (accessed Jan. 2008).

23. Calligaris, *Hello Brasil!* 15.

24. Roland Chemama, "Où s'invente le Brésil?" *Freud-Lacan,* Association Freudienne
Internationale (May 28, 2002), http://www.freud-lacan.com/articles/article.php?id_article
=00259 (accessed Aug. 28, 2008).

25. Manoel T. Berlinck, "Insuficiência Imunológica Psíquica," in *Psicanálise e Colo-
nização, Leituras do Sintoma Social no Brasil,* ed. Edson L. de Sousa (Porto Alegre, Brazil:
Artes e Ofícios, 1999), 240–51.

26. Maria Dakolias, "Court Performance Around the World: A Comparative Perspective," *Yale Human Rights Development Law Journal* 2, no. 1 (1999), http://islandia.law.yale.
edu/yhrdlj/contents.html#vol2; also at The World Bank, WTP 430, 1999/07/31, http://
www-wds.worldbank.org/servlet/WDS_IBank_Servlet?pcont=details&eid=000094946
_99090805303789.

27. Lourenço Stelio Rega, *Dando um Jeito no Jeitinho: Como Ser Ético sem Deixar de
Ser Brasileiro* [Fixing Institutionalized Graft: How to Be Ethical Without Ceasing to Be
Brazilian] (São Paulo: Mundo Cristão, 2000), 105, 110.

28. Luiz Celso de Piratininga, "A Redescoberta da Lei de Gerson," *Boletim* (Ética e
Sociedade) 119 (May 1999), Conselho Nacional de Auto-Regulamentação Publicitaria,
http://www.conar.org.br/opiniao/gerson.html (accessed Jan. 18, 2006).

29. Roberto DaMatta, "Você Sabe com Quem Esta Falando?" *Carnavais, Malandros
e Heróis* (Rio de Janeiro: Zahar, 1980).

30. For instance, in the Press and Poster category of the 2001 Cannes advertising
award, Brazil took five Gold Lion awards, the same number as the USA-based agencies,
while the United Kingdom achieved two.

31. Richard Thompson et al., *Organizational Change: An Assessment of Trust and
Cynicism,* Report DOT/FAA/AM-00/14 (Washington, DC: Office of Aviation Medicine,
May 2000), 1.

32. Contardo Calligaris, "Maluf na Cabeça," *Folha de São Paulo* (May 23, 2002): E8.

CHAPTER 9

1. Alida C. Metcalf, *Go-Betweens and the Colonization of Brazil 1500–1600* (Austin:
University of Texas Press, 2005); Judy Bieber, book review, *Luso-Brazilian Review* 44, no.
1 (2007): 177–79, http://www.muse.jhu.edu /login?uri=/journals/luso-brazilian_review/
v044/44.1bieber.html.

2. Ana Elena Porras, *Cultura de la Interoceanidad, Narrativas de Identidad Nacional de
Panamá* (Panama City: Editorial Universitaria "Carlos Manuel Gasteazoro," 2005), 72–73.

3. For a fuller account of the Pocahontas tale, see Ann Uhry Abrams, *The Pilgrims and
Pocahontas: Rival Myths of American Origin* (Boulder, CO: Westview, 1999), esp. 4, 51ff.

4. Ralph Waldo Emerson, "Self-Reliance," as quoted in William Mackintire Salter,
Ethical Religion (Boston, 1889; London: Watts & Co., 1905).

5. Alberto Alessina, Edward Glaesser, and Bruce Sacerdote, "Why Doesn't the USA Have a European-Style Welfare State?" *Brookings Papers on Economic Activity* 2 (2001): 189, 195.

6. In 1895 the U.S. courts declared income tax to be unconstitutional, and it took a constitutional amendment to reinstate it.

7. Alessina, Glaesser, and Sacerdote, "Why Doesn't the USA Have a European-Style Welfare State?" 189.

8. Ibid.

9. See Robert Bellah et al., *Habits of the Heart* (Berkeley: University of California Press, 1985). For a distinction between American individualism and egalitarianism, see Aaron Wildawsky, *The Rise of Radical Egalitarianism* (Washington, DC: American University Press, 1991).

10. The significance of recognition is wonderfully captured by Pierre Bourdieu: "There is no worse dispossession, no worse privation, perhaps, than that of the losers in the symbolic struggle for recognition." Pierre Bourdieu, *Pascalian Meditations* (Stanford, CA: Stanford University Press, 2000), 241.

11. John Gillin, "Ethics Components in Modern Latin American Culture," *American Anthropologist* 57 no. 3 (June 1955): 488–500, esp. 491.

12. Allain de Botton, *Status Anxiety* (London: Hamish Hamilton, 2004), 115.

13. Madariaga, in attempting to differentiate English and French thought processes from the Spanish one, has noted that British mentality is oriented by empiricism and utilitarian pragmatism, French thinking is oriented to logic and deductive conceptualization, while Spanish thought is dominated by passion. See Salvador de Madariaga, *Englishmen, Frenchmen, Spaniards* (Oxford: Oxford University Press, 1931).

14. F. S. C. Northrop, *Philosophical Anthropology and Practical Politics* (New York: Macmillan, 1960), 136.

15. Interview of General Nikolai S. Leonov by Igor Gielow, "Mais!" *Folha de São Paulo* (Jan. 13, 2008): 5.

16. "Argentina and the IMF Knife-Fights," *The Economist* (Mar. 11, 2004); "Who Blinked?" *The Economist* (Mar. 10, 2004).

17. The successful Brazilian soccer player, Romário, while playing for a European club, was entitled to extrinsic incentives such as bonuses and perks if he succeeded in meeting goals-per-match targets. Upon returning to Brazil, he mistakenly believed that his success would entitle him to different treatment than that of his colleagues; it did not. His insistence on star treatment promptly alienated him from his teammates and supporters. See Lívia Barbosa, "Meritocracia à Brasileira: O Que É Desempenho no Brasil?" *Revista do Serviço Público Ano 47* 120, no. 3 (Sept.–Dec. 1996): 58–102, esp. 90–91.

18. Exaggerated responses to criticism would be yet another expression of the latent susceptibility among Latin Americans. A British scholar once asked me, "Alfredo, why do Latin Americans have such prickly egos?" There is no quick answer, but a fruitful search should come close to the concept of inferiority complex, discussed in "The Search for Identity" in Chapter 8.

19. Such treatment defers to customers' status—*pessoa diferenciada*, in Portuguese—as opposed to a member of the masses. There may well be a class dimension to this dynamic, which I will tackle at another time.

20. Handbooks designed as a lifeline to American executives abroad seldom go into any depth of analysis. However, at least one has grasped the feeling of "uniqueness" among Latins in at least four countries: Terri Morrison, Wayne A. Conway, and F. A. Barden, *Kiss, Bow or Shake Hands* (Avon, MA: Adams Media, 1994), 48 (Chile), 71 (Costa Rica), 304 (Portugal), and 414 (Uruguay).

21. Michael Herzfeld, "Honor and Shame, Problems in the Comparative Analysis of Moral Systems," *Man* 15, no. 12 (June 1980): 342.

22. Clarence H. Haring and Bureau of International Research of Harvard University and Radcliffe College, *South America Looks at the United States* (New York: Ayers Publishing, 1970 [1928]), 4.

23. Ibid., 63–64.

24. Scott McCartney, "Teaching Americans How to Behave Abroad," *Wall Street Journal Online*, http://www.careerjournal.com/myc/workabroad/20060413-mccartney.html (accessed Apr. 23, 2006). I thank Flavio Cabaleiro for calling my attention to this article.

25. Glenn Rifkin, "Building Better Global Managers," *Harvard Management Update* (Mar. 2006): 3–5.

26. Roberto Mangabeira Unger, *The Self Awakened Pragmatism Unbound* (Cambridge, MA, and London: Harvard University Press, 2007), 1; also available at http://www.hup.harvard.edu/pdf/UNGSEL_final.pdf and http://c1blog.blogspot.com/2007/04/roberto-mangabeira-ungers-self-awakened.html (both accessed Oct. 8, 2008).

27. Martin Blinkhorn, "Spain: The Spanish Problem," *Journal of Contemporary History, Imperial Hangovers* 15, no. 1 (Jan. 1980): 5–25, esp. 13–14.

28. Rodó's *Ariel* is available in full on the Internet in Spanish at various locations; excerpts in English may be found at http://www.humanistictexts.org/rodo.htm (accessed Feb. 9, 2006). For a modern translation in print, see José Enrique Rodó, *Ariel* (Austin: University of Texas Press, 1988).

29. Haring, et al., *South America Looks at the United States*, 69.

30. Ibid., 75.

31. David T. Ábalos, "Transforming the Personal, Political, Historical, and Sacred Faces of the Latino Male," *Journal of Men's Studies* 13, no. 2 (Winter 2005): 155–67.

32. Luis H. Zayas, "Why Do So Many Latina Teens Attempt Suicide? A Conceptual Model for Research," *American Journal of Orthopsychiatry* 5, no. 2 (2005): 275–87.

33. Catherine L. Caldwell-Harris and Ayse Ayçiçegi, "When Personality and Culture Clash: The Psychological Distress of Allocentrics in an Individualist Culture and Idiocentrics in a Collectivist Culture," *Transcultural Psychiatry*, 43, no. 3 (2006): 331–61.

34. Thomas Page's memories of the Southern plantations in the United States are reminiscent of Joaquim Nabuco's memories of plantation life in the Brazilian Northeast.

Carolina Nabuco, *Retrato dos Estados Unidos à Luz da Sua Literatura* (Rio de Janeiro: Nova Fronteira, 2000), 93.

35. Göran Therborn, *Sexo e Poder* (São Paulo: Contexto, 2006), 59.

36. Verena Martinez Alier, *Marriage, Class and Color in Nineteenth-Century Cuba: A Study of Racial Attitudes and Sexual Values in a Slave Society* (New York and Cambridge: Cambridge University Press, 1974), xv, 20.

37. "Thomas Jefferson and Sally Hemings: A Brief Account," *The Jefferson Monticello* (online), http://www.monticello.org/plantation/hemingscontro/hemings-jefferson_contro.html (accessed Jan. 5, 2008).

38. For an admirable rendition of the poem by Glaisma Pérez-Silva, see http://www.favoritepoem.org/videos.html (accessed Sept. 11, 2008).

39. Lee Ross and Richard E. Nisbett, "Culture, Ideology, and Construal," *The Person and the Situation: Perspectives of Social Psychology* (Boston: McGraw-Hill, 1999), 184–89.

40. Euclides da Cunha, *Os Sertões—Campanha de Canudos* (Rio de Janeiro: Laemmert, 1902).

41. Andrew Weever et al., "Religion and Spirituality in Three Major General Medical Journals from 1998 to 2000," *Southern Medical Journal* 97, no. 12 (Dec. 2004): 1245–49.

42. Law 16.274 of July 6 of 1992, commented by David Parker, "Uruguay's Dueling Law, 1920–1992: Tolerance or Regulation?" (paper presented at the Canadian Association for Latin American and Caribbean Studies 2008 Conference, Vancouver June 4–7, 2008), http://www.sfu.ca/las/calacs-2008/.

43. Thousands of men followed the precept of Andrew Jackson's "little, dumpy, red-headed Irish" mother. Arthur Palmer Hudson, *Humor of the Old Deep South*, Roy J. Friedman Mark Twain Collection, Library of Congress (New York: Macmillan, 1936), 411.

44. Ibid., 410.

45. Peter Laslett, "Sir Robert Filmer: The Man Versus the Whig Myth," *William and Mary Quarterly* 5 (Oct. 1948): 523–46.

46. Barbara Myloni, Anne-Will Harzing, and Hafiz Mirza, "Have the Colours of Culture Faded Away?" *International Journal of Cross Cultural Management* 4, no. 1 (Apr. 2004): 59–76.

CHAPTER 10

1. J. Valerie Fifer, *United States Perceptions of Latin America, 1850–1930: A "New West" South of Capricorn?* (Manchester: Manchester University Press 1991), 32–43.

2. While retention of Italian and Spanish immigrants in the USA was lower than for other nationalities, Argentina's immigrant retention rates of Italians were about the lowest in the New World, to the point that Italians were referred to as "birds of passage." Timothy J. Hatton and Jeffrey G. Williamson, *The Age of Mass Migration: Causes and Economic Impact* (New York: Oxford University Press, 1998), 9.

3. Jeremy Adelman, "The Social Basis of Technical Change: Mechanization of the Wheatlands of Argentina and Canada, 1890–1914," *Comparative Studies in Society and History* 32, no. 2 (Apr. 1992): 271–300.

4. The country of origin effect (COE) attempts to capture the array of unconscious resistance to purchase products or services from a foreign country without a prior reputation in the field.

5. Jacquie D. Vorauer, Kelley J. Main, and Gordon B. O'Connell, "How Do Individuals Expect to Be Viewed by Members of Lower Status Groups? Content and Implications of Meta-stereotypes," *Journal of Personality and Social Psychology* 75, no. 4 (Oct. 1998): 917–37.

6. Octavio Souza, *Fantasia do Brasil* (São Paulo: Escuta, 1994), 109.

7. A high executive of one of the largest Brazilian software houses producing some of the most internationally competitive Brazilian products told a journalist that he hoped his company would be invited by the head office of a foreign bank once it realized how clever his company's software solution for its Brazilian operation had been, and he justified why the software house would not take the initiative to sell abroad: "It is hard to venture abroad unprotected, it is hard to wear off the prejudice against a developing country with an image not linked to technology production." *O Estado de São Paulo* (May 12, 2002), B12.

8. Tzvetan Todorov, *A Conquista de América: A Questão do Outro* (São Paulo: Martins Fontes, 1999), 18–19.

9. Brazilian Ministry of Labor and Employment, RAIS statistics, 2001.

10. Telegeography and World Bank data for 2000.

11. The Airports Council International data, standardized by World Bank GDP data, refer only to international passengers, independent of their nationalities. It does not allow ascertaining who travels.

12. During an unfortunate 1996 interview with the Portuguese press, President Cardoso referred to Brazil's population as "hillbillies" (*caipiras*) when attempting to offer an explanation for his people's resistance to globalization; http://www.convest.unicamp.br/vest97/provas/fase1/fase1.htm (accessed Aug. 29, 2008).

13. Robert M. Sherwood, Geoffrey Shepherd, and Celso Marcos De Souza, "Judicial Systems and Economic Performance," *Quarterly Review of Economics and Finance* 34 (1994): 101–16.

14. Kathryn Hendley, Barry Ickes, and Randi Ryterman, "Observations on the Use of Law by Russian Enterprises," *Post-Soviet Affairs* 13, no. 1 (Jan.–Mar. 1997): 19–41, esp. 38–39.

15. Robert Shapiro, "The IT Split: Why Japan's Tech Industry Bombed While America's Boomed," *Slate* (Aug. 21, 2002), http://slate.msn.com/id/2069718/ (accessed Aug. 29, 2008).

16. Customers attach stereotyped images to countries of origin of the products they consider purchasing. These images condition the decision to buy and the price to pay for the goods and services under consideration. See Nicolas G. Papadopoulos and Louise

Heslop, *Product-Country Images: Impact and Role in International Marketing* (Binghamton, NY: Haworth Press, 1992), 3.

PART 4

1. Geert Hofstede, *Culture's Consequences, International Differences in Work-Related Values* (Thousand Oaks, CA: Sage, 1980).

2. Fons Trompenaars, *Riding the Waves of Culture* (London: Nicholas Brealey, 1995).

CHAPTER 11

1. Ruth Benedict, *Patterns of Culture* (Boston: Houghton Mifflin, 1934) and *The Chrysanthemum and the Sword: Patterns of Japanese Culture* (Boston: Houghton Mifflin, 1946); Margaret Mead, *And Keep Your Powder Dry: An Anthropologist Looks at America* (New York: Morrow, 1942) and "National Character," in *Anthropology Today: An Encyclopedic Inventory*, ed. Alfred L. Kroeber (Chicago: University of Chicago Press, 1953); Geoffrey Gorer, *The American People: A Study in National Character* (New York: Norton, 1948) and *Exploring English Character* (New York: Criterion, 1955).

2. Joel Lefkowitz, *Ethics and Values in Industrial-Organizational Psychology* (Mahwah, NJ: Erlbaum, 2003), 137–38.

3. Much of what we will see in terms of cross-cultural management surveys is grounded in value-belief theory, which claims that values and beliefs held by members of a society guide their actions, providing the members agree on the fairness and effectiveness of these values. In terms of causality, this theory purports that culture affects beliefs and values and that these influence individual behavior. It is not the only theory; a competing one is the implicit motivation theory, which purports that it is nonconscious motives such as achievement, affiliation, and power that influence behavior and that values and beliefs have their relevance restricted to short-term goals under invariant circumstances. See, for example, Douglas McGregor, *The Human Side of Enterprise* (New York: McGraw-Hill, 1960).

4. Clyde Kluckhohn, "Values and Value Orientation in the Theory of Action," in *Toward a General Theory of Action*, ed. T. Parsons and E. Shils (Cambridge, MA: Harvard University Press, 1952), 395.

5. Milton Rokeach, *The Nature of Human Values* (New York: Macmillan, 1973).

6. Rene V. Dawis, "Vocational Interests, Values, and Preferences," in *Handbook of Industrial and Organizational Psychology*, vol. 2, ed. Marvin D. Dunnette, and Leaetta M. Hough (Palo Alto, CA: Consulting Psychologists Press, 1991), 833–71.

7. William A. Cook, "How Customers Think: Essential Insights into the Mind of the Market," *Journal of Advertising Research* 44, no. 2 (2004).

8. Dov Elizur and Abraham Sagie, "Facets of Personal Values: A Structural Analysis of Life and Work Values," *Applied Psychology: An International Review* 48 (1999): 73–87.

9. Shalom H. Schwartz, "A Theory of Cultural Values and Some Implications for Work," *Applied Psychology: An International Review* 48 (1999): 23–47.

10. Geert Hofstede, *Culture's Consequences: Comparing Values, Behaviors, Institutions, and Organizations Across Nations* (Thousand Oaks, CA: Sage, 2001); and Geert Hofstede, Brian Neuijen, Denise-Daval Ohayv, and Geert Sanders, "Measuring Organizational Cultures: A Qualitative and Quantitative Study Across Twenty Cases Administrative," *Science Quarterly* 35 (1990): 286–316.

11. Joel Lefkowitz, *Ethics and Values in Industrial-Organizational Psychology* (Mahwah, NJ: Lawrence Erlbaum, 2003), 154.

12. Mattei Dogan, ed., *Comparing Pluralist Democracies: Strains on Legitimacy* (Boulder, CO: Westview, 1988), 2–3.

13. Robert D. Putnam et al., "Explaining Institutional Success: The Case of Italian Regional Government," *American Political Science Review* 77 (1983): 55–74, and "Institutional Performance and Political Culture: Some Puzzles About the Power of the Past," *Governance* 1, no. 3 (July 1988): 221–42.

14. Michael Thompson, Richard Ellis, and Aaron Wildavsky, *Cultural Theory* (Boulder, CO: Westview Press, 1990), 105, 215.

15. D. Douglas Caulkins, "Is Mary Douglas's Grid/Group Analysis Useful for Cross-Cultural Research?" *Cross-Cultural Research* 33, no. 1 (Feb. 1999): 108–28.

16. Mary Douglas, "Cultural Bias," in *In the Active Voice*, ed. Mary Douglas (London: Routledge and Kegan Paul, 1982), 190–92, 201–3.

17. Ibid., 192, 203.

18. Ibid., 191, 202.

19. Clyde Kluckhohn, "Values and Value-Orientations in the Theory of Action: An Exploration in Definition and Classification," in *Toward a General Theory of Action*, ed. T. Parsons and E. A. Shils (Cambridge, MA: Harvard University Press, 1951), 395.

20. Milton Rokeach, *Beliefs, Attitudes, and Values: A Theory of Organization and Change* (San Francisco: Jossey-Bass, 1972), 159ff.

21. Geert Hofstede, "A Case for Comparing Apples with Oranges: International Differences in Values," *International Journal of Comparative Sociology* 39, no. 1 (1998).

22. Alex Inkeles and Daniel J. Levinson, "National Character: The Study of Modal Personality and Sociocultural Systems," in *Handbook of Social Psychology*, vol. 2, ed. G. Lindzey (Cambridge, MA: Addison-Wesley, 1954), 977–1020.

23. Hofstede, "A Case for Comparing Apples with Oranges."

24. Ton van Nimwegen, *Global Banking, Global Values: The In-house Reception of the Corporate Values of ABN-AMRO* (Delft, Netherlands: Eburon, 2002), 37.

25. Hofstede, "A Case for Comparing Apples with Oranges."

26. Ibid.

27. Ibid.

28. Harry C. Triandis, *Individualism and Collectivism* (Boulder, CO: Westview 1995).

29. Rhy-song Yeh and John J. Lawrence, "Individualism and Confucian Dynamism: A Note on Hofstede's Cultural Root to Economic Growth," *Journal of International Business Studies* 26, no. 3 (1995): 655–69; Harry G. Barkema and Freek Vermeulen, "What Dif-

ferences in the Cultural Backgrounds of Partners Are Detrimental for International Joint Ventures?" *Journal of International Business Studies* 28, no. 4 (1997).

30. Barbara Krug, ed., *China's Rational Entrepreneurs: The Development of the New Private Business Sector* (New York: Routledge, 2004), 99.

31. Lawrence S. T. Tai, "Doing Business in the People's Republic of China: Some Keys to Success," *Management International Review* 28 (1988): 5–9.

32. Harry G. Barkema and Freek Vermeulen, "What Differences in the Cultural Backgrounds of Partners Are Detrimental for International Joint Ventures?" *Journal of International Business Studies* 28, no. 4 (1997).

33. Fons Trompenaars and Charles Hampden-Turner, "Riding the Waves of Culture," 2nd ed. (London: Nicholas Brealey, 1998); and Charles Hampden-Turner and Fons Trompenaars, *Building Cross-Cultural Competence* (Chichester, UK: Wiley, 2000).

34. Florence Rockwood Kluckhohn and Fred L. Strodtbeck, *Variations in Value Orientations* (Evanston, IL: Row, Peterson, 1961).

35. I will address the topics of polychronic and monochronic concepts of time in Chapter 16.

36. Shalom H. Schwartz, "A Theory of Cultural Values and Some Implications for Work," *Applied Psychology: An International Review* 48, no. 1 (1999): 23–47.

37. For an explanation of the interpretation of coplotted data, see Dena M. Bravata et al., "CoPlot: A Tool for Visualizing Multivariate Data in Medicine," *Statistics in Medicine* 27, no. 12 (Oct. 22, 2007): 2234–47.

38. Samuel Huntington, *The Clash of Civilizations and the Remaking of World Order* (New York: Simon & Schuster, 1997).

39. Anne-Wil Harzing, "Does the Use of English-language Questionnaires in Cross-National Research Obscure National Differences?" *International Journal of Cross-Cultural Management* 5, no. 2 (2005): 213–24.

40. Geert Hofstede, *Culture's Consequences: Comparing Values, Behaviors, Institutions and Organizations Across Nations*, 2nd ed. (Thousand Oaks, CA: Sage, 2003), 146–48; Sanders Wennekers, Lorraine M. Uhlaner, and Roy Thurik, "Entrepreneurship and Its Conditions: A Macro Perspective," *International Journal of Entrepreneurship Education* 1, no. 1 (2002): 25–65, esp. 45.

41. *Folha de São Paulo* (May 30, 2006), C5.

42. "Associação Quer Espiritualizar o Judiciário," *Folha de São Paulo* (May 19, 2006), http://www1.folha.uol.com.br/folha/cotidiano/ult95u403207.shtml (accessed Oct. 12, 2008).

43. Instituto Emprendedor Endeavour, *Como Fazer Uma Empresa Dar Certo em um País Incerto* (São Paulo: Campus, 2005), 4.

44. Donald Sull and Martin Escobari, *Sucesso Made In Brasil: O Segredo das Empresas Brasileiras Que Dão Certo* (Rio de Janeiro: Campus, 2004).

45. Edgar Schein, *Organizational Culture and Leadership* (San Francisco: Jossey-Bass, 1985).

46. Peter Smith, Mark Peterson, and Zhong Ming Wang, "The Manager as Mediator of Alternative Meanings: A Pilot Study from China, the USA, U.K.," *Journal of International Business Studies* 27, no. 1 (1966): 115–37, esp. 133.

47. The best survey analysis may seek to control by age and specialization of the respondents; younger ages tend to encourage footlessness underscored by lack of specialization. But surveys cannot control for the phase of the economic cycle under which the respondents are answering, and tight labor markets also encourage higher turnover. Asking respondents whether they are willing to hold on to their jobs despite the tension it brings them may not express aversion to uncertainty as much as the certainty that the job they have is the best job they can hope for under the current economic circumstances.

48. About 580,000 people left Uruguay between 1963 and 2004, meaning that almost 15 percent of Uruguayan nationals live abroad. Wanda Cabella and Adela Pelegrino, *Una Estimación de la Emigración Internacional Uruguaya entre 1963 y 2004*, Serie Documentos de Trabajo, no. 70 (Montevideo: Facultad de Ciencias Sociales, Nov. 2005).

49. ISR (Towers Perrin) Survey on Empowerment, *Folha de São Paulo* (Feb. 19, 2006), Employment sec-6.

50. Patricia M. Greenfield, "You Can't Take It with You: Why Ability Assessments Don't Cross Cultures," *American Psychologist* 52, no. 10 (Oct. 1997): 1115–24.

51. Hilal is nonetheless working along these lines, adapting a Hofstede questionnaire with a view to analyze the southern Latin American work environment within one Brazilian corporation operating in seventeen cities of Brazil, plus the capital cities of Argentina, Chile, and Paraguay. For a preliminary assessment, see Adriana Garibaldi de Hilal, "JIBS—Organisational Culture Dimensions: Findings from a Brazilian Company," http://www.tilburguniversity.nl/globus/seminars/sem03.03.pdf (accessed Dec. 15, 2005).

52. Tomasz Lenartowicz and James P. Johnson, "A Cross-National Assessment of the Values of Latin America Managers: Contrasting Hues or Shades of Gray?" *Journal of International Business Studies* 34, no. 3 (May 2003): 266–81.

53. Tomasz Lenartowicz and Kendall Roth, "Does a Sub-culture Within a Country Matter? A Cross-Culture Study of Motivational Domains and Business Performance in Brazil," *Journal of International Business Studies* 32, no. 2 (2001): 305–25.

54. The meaning to be drawn from images is, of course, also culturally contingent. But one cannot but feel impressed by the cunningness of the proposal attempting to match people through their preferences as expressed through the choice of images, as in http://dna.imagini.net/friends/ (accessed Jan. 10, 2008).

55. Kuo-Shu Yang, "Will Societal Modernization Eventually Eliminate Cross-Cultural Psychological Differences?" in *The Cross-Cultural Challenge to Social Psychology*, ed. Michael Harris Bond (Thousand Oaks, CA: Sage, 1988), 67–85.

56. Harry C. Triandis, *Individualism and Collectivism* (Boulder, CO: Westview, 1995), 82.

PART 5

1. Richard Morse, *O Espelho de Próspero* (São Paulo: Companhia das Letras, 1988), 72.

2. See Bolívar's 1824 call for the Congress of Panama of 1826 in "El Congreso Anfictiónico de Panamá a 180 Años de su Instalación," http://www.minci.gob.ve/opinion/7/6573/el_congreso_anfictionico.html (accessed Oct. 8, 2008).

3. Oded Zenka and Yoram Sheram, "Role Conflict and Role Ambiguity of Chief Executive Officers in Joint International Ventures," *Journal of International Business Studies* 239, no. 1 (1992): 55–75; Harry G. Barkema et al., "Foreign Entry, Cultural Barriers and Learning," *Strategic Management Journal* 17 (1996): 151–66.

4. John Stopford and Louis Wells, *Managing the Multinational Enterprise* (New York: Basic Books, 1972).

5. Joseph Soetesr and Heinz Schreuder, "The Interaction Between National and Organizational Cultures in Accounting Firms," *Accounting Organizations and Society* 13 (1988): 75–85.

6. Barbara Myloni, Anne-Will Harzing, and Hafiz Mirza, "Have the Colours of Culture Faded Away?" *International Journal of Cross Cultural Management* 4 (Apr. 2004): 1.

7. There are survey-based indications of what happens in Latin America, such as suggestions that family orientation may be paramount, followed by a quest for power and short-term orientation. See Geert Hofstede et al., "What Goals Do Business Leaders Pursue? A Study in Fifteen Countries," *Journal of International Business Studies* 33, no. 4 (2002): 797, or for a thorough comparison of Brazilian, Indian, and others of more advanced countries, see Betania Tanure de Barros and Sumantra Ghoshal, *Estratégia e Gestão Empresarial: Construindo Empresas Brasileiras de Sucesso* (São Paulo: Campus, 2004).

8. Geert Hofstede, "The Interaction Between National and Organizational Value Systems," *Journal of Management Studies* 32 (1985): 347–57.

9. Harry G. Barkema and Freek Vermeulen, "What Differences in the Cultural Backgrounds of Partners Are Detrimental for International Joint Ventures?" *Journal of International Business Studies* 28, no. 4 (1997).

CHAPTER 12

1. "EMICs and ETICS of Culturally-Endorsed Implicit Leadership Theories: Are Attributes of Charismatic/Transformational Leadership Universally Endorsed?" GLOBE Project, http://www.thunderbird.edu/wwwfiles/ms/globe/publications_2001.html (accessed Mar. 16, 2006). Much of the work of the GLOBE project quoted in this book has been also published in *Journal of World Business* (special edition) 37 (2002).

2. To collectivists the transactional leadership style may seem like a second-order style of leadership. However, it may lead to more effective results with collectivists, as in the case of brainstorming. See Dong Jung and Bruce Avolio, "Effects of Leadership Style and Cultural Orientation on Performance in Groups and on Individual Tasks Conditions," *Academy of Management Journal* 42, no. 2 (Apr. 1999): 208–18.

3. Robert G. Lord and Karen J. Maher, *Leadership and Information Processing* (London: Routledge, 1991).

4. Peter Smith, Mark Peterson, and Zhong Ming Wang, "The Manager as Mediator of Alternative Meanings: A Pilot Study from China, the USA, U.K.," *Journal of International Business Studies* 27, no. 1 (1966): 133.

5. Robert J. House, Paul J. Hanges, Mansour Javidan, and Peter W. Dorfman, *Culture, Leadership, and Organizations: The GLOBE Study of 62 Societies*, Global Leadership and Organizational Behavior Effectiveness Research Program (Thousand Oaks, CA: Sage, 2004); Jagdeep S. Chhokar, Felix C. Brodbeck, and Robert J. House, *Culture and Leadership Across the World: The Globe Book of In-depth Studies of 25 Societies* (Mahwah, NJ: Lawrence Erlbaum, 2007).

6. EMICs and ETICS, 12.

7. Ibid., 23.

8. Paul L. Koopman, Deanne N. Den Hartog, and Edvard Konrad, "National Culture and Leadership Profiles in Europe: Some Results from the GLOBE Study," *European Journal of Work and Organizational Psychology* 8, no. 4 (1999): 503–20.

9. It is useful to remember my closing remarks in the section titled "Which Model to Use?" in Chapter 11. There I stated that the Shalom Schwartz coplotting approach helped bring to the foreground the importance of geographical proximity in the diffusion of cultural attitudes and in the statistical clustering of countries.

10. James Lockhart and Stuart B. Schwartz, *A History of Colonial Spanish America and Brazil* (Cambridge: Cambridge University Press, 1983), 7.

11. Ibid., 16.

12. Antonio Fernando de Franchesci, *Os "Reclames" de Fulvio Pennacchi* (São Paulo: Instituto Moreira Salles, 2005), 9.

13. Francis Fukuyama, *The End of History and the Last Man* (Los Angeles: Avon Books, 1992), 165–68.

14. Pierre Bourdieu, *Pascalian Meditations* (Stanford, CA: Stanford University Press, 2000), 242.

15. Eduardo B. Davel and J. B. Vasconcelos, "Gerencia de Autoridade nas Empresas Brasileiras: Uma Reflexão Histórica e Empírica sobre a Dimensão Paterna nas Relações de Trabalho," in *Cultura Organizacional e Cultura Brasileira*, ed. Fernando P. Motta and Miguel P. Caldas (São Paulo: Atlas, 1977), 94–110.

16. Zeynep Aycan, "Paternalism: Towards Conceptual Refinement and Operationalization," in *Scientific Advances in Indigenous Psychologies: Empirical, Philosophical, and Cultural Contributions*, ed. K. S. Yang, K. K. Hwang, and U. Kim (London: Cambridge University Press), 445–66.

17. Betânia Tanure de Barros and Marco Aurélio Spyer Prates, *O Estilo Brasileiro de Administrar* (São Paulo: Atlas, 1996), 88.

18. Mathew D. Lieberman, "Intuition: A Social Cognitive Neuroscience Approach," *Psychological Bulletin* 126, no. 1 (2000): 109–37, esp. 111.

19. That there is admittedly little room for intuition in American business does not mean that it should not be taken into consideration in studies of Latin American leadership, particularly when it has already been mentioned as relevant, as in H. Gómez and C. Dávila, guest eds., "Innovation, INTERMAN, and International Business in Latin America," *International Executive* (special issue) 36, no. 6 (Nov.–Dec. 1994): 671–88. The relevance of intuition was also acknowledged by a contributing author to the GLOBE project, Colombian Enrique Ogliastri, PhD, who nonetheless did not follow up in his text, which focused on the results of an American-designed survey. See Enrique Ogliastri, "Culture and Organizational Leadership in Colombia," Universidad de los Andes (revised July 5, 1998), http://www.fh-fulda.de/fileadmin/Fachbereich_SW/Downloads/Profs/Wolf/Studies/colombian/colombian.pdf (accessed Oct. 15, 2008).

20. Rob Goffee (presentation to the London Business School's Alumni Summit, June 4–5, 2004); and Robert Goffee and Gareth Jones, *Why Should Anyone Be Led by You?* (Cambridge, MA: Harvard Business School Press, 2006), 88–89.

21. "Anthropologists during the time of colonialism usually studied 'down' (meaning that they worked with informants who had less power, prestige, access to media and technology, etc. than they did)." Course syllabus for "Colonialism, Postcolonialism, and Anthropology—Anthropologists: Heroes or Villains?" (Fall 2002), University of Alabama at Birmingham, http://www.dpo.uab.edu/~svan/ANTH302syllabus-fall2002.html (accessed Mar. 17, 2006).

22. Robert Borofsky and Bruce Albert, *Yanomami: The Fierce Controversy and What We Can Learn from It* (Berkeley: University of California Press, 2005).

23. In fact, in Brazil I know only three success stories: The former international executive of the Bank of Boston, Henrique Meirelles, later became a congressional representative and president of Central Bank. More recently, Antonio Maciel Neto, in May 2006, left a position as vice president of Ford for Latin America to join Aracruz Celulose. Then we have José Carlos Grubisich, whose career was mostly associated with Rhodia and the French Rhône-Poulenc group. Vicente Fox is also an example, in Mexico, in that he rose to president after a successful career as a Coca-Cola executive. But those cases are few and far between.

24. Patricia Pitcher, *Artists, Craftsmen, and Technocrats: The Dreams, Realities, and Illusions of Leadership* (Quebec: Stoddart, 1997).

25. Leadership styles must match corporate culture, and the latter depends on the corporation's maturity phase. Mature corporations may rely more readily on controlling minds for leadership, as is more fitting of "mercenary" corporate cultures. For a discussion of corporate culture and phases, see Robert Goffee and Gareth Jones, *The Character of a Corporation: How Your Company's Culture Can Make or Break Your Business* (London: Profile Books, 2002).

26. The Internet Movie Database (IMDb), www.imdb.com/title/tt350258/combined (accessed Oct. 8, 2008).

27. Luciana G. Amiky, Gedival Magalhães, Kattia Muraro Mirabello, and Renato Guazzelli, "Cross-Over Entre Líderes de Empresas Nacionais e Multinacionais" ("Cross-Cultural

Management" coursework, IBMEC São Paulo, 2006). A regression analysis of the data, seeking to explain the presidencies of multinationals based only on presidents' affiliations to the same or another multinational immediately prior to their promotions rendered a coefficient of 0.9375 and Student t value of 15.16575 in a regression with R^2=0.833333.

28. The survey itself was part of coursework undertaken by IBMEC EMBA students Mauro E. R. Persona, Michel Itkes, and Alexsandro B. X. Pinto. The author wishes to acknowledge the impressive effort deployed by these professionals, as well as to thank the anonymous respondents who made this survey possible.

29. The survey in English may be viewed at http://www.surveymonkey.com/s.aspx?s m=RmjrCcI4Foqjr_2b49iPs5JA_3d_3d (accessed Oct. 13, 2008).

30. Nalini Ambady and Robert Rosenthal, "Half a Minute: Predicting Teacher Evaluations from Thin Slices of Nonverbal Behavior and Physical Attractiveness," *Journal of Personality and Social Psychology* 64 (1993): 431–41. Similarly, nonverbal cues were found to be positively related to liking, trust, and judgment on performance in Tim DeGroot and Stephan J. Motowidlo, "Why Visual and Vocal Interview Cues Can Affect Interviewers' Judgments and Predict Job Performance," *Journal of Applied Psychology* 84, no. 6 (1999): 986–93. As this book goes to print, Nalini Ambady and Nicholas Rule have made further important tests measuring students' significant appreciation of corporate profitability based on face characteristics of business leaders. Nalini Ambady and Nicholas O. Rule, "The Face of Success: Inferences from Chief Executive Officers' Appearance Predict Company Profits," *Psychological Science* 19, no. 2 (0956-7976) (Feb. 1, 2008): 109–111.

See also, "Face Value," *The Economist* (Jan. 24, 2008).

31. Matthew D. Lieberman, "Intuition: A Social Cognitive Neuroscience Approach," *Psychological Bulletin* 126, no. 1 (2000): 110.

32. Incidentally, there must be some common ground to lead to an evaluation, however fuzzy. Adult judges unfamiliar with the teacher-student interaction underperformed students in a similarly controlled experiment at the Hebrew University of Jerusalem. Elisha Babad, "Guessing Teachers' Differential Treatment of High- and Low-Achievers from Thin Slices of Their Public Lecturing Behavior," *Journal of Nonverbal Behavior* 29, no. 2 (June 2005): 125–34.

33. Professor Sebastian Steizel of the University of San Andrés, Buenos Aires, personal communication (Oct. 9, 2007).

CHAPTER 13

1. Carl G. Jung, "The Archetypes and the Collective Unconscious," *The Collected Works of C. G. Jung*, vol. 9 (London: Routledge, 1959), part 1, par. 3.

2. Norris Brock Johnson, "Primordial Image and the Archetypal Design of Art," *Journal of Analytical Psychology* 36 (1991): 371–92.

3. Anthony Stevens, "Jungian Approach to Human Agression with Special Emphasis on War," *Aggressive Behaviour* 21 (1995): 3–11, esp. 4, 6.

4. James Smith Allen, "History and the Novel: Mentalité in Modern Popular Fiction," *History and Theory* 22, no. 3 (Oct. 1983): 248–49.

5. Wolfgang Iser, "The Reading Process: A Phenomenological Approach," in *Reader-Response Criticism: From Formalism to Post-structuralism*, ed. Jane P. Tomkins (Baltimore, MD: Johns Hopkins University Press, 1990), 50–69.

6. James Smith Allen, "History and the Novel: Mentalité in Modern Popular Fiction," *History and Theory* 22, no. 3 (Oct. 1983): 233–52.

7. Beatriz Sarlo, *El Imperio de los Sentimientos* (Buenos Aires: Editorial Norma, 2004), 37.

8. Stanley Solomon, *Beyond Formula: American Film Genre* (New York: Harcourt, 1976), 3.

9. See John Hellman, "Vietnam and the Hollywood Genre Film: Inversions of American Mythology in *The Deer Hunter* and *Apocalypse Now*," *American Quarterly* 34, no. 4 (Autumn 1982): 418–39, esp. 419n3.

10. Beatriz Sarlo, "Borges, un Escritor en las Orillas," J. L. Borges Center for Studies and Documentation, University of Pittsburgh, http://www.borges.pitt.edu/bsol/bse7. php (accessed Oct. 16, 2008).

11. The word "gaucho" is most probably derived from *guacho*, from the Guarani indigenous language, meaning "without a (known) father."

12. Alan Maloney, "Preference Ratings of Images Representing Archetypal Themes: An Empirical Study of the Concept of Archetypes," *Journal of Analytical Psychology* 44 (1999): 101–16, esp. 102, 103.

13. For an insight regarding the gaucho and his times, you may wish to read a collection of documents by Eduardo J. Míguez, *El Mundo de Martín Fierro* (Buenos Aires: Eudeba, 2005).

14. Quoted by Martin Aguinis, "Incorrigibles Argentinos" (May 14, 2007), http://liberpress.blogspot.com/2007/05/incorregibles-argentinos.html (accessed Aug. 30, 2008).

15. Roberto Fontanarrosa, *Inodoro Pereyra*, no. 7 (Buenos Aires: Ediciones La Flor, 1997).

16. Leopoldo Lugones, *El Payador* (Buenos Aires: Stockcero, 2004).

17. Ricardo Güiraldes, *Don Segundo Sombra: Shadows on the Pampas*, trans. Harriet De Onís (New York: New American Library, 1966).

18. Yvonne Bordelois, *Un Triángulo Crucial: Borges, Güiraldes y Lugones* (Buenos Aires: Eudeba, 1999), 94–95.

19. Ibid., 124.

20. In "El Fin," *La Nación* (Buenos Aires, Oct. 11, 1953), sec. 2-1, Borges introduces an infinite twist to the same duel in Martín Fierro. Rather than an account of a duel that took place, the courage of the fugitive gaucho recurrently finds similar expression.

21. Marcos Aguinis, *El Atroz Encanto de Ser Argentinos* (Buenos Aires: Planeta, 2001), 82–83.

22. Borges acknowledged that, in his juvenile years, to address someone as a "gaucho" was more of an insult than a commendation. In Bordelois, *Un Triángulo Crucial*, 122–23.

23. Domingo F. Sarmiento, introduction to *Facundo*, http://www.cervantesvirtual.com/servlet/SirveObras/01474062099103040832268/p0000001.htm (accessed Aug. 29, 2008).

24. United States Department of Agriculture (Mar. 2006), http://www.fas.usda.gov/dlp/circular/2006/06-03LP/bpppcc.pdf (accessed Oct. 7, 2008).

25. "Borges works on the character [Martin Fierro] to find in him the past and archaic image of a *guapo* the dweller of that new [urban] literary scene he is creating: *las orillas.*" Beatriz Sarlo, "Borges: Tradition and the Avant-garde," J. L. Borges Center for Studies and Documentation, University of Pittsburgh, http://www.borges.pitt.edu/bsol/bsbt.php (accessed Aug. 29, 2006).

26. Caleb Bach, "Ricardo Piglia: Between the Lines of a Literary Detective Writer Ricardo Piglia Creates a Fascinating Amalgam, Mixing Genres and Styles That Reflect Historical and Social Circumstances of His Native Argentina," *Americas* (English edition, May–June 2002).

27. After Raymond Carr's reference to the Spaniards rejoicing at the triumph of General O'Donell's incursion on Morocco in 1859–60. War, as in *montoneras* or bullfighting, may be the expression of a national character that needs not seek bounty. The reward is in the recognition for displaying uniqueness by defying tragedy. For the Morocco incursion, see Raymond Carr, *Spain, 1808–1975*, 2nd ed. (Oxford: Clarendon Press, 1982), 261.

28. "'I am truly surprised,' said Costa Méndez, former Secretary of State of Argentina, 'that the British will go to war for such a small problem as these few rocky islands.'" Quoted in Alexander M. Haig, Jr., *Caveat: Realism, Reagan and Foreign Policy* (New York: Macmillan, 1984); see excerpt at http://www.time.com/time/printout/0,8816,952421,00.html (accessed Oct. 7, 2008).

29. *Folha de São Paulo* (Apr. 30, 2006), A17.

30. http://www.thunderbird.edu/wwwfiles/ms/globe/publications_2001.html (accessed Mar. 16, 2006). Much of the work of the GLOBE project quoted in this book has also been published in *Journal of World Business* (special edition) 37 (2002).

31. This impression is confirmed by the preliminary data on pages 14–15 by Adriana Garibaldi de Hilal, in which Argentines, Chileans, and Paraguayans showed a higher preference for "autocratic, paternalistic" styles of leadership, in contrast to the Brazilian preference for a more "consultative or participative" leadership style; http://www.tilburg university.nl/globus/seminars/sem03.03.pdf (accessed Dec. 15, 2005).

32. "Jorge Luis Borges once wrote of the power of tango to conjure an imagined past, 'stoic and orgiastic, in which I have challenged and fought, in the end to fall silently in an obscure knife-fight.'" *The Economist* (Mar. 13, 2004): 75.

33. Vicente Palermo believes that Argentine nationalism is more "toxic" than the Brazilian variety, and refers to Brazil's much calmer 2008 reaction to Bolivia's high-handed unilateral suspension of natural gas deliveries to Brazil vis-à-vis Argentine attitudes to

weaker Uruguay regarding the 2007 dispute over potentially polluting paper mills to be deployed by Uruguay alongside the border river Uruguay. See Vicente Palermo, "Algunas Hipótesis Comparativas: Brasil Argentina Siglo XX" (paper presented at the seminar Política e Sociedade na Argentina e no Brasil: Estado, Democracia e Cultura, Departamento de Ciéncia Política, Universidade Federal de Minas Gerais, June 2008), par. 6.

34. Theodore Zeldin, personal communication (Feb. 22, 2006).

35. "Maradona claimed it was 'the Hand of God,' not his own, which had guided the ball to the English goal. Argentina went on to win 2-1 and eventually lift the World Cup in 1986. Since then the incident has irked English supporters, but given satisfaction to Argentine fans. . . . That first Argentine goal will remain among the most controversial episodes in football history. From the referee's angle it looked as though Maradona had headed the ball into the back of the net, but Maradona had actually used his hand. After scoring during the quarter-final match, Maradona said the boys came over to celebrate. 'They were quite timid. They came over to embrace me but it was as if they were saying: "We've robbed them,"' he said. 'But I said to them: "Whoever robs a thief gets a 100-year pardon."' The player was apparently referring to the Falklands War, fought unsuccessfully by Argentina against the UK to take control of the islands it claimed as its own." BBC (Aug. 31, 2005), http://news.bbc.co.uk/hi/spanish/learn_english/newsid_4200000/4200194. stm (accessed Feb. 12, 2006).

36. In *The Kiss of the Spider Woman*, Manuel Puig, writing in 1979 Argentina—about a century after Martin Fierro—replays the dynamics of two men in the absence of women. For an analysis, see Mira Weigman, "Re-visioning the Spider Woman Archetype in *The Kiss of the Spider Woman*," *Journal of Analytical Psychology* 49 (2004): 397–412. Also of interest is Diana Taylor, *Disappearing Acts: Spectacles of Gender and Nationalism in Argentina's "Dirty War"* (Durham, NC: Duke University Press, 1997).

37. Warren Coleman, "Tyrannical Omnipotence in the Archetypal Father," *Journal of Analytical Psychology* 45 (2000): 521–39.

CHAPTER 14

1. Paulo Prado, *Retrato do Brasil* (São Paulo: Companhia das Letras, 1997), 62.

2. Gilberto Freyre, *New World in the Tropics: The Culture of Modern Brazil*, 1st ed. (New York: Knopf, 1959), 48–49.

3. Ibid., 55.

4. Pedro Correia, who had lived in Brazil since 1534, wrote that it was an established custom in São Vicente that married men had twenty or more Indian women, some slaves, some not, all of whom were their "women." Alida C. Metcalf, *Go-Betweens and the Colonization of Brazil 1500–1600* (Austin: University of Texas Press, 2005); Judy Bieber, book review, *Luso-Brazilian Review* 44, no. 1 (2007): 177–79, http://www.muse.jhu.edu/login?uri=/journals/luso-brazilian_review/vo44/44.1bieber.html.

5. Fernando de Azevedo, *Brazilian Culture: An Introduction to the Study of Culture of Brazil,* trans. William Rex Crawford (New York: Macmillan, 1950), 118.

6. Humberto de Campos, *Crítica* (1st series), 2nd ed. (São Paulo: Marisa, 1933).

7. Paulo Prado, *Retrato do Brasil* (São Paulo: Companhia das Letras, 1997), chaps. 1, 2.

8. Afonso Arino de Melo Franco, *Conceito de Civilização Brasileira*, vol. 70 (São Paulo: Companhia Editora Nacional—Brasiliana, 1936).

9. Azevedo, *Brazilian Culture*, 120, 126.

10. Euclydes da Cunha, *Rebellion in the Backlands* (Chicago: University of Chicago Press, 1944), 2.

11. Miranda Reis, *Boletim do Ariel* 6, no. 4 (Jan. 1937).

12. Flight is not necessarily wrong if fight will not resolve the threat. Capitulation to chance is another matter altogether and is an expression of flight, but one that barely entails a disposition to fight and can thus hardly claim to grant a solution. Exploration for gold has strong elements of chance, as does oil exploration. Only a narrow gray area separates each from gambling. See Theodore Zeldin, *An Intimate History of Humanity* (London: Sinclair-Stevenson, 1994), chap. 13.

13. The data do not provide information regarding the odds of gambling in each country. See National Gambling Board of South Africa, "Comparison of the South African Gambling Industry with that of Selected Countries," 125–26, http://www.ngb.org.za/uploads/30_Chapter%205.pdf (accessed Feb. 16, 2006).

14. Azevedo, *Brazilian Culture*, 120.

15. Tristão de Ataíde, "Traços da Psicologia do Povo Brasileiro," *A Ordem* (Rio de Janeiro, Feb. 1934).

16. Azevedo, *Brazilian Culture*, 123.

17. Ibid., 121.

18. Clodomiro Vianna Moog, *Bandeirantes e Pioneiros: Paralelos entre Duas Culturas* (Rio de Janeiro: Civilização Brasileira, 1964), 246–47.

19. Also see the discussion of Sebastianism in Chapter 4.

20. For a more skeptic view of the manifestation of Sebastianism at Canudos, as per Euclydes da Cunha's *Rebellion in the Backlands*, see Roberto Ventura, "Canudos como Cidade Iletrada: Euclides da Cunha na Urbs Monstruosa," in *Revista de Antropologia* (São Paulo) 40, no. 1 (1997). For an endorsement of the application of Sebastianism at Canudos, see Maria Isaura Pereira de Queiroz, "D. Sebastião no Brasil: O Imaginário em Movimentos Messiânicos Nacionais," http://www.usp.br/revistausp/n20/fisauratexto.html (accessed Jan. 18, 2006).

21. Padre Cícero (1844–1934) was a defrocked Catholic priest, who in the early twentieth century attracted thousands to the town of Juazeiro, Ceará, Brazil. In Juazeiro, most lived in piety and devotion to Padre Cícero, who is still worshiped today.

22. Azevedo, *Brazilian Culture*, 127.

23. Mílton Rodrigues Silva, *Educação Comparada* (São Paulo: Nacional, 1938), 233–45.

24. Azevedo, *Brazilian Culture*, 131.

25. Octavio Ianni, "Tipos e Mitos do Pensamento Brasileiro," *Sociologias* (Porto Alegre) 4, no. 7 (Jan.–June 2002): 176–87.

26. Manuel de Almeida first published his story in the Rio de Janeiro newspaper *Correio Mercantil* between 1852 and 1853, available in Portuguese from the São Paulo publishing house, Ática (1997).

27. Amácio Mazzaropi played Jeca Tatú in one film and characterized similar peasants in seven films altogether, until 1958. Joaquim Pedro de Andrade directed the film *Macunaíma* in 1969. In addition, while not a literary character, one could add to these the comic strip *O Amigo da Onça* (The False Friend), which Péricles contributed to the magazine *O Cruzeiro* from the 1940s until the 1960s.

28. Betty Milan, *O Pais da Bola* (São Paulo: RCB, 1998).

29. Joaquim Pedro de Andrade, "Por Él Mismo," *Cine y Médios en Argentina* 2, no. 5 (1971): 24.

30. Gustavo Lins Ribeiro, *Macunaíma: To Be and Not to Be, That Is the Question* (Brasília: Série Antropologia, UNB, 1993), 12.

31. Jacy Seixas, *Tênues Fronteiras de Memórias e Esquecimentos* (São Paulo: Fronteiras, UNESP, 2003), 175–81.

32. Fifty thousand copies of the first issue of *O Cruzeiro* appeared in Rio de Janeiro in November 1928; two weeks earlier it had been announced by four million leaflets dropped from high-rise buildings, amounting to about four leaflets per inhabitant. By 1944 it had grown to innovate in photographic styles. The magazine's eighteen-page article on an attack by the Xavantes Indian tribe was also published in sixty countries. See Marialva Barbosa, "O Cruzeiro: Uma Revista Síntese de uma Época da História da Imprensa Brasileira," *Ciberlegenda* 7 (2002), http://www.uff.br/mestcii/marial6.htm (accessed Apr. 2, 2006).

33. Not all is courage and defiance in José Hernández's "Martin Fierro," either. There, Hernández wisely preserves Fierro and confines evasion tactics to the advice of a deleterious character: Viejo Vizcacha. The latter issues pearls of evasion wisdom, such as the recommendation to befriend the judge, because one never knows when one may need him.

34. A samba school does more than teach how to dance samba. It consists of a social organization that conceives, develops, and delivers its parade during Carnival. It can be as small as five hundred members but more frequently runs into the thousands. The members are mostly residents of a given neighborhood, and the samba school often develops assistance and recreational facilities for its neighbors all year round.

35. Alexandre Borges de Freitas, "Traços Brasileiros para uma Analise Organizacional," *Cultural Organizacional e Cultura Brasileira*, ed. Fernando C. Motta and Miguel Caldas Prestes (São Paulo: Atlas, 1997), 38–54; Marco Aurélio Spyer Prates and Betania Tanure de Barros, "O Estilo Brasileiro de Administrar," ibid., 55–69.

36. Ibid., 68.

37. Ibid., 44.

38. Those interested in building further along these lines may want to browse over the work of Loretta Lynn Murphy, who applied the Borges de Freitas classification to compare Brazilian and Canadian managers, the latter who are made to appear as a "stiff-upper-lip" version of managers in the United States. See Loretta Lynn Murphy, "Canadian and

Brazilian Management Techniques: Strait-Jacket Commandeering Versus Fire Jumping," coursework, Specialization Course in Business Administration, School of Business, Federal University of Bahia, http://www.fgvsp.br/iberoamerican/Papers/0124_Canadian%20 and%20Brazilian%20Management%20Techniques.pdf (accessed Nov. 20, 2005).

39. Exaggerated hierarchy, with the ensuing roguery and impunity, is usually taken to breed distrust among followers; but it may also "bite" partners. Latin American minority partners suffer when corporate profits are siphoned off to corporations controlled by majority owners. This is not only a Brazilian problem. See Luis Sanz and Martín de Pablo Holan, "Recupere la Confianza de Sus Accionistas Minoritarios," *Harvard Business Review, América Latina* 82, no. 11 (2004): 40–45.

40. Albert O. Hirschman, *Exit, Voice and Loyalty: Response to Decline in Firms, Organizations, and States* (Cambridge, MA: Harvard University Press, 1970).

41. Roberto DaMatta, *Carnivals, Rogues, and Heroes: An Interpretation of the Brazilian Dilemma* (Notre Dame, IN: University of Notre Dame Press, 1991).

42. In fact, gambling for a future, as a cultural trait, appeared only in the Latin American cluster; see Geert Hofstede et al., "What Goals Do Business Leaders Pursue? A Study in Fifteen Countries," *Journal of International Business Studies* 33 (2002): 797.

43. Moog, *Bandeirantes e Pioneiros*, 246–47.

44. José Wilson Armani Paschoal, *A Arte de Gerir Pessoas em Ambientes Creativos* (São Paulo: Record, 2005).

45. Cecília Bergamini, *Motivação nas Organizações* (São Paulo: Atlas, 1986), 35.

46. The Brazilian cosmetics corporation Natura seeks to develop personnel management techniques attuned to its corporate culture. See Betania Tanure and Roberto G. Duarte, "Leveraging Competitiveness upon National Cultural Traits: The Management of People in Brazilian Companies," *International Journal of Human Resource Management* 16, no. 12 (Dec. 2005): 2201–17.

47. "The Beauty Top Hundred," *Who's Who of Cosmetics* 39, http://www.scribd.com/doc/3719687/BRI-Top-100-Beauty-Company-Report (accessed Oct. 6, 2008).

48. "NRF Chairman Arnold Zetcher, left, presents O Boticario President Miguel Krigsner with the NRF International Retailer of the Year Award at the National Retail Federation 95th Annual Convention in New York City January 17, 2006" (photo caption), http://www.nrf.com/Press/Annual2006Photos.asp (accessed Apr. 25, 2006).

49. Betania Tanure and Robreto G. Duarte, "Leveraging Competitiveness upon National Cultural Traits: The Management of People in Brazilian Companies," *International Journal of Human Resource Management* 16, no. 12 (Dec. 2005): 2201–17, esp. 2204. This article focuses exclusively on the Natura case.

50. Tanure and Duarte, "Leveraging Competitiveness," 2209.

51. I am grateful to Francisco A. Leguizamón for sharing INCAE's work on the Grupo San Nicolás.

52. Tanure and Duarte, "Leveraging Competitiveness," 2211.

53. Ibid., 2211, 2212.

54. Such was the case for a 100-gram Natura product, "vegetable soap for mother and child," dispatched to an address in the Higienópolis neighborhood in São Paulo on June 12, 2006.

55. Roberto Mangabeira Unger, *The Self Awakened: Pragmatism Unbound* (Cambridge, MA: Harvard University Press, 2007), 11; also available at http://www.hup.harvard.edu/pdf/UNGSEL_final.pdf (accessed Oct. 8, 2008).

CHAPTER 15

1. Edward T. Hall, *Beyond Culture* (New York: Anchor/Doubleday, 1971).

2. Jenai Wu and David Laws, "Trust and Other-Anxiety in Negotiations: Dynamics Across Boundaries of Self and Culture," *Negotiation Journal* (Oct. 2003): 329–67.

3. Edward T. Hall, *The Silent Language* (Garden City, NY: Doubleday, 1959).

4. Edward T. Hall and Mildred Reed Hall, *Hidden Differences: Doing Business with the Japanese* (Garden City, NY: Anchor Press/Doubleday, 1987).

5. Carol J. Kaufman, Paul M. Lane, and Jay D. Lindquist, "Exploring More than Twenty-Four Hours a Day: A Preliminary Investigation of Polychronic Time Use," *Journal of Consumer Research* 18 (Dec. 1991): 392–401.

6. Lalita Manrai and Ajay Manrai, "Effects of Cultural Context, Gender, and Acculturation on Perceptions of Work Versus Social/Leisure Time Usage," *Journal of Business Research* 32, no. 2 (1995): 115–28.

7. In particular, Hall studied the amount of space that different peoples seemed to be comfortable with in human interaction, whether private or public. It pays to keep tabs of this, considering that North American businesspeople generally require more space than their Latin American counterparts when holding face-to-face conversations. See Edward T. Hall, *The Hidden Dimension* (Garden City, NY: Doubleday, 1966).

8. Yeon-Koo Che and Yeong Seung Yoo, "Optimal Incentives for Teams," *American Economic Review* 91, no. 3 (June 2001): 525–41.

9. Csey Ichniowski and Kathryn Shaw, "The Effect of Human Resource Management Systems: An International Comparison of U.S. and Japanese Plants," *Management Science* 45, no. 5 (May 1999): 704–21.

10. Human resources practices among foreign multinationals operating in Greece are applied by Greek staff, watering down the foreignness of those practices. Barbara Myloni, Anne-Wil Harzing, and Hafiz Mirza, "Have the Colours of Culture Faded Away?" *International Journal of Cross Cultural Management* 4, no. 1 (Apr. 2004): 59–76, esp. 59, 69.

11. Kathryn M. Bartol and Laura L. Hagmann, "Team-based Pay Plans: A Key to Effective Teamwork," *Compensation and Benefits Review* 24, no. 6 (1992): 24–49.

12. Susan Albers Mohrman, Susan G. Cohen, and Allan M. Mohrman, Jr., *Designing Team-based Organizations: New Forms of Knowledge Work* (San Francisco: Jossey-Bass, 1995), 344.

13. Tony Clelford and Amanda Hopkins, "Sizing the Slice: Assessing Individual Performance in Group Projects," Centre for Education in the Built Environment, www.cebe.ltsn .ac.uk/learning/casestudies/case_pdf/TonyClelford2004.pdf (accessed Oct. 15, 2008).

14. Steven E. Gross, *Compensation for Teams: How to Design and Implement Team-based Reward Systems* (New York: American Management Association, 1995), 191.

15. Individual merit rewards in multiple-objective, team-based production organizations such as secondary schools are known to have backfired: although student retention increased, so did the number of failing students; grade averages did not improve, and daily attendance fell. See Randall Eberts, Kevin Holembeck, and Joe Stone, "Teacher Performance Incentives and Student Outcomes," *Journal of Human Resources* 37, no. 4 (Autumn 2002): 913–27.

16. S. E Kruck and Harry L. Reif, "Assessing Individual Student Performance in Collaborative Projects: A Case Study," *Information Technology, Learning, and Performance Journal* 19, no. 2 (Fall 2001): 37–47.

17. Clelford and Hopkins, "Sizing the Slice."

18. James E. Ettaro, "Assessing Individual Student Performance in Teams," *Journal of Industrial Technology* 16, no. 3 (May–July 2000): 2–7.

19. Elizabeth A. Farmer et al., "Assessing the Performance of Doctors in Teams and Systems," *Medical Education* 36, no. 10 (Oct. 2002): 942–48.

20. Harry Levinson, "Asinine Attitudes Toward Motivation," in *Ultimate Rewards: What Really Motivates People to Achieve*, ed. Steven Kerr (Cambridge, MA: Harvard Business School Press, 1997): 3–14.

21. Steven E. Gross explicitly recommends that the primary recognition of individuals' performance in teams be noncash. Gross, *Compensation for Teams*, 140.

22. Cecilia W. Bergamini has carried out research on motivation in Brazilian companies and has offered valuable insights. See her book, *Motivação nas Organizações* (São Paulo: Atlas, 1986), 185ff.

23. Sanjeev Agarwal, Thomas E. DeCarlo, and Shyam B. Vyas, "Leadership Behavior and Organizational Commitment: A Comparative Study of American and Indian Salespersons," *Journal of International Business Studies* 30, no. 4 (1999): 727–43.

24. Sanford E. DeVoe and Sheena S. Iyengar, "Managers' Theories of Subordinates: A Cross-Cultural Examination of Manager Perceptions of Motivation and Appraisal of Performance," *Organizational Behavior and Human Decision Processes* 93 (2004): 47–61, esp. 59.

25. Alfie Kohn, "Why Incentive Plans Cannot Work," in Kerr, *Ultimate Rewards*, 15–24.

26. "Rethinking Rewards: Perspectives on Alfie Kohn's 'Why Incentive Plans Cannot Work,'" in Kerr, *Ultimate Rewards*, 25–41.

27. Douglas McGregor, "Behind Every Managerial Decision or Action Are Assumptions About Human Nature and Human Behavior," *The Human Side of Enterprise* (New York: McGraw-Hill, 1960), 33.

28. Incidentally, Martin Luther King's "I Have a Dream" speech also focused on the grievances of Afro-Americans being exiled in their own land.

CHAPTER 16

1. Peter C. Emmer, "The First Global War: The Dutch Versus Iberia in Asia, Africa and the New World, 1590–1609," *e-Journal of Portuguese History* 1, no. 1 (Summer 2003): 2.

2. Pedro Picaluga Nevado, "The Internationalization of Small and Medium-Size Companies: A Complementary Framework for International Strategies" (EIASM 5th workshop on International Management, Koç University, Istanbul, Turkey, Sept. 29–30, 2007), 5.

3. "Spanish Companies Go Overseas," *The Economist* (Feb. 16, 2006).

4. Mauro F. Guillén, *The Rise of Spanish Multinationals: European Business in the Global Economy* (London: Cambridge University Press, 2005), 4–6.

5. *Global Entrepreneurship Monitor (GEM) Global 2004 Launch Conference: Overview of Entrepreneurial Activity in North and South America* (Jan. 20, 2005), http://www.gemconsortium.org/download.asp?fid=381 (accessed Oct. 16, 2008).

6. Bernard Rosen, "Socialization and Achievement Motivation in Brazil," *American Sociological Review* 27, no. 5 (Oct. 1962): 612–24.

7. Ibid., 619.

8. Simone Echeveste, Berenice Vieira, Débora Viana, Guilherme Trez, and Carlos Panosso, "Perfil do Executivo no Mercado Globalizado," *Revista de Administração Contemporânea (ANPAD-RAC)* 3, no. 2 (May–Aug. 1999): 184.

9. Maria Fernanda Teixeira da Costa, "Sistema de Crenças e Valores de Empresários Brasileiros Exportadores" (Master's thesis, Institute of Psychology of the University of São Paulo, Department of Social and Labor Psychology, 2005), 52, 53, 55.

10. Christopher Peterson and Martin E. P. Seligman, *Character Strengths and Virtues: A Handbook and Classification* (New York: APA and Oxford University Press, 2004).

11. Rhodia and Siemens seem to be exceptions in that they regularly buy Brazilian technology.

12. The flows were estimated at $700 million in 2000. See the (American) National Science Foundation data, *Science and Engineering Indicators, 2004: Volume 1*, http://www.nsf.gov/statistics/seind04/pdf/volume1.pdf, page 4-66, fig. 4.34 (accessed Oct. 16, 2008).

13. Some emerging markets such as China, Israel, Ireland, and Singapore managed to attract $500 million or more each; that is still only one-tenth of what American multinationals invested abroad in R&D in 2000. See *Science and Engineering Indicators, 2004: Volume 1*, http://www.nsf.gov/statistics/seind04/pdf/volume1.pdf, page 4-69, table 4.26 (accessed Oct. 16, 2008).

14. International Patent Documentation Center (INPADOC), 1992–95. Also see "Patenting by Geographic Region (State and Country); Breakout by Organization: Count of 2003–2007 Utility Patent Grants, by Calendar Year of Grant," United States Patent and Trademark Office (USPTO), http://www.uspto.gov/go/taf/asgstc/brx_ror.htm (accessed Oct. 16, 2008).

15. Peter Smith, Mark Peterson, and Zhong Ming Wang, "The Manager as Mediator of Alternative Meanings, a Pilot Study from China, the USA, U.K," *Journal of International Business Studies* 27, no. 1 (Mar. 1996): 133.

16. "Bush Aide 'Is Source of CIA Leak,'" BBC, http://news.bbc.co.uk/1/hi/world/americas/4691367.stm (accessed July 2005). For a follow-up, see also "Ex-Bush Aide Contradicts Libby on C.I.A. Agent," http://www.nytimes.com/2007/01/29/washington/29cnd-libby.html (accessed June 17, 2006).

17. Mary F. Sully de Luque and Steven M. Sommer, "The Impact of Culture on Feedback-Seeking Behavior: An Integrated Model and Propositions," *Academy of Management Review* 25 (2000): 829–49.

18. In collectivist societies, asking "how did 'we' do?" may lead to more revealing answers. Christopher P. Earley, Christina B. Gibson, and Chao C. Chen, "How Did I Do Versus How Did We Do: Intercultural Contrasts of Performance Feedback Search and Self-Efficacy in China, Czechoslovakia, and the United States," *Journal of Cross-Cultural Psychology* 30 (1999): 594–619.

19. I wish to acknowledge the helpful comments of Flavio Cabaleiro on this section.

20. Here I focus only on attitudes regarding denunciation in business, not in civic life. The system is also heavily frowned upon in Latin America, where bounty hunters never had a foothold in the administration of justice, as they did in the USA. See, for instance, the fierce refusal in Colombia of cash rewards for hunting down guerrillas; Luis Ramírez, "La administración de los Ilegalismos," *Rebelión* (June 26, 2008), http://www.rebelion.org/noticia.php?id=69430 (accessed Oct. 15, 2008).

21. Julio Sergio Ramírez, "El papel de la ética en el servicio civil de carrera," Harvard Institute for International Development, http://www.gobierno-digital.gob.mx/work/sites/SFP/resources/PPTContent/1739/2/frame.html (accessed Sept. 11, 2008).

22. The Jesuit order implemented delation as a means of internal control during the sixteenth century. Every inmate of a Jesuit house could launch secret accusations against his superior. All were subject to delation. The Dominican order provided the rank and file of the Inquisition, but it was the founder of the Jesuits who supported the erection of the tribunal in Portugal (1545–46), and it was Cardinal F. Nithard, a Jesuit, who became Inquisitor-General in Portugal in 1655.

23. The privatization of law enforcement has seen an academic resurgence since Gary S. Becker and George C. Stigler, "Law Enforcement, Malfeasance, and Compensation of Enforcers," *Journal of Legal Studies* 3 (Jan. 1974): 1–18, and has yielded instruments such as the "Trojan Horse," which decriminalizes some instances of law enforcement while still resorting to delation. See Omri Yadlin, "The Conspirator Dilemma: Introducing the 'Trojan Horse' Enforcement Strategy," Berkeley Program in Law & Economics, Working Paper Series, paper 48 (Apr. 2, 2002), http://www.bepress.com/blewp/default/vol2001/iss1/art2 (accessed Dec. 8, 2005).

24. Rights acquired the strength of common law and could no longer be subjected to the whimsical interpretation of kings. Harold Hulme, *The Life of Sir John Eliot, 1592 to 1632: Struggle for Parliamentary Freedom* (London: Allen & Unwin, 1957), 255.

25. Ibid., 227.

26. Personal communication, Beatriz Rivera, University of Puerto Rico (Apr. 6, 2006): "Some people here would tell you we are U.S. and therefore work under U.S. rules, but the truth is that culturally we are very different."

27. Alfredo Behrens, "Brazil," in *The Software Industry in Emerging Markets*, ed. Simon Commander (London: Elgar, 2005), 195.

28. J. Daniel Couger, "Key Human Resource Issues in the 1990s: Views of IS Executives Versus Human Resource Executives," *Information and Management* 14, no. 4 (1988): 161–74.

29. Joel Dreyfus, "Get Ready for the New Workforce," *Fortune* (Apr. 23, 1990): 165–91.

30. Fred Niederman, James C. Brancheau, and James C. Wetherbe, "Information Systems Management Issues for the 1990s," *MIS Quarterly* 15, no. 4 (Dec. 1991): 475–500, esp. 491.

31. Behrens, "Brazil," 207–10.

32. *ComputerWorld*, São Paulo (Aug. 5, 2005), http://computerworld.uol.com. br/AdPortalV5/adCmsDocumentShow.aspx?GUID=06201AC9-97D4-49E8-AB74-AF452FF07B7D&ChannelID=20 (accessed Dec. 5, 2005).

33. A recent Brazilian study on 1,200 companies operating in fourteen sectors in São Paulo found a consistent negative relationship between the level of outsourcing and growth and profitability. Luis A. L. Brito, Alexandre L. C. M. Duarte, and Luis C. Di Serio, "Práticas Operacionais e o Desempenho: Uma Análise Impírica das Impresas Paulistas," in *XXXI Encontro Anual da Associação Nacional de Pós-Graduação em Administração, Rio de Janeiro, Anais* (Rio de Janeiro: ANPAD, 2007).

34. Christopher Sten, *Sounding the Whale: Moby-Dick as Epic Novel* (Kent, OH: Kent State University Press, 1996), 3.

35. John Hellman, "Vietnam and the Hollywood Genre Film: Inversions of American Mythology in *The Deer Hunter* and *Apocalypse Now*," *American Quarterly* 34 (1982): 418–39.

36. I will avoid contentious issues here by not alluding to the U.S. leadership's obsession with Fidel Castro, to the point of risking more than one CIA operative to deprive Castro of his beard. See Marshall Blonsky, *On Signs* (Baltimore, MD: Johns Hopkins University Press, 1985), 12. But Castro's capacity to outlive the American establishment's dislike since the time of President Eisenhower brings to mind the relationship of Chuck Jones's cartoon dyad, Wile E. Coyote and the Roadrunner. In true Roadrunner style, Castro's defiant billboard facing the U.S. Interests Section in Havana reads: "Mr. Imperialists: We are absolutely not afraid of you" (Señores Imperialistas: No les tenemos absolutamente ningun miedo!). Perhaps the Roadrunner role is more befitting the Latin American temperament, while the role of the obsessive, pragmatist Coyote is more befitting the USA. After all, close to three-quarters of my Brazilian MBA students systematically side with Roadrunner, despite Chuck Jones having designed the dyad to sway audience sympathy toward

Coyote. See http://looneytunes.warnerbros.com/stars_of_the_show/wile_roadrunner/wile_story.html (accessed Sept. 6, 2008).

37. Betania Tanure de Barros, Paul Evans, and Vladimir Pucik, *Virtudes e Pecados Capitais: A Gestão de Pessoas no Brasil* (Rio de Janeiro: Elsevier, 2007).

38. Andy Chui, Allisson Lloyd, and Chuck C. Y. Kwok, "The Determination of Capital Structure: Is National Culture a Missing Piece to the Puzzle?" *Journal of International Business Studies* 33, no. 1 (2002): 99–127.

39. Harry G. Barkema and Freek Vermeulen, "What Differences in the Cultural Backgrounds of Partners Are Detrimental for International Joint Ventures?" *Journal of International Business Studies* 28, no. 4 (1997).

40. Sidney J. Gray, "Toward a Theory of Cultural Influences on the Development of Accounting Systems Internationally," *Abacus* 24 (Mar. 1988): 1–15.

41. Elionor Farah Jreige Weffort, *O Brasil e a Harmonização Contábil Internacional*, Serie PriceWaterhouseCoopers—Academia-Empresa, no. 3 (São Paulo: Atlas, 2005), 167.

INDEX